TEACHING LITERATURE AND WRITING IN PRISONS

TEACHING LITERATURE AND WRITING IN PRISONS

Edited by

Sheila Smith McKoy and
Patrick Elliot Alexander

The Modern Language Association of America
New York   2023

To order MLA publications, visit www.mla.org/books. For wholesale and international orders, see www.mla.org/bookstore-orders.

The MLA office is located on the island known as Mannahatta (Manhattan) in Lenapehoking, the homeland of the Lenape people. The MLA pays respect to the original stewards of this land and to the diverse and vibrant Native communities that continue to thrive in New York City.

Thanks to Nolan Alexander for inspiration for this volume's cover design.

Library of Congress Cataloging-in-Publication Data

Names: Smith McKoy, Sheila, editor. | Alexander, Patrick Elliot, 1983– editor.
Title: Teaching literature and writing in prisons /
   edited by Sheila Smith McKoy and Patrick Elliot Alexander.
Description: New York : The Modern Language Association of America, 2023. |
   Includes index. | Includes bibliographical references.
Identifiers: LCCN 2023006991 (print) | LCCN 2023006992 (ebook) |
   ISBN 9781603295901 (hardcover) | ISBN 9781603295918 (paperback) |
   ISBN 9781603295925 (EPUB)
Subjects: LCSH: Prisoners—Education. | Prisoners—Vocational education. |
   Prisoners' writings.
Classification: LCC HV8875 .T43 2023 (print) | LCC HV8875 (ebook) |
   DDC 365/.666—dc23/eng/20230328
LC record available at https://lccn.loc.gov/2023006991
LC ebook record available at https://lccn.loc.gov/2023006992

We dedicate this volume to our colleague Ben Hall, who was released from Oregon State Penitentiary in April 2020 after serving twenty-two years there. Ben then enrolled at Portland State University for the fall 2020 semester. Though Ben transitioned on 20 December 2020, we are grateful that his spirit, energy, and critical thought inform the work of this volume.

Contents

Part Two: Practices

Introduction

Sheila Smith McKoy and Patrick Elliot Alexander

American literature and letters have had an enduring and intimate connection with prisons, in part because of the myriad ways that writers have often found themselves working to address social inequalities. Those who have shared the experience of raising social consciousness from jail or prison include Henry David Thoreau; Chester Himes; Ezra Pound; Malcolm X; Martin Luther King, Jr.; Etheridge Knight; Piri Thomas; Jimmy Santiago Baca; George Jackson; Angela Y. Davis; Ericka Huggins; Assata Shakur; Safiya Bukhari; and Mumia Abu-Jamal, to name only a few. It is also worth noting that for the underserved and undervalued in our social system, imprisonment becomes the locus of education. Yale University's Beinecke Rare Book and Manuscript Library now holds the oldest known artifact of African American prison writing. Austin Reed's autobiographical narrative, *The Life and Adventures of a Haunted Convict*, provides an example of prison education as defined by both the acquisition of critical literacy skills and direct confrontation with the social inequalities that precede and characterize incarceration. In his autobiography and exploration of prison education, Malcolm X notes:

> I have often reflected upon the new vistas that reading opened to me. I knew right there in prison that reading had changed forever the course of my life. As I see it today, the ability to read awoke inside me some long dormant craving to be mentally alive. . . . Not long ago, an English writer telephoned me from London, asking questions. One was, "What's your alma mater?" I told him, "Books." (182)

As Reed and Malcolm X reveal, literature and writing have long been a means by which incarcerated people not only receive an education but also impart to others a reeducation. This reeducation spreads far and wide, as the former political prisoner, renowned scholar, and antiprison activist Angela Y. Davis illustrates so well in her acclaimed autobiography, which she published shortly after her acquittal by an all-white jury for three capital crimes that she did not commit. In *Angela Davis: An Autobiography*, Davis—whose jail confinement in New York and later in California followed her high-profile appearance on the FBI's Ten Most Wanted Fugitives list in 1970—writes about continuing her career as a young college professor during her many months of wrongful incarceration. Davis managed to cultivate informal educational meetings among fellow incarcerated women during her jailing, and these meetings often focused on the women's interest in the literature of the Black liberation movement, including books like the imprisoned intellectual George Jackson's collection of prison letters, *Soledad Brother*. Davis remarked that copies of Jackson's *Soledad Brother* were "always in demand and were widely read" by the disproportionately Black and poor incarcerated women she taught and that this book helped them better comprehend how deeply racial injustice and economic exploitation were ingrained in a bail system that made their pretrial detentions unusually lengthy (62). Yet Davis also recalled writing Jackson a letter about his book's problematic treatment of women after observing that the women incarcerated with her at the New York Women's House of Detention began to see themselves as teachers—and not only students—after they exchanged with one another their own detailed analyses of Jackson's sexist and misogynist conceptions of social transformation throughout *Soledad Brother*. She reports in her autobiography, "When my message reached George that the women were exhilarated by [his] book but disturbed by his . . . uncomplimentary remarks about Black women, he apologized and wanted them all to understand his misjudgment" (317).

Reed, Malcolm X, Davis, and so many others have demonstrated the power of literature and writing to teach themselves and their readers how to better interrogate the past, acknowledge the social injustices of the present, and imagine a future in which these negotiations are no longer necessary. They have also illustrated well an important intersection between the long history of prison education in literary studies and nuanced understandings of imprisoned intellectualism that have emerged recently in the field of critical prison studies. In her 2018 summary of the field, Micol Seigel notes that critical prison studies scholarship has expanded along with "the tremendous growth in the prison population in the United States since the 1970s." According to Seigel, the field of critical prison studies has enabled outside scholars and "incarcerated thinkers" to build cogent, viable, and transformative theories regarding our cultural understanding of race, gender, crime, and punishment (124). Still, alongside this more contemporary American history of mass incarceration and prison education or reeducation is a distressing lack of resources for instructors teaching in jails and prisons. Despite the growth of critical prison studies and our current historical moment, in which national attention to social justice issues has led to the expansion of prison education programs designed by individual professors and university-based programs (Weissman), there are limited pedagogical resources available for those teaching literature courses, offering writing workshops, or leading reading groups in prisons.

Teaching Literature and Writing in Prisons is designed to provide the necessary pedagogical resources for instructors teaching in prisons and for those who seek to engage in this important work. This collection provides resources for both experienced and novice teachers, including information related to course development, pedagogical strategies, publication of incarcerated students' writing, and public presentation of imprisoned students' scholarly and creative work. As importantly, this volume incorporates the perspectives of both incarcerated and nonincarcerated teachers and students, and it centers critical prison studies scholarship in its explorations of how democratic and supportive reading and writing environments are established and maintained in today's jails and prisons.

Historical Context of Prison Education

In the passages cited most frequently from his first and best-known narrative, the prominent African American abolitionist and orator Frederick Douglass boasts of having "succeeded in learning to read and write" while enslaved in nineteenth-century Maryland (147). Indeed, for the unlettered Douglass, literacy acquisition was unforeseeable precisely because he was a slave: a crucial dimension of slavery lay in its practitioners' withholding of books, teachers, intellectual stimulation, and educational community from enslaved populations. Yet Douglass learned to read and write and imparted his love of literary expression to fellow enslaved learners. Ever determined, Douglass thus discovered what he called "the pathway from slavery to freedom" even before he fled the plantation: he freed his mind by unfettering his and other enslaved people's systemically restricted access to knowledge of the written word (143). In sum, Douglass's establishment of a literary learning community within slavery's world of confinement afforded him and countless others whom society had labeled "slaves" the rare opportunity to see and express themselves as "scholars" (197).

Teaching Literature and Writing in Prisons examines the teaching practices that animate literary learning communities in today's razor-wire world of confinement: the contemporary U.S. prison. Contributors to this volume teach literature and writing in prisons and jails of different security levels in disparate regions of the nation, and they do so with a critical awareness of the power and historical significance of literary study and writing for adults and children whose learning takes place in environments typified by confinement. Just as enslaved learners fought to understand and be understood beyond the limiting terms of their confinement, today's incarcerated learners have disproportionately experienced systemic undereducation prior to incarceration and constitute the fastest-growing population of Americans with limited or no access to reading, writing, higher education opportunities, or learning communities. In this regard, Kaia Stern, director of the Prison Studies Project and visiting lecturer in the Department of Sociology at Harvard University, who has spent more than two decades teaching in prison, underscores the importance of contextualizing the relationship between systemic undereducation in the so-called free world and its frequent continuation in the world of incarceration and captivity: "[O]nly a minute fraction of all people in prison even have access to a postsecondary education. The vast majority struggle to read the information about basic supplies, like soaps and stamps, on prison commissary lists because they have been failed by the public school systems that were meant to serve them" (196). Relatedly, the legal scholar Michelle Alexander, author of the widely read *The New Jim Crow: Mass Incarceration in the Age of Colorblindness*, has observed how the school, in the urban ghetto, is all too often an oppositional, militarized space for policing and punishing the disproportionately Black, brown, and poor populations that eventually end up confined within our nation's mind-numbing jails and prisons: "Schools located in ghetto communities more closely resemble prisons than places of learning, creativity, or moral development" (167).[1]

The history of prison education itself has also influenced the development and spurred the urgency of this volume. On the one hand, the 2010s and 2020s represent a time period in which incarcerated reading and writing groups have gradually expanded, especially with the rise of privately funded and volunteer-supported college-in-prison programs. However, this modest growth should be understood in the larger context of the aftermath of Congress's passage of the Violent Crime Control and Law

Enforcement Act in 1994. That law, by eliminating the possibility of Pell Grants for imprisoned students, effectively terminated public funding for the many college-in-prison programs then in existence (Lagemann 9).[2] To reiterate, Ellen Condliffe Lagemann, a Bard College professor and distinguished fellow of the Bard Prison Initiative, reminds us, "While in the early 1990s 772 college-in-prison programs operated in 1,287 correctional facilities across the United States, almost all of them were closed down after the passage of the 1994 crime bill" (9). Since that time, a fair number of college-in-prison programs have been founded that regularly offer courses in literature and writing—including programs whose instructors are represented in this volume, such as Mount Tamalpais College at San Quentin State Prison (formerly known as the Prison University Project and Patten University at San Quentin), Cornell University's Cornell Prison Education Program (which operates in four New York prisons), the University of Mississippi and Mississippi College's Prison-to-College Pipeline Program at the Mississippi State Penitentiary at Parchman and Central Mississippi Correctional Facility, and Stetson University's Community Education Project at Tomokoa Correctional Institution. We find ourselves at a historical moment, in other words, in which a sizeable population of incarcerated people are taking literary courses, enrolling in writing workshops, or joining literary discussion groups—and as such, questions have arisen among instructors not only about what books one might assign for students to read, but also how one might go about curriculum development, learning activities, lesson planning, and even formal assessment within prison and jail environments typified by ever more harrowing forms of harm, social isolation, and educational deprivation. These concerns have led to robust paper and panel presentations on teaching literature and writing in prisons at many national conferences in the past decade—such as the annual meeting of the National Conference on Higher Education in Prison, Vanderbilt University's Rethinking Prisons conference in 2013, the University of Mississippi's Rethinking Mass Incarceration in the South conferences in 2014 and 2016, the Southeastern American Studies Association conferences in 2015 and 2019, the American Studies Association conference in 2017, the "Corrections, Rehabilitation, and Reform" conference that Mount Tamalpais College held onsite at San Quentin State Prison in 2018, and the Making and Unmaking Mass Incarceration Conference at the University of Mississippi in 2019.

Teaching Literature and Writing in Prisons critically revisits and builds on these conference presentations, especially as increasing numbers of scholars across the disciplines are drawn as much to research about mass incarceration and prison teaching as to considering what it means to do such work during our era of the prison-industrial complex,[3] an era in which imprisonment is both a method of racialized social control and a profit-driven industry (Davis, *Are Prisons Obsolete?* 84) that is responsible for the punitive confinement of one in every ninety-nine adults in the United States (Liptak) and more Black men than were enslaved in 1850 (Lu). When nearly two million Americans are confined in overcrowded "correctional" facilities, plantation prisons, and six-foot-by-eight-foot Security Housing Units in a system that has been shown to be not only not rehabilitative but also typified by racial bias, discriminatory sentencing practices, political repression, state violence, sexual abuse, medical neglect, corporate greed, and the increasingly privatized warehousing of Black, brown, poor, and mentally ill people, teaching literature and writing in prisons has as much socially transformative potential as it did for Douglass and others on nineteenth-century slave plantations (Sawyer and Wagner). Indeed, this volume aims to address whether and how approaches to teaching literature and writing in prisons undermine the logic of incapacitation and dehumanization that critical prison studies scholars like Davis, Dylan Rodríguez, and Victoria Law, and legal studies scholars like Michelle Alexander, Colin Dayan, and Mona Lynch, have shown to be disturbingly ordinary in prisons, jails, and youth detention facilities since at least 1970. For this reason, incarcerated teachers and students are contributors to this volume, as are outside instructors. Collectively, this volume's contributors consider the extent to which course development, teaching strategies, learning activities, and curricula not only foster an appreciation of literature and writing that lessens the psychological toll of the prolonged social isolation and educational deprivation that have become endemic in today's prisons and jails but also constitute an abolitionist intervention against the system of injustice and incarceration that defines our era.

Structure of the Volume and Overview of Essays

We have organized this volume around two central questions: What is the purpose of literary study, writing, and the performed word in jail and prison classrooms? What are specific pedagogical strategies for teaching literature and writing in particular carceral classroom contexts? In answer to the first question, contributors share theoretical frameworks and teaching experiences. In part one of the volume, they interrogate assumptions about rehabilitation, literacy, and transformation that frame our conceptions of jail and prison classrooms. Additionally, and at times alternatively, these essays explore the limits and possibilities of critical pedagogies when teaching literature, writing, and the performed word behind bars. The second part of the volume highlights practices—particular instructional approaches to literary study or writing in jails and prisons—by emphasizing specific pedagogical strategies that nonincarcerated instructors might adopt to honor the intellectual curiosities, personal concerns, and expressed needs of incarcerated learners. These essays illuminate teaching styles that actively undermine the practices of social isolation and silence that define everyday life for people confined behind concrete walls and razor wire. In keeping with our goals in *Teaching Literature and Writing in Prisons* of using language that is humanizing and respectful, not stigmatizing or repetitious in referencing the terrain of punitive isolation, we most frequently use the terms *outside, outside instructor*, and *outside student* to refer to nonincarcerated people; we use the terms *inside, inside instructor*, and *inside student* to refer to incarcerated people.

Part One: Purposes

The first essay in *Teaching Literature and Writing in Prisons* engages directly with the question of the purpose of literary study, writing, and performance in jail and prison classrooms. The outside instructor Jess A. Goldberg's essay "Riotous Study: Black Studies, Academic Unfreedom, and Surveilled Pedagogy in Prison Education" addresses methods of "employ[ing] what Fred Moten might call the 'fugitivity' of Black studies pedagogy . . . through seemingly innocuous course texts" and reveals how literary study in the prison classroom can be as much a surreptitious opposition to the prison's censorship, book-banning, and surveillance practices as an on-site critical interrogation of the carceral power dynamics of the jail, prison, and carceral state. In "Power Mapping the Capitol: Notes on Abolitionist Pedagogy and Captive Study," Meghan G. McDowell and Alison Rose Reed offer a related perspective on the specific purpose of abolitionist literary study. McDowell and Reed, outside instructors, argue for an understanding of the liberatory power of shared laughter and interpersonal closeness accomplished in the communal act of studying literature, including Suzanne Collins's bestseller *The Hunger Games* and Marita Bonner's Black feminist play *The Purple Flower*, within a Virginia jail classroom.

The next several essays are in conversation about the possibilities and limits of transformation. Anastazia Schmid's "The Sacred Writing Circle: Pedagogical Challenges of Creative Writing and Teaching among

Incarcerated Women" focuses on the "transformational healing" possible in a writing group at the Indiana Women's Prison through commitment to communal uplift and opposition to the savior mentality and stereotyped thinking about incarcerated students that outside instructors often bring to the prison classroom. In "Of Toothbrushes, Bread, and Beanstalks: Freedom and Kinship Inside," Ann E. Green, Richard Sean Gross, and Rachel Swenarton—an outside instructor, inside student, and outside student, respectively—reflect on applying principles of critical service-learning in the Inside-Out Prison Exchange Program within sites of incarceration in Pennsylvania as they argue for prioritizing the power of intentional presence, not individual transformation, in the carceral classroom. The work that Anna Plemons presents in "Relational Methodologies and Decolonial Outcomes for the Prison Writing Classroom" also embraces a co-created learning space. For Plemons, when outside instructors strategically honor incarcerated students' agency and leadership in the classroom, their collaborations simultaneously engage the writing process and dispel the myth that incarcerated students need a nonincarcerated instructor to use writing to transform morally and intellectually. Focusing on the consistent undermining of the prison system's power dynamics in "The Brain Is Wider than the Sky," David Bennett, who is imprisoned, and Courtney Rein, a nonincarcerated instructor, show how inside and outside participants in the Prison University Project at San Quentin State Prison collaborate in course development and teaching styles to maintain genuinely democratic, diverse, and inclusive learning communities within the prison classroom where "teachers—both incarcerated and free—can liberate one another from the mental shackles of preconceived notions about what education is and should be."

Several essays then consider the role of performance in transforming understandings of the purpose of literary study and writing in jails and prisons. Elizabeth Hawes's "Meteorite" candidly illustrates, from the author's own experience, the daily challenges that incarcerated writers face and draws attention to the "transformative effect" that is possible through the work of outside organizations that unite incarcerated writers with the broader public through performance. Jenna Dreier's "Shakespeare with Survivors: Learning from Incarcerated Women in the Me Too Era" explores how the Detroit Public Theatre's Shakespeare in Prison program's approaches to performing William Shakespeare's plays *The Taming of the Shrew* and *Othello* at Women's Huron Valley Correctional Facility help expose and oppose the "open secret of abuse" in women's prisons while creating for imprisoned survivors of sexual assault desired opportunities for expression. In "Playwriting across the Walls as Abolitionist Practice," Rivka Eckert focuses on the abolitionist practices that infuse the Plays Across the Walls Festival, a theater-making model that Eckert established collaboratively with incarcerated students and university actors in New York State.

The final five essays in the first part of the volume deeply interrogate questions of individual and social transformation surrounding literary study and writing in jail and prison classrooms. C. Fausto Cabrera makes a case in "Cracks in the Glass Ceiling" for understanding the impact of writing communities that imprisoned people establish and lead. In "Rethinking the Hero Narrative of Critical Pedagogy: Teaching Creative Writing with and for Women at the County Jail," Molly Dooley Appel and Shannon Frey critically reflect on their experiences with team-teaching and learning from a class of incarcerated women writers, suggesting that outside instructors' introduction of critical pedagogy in the jail or prison classroom has undeniable limits and that "[r]aising consciousness might end in greater restrictions instead of greater freedom, especially in the extremely rigid jail environment." Paméla Cappas-Torro, Antonio Rosa, and Ken Smith also interrogate the utility of critical pedagogy as a guiding logic for the teaching of language in prison in "Spanish Co-instruction in Prison: A Dialogue on Language, Identity, and Pedagogy." Cappas-Torro, Rosa, and Smith highlight the barriers that Rosa and Smith face as imprisoned co-instructors as, unsettlingly, a fundamental part of this collaborative instruction experience. Seth Michelson's essay, "Poetic Difference: How Emplaced Writing Influences Lives in Prison," adds another layer to this discussion. While Michelson is aware of the at best temporary undermining of carceral power dynamics that his facilitation of poetry workshops for undocumented children at a maximum security detention center represents, he also draws attention to the possibility of transformational outcomes—such as the publication of workshop participants' bilingual anthology, *Dreaming America: Voices of Undocumented Youth in Maximum-Security Detention*, whose sales support a legal defense fund for the children at the facility. Finally, in "Unsettling Literacy: Querying the Rhetorics of Transformation," Anne Dalke calls into question both the reductive conceptions of "transformation" in the carceral classroom and the myth of literacy acquisition surrounding the teaching of literature and writing in jail and prison classrooms, all while arguing for "an awareness of the multilayered complexities and possibilities of [these] particularly constrained and conflicted site[s]. . . [and] the subversion possible amid [their] complicated interactions."

Part Two: Practices

The first two essays in the volume's second part consider the prioritization of incarcerated students' concerns and intellectual curiosities as a specific pedagogical approach for teaching literature and writing in college-level carceral classrooms. In "Liberators in Theory, Collaborators in Deed: Navigating the Constraints of the Prison Classroom," R. Michael Gosselin, an outside instructor at Attica Correctional Facility, revisits revelatory observations of incarcerated students in the light of popular teaching-in-prison narratives and advises nonincarcerated teachers how to best serve students enrolled in literature and writing courses in college-in-prison programs. In conversation with Gosselin's essay, James King and Amber Shields's "Collaborating to Reimagine Knowledge Sharing in the Prison Classroom" challenges outside instructors to recognize, reveal, and resist course development and classroom practices that are assimilationist, colonizing, or white supremacist in nature and to adopt pedagogical approaches that genuinely affirm the expressed learning goals of incarcerated program participants.

Rachel Boccio's "Disrupting the Time of Incarceration: Close Reading in a Justice-Oriented Prison Classroom" and the two essays that follow it address text-specific teaching approaches or group facilitation approaches in distinct carceral learning communities. Boccio reflects on teaching *Live from Death Row*—the best-known work of the longtime Black revolutionary journalist, imprisoned radical intellectual, and cause célèbre Mumia Abu-Jamal—at a maximum security youth facility in Connecticut, emphasizing a collaborative teaching methodology that "draws upon established foundations for social justice education and from a theory of close reading that articulates interactive and experimental aspects of the literary practice." In "Reading and Writing between the Devil and the Deep Blue: The Appalachian Prison Book Project," Katy Ryan, Valerie Surrett, and Rayna Momen critically revisit their group reading experiences in a West Virginia women's federal prison and consider the solidarity that results from the dialogue-driven approaches incorporated into their book club's in-prison engagement with acclaimed novels and poetry. In "Narrating Captivity, Imagining Justice: Reading Mary Shelley's *Frankenstein* in Prison," Laura E. Ciolkowski focuses on imprisoned students' classroom leadership while demonstrating that *Frankenstein*—which she taught in a medium security New York women's prison—can become an indispensable tool for rethinking the construction of monstrosity and the practice of gendered anti-Black racism in the contemporary carceral state.

The next three essays in this part address self-assessment and self-publication as classroom practices that destabilize carceral power and promote incarcerated students' desired learning outcomes. In "From a Public Defender Office to a Prison Classroom: Why I Teach Writing in Prison," Patrick Filipe Conway observes how working as a criminal investigator in a public defender office redirected his career path and transformed his teaching strategies. Benjamin J. Hall, Rhiannon M. Cates, and Vicki L. Reitenauer's "Writing Our Lives into the World" probes deeper into the prioritization of students' self-directed learning and self-assessment in college-level writing courses in prison. Hall, Cates, and Reitenauer define themselves as "a currently incarcerated student and teaching assistant, a university staff member with experience as a student and teaching assistant, and an instructor of women, gender, and sexuality studies." Their classroom identities underscore the efficacy of their approach to combating the asymmetrical power dynamics of the prison and the outside-instructor-led carceral classroom through various methods of honoring students' agency in writing classrooms. Adding another illuminating dimension to this conversation, Sarah Shotland, in "Erasure or Exploitation? Considering Questions in Prison Publications," urges outside instructors of writing courses to support the desires of incarcerated students, their families, and their loved ones related to publication of their original work. In Shotland's words, "It is important to reserve class time for a full discussion and deliberation about the risks and rewards of creating and distributing a publication on any scale. . . . This kind of instruction increases students' understanding of publishing and editorial standards as well as their agency in framing and broadcasting their stories and images, no matter the scale or scope."

The second part of the volume closes with a focus on the need for self-care—particularly for outside instructors and outside students working with inside instructors and inside students—in the spirit of preserving the well-being of all participants in carceral classrooms. In "Self-Care as Ethical Practice for Teachers and Volunteers Working with Writers behind Bars," Shelby D. Tuthill and Tobi Jacobi draw from extensive interviews with participants in a community-based writing initiative that supports incarcerated writers in Colorado to make a case for "recognizing the compassion fatigue, collective trauma, and feelings of alienation, allyship, anger, empathy, and helplessness that often arise with working in contexts like prison" while also ensuring "[a]ccess to ongoing and varied self-care strategies [that] can provide the support that prison teachers and students require."

Amid this volume's intentional examinations of race, gender, class, sexuality, (racial) capitalism, and homophobia as elements of the carceral system, the perspective of trans and gender nonconforming teachers and students is, regrettably, not specifically addressed, though these perspectives and identities shape the experiences of the jail and prison classroom for both inside and outside instructors, teachers, and group facilitation leaders. It is our hope that this volume will inspire other work that will highlight these identities and experiences as they relate to scholars, instructors, students, and prison abolitionists. It is critically important to our understanding the full impact of this work and its transformative possibilities.

Acknowledging Terminology, Volume Contributors, and Current Events

We and all nonincarcerated contributors have made every effort to ensure that our terminological references to incarcerated people within this introduction and within each essay reflect language that is humanizing and respectful, not implicitly or explicitly stigmatizing. In this regard, we follow the thinking of the late Eddie Ellis, a formerly incarcerated community organizer and founder of the Center for NuLeadership on Human Justice and Healing, who writes in his "Open Letter to Our Friends on the Question of Language" of the importance of using person-first language when referring to incarcerated and formerly incarcerated people:

> When we are not called mad dogs, animals, predators, offenders and other derogatory terms, we are referred to as inmates, convicts, prisoners and felons—all terms devoid of humanness which identify us as "things" rather than as people. These terms are accepted as the "official" language of the media, law enforcement, prison industrial complex and public policy agencies. However, they are no longer acceptable for us and we are asking people to stop using them. . . . [W]e are asking everyone to stop using these negative terms and to simply refer to us as PEOPLE. People currently or formerly incarcerated, PEOPLE on parole, PEOPLE recently released from prison, PEOPLE in prison, PEOPLE with criminal convictions, but PEOPLE.

The rare instances in which any of the disavowed terms that Ellis lists—"inmates, convicts, prisoners and felons"—are included in *Teaching Literature and Writing in Prisons* occur within essays authored by individual incarcerated or formerly incarcerated contributors. On these limited occasions, we have honored the ethical position that i legitimate place to tell incarcerated or formerly incarcerated p to refer to the experience of incarceration.

We also wish to express our deep appreciation for incarcerated and formerly incarcerated essayists' significant contributions to this volume. When we issued our call for papers for *Teaching Literature and Writing in Prisons*, we did so with a specific invitation for essay proposals from incarcerated and formerly incarcerated teachers and students. Our invitation reflected our shared awareness, as nonincarcerated instructors, of how profoundly our teaching of literature and writing in prisons has been shaped by incarcerated and formerly incarcerated teachers' and students' pedagogical philosophies and astute assessments of our class meetings and courses—which one of us has discussed at length in published work.[4] The invitation was also informed by this observation by Davis: "People in [jails and] prisons . . . have a right to participate in transformative projects" (*Meaning* 54). Whether or not the present volume proves transformative, we believe that its complex and wide-ranging perspectives on teaching literature and writing in jails and prisons depend upon our commitment to honoring incarcerated and formerly incarcerated teachers' and students' "right to participate" in this particular project. Moreover, the enormous barriers to preparing drafts, reviewing feedback, and submitting revisions that our incarcerated and formerly incarcerated contributors faced cannot be understated. With no access to e-mail and limited or no access to computers, they enlisted outside supporters to work with us so that we could collectively ensure that the best version of their essays would be included in this volume. We express our sincere gratitude to the incarcerated and formerly incarcerated essayists whose single-authored or coauthored work appears in *Teaching Literature and Writing in Prisons*: for you and your outside supporters' tireless efforts and for your undying commitment to continue writing and revising amid limited or no resources, we humbly thank you. This volume is undoubtedly better not only because it includes your perspectives but also because it celebrates your persistence.

Finally, at the time of the writing of this volume, neither we nor our contributors could have foreseen two world-changing phenomena that will inevitably shape its reception and cultural significance: first, the global COVID-19 pandemic and its incalculably crushing public health, economic, and racialized premature death impacts; and, second, the exposure and international condemnation of lethal acts of racist and gendered state violence against the unarmed Black citizens Ahmaud Arbery, Breonna Taylor, and George Floyd. These galvanizing incidents and others like them (see Dungca et al.) reflect a centuries-long practice of white supremacist and patriarchal social control that has caused new devastation as the coronavirus has spread through incarcerated populations. As revealed in the recent work of scholars like Dan Berger and Marc Lamont Hill and organizations like the Equal Justice Initiative ("COVID-19's Impact") and Prison Policy Initiative ("Most Significant Criminal Justice Policy Changes"), various forms of state violence behind bars, general medical neglect, the inability to quarantine or social-distance in sites of large-scale punitive confinement, and the distressing lack of response by the federal, state, and local governments to the impacts of COVID-19 on those held in already overcrowded prisons, jails, immigration detention centers, and youth facilities have exacerbated the spread of coronavirus infections and rapidly increased injury, mental illness, and premature death among incarcerated people, whose labor all the while continues to be exploited: the latter has been evidenced in jailed and imprisoned people sewing face masks and bottling hand sanitizer for nonincarcerated communities while having no access to these COVID-19 prevention mechanisms themselves (Berger 129–30; Hill 37–38). More specific to the context of this volume, the coronavirus and widespread indifference toward the education and well-being of incarcerated teachers and learners has led to massive abrupt cancellations of what was already a limited number of courses, group meetings, and academic support services that had provided some consistent experience of human community inside jails and prisons. Of equal concern has been the drastic decrease in or wholesale elimination of funding support for learning communities within sites of incarceration (Lewis). Tanya Erzen, associate professor at the University of Puget Sound and faculty director of the Freedom Education Project Puget Sound college-in-prison program, has noted,

> Unlike most higher education programs in prisons across the country, we are extremely fortunate that we can still send messages to students through the internal communication system. Morale among students is low. They feel isolated and terrified. They struggle to complete work without the accountability of peers and professors. They miss being in a classroom with their fellow students because most can't leave their units. They crave connections to the outside world. They write of loss and mourning.

We remain grateful that, at the time of this writing, some of our contributors who are incarcerated have survived this nightmare and have been released. We also hope that the contributors who are not yet free shall be as fortunate. Their stories are a part of the longer narrative of injustice and inequity, transformation and hope that defines this work. With these considerations in mind, we ask that all who read this volume understand that it is informed by both these most recent grim realities and the remarkable resilience that has shaped the important work collected here.

NOTES

1. For more on the understaffed, underresourced, and overtly militarized learning environments that precede and accompany too many incarcerations, see Rios; Heiner and Mangual.

2. On the movement toward the reestablishment of Pell Grants for imprisoned people, see Weissman.

3. "Prison-industrial complex" is a term coined by the social historian Mike Davis, but Angela Y. Davis popularized it. For Davis, the term refers to a method of conceptualizing late-twentieth- and early-twenty-first-century imprisonment as an industry, increasingly with private investment. The supply of raw materials for this "punishment industry"—disproportionately, Black, brown, and poor bodies—is made available by social factors that cannot be reduced to crime, especially ideologies of racism and corporate agendas premised on global capitalism. For more, see Davis, *Are Prisons Obsolete?* 84–104.

4. This published work on teaching literature and writing in prisons includes P. Alexander, "'To Live,'" "Education as Liberation," and "Radical Togetherness."

WORKS CITED

Alexander, Michelle. *The New Jim Crow: Mass Incarceration in the Age of Colorblindness.* The New Press, 2010.

Alexander, Patrick Elliot. "Education as Liberation: African American Literature and Abolition Pedagogy in the Sunbelt Prison Classroom." *South: A Scholarly Journal*, vol. 50, no. 1, 2017, pp. 9–21.

———. "Radical Togetherness: African-American Literature and Abolition Pedagogy at Parchman and Beyond." *Humanities*, vol. 9, no. 2, 2020, https://doi.org/10.3390/h9020049.

———. "'To Live and Remain outside of the Barb[ed] Wire and Fence': A Prison Classroom, African American Literature, and the Pedagogy of Freedom." *Reflections: A Journal of Writing, Service Learning, and Community Literacy*, vol. 11, 2011, pp. 88–108.

Berger, Dan. "Why Has COVID-19 Not Led to More Humanitarian Releases?" *The Politics of Care: From COVID-19 to Black Lives Matter.* Boston Review and Verso Books, 2020, pp. 128–35.

"COVID-19's Impact on People in Prison." *Equal Justice Initiative*, 21 Aug. 2020, eji.org/news/covid-19s-impact-on-people-in-prison/.

Davis, Angela Y. *Angela Davis: An Autobiography.* International Publishers, 1974.

———. *Are Prisons Obsolete?* Seven Stories Press, 2003.

———. *The Meaning of Freedom: And Other Difficult Dialogues.* City Lights Books, 2012.

Dayan, Colin. *The Law Is a White Dog: How Legal Rituals Make and Unmake Persons.* Princeton UP, 2011.

Douglass, Frederick. *The Narrative of the Life of Frederick Douglass, An American Slave, Written by Himself: A New Critical Edition.* Edited by Angela Y. Davis, City Lights, 2009.

Dungca, Nicole, et al. "A Dozen High-Profile Fatal Encounters That Have Galvanized Protests Nationwide." *The Washington Post*, 8 June 2020, www.washingtonpost.com/investigations/a-dozen-high-profile-fatal-encounters-that-have-galvanized-protests-nationwide/2020/06/08/4fdbfc9c-a72f-11ea-b473-04905b1af82b_story.html.

Ellis, Eddie. "An Open Letter to Our Friends on the Question of Language." Center for NuLeadership on Urban Solutions, July 2017, cmjcenter.org/wp-content/uploads/2017/07/CNUS-AppropriateLanguage.pdf.

Erzen, Tanya. "Unlocking the Potential of Prison Education." *Inside Higher Ed*, 15 July 2020, www.insidehighered.com/views/2020/07/15/pandemic-has-exacerbated-all-inequities-already-existed-prison-education-programs.

Heiner, Brady Thomas, and Ariana Mangual. "The Repressive Social Function of Schools in Racialized Communities." *States of Confinement: Policing, Detention, and Prisons*, edited by Joy James, Palgrave, 2000, pp. 222–29.

Hill, Marc Lamont. *We Still Here: Pandemic, Policing, Protest, and Possibility.* Haymarket Books, 2020.

Lagemann, Ellen Condliffe. *Liberating Minds: The Case for College in Prison.* The New Press, 2016.

Law, Victoria. *Resistance behind Bars: The Struggles of Incarcerated Women.* PM Press, 2009.

Lewis, Nicole. "Can College Programs in Prison Survive COVID-19?" *The Marshall Project*, 4 May 2020, themarshallproject.org/2020/05/04/can-college-programs-in-prison-survive-covid-19.

Liptak, Adam. "1 in 100 U.S. Adults behind Bars, New Study Says." *The New York Times*, 28 Feb. 2008, www.nytimes.com/2008/02/28/us/28cnd-prison.html.

Lu, Thoai. "Michelle Alexander: More Black Men in Prison than Were Enslaved in 1850." *Colorlines*, 30 Mar. 2011, www.colorlines.com/articles/michelle-alexander-more-black-men-prison-were-enslaved-1850.

Lynch, Mona. *Sunbelt Justice: Arizona and the Transformation of American Punishment.* Stanford UP, 2009.

Malcolm X and Alex Haley. *The Autobiography of Malcolm X: As Told to Alex Haley.* 1966. Ballantine, 1987.

"The Most Significant Criminal Justice Policy Changes from the COVID-19 Pandemic." *Prison Policy Initiative*, 24 Nov. 2020, www.prisonpolicy.org/virus/virusresponse.html.

Reed, Austin. *The Life and Adventures of a Haunted Convict.* 1858. Modern Library, 2016.

Rios, Victor M. "The Hyper-criminalization of Black and Latino Male Youth in the Era of Mass Incarceration," *Souls: A Critical Journal of Black Politics, Culture, and Society*, vol. 8, no. 2, 2006, pp. 40–54.

Rodríguez, Dylan. *Forced Passages: Imprisoned Radical Intellectuals and the U.S. Prison Regime.* U of Minnesota P, 2006.

Sawyer, Wendy, and Peter Wagner. "Mass Incarceration: The Whole Pie 2022." *Prison Policy Initiative*, 14 Mar. 2022, prisonpolicy.org/reports/pie2022.html.

Siegel, Micol. "Critical Prison Studies: Review of a Field." *American Quarterly*, vol. 70, no. 1, 2018, pp. 123–37.

Stern, Kaia. *Voices from American Prisons: Faith, Education, and Healing.* Routledge, 2014.

Weissman, Sara. "Education behind and beyond Bars." *Inside Higher Ed*, 18 May 2021, insidehighered.com/news/2021/05/18/new-moment-prison-education.

PART ONE
PURPOSES

Riotous Study: Black Studies, Academic Unfreedom, and Surveilled Pedagogy in Prison Education

Jess A. Goldberg

In his 1829 *Appeal . . . to the Coloured Citizens of the World*, one of the central arguments the Black abolitionist writer David Walker makes is that, contra Thomas Jefferson's writings on the intellectual incapacities of Africans in "Query 14" of his *Notes on the State of Virginia*, Black people are capable of literacy should they simply be given the opportunity to attain an education in reading and writing. From his assertion of ability, Walker exhorts Black people to become literate and use education to prove to the world that the Black race is indeed Human.[1] Alongside this, Walker argues that Black people are kept from literacy education primarily because enslavers know that the more reading an enslaved person does, the harder that enslaved person—that chattelized Black human being—becomes to mentally control. He reflects specifically on the censorship applied to his *Appeal* itself and the surveillance mechanisms employed to keep it out of the hands of Black people in the South especially:

> Why do the Slave-holders or Tyrants of America and their advocates fight so hard to keep my brethren from receiving and reading my Book of Appeal to them?—Is it because they treat us so well?—Is it because we are satisfied to rest in Slavery to them and their children?—Is it because they are treating us like men, by compensating us all over this free country!! for our labours?—But why are the Americans so very fearfully terrified respecting my Book?—Why do they search vessels, &c. when entering the harbours of tyrannical States, to see if any of my Books can be found, for fear that my brethren will get them to read. Why, I thought the Americans proclaimed to the world that they are a happy, enlightened, humane and Christian people, all the inhabitants of the country enjoy equal Rights!! America is the Asylum for the oppressed of all nations!!!

Through an accumulation of references, allusions, and pointed rhetorical questions, Walker makes clear that censorship of reading materials available to the oppressed is directly linked with the oppressor's fear of a rebellion or revolution that the oppressor knows is justified and so must be vehemently cut off before it can begin.

If we follow the work of Angela Y. Davis, Ruth Wilson Gilmore, Saidiya Hartman, Douglas Blackmon, Dennis Childs, Patrick Elliot Alexander, and numerous other scholars and writers thinking about the prison-industrial complex as an afterlife of slavery, we can hear in Walker's early-nineteenth-century argument a diagnosis of mechanisms of surveillance within twenty-first-century prisons. In this essay, I examine censorship and academic unfreedom in prison education with Walker in mind as I reflect on my own experience teaching literature and writing in prisons in central New York State from 2016 to 2018. As a point of departure, I am revisiting a defining moment in that teaching experience, a moment enmeshed in a five-word sentence that invoked a centuries-old fear of rebellion.

"This will incite a riot."

That's apparently what a figure of authority at the prison at which I was supposed to teach World Literature I in summer 2017 said when she told my coordinator that my entire syllabus was rejected. I would be given a weekend to create a new, acceptable syllabus or the course would be dropped for the summer and students would have to wait an entire semester to take this class that was required for their associate's degrees.

In the ensuing pages, I flesh out this experience and connect it to critical discourse around book censorship in jails and prisons to think through the problem of academic unfreedom and surveilled pedagogy in prison education, especially and specifically for literature and writing professors teaching in the field of Black studies. Through reflection on the classroom experiences I have shared with my students, I hope to sketch out how those of us who work with incarcerated students can attempt to employ what Fred Moten might call the "fugitivity" of Black studies pedagogy (see "Taste" and "Knowledge") through seemingly innocuous course texts. In its very attempt to censor, I argue, the prison invites resistance discourse in through the back door, because that discourse was already there to begin with. That is, while censorship in a prison environment is often articulated by agents of the state as proactive or preventive, it is a fundamentally reactionary mechanism; because resistance to carceral control precedes censorship in the first place, censorship is always attempting to catch up to discourses and knowledges already beyond its reach.

I taught my first prison class in summer 2016 inside a men's maximum security state "correctional facility"[2] in central New York. The course was an introductory English class, and in it I assigned Junot Diaz's short story collection *Drown*, Toni Morrison's novel *A Mercy*, Zora Neale Hurston's novel *Their Eyes Were Watching God*, and Marjorie Chan's play *A Nanking Winter*. These texts all highlight, to different degrees, issues including racism, sexism, sexuality, war, and violence. They also make use of multiple levels of narration or multiple narrators to create conversation on the page. In designing the syllabus around the theme of writing with and against other voices, I selected these works to attune students to the ways in which writing is a conversation that happens with, against, and around others. The course's content was thus aligned with my pedagogical commitment to helping students transform the classroom space into a community of collective learning—a task that is particularly inflected and important in a prison classroom, wherein students often have very diverse educational backgrounds. Despite the fact that students were accustomed, in the everyday workings of the prison, to being addressed by officers as "inmate" rather than by name—just one of many ways in which the law, in Colin Dayan's words, can "make and unmake persons"—the classroom was to be a place and class itself was to be a time in which they would be recognized as the full persons they still were. This recognition is not an appeal by an individual civil subject to an authority or power—either the state or, in the case of a college class, the teacher—but rather a collectively weaved communal project. Reflecting on the multilayered narration of *Their Eyes Were Watching God*, one student posited that because within the third-person framing narrative the protagonist, Janie, is telling her story to her friend, whom she empowers to tell the rest of the town, the novel winds up "creating a communal voice to tell its story." In so doing, the work models communal voice in the prison classroom, where the surrounding infrastructure seeks to obliterate all forms of community and sociality.

Hurston's text even opened space for the students to have a deep and powerful conversation about masculinity, violence, and the prison environment. For example, the character Tea Cake demonstrates throughout the novel a charm and masculine swagger that often makes him attractive to readers, and for most of his time with Janie he is a compassionate partner to her. So students were alarmed when, near the end of the novel, Tea Cake strikes Janie after he perceives another man as flirting with her. Some students in the class tried to defend this moment as understandable even if not excusable, arguing that Tea Cake hit Janie because he loved her so much he didn't want to lose her to someone else. I asked the students why Tea Cake might think that hitting the woman he loves is a proper expression of love, and they talked about how men are sometimes socialized to believe in love as a kind of "owning," and physical violence as the proper way to "protect" what's yours. I should say here that part of my teaching persona is to perform my own queer, ambivalent relation to masculinity with students, to invite reflection on vulnerability and notions of power. But without my prompting, this conversation about Tea Cake eventually pivoted to critical reflections on the ways in which violence and masculinity go hand in hand for these students in the prison. In the following weeks, our class continued to return to the idea of masculinity, and to this day these students have, as a group, provided me with the deepest critical interrogations of masculinity I have been a part of as a teacher in my career. It wasn't because I brought them an essay on feminist or queer theory or snuck in a manifesto past the guards. It was because we worked together to build a community of learners willing to see each other in ways in which the guards patrolling outside our classroom refused to see us.

The following summer, 2017, the teachers from my program returned to find that the same prison had banned Hurston's novel, as well as a number of other texts by Black authors that had previously been successfully taught in college courses at the prison, including James Baldwin's *The Fire Next Time* and Charles W. Chesnutt's *The Marrow of Tradition*. When we asked for an explanation, we were told that in the case of Hurston's book, since it was written in dialect rather than standard (the word used by prison staff was "proper") English, it actually hurt the students' academic progress because they would think it was acceptable to write that way. Never mind that this judgment was made for us, the teachers and content experts, by prison officials; its appeal to the rigors of standard written English quickly unraveled as the prison's logic of censorship revealed itself in response to my proposed world literature syllabus.

I am not a world literature scholar, but because the course is required for the associate's degree in liberal arts toward which students in the Cornell Prison Education Program work, many students needed the class to complete their degrees, and I offered to teach it. To keep the content somewhat in my intellectual wheelhouse, I leaned on principles of academic freedom that I often take for granted and decided to design a syllabus organized around African diaspora literature, a global force that has touched every continent. After looking at the texts on my syllabus, however, prison officials barred the entire course and told me that I had less than a week to come up with an entirely new syllabus. They had noticed that one of the texts had the word *negro* in it, which alarmed them since they thought the word inappropriate for the classroom, then looked through all of the texts and realized that some—though not all—of them discussed slavery and, I believe more importantly, slave rebellions. "This," they pronounced, "could incite a riot."

After meeting with the program director at the university early on a Friday morning, I crafted an entirely new syllabus over the weekend, redesigning the course as a global theater survey featuring classic plays from *The Wadsworth Anthology of Drama* (Worthen), and sent it to my supervisors on Monday afternoon. That syllabus was approved.

Like a Trojan horse, the bulky, standard-looking anthology housed pedagogical and conceptual remnants from the African diaspora course I had originally designed. Despite the fact that African writers are underrepresented in the anthology, as are women in general, the original course's themes emerged through the concerns raised by the canonical plays that I wound up teaching and the inflection those plays took on within a prison setting. Two class discussions in particular can be usefully considered within one theoretical framework of Black studies and the structural antiblackness of the prison-industrial complex.

The course opened with Aeschylus's *Oresteia*, the trilogy including *Agamemnon, The Libation Bearers*, and *The Eumenides*. These plays, which are often taught as some of the first works in the Western canon of drama and would be conspicuous in their absence from a global theater course, tell the stories of the murder of Agamemnon by Clytemnestra, the murder of Clytemnestra by Orestes, and then the trial of Orestes, through which the goddess Athena inaugurates the rule of law by trial in Greek society. Throughout our discussions of the three plays, students were drawn to the themes of revenge and violence as methods of achieving justice. (Such themes are of great interest to David Walker as well, but we shall return to that connection.) During our study of the first play in the trilogy, I asked which character seemed like the most important one to the plot, and without even waiting to raise their hands nearly all the students quickly suggested Clytemnestra. "So why isn't the play called *Clytemnestra* instead of *Agamemnon*?" I asked. Since I had introduced the basic literary concept of the absent center and used our first class meeting to discuss the historical processes of canonization that underpin literature surveys like the one in which the students found themselves, they had been primed to think about the mechanisms by which any set is structured both by what is there and by what is not. That is, the meaning of a narrative literary text depends just as much on what is excluded from the narrative's attention or focalization as it does on what is explicitly included. The best explanation, I believe, comes from Toni Morrison's

"Unspeakable Things Unspoken: The Afro-American Presence in American Literature," which states that "a void may be empty, but it is not a vacuum; certain absences are so stressed, so ornate, so planned, they call attention to themselves . . . " (210). There is nothing inherently radical about this idea, of course. One could also point to Susan Glaspell's 1916 play *Trifles* as emplotting the concept especially clearly through gender. It is a fundamental analytic tool within literary and performance studies and thus a necessary component of any college-level course in these disciplines that has nothing inherently to do with race, gender, class, sexuality, or any other mode of human difference. Whether or not one chooses to focus their teaching on social inequalities that frighten prison officials, the study of meaning and interpretation must by necessity address the absences that allow meaning to cohere.[3]

That is why one question, "Why isn't the play called *Clytemnestra?*," sparked a forty-five-minute discussion about the exclusion of women from the play's conceptions of justice and how the murder of Iphigenia, Clytemnestra's daughter, goes unaccounted for until her mother takes it upon herself to seek retribution. This line of thinking reemerged and sharpened when we confronted Clytemnestra's ghost in *The Eumenides*. In this final play of the trilogy, Clytemnestra's ghost appears to provoke the Furies to chase Orestes and exact punishment on him for his crime of matricide. I introduced students to some theoretical vocabulary on hauntology and pushed them to think about the literary meanings of ghosts as those which return to make a demand.[4] Prompted by a student who had taken a political science course in an earlier semester, we fleshed out Thomas Hobbes's idea of the social contract in examining Athena's declaration that trials by law exist to determine order and justice in the future rather than to exact personal revenge, which, the students all agreed, seems like a very good idea. But the ghost soon reappeared in our discussion (one student even pointed out how the ghost's return after having been left behind in our own classroom conversation paralleled her return in the play). The ghost, one student said, reminds us of who is left out of the contract. Thus, the class concluded, the ghost tells us how the contract is a sham. In this moment, the students had, without knowing it, aligned Aeschylus's play with Walker's *Appeal* in identifying this critique of the so-called social contract and offering an account of justifiable vengeance as a kind of justice. The students then began theorizing how the social contract as a political fiction depends upon the exclusion of certain persons from its terms to maintain order, be it women in Greece or Black people or poor people in the United States—as they saw for themselves in prison. I must confess I was hoping this would come up, but I did not anticipate one student's insightful closing remarks of the day: "The ghost is an activist. She draws our attention to injustice so we can do justice outside the law."[5]

What happened in that class was both more than and dependent on the content of the texts I was able to bring into the classroom under the surveilling eye of the state. In the most obvious sense, my selection of *The Wadsworth Anthology* was a performance of deference to the prison's regime of surveillance, made necessary by my primary goal as a teacher: help the incarcerated students earn college credits. It is not necessarily the job of the prison educator to teach about prisons or systems of justice and injustice. And it is necessary to state clearly that teachers who come to prison education with a heroic sense of self as The One who will bring revelation to the darkened minds of those inside the prison walls are not the teachers who should be doing this work. Prison teaching, perhaps even more than teaching outside the carceral institution, is a collaborative and collective endeavor in which the teacher is as much a learner as a teacher and every student is as much a teacher as a learner. With that in mind, at the end of the day, my goal was not to teach incarcerated people about their own experiences—to do so would be presumptuous at least—but to achieve the concrete task of facilitating the students' earning credits toward a degree, because I was fortunate enough to work in a program with the means of providing those resources. That goal was more important than picking a fight about my own academic freedom as a scholar, and so I chose to teach from a collection of canonical works by primarily white and primarily male authors. That anthology got me in the door to facilitate the practical side of the students' education. That was step one.

Step two was about what happens after getting by the surveilled gate and into the surveilled classroom. While there were no officers in the classroom with me as I taught, there were always officers just outside the classroom, peering through the glass window and taking visual note of our class. What this meant was that all pedagogy in that classroom was surveilled pedagogy. In the context of such an overpowering regime of surveillance, I had to draw on my method of course design to craft my teaching practices. That is, just as I responded to the state's flexing of its (illogical) power over my syllabus in a manner that allowed me to attempt to remain an agent *in but not of* the carceral regime (the prison teacher cannot escape being part of the history of prison reform used to justify the very existence of the prison-industrial complex, even those of us who are, politically, prison abolitionists), I had to organize my teaching to facilitate community-building and critical questioning without appearing

to fly in the face of institutional rules or to challenge those rules' enforc-
ers (even when they delayed or disrupted our class).[6] Building on student
interests, approaching students as potential teachers, and remaining always a learner oneself allows one to maneuver one's academic unfreedom through a pedagogy that remains out of reach of the law.

Such academic unfreedom, of course, is part of a larger issue of censorship in prisons that exceeds education programs and recent headlines.
As reporting by the Vera Institute documents, the practice of banning
books is ubiquitous throughout the United States and is accomplished
through a number of different policy mechanisms, including blatant censorship lists, strict rules about who is permitted to send or receive materials to and from incarcerated individuals, and vague guidelines of criteria
according to which individual officers can reject reading materials sent
or brought into a carceral facility (Dholakia). According to most activists
and organizers working to get books into carceral facilities, these various
mechanisms for keeping books out of the hands of incarcerated people
are indicative of the fear, often explicitly articulated by the prison workers who are rejecting and banning materials, that reading materials pose
a threat to the order of the prison. In the case of my specific teaching
experience, the declaration that the texts on my syllabus could "incite a
riot" is more than a frustrating imposition of arbitrary law, like so many
of the orders given by correctional officers in the course of a day. There
was enough sense of threat to an institution where revolutionary books
like *The Autobiography of Malcolm X* were already available through the
prison's library that the logic of riot-quelling was employed as justification for the obliteration of academic freedom. Grant Farred writes in *In
Motion, at Rest: The Event of the Athletic Body* that "the law knows itself
as, before all else, vulnerable" (11). That is, the state's surveillance is as
much an indication of its awareness of its own possible undoing as it is
an instance of the exercise of power. Why did my syllabus, more than a
library book, suggest that undoing?

It is not the text alone that the deputy fears; it is the community solidarity built by common study—perhaps what Stefano Harney and Fred
Moten would call "black study" in the "undercommons." The crude carceral epistemology of surveillance does not discern, however, that Black
study is not merely about the objects of analysis but about a disposition
toward fugitivity that exceeds any biologically, culturally, or epidermally
essentialized blackness. Blackness, for Moten, is not an object of study
but a force of escape that exceeds the grasp of the law ("Blackness").
So while the prison-industrial complex reveals in this logic of surveillance that its antiblackness is not only a mode of locking Black bodies in

cages but also a mode of attempting to obliterate Black thought, it remains true that just as Black life always continues despite the legal imposition of social death, Black study cannot be snuffed out by censorship. Black study blackens the most canonical European texts. One of my colleagues correctly pointed out that banning discussion of slavery or rebellion is essentially banning Black studies, and in a fundamental way she is absolutely correct. But what if some stuff slips through?

Our pedagogy may not be able to directly confront the force of law, but it is precisely in refusing the direct confrontation, perhaps, if we follow Harney and Moten's logic, that the possibility for radical abolition emerges through a refusal to be recognized by the institution's attunement to resistance. I'll close, then, by asking those of us who do the work around which this volume is organized, the work of teaching literature and writing in prisons, to also do the work of cultivating an undercommons. Let us do the work of fugitive planning. Let us do the work of Black study—work that exceeds, in Moten's theorization, our epidermalization. I would urge those of us in (but not of) the academy, and those of us in excess of the academy, who care about the surveilled pedagogies of prison classrooms to think about the possibility of fugitive pedagogy that is *in but not of* the prison. In the absence of academic freedom, and in the face of unapologetic antiblackness, how might we do Black study, which is nothing if not the study toward a freedom that exceeds the academic, inside the concrete walls of carcerality?

NOTES

1. Drawing on a rich body of scholarship in Black studies, I employ the capitalized "Human" to intentionally differentiate the socially constructed figure of "the Human" imagined through European humanist thought from the biological designation "human being"; that is, not all humans (with a small *h*) are included in the socially, juridically, and politically constructed category of the Human (with a capital *H*).

2. New York State officially designates prisons and jails as "correctional facilities" in its naming conventions. Like most carceral studies scholars and prison abolitionists, I reject the logic of "corrections" denoted by this naming. Prisons and jails are penal institutions. They exacerbate social problems; they do not "correct" anything.

3. If permitting the construction of meaning around an absence sounds like a fundamental function of prisons themselves, it should. As Davis writes, "The prison therefore functions ideologically as an abstract site into which undesirables are deposited, relieving us of the responsibility of thinking about the real issues afflicting those communities from which prisoners are drawn in such

disproportionate numbers. This is the ideological work that the prison performs—it relieves us of the responsibility of seriously engaging with the problems of our society, especially those produced by racism and, increasingly, global capitalism. . . . The prison has become a black hole into which the detritus of contemporary capitalism is deposited" (*Are Prisons Obsolete?* 16).

4. The signal theory text for me in referencing hauntology is Jacques Derrida's *Specters of Marx*.

5. This series of class discussions on the *Oresteia* trilogy and my brief introduction of Derrida—traditionally characterized as a particularly difficult thinker within critical theory—exemplify the kind of powerful analysis and critical thinking I have observed during courses inside carceral facilities. I am often deeply frustrated in conversation with other teachers or academics when I encounter the assumption that incarcerated students are somehow less capable of handling difficult material or engaging in critical thinking or that, in the words of one colleague, conversations are "more emotional and less analytical" inside prison classrooms. I wouldn't feel the need to note this here had I not heard it enough times that I can hear it coming before it is said in some conversations. I hope readers coming to this anthology without previous experience teaching inside prisons walk away from this scene of class discussion committed to setting aside preexisting assumptions about which kinds of students are or are not capable of what "levels" of academic work. The prison infrastructure certainly imposed limitations, but those limitations are not inherent to the students.

6. Stefano Harney and Fred Moten theorize the *in but not of* formulation in "The University and the Undercommons," writing, "Yet the maroons refuse professionalization, that is, to be against the university. The university will not recognize this indecision, and thus professionalization is shaped precisely by what it cannot acknowledge, its internal antagonism, its wayward labor, its surplus" (31–32). Similarly, it is the job of the prison teacher to refuse professionalization—to refuse to be against the prison in which they teach. Such confrontation risks retaliation against the students, who cannot leave the prison after class. In contrast, to operate in the indecision that Moten and Harney designate is to neither confront nor capitulate to the surveillance regime.

WORKS CITED

Aeschylus. *The Oresteia. The Wadsworth Anthology of Drama*, edited by W. B. Worthen, 6th ed., Wadsworth, 2011, pp. 28–74.

Dayan, Colin. *The Law Is a White Dog: How Legal Rituals Make and Unmake Persons*. Princeton UP, 2011.

Derrida, Jacques. *Specters of Marx: The State of the Debt, the Work of Mourning, and the New International*. Translated by Peggy Kamuf, Routledge, 1993.

Dholakia, Nazish. "The Cruel Practice of Banning Books behind Bars." *Vera Institute*, 4 Apr., 2022, vera.org/news/the-cruel-practice-of-banning-books-behind-bars.

Farred, Grant. *In Motion, at Rest: The Event of the Athletic Body.* U of Minnesota P, 2014.

Glaspell, Susan. *Trifles.* 1916. Samuel French, 2010.

Harney, Stefano, and Fred Moten. "The University and the Undercommons." *The Undercommons: Fugitive Planning and Black Study*, by Harney and Moten, Minor Compositions, 2013, pp. 22–43.

Hurston, Zora Neale. *Their Eyes Were Watching God.* 1937. Harper Perennial, 2006.

Jefferson, Thomas. *"Notes on the State of Virginia:* Query 14." 1781. *Teaching American History*, Ashland University, 2023, teachingamericanhistory .org/document/notes-on-the-state-of-viriginia-query-xiv-justice/.

Morrison, Toni. "Unspeakable Things Unspoken: The Afro-American Presence in American Literature." *The Source of Self-Regard: Selected Essays, Speeches, and Meditations*, Penguin Random House, 2019, pp. 161–97.

Moten, Fred. "Blackness and Nothingness (Mysticism in the Flesh)." *South Atlantic Quarterly*, vol. 112, no. 4, 2013, pp. 737–80.

———. "Knowledge of Freedom." *CR: The New Centennial Review*, vol. 4, no. 2, 2004, pp. 269–310.

———. "Taste Dissonance Flavor Escape: Preface for a Solo by Miles Davis." *Women and Performance*, vol. 17, no. 2, 2007, pp. 217–46.

Walker, David. *Walker's Appeal, in Four Parts, Together with a Preamble, to the Coloured Citizens of the World, but in Particular, and Very Expressly, to Those of the United States of America.* 1830. *Documenting the American South*, 2001, docsouth.unc.edu/nc/walker/walker.html.

Power Mapping the Capitol: Notes on Abolitionist Pedagogy and Captive Study

Meghan G. McDowell and Alison Rose Reed

Our riotous laughter echoed down the corridor, pricking the ears of the guards as it reached their station. The three guards seemed to turn their heads in unison, squinting as they stared down the hallway to our small group, six students and two professors gathered around tables bolted to the floor. It felt as though the guards were trying to determine whether our laughter was a conspiracy of conviviality, a seeding of intimacy to be stamped out, or just a harmless joke. Wondering, they sauntered closer, enclosing us in a semicircle. They feigned interest, asking what we were reading, made small talk, and eventually went back to their guard station. A jailed student had made a particularly funny comment about the Peacekeepers—the police force that terrorizes residents in Suzanne Collins's dystopian bestseller *The Hunger Games*. While neither of us can recall the exact joke, the guards' response to our laughter is unforgettable, as it marked the only time they approached us that semester.

We were gathered that day as part of the inaugural reading group for Humanities Behind Bars (HBB). HBB began in 2016 and is dedicated to cultivating inside-outside alliances and imagining a world without cops, cages, or mass criminalization. Our work is rooted in community-based study, mutual aid, and organizing that centers formerly and currently incarcerated people and their loved ones throughout the Tidewater region.[1] Like all outside programming in jails and prisons, HBB is subject to a laundry list of rules that govern our conduct as designated "volunteers" (a term that implies a charity model of which HBB remains critical) and that of jailed students. The felt experience of these rules is often one of arbitrariness and uneven enforcement contingent on a rookie guard or the weather or a "security threat." Either way, the tempo of discipline is arrhythmic, frustrating the lesson plan but never the plot. Why did our shared laughter solicit a response from the guards? Did our laughter contain a threat? What, if anything, can such moments teach us about the possibilities of building inside-outside alliances under conditions of capture? The guards' proactive response seemed to suggest that our laughter was perceived as inappropriate conduct, as an affective exchange unfitting to educational programming inside a jail.

In this essay, we build from and with this moment of shared laughter to examine the potentiality of conviviality, "elective affinities" (Condorelli, "Company" [Part Two]), and resistance to carceral state power that is generated through the collective study of literature. Our use of the term *study* is aligned with Stefano Harney and Fred Moten's articulation of study as a fugitive form of sociality—a being *with* and *for*—and as a method of analysis that makes visible and disarticulates the logics of antirationality, war, theft, erasure, and debt foundational to the university itself. Following recent contributions theorizing resistance, abolition, and friendship, or what Nick Montgomery and Carla Bergman call "joyful militancy," we ask how the collective study of literature can cultivate intimacies that enable us to feel the texture of an abolitionist present and build collective autonomy amid conditions of captive study.

To examine this and related questions, we begin by reviewing antifraternization policies standard in jails and prisons across the country. We suggest that these policies are expressions of carceral power rooted in antiblackness, an outgrowth of earlier laws that attempted to deny enslaved people freedom of association, the ability to gather, plan, plot, and execute. We then turn to contemporary imprisoned intellectuals as they theorize the potential embodied in the "queer logics" (Varner 211) of intimacy and affinity in prison. Finally, we build on these insights by examining our experience studying *The Hunger Games* and Marita Bonner's Black feminist play *The Purple Flower* with students warehoused at a jail in Norfolk, Virginia. We argue that literature, read through the lens of critical prison studies, provides what we elsewhere identify as a "Trojan horse tactic" for building countercarceral forms of intimacy that enable us to pursue a critique of the carceral state and neoliberal college-in-prison programs (McDowell and Reed 159). We extend Avery Gordon and Céline Condorelli's theorization of friendship, as a relational and affective positionality of "both 'being close to' and 'making common cause'" (Condorelli, "Company" [Part Two]), to the collective study of literature with incarcerated students, understanding the power dynamics that shape the scene of teaching.

No Friendships Here: Antifraternizing Regulations and Carceral Power

The sociality of laughter, often contagious and occasionally conspiratorial, gestures toward bonds of association that are expressly prohibited by anti-fraternization policies in detention facilities. These regulations ostensibly govern interactions between staff and prisoners (and extend to educators and other outside volunteers as well). The Virginia Department of Corrections policy defining *fraternization* provides a fairly typical example:

> Employee association with offenders, or their family members, or close friends of offenders outside of employee job functions, that extends to unacceptable, unprofessional, and prohibited behavior; examples include non-work-related visits between offenders and employees, non-work-related relationships with family members or close friends of offenders, connections on social media, discussing employee personal matters (marriage, children, work, etc.) with offenders, and engaging in romantic or sexual relationships with offenders. ("Operating Procedure" 7)

On the one hand, the effort to regulate a divergent set of associations and to develop a juridical concept of intimacy within carceral institutions could be said to reflect the best impulses of a liberal-reformist state—a state that, through antifraternizing policies, recognizes that consent is simply not possible between staff and imprisoned people, as the very terms of association and intimacy are always already saturated by the intersecting forms of violence that cohere the prison regime. Yet, on the other hand, staff, outside volunteers, and people warehoused in jails and prisons across the United States are not legal abstractions but share what Gordon terms "complex personhood," the idea that "even those who live in the most dire circumstances possess a complex and oftentimes contradictory humanity and subjectivity that is never adequately glimpsed by viewing them as victims or . . . superhuman agents" (4).

To be clear, we are not suggesting that sexual relationships between staff or volunteers and imprisoned people be sanctioned; rather, we are concerned with the countercarceral forms of relationality these policies attempt to extinguish. For example, Lyle May, held captive on North Carolina's death row, writes beautifully about the complexities of intimacy in carceral spaces, arguing that while policies against romantic fraternization between guards and prisoners "is understandable," these rules also deny the fact that "human beings just insist on being social creatures, and no matter how much you indoctrinate or denigrate them, they remain as such." Throughout his essay, May expands on this point, discussing the consequences for staff and volunteers who break the "unwritten rules" governing death row: disinterest, allegiance to policy, frequent staff turnover to reduce familiarity, and, above all, a belief in the status quo. Staff and volunteers who refuse these terms and instead relate to prisoners with kindness, respect, compassion, and patience are "scrutinized for their friendliness" and eventually fired or transferred by prison administrators. "The problem with [staff's] recognition and nurturing of our humanity," May concludes, "is that it, too, ignored the unwritten rules."

Similarly, the formerly incarcerated scholar Deena Varner examines "the queer logic" of intimacies that traffic between and among jailers and the jailed. While not ignoring the institutional violence that makes and remakes the jail, or denying its Foucauldian effort "to produce normative subjects," Varner directs our attention to the ways imprisoned folks "co-construct queer logics of sex, sexuality, work, play, and leisure," thereby resisting the "domination of a system designed to efface them" (211). Namely, Varner takes issue with the prevailing idea that the structural conditions of jail or prison foreclose the possibility for detainees to seek authentic agential pleasure. This premise, Varner suggests, is false on two accounts. First, it erroneously imagines detainees as subjects that can only be acted upon. Second, it assumes, and therefore reproduces, a binary between the inside and the outside world, where the violence of the prison is an exception to, or in excess of, the liberal democratic order. Varner joins a long list of jailhouse theorists who have argued against this binary, repositioning the United States writ large as a "prison regime," to borrow a phrase from Dylan Rodríguez, or, as one incarcerated student put it during class discussion, "Jail? It's a jail out there!"

Instead, Varner reminds us that "all [prisoners] have histories, families, and sexualities"—what we might name here collectively as intimacies—"that exceed the putative boundaries of the prison." Therefore, the nondistinction between the inside and outside world, "and the excess that is constitutive of it," Varner explains, is further unmasked by policies that seek to extinguish incarcerated people's capacity for intimacy: "The very existence of a prohibition against 'fraternization' implies the constructedness of the difference between punished and punisher, insider and outsider, and reveals the flimsiness of the foundation on which such a distinction is built" (214). Jails and prisons, then, not only warehouse people's productive capacities; through antifraternization policies, these institutions also attempt to break bonds of association that "nurture our humanity" and recognize our insistence on "being social creatures," to return to May's evocative phrasing. Indeed, racial capitalism, the system that jails and prisons serve, has always waged war "on collective life itself" (Melamed 78), using racism—"the state-sanctioned or extralegal production and exploitation of group-differentiated vulnerability to premature death"—to differentiate between valued, value-producing, and valueless forms of human life (Gilmore 28).

Both Melamed's and Gilmore's analyses of racial capitalism necessitate a rereading of antifraternization policies, one that moves away from liberal-democratic efforts to eliminate sexual violence in prisons and instead asks us to examine these regulations through the logics of chattel slavery—understanding the prison *as* sexual violence. The prison abolitionist scholar and activist Angela Y. Davis has written extensively about the relationship between slavery and incarceration, noting that enslaved people were denied freedom of association and that social death is predicated on the kinship-destroying practices of human commodification (see, for example, *Meaning of Freedom*). Post-Emancipation, Davis argues, the criminal legal system absorbed these racialized punishment practices, determining "that Black people were to be socially defined in large part by re-created conditions of slavery" ("Racialized Punishment" 101). Just as bonds of association were the foundation of enslaved people's rebellions and general strike against slavery, so too are contemporary imprisoned people's efforts to contest their state-sanctioned premature death.

Recontextualizing antifraternization policies through the lens of critical prison studies not only helps clarify how carceral power operates but also points toward a fugitive politics of possibility premised on Harney and Moten's definition of study as a mode of being *with* and *for*. This is how Montgomery and Bergman, too, understand affinity, as a form of sociality "based in shared commitments and desires without erasing differences [or] trampling on each other's autonomy" (108–09). While risky and fraught with myriad forms of neoliberal entrapment, devising pedagogical practices that center study remains an ethical imperative if we are to work against the violent aspiration, shared by universities and jails alike, of education as preparation for assimilating into an antirelational racial capitalist society. Instead, an abolitionist orientation toward pedagogy thrives in the transformative zones of social encounter. We thus see affinities expressed through shared laughter as deeply radical acts in the context of a state that attempts to systematically sever social relations, an argument we explore in the following section.

Bridging Vulnerabilities: *The Hunger Games* and *The Purple Flower*

Our two case studies, Collins's *The Hunger Games* and Bonner's *The Purple Flower*, illustrate how friendship as a modality of abolitionist pedagogy functions in classroom spaces. Engaging with the work of critical prison studies scholars such as Davis, Rodríguez, and Patrick Elliot Alexander, our reference to abolitionist pedagogy describes group-based study that centers the transformative possibilities of collective knowledge production and interrupts state-sanctioned forms of social isolation and "educational deprivation" rooted in white supremacy (Alexander 10). We also follow this scholarship's critique of the way college-in-prison programs can reproduce neoliberal models of education for assimilation into—rather than transformation of—existing institutions (see Harkins and Meiners; McDowell and Reed; Meyerhoff). Abolitionist pedagogy not only serves as an indictment of the harmful and harm-inducing logics that govern neoliberal educational models in universities and prisons alike but also suggests ways to build alternative praxes guided by the Black radical tradition's emphasis on improvisation, self-determined action, and nonhierarchical, movement-oriented collective study.

While many readers will be familiar with *The Hunger Games*, we offer a brief synopsis here. Published to critical acclaim in 2008, the trilogy is set in Panem, a futuristic world destroyed by human-induced climate change. There are twelve districts in Panem, controlled by the Capitol, the seat of an authoritarian government. President Snow rules over Panem, a racially and economically stratified society. The rich and famous live in the Capitol, where resources are reliably abundant. The remaining twelve districts are run as labor camps, geographically bound areas whose impoverished workers mine the resources that enrich the Capitol. Wealth and political power are concentrated in the hands of Snow, whose Orwellian Peacekeepers use surveillance and violence to manage productivity and repress uprisings in the districts.

Each year the Capitol hosts the Hunger Games, a televised event where pairs of "tributes" from each district compete to the death, the final survivor winning fame and fortune. The tributes are selected by a lottery and can only be replaced by a family member. In the first novel, we are introduced to the central heroine, sixteen-year-old Katniss Everdeen, who saves her sister's life by volunteering to take her place in the games. The book goes on to chronicle Katniss's effort to not only survive but ultimately subvert the games, seeding a multidistrict rebellion against the Capitol. Despite its limitations (see Siddiquee), the novel allows for a robust study of racial capitalism, state violence, solidarity, and resistance.

One of the first exercises we did as a group was to make a power map of Panem. Power mapping is often used in popular education and organizing campaigns to identify points of pressure, those people and institutions that must be leveraged to create change. In our class, it was useful to sketch out the Capitol's methods of consolidating and maintaining power. Through power mapping we were able to answer important questions, such as, What prevents the districts from rebelling? How does the Capitol maintain control when they are outnumbered by people in the other districts? Just as significantly, we were also able to map relationships of power between otherwise discrete ideologies and institutions. For example, in response to the question about how the Capitol maintains control, jailed students emphasized how material and ideological forces meld to create a carceral society. Students described this society as one where spectacular forms of violence—like raids by the Peacekeepers, or tributes fighting to the death in the Hunger Games—are paired with the systematic suffering caused by segregation, poverty, bodily disintegration from years of forced manual labor, and psychological weariness, as many people living in the Districts accepted their material conditions as fate. "You suppress yourself," as one student put it.

Similar to jail or prison, the arena where the Hunger Games are played is not an exceptional space in an otherwise democratic society but rather reflects and consolidates the conditions of everyday life in Panem. The Hunger Games, students quickly realized, are a hyperrealization of the carceral logics that govern all of Panem: disposability, extraction, spectacle, segregation, and premature death. The games attempt to reproduce a particular way of relating to one another premised on individuality, competition, and fear, spokes in a wheel of antirelationality. In *Joyful Militancy*, Montgomery and Bergman explain how empire strives to eradicate interdependent relationships, or what they call "a dangerous closeness," by making intimacy legible through white supremacist, heteropatriarchal norms and "through relentless violence, division, competition, [and] management" (82). Students described this as being "taught to hate each other but love wealth" and spoke of being "trapped" in a country "chasing a mythical dream" but knowing "it's not my dream."

Perhaps the single most important lesson from our power mapping exercise was the recognition that "the state," "violence," "dehumanization," "labor," and "segregation," for example, are not mere abstractions or fate or an experience that some have and others do not; rather, they are relationships between people, places, and things. "The state is a social relationship," argues the political theorist Gustav Landauer, "a certain way of people relating to one another. It can be destroyed by creating new relationships" (qtd. in Montgomery and Bergman 106). For Landauer, revolutionary transformation is an "immediate, situated, ethical project" that begins by remaking ourselves and "undoing the state's hold on our relationships" (106).

A pivotal scene in *The Hunger Games* brings Landauer's point to life. Amid the imperative to kill or be killed, Katniss forms an unlikely bond with Rue, a competitor from one of Panem's poorest districts. Rue and Katniss work together to protect each other, gathering and sharing resources and hatching a plot to beat the Careers, tributes from the Capitol who have spent their entire lives training for the games. Despite their efforts, Rue eventually dies at the hands of another tribute. Rue's death ignites Katniss and foreshadows the Capitol's undoing, as the heroine no longer intends to merely survive the games but instead vows to overthrow the Capitol by uniting the districts. Katniss's revolutionary praxis, however, begins with honoring Rue's life—and openly affirming their alliance—by placing flowers on Rue's body. Katniss concludes the ritual by bringing her fingers to her lips and then holding them out toward the sky, in a gesture of respect and solidarity with Rue's district.

We spent a long time meditating on this passage in class. The scene prompted us to consider the parts of the tribute that are "un-ownable," as one student phrased it. There was an elective affinity between Katniss and Rue that the Capitol could not corrupt, suggesting that intimacy can seed "form[s] of life that cannot be totally capitalized upon" (Condorelli, "Company" [Part Two]). Katniss and Rue's willingness to nurture and defend their relationship is an example of the "queer logic" of intimacy in spaces of domination, or what Montgomery and Bergman call "relational ethics" (43). Katniss fraternized with "the enemy," making collective life over and against the "technologies of antirelationality" (Melamed 78) that structure the games. "You can't own what people have in their hearts," a student concluded. "You have to realize there is love out there too."

Through our collective study of *The Hunger Games*, we developed a specific "intimacy in relation to issues," to use Condorelli's phrase ("Company" [Part One]). The novel gave us a language for speaking about the prison regime without ever referring to it by name. We adopted Collins's name for the guards as Peacekeepers and referred to the sheriff as Snowden; local politicians were called Gamemakers, Panem stood in for the United States, and jailed students saw themselves in the tributes, searching for ways to make life amid social death. In this instance, literature functioned as a "bridging" device, a concept developed by the

Chicana feminist theorist Gloria Anzaldúa to describe those texts, actions, moments, and places that open us up to one another and allow for the possibility of creating shared principles and commitments. "To bridge," Anzaldúa writes, "is to attempt community, and for that we must risk being open to personal, political, and spiritual intimacy, to risk being wounded" (246). The elective affinities we built with jailed students during our reading of *The Hunger Games* linger now as a lesson about whether we can alter, disrupt, or refuse the order of things "through intimate associations and small-scale closeness" (Condorelli, "Company" [Part Two]) and whether group-based study under uneven conditions of capture can or should produce what Donna Haraway calls "earthquakes in kin making" as an explicit abolitionist and pedagogical desire (208).[2] On our final day of discussion, we asked, What would happen without the Capitol? It stands as an open question.

We now turn to the collaborative study and acting out of Bonner's one-act surrealist play *The Purple Flower* in HBB's fall 2018 seminar, Soundtracks of Struggle: The Poetics and Politics of US History. Published in the NAACP's *Crisis* magazine in 1928, the play critiques the specific spatial arrangement of power under Jim Crow, but its allegorical exploration of the need for a transformed society, expressed through biblical and historical allusion, is at once prophetic and diagnostic of power relations more generally. The surrealistic setting and characters unfold in rich, poetic detail and layered meanings: above a horizontal dividing line, White Devils reside on a hill called Somewhere and deny admittance to the Us except as day laborers. As the Us strategize how to access the Flower-of-Life-at-Its-Fullest, guarded by the White Devils on the hill, they reside in and cultivate the valley below the line, having been rebuffed for "merely asking permission to go up" to the land they themselves made habitable (192). The White Devils cannot stand to imagine a version of identity and reality not predicated on violent exclusion and subordination; meanwhile, the Us scheme and dream otherwise. The ensuing communal conversations, out of which intergenerational tensions and tenderness emerge, stage a debate between the old guard and the "New Negro" writers of the Harlem Renaissance (Locke); this debate highlights ongoing, generative conversations on the relationship between art and activism, and the revolutionary possibilities immanent to their intersection.

In interrogating what it means to confront whiteness as a racial identity, the revolutionary ethos of *The Purple Flower* imagines a radical redistribution of spatial and racial privilege as a bloodletting; since empires are built on the blood and labor of Indigenous and Black people, Bonner's play, which anticipates the radical politics of the Black liberation struggle, uses the biblical metaphor of blood sacrifice to foreshadow the limits of civil rights rhetoric and reform. Bonner contemplates the urgent need for white people to take responsibility for individual, interpersonal, and institutional forms of racism and imagines a transformed society of communal self-determination that redistributes resources and dissolves hierarchy.

The Purple Flower's surrealism and parable of settler racial capitalism allowed for the study of concrete social problems through the "Trojan horse tactic" of political allegory. Just as The Hunger Games uses fantasy as a means to explore dystopian social realities, Bonner roots her play in material particularities at the same time as she gestures toward the universal by exploring power on a global scale. That is to say, Bonner universalizes liberation struggles with the symbolic weight of the purple flower, the Flower-of-Life-at-Its-Fullest, but also makes specific reference to US history, as one of the Us recalls over "two hundred years of slavery" (193).

Although this experimental drama won the 1927 Crisis award for Literary Art and Expression, it was never staged in its day, and few contemporary productions have been reviewed to date. As Allison Berg and Meredith Taylor note in their discussion of performing it in an undergraduate literature classroom, most analyses of the play focus on reading, not performance. Given the historical conditions of Jim Crow under which The Purple Flower was created, it is no surprise the play was controversial in its day: Bonner frames a legacy of violence, criminalization, exploitation, and the persistence of white racial domination after US chattel slavery's formal abolition. The onstage restriction of movement enforced by the elaborate vertical structure of the scenery strikes immediate parallels to the way the carceral landscape confines and constricts mobility through surveillance, policing, and imprisonment. In class, these crucial elements of the setting led to a discussion of the spatialization of racial power and privilege. Students first drew the layout of the stage on the whiteboard in our classroom, with its leaky walls and antiquated blue carpet, while the clanging of the kitchen crew rattled through the pipes overhead.

After identifying and discussing key elements of the setting and the gravity of the stage directions, which further elaborated Bonner's critique of institutional racism, we ventured into a conversation about the playwright's description of the White Devils, who have horns and tails, and of the Us, who may be "white as the White Devils" or "brown as the earth" (191). The play's specific references to enslavement left students in no doubt that the Us were Black Americans; some ventured to suggest

that the Us could also include other people of color who experience institutional barriers—from entrenched, ongoing histories of settler colonialism and immigration policy—to entrance into the myth of the American
Dream, which the purple flower represents as symbolic ascendency to
power and privilege premised on violence. The Us, then, in their spatial
arrangement onstage, embody a shared relationship to state power and
shape the struggle for its revolutionary overturning. Between those with
access to the flower and those denied its assimilationist aroma exist the
White Devils who possessively protect it, concretizing whiteness as a social construction with violent material manifestations.

Bonner also theorizes the instability of racial regimes through her
concept of the Thin-Skin-of-Civilization, which points to what Cedric
Robinson would describe as the gaps and ruptures in power, since in
Bonner's words a "thought can drop you through it" (192). Before staging the play, then, students critiqued the arbitrary assignment of degrees
of "civilization" (according to racist fallacies of biology attached to skin
color) and challenged the violent premise of symbolic, albeit limited, access to whiteness as a point of view. The precariousness of this arbitrary
divide enforcing racial power harked back to previous discussions of the
law of hypodescent, US chattel slavery's legacies of sexual violence, and
the ideology of purity. Yet, as with W. E. B. Du Bois's famous notion of
"double-consciousness" (11), the play's duality is not between blackness
and whiteness but between the social construction of race and citizenship, with its powers of exclusion—critiquing the tenacity with which
Americanness remains sutured to whiteness. In a setting that represents
privilege as a hilly, open plain, the White Devils use violent tactics to
keep the Us from getting up the hill to the purple flower. Ultimately, Bonner calls for white people to take responsibility for racism and the ways
they benefit from it structurally; the play serves as a vital parable of the
possibilities and pitfalls of coalition politics.

Students identified some historical strategies for gaining access to
the purple flower proposed in the play, such as labor, book learning, re-
ligion, money, and politics (specifically, elite leadership). The Young Us,
representing the "New Negro" or Harlem Renaissance writers, implicitly
stage a critique of the old guard's political strategies. Work, education,
God, money, and politics alone, they argue, cannot be a means of salvation when historically used as tools of subjection. The prison educational
setting also brought into stark relief the play's critique of the limitations
of books, or knowledge, as state power censors or bans radical content.
When these means of accessing the flower don't work, the Us turn to grassroots community organizing and the study of history, as dust in the play

summons embodied memory. They also call for white people to make a radical sacrifice, symbolically relinquishing their unearned advantages as a bloodletting. In particular, the Us plan to lure White Devils out of the bushes with music, aware of what temptations might entice culture vultures who appropriate and capitalize on Black creative genius. Finally, we discussed the play's revolutionary ethos, specifically the last warning the Us make to the White Devils: "You have taken blood. You must give blood . . . there can be no other way" (198–99). In summary, Bonner asks what it means to confront whiteness as a racial identity—when white people are unwilling to relinquish the constitutively violent privilege and power attached to whiteness. She imagines this relinquishing of privilege as a symbolic bloodletting: "Now they need blood for birth so the New Man can live" (198). This new person must rise from the ashes of the equally destructive white liberal and white supremacist forces that perpetuate global racial capitalism. What, more specifically, must be given up in order to make room for this concept of personhood?

The Purple Flower refuses an easy answer, for positing one solution ignores that in the struggle for social transformation, organizers craft many tools. Instead, Bonner's play elicits debate over its multiplying sites of meaning. The play's ending echoes this ambiguity and call to action: "*All the Us listen. All the valley listens. Nowhere listens. All the White Devils listen. Somewhere listens. Let the curtain close leaving all the Us, the White Devils, Nowhere, Somewhere, listening, listening. Is it time?*" (199). Bonner's text thus necessitates a different kind of reading and of listening, refusing dramatic catharsis in favor of awakening a critical consciousness and desire to build a new world. To recognize the so-called American Dream as a nightmare necessarily upends postracial fables popularized during the Obama era, and the general discomfort around discussing racism despite its obvious and ubiquitous presence.

While on college campuses the term "White Devils" can spark a selective outrage that seeks to shut down uncomfortable conversations about what it means to confront whiteness as a racial identity, at the jail it worked not only as an opportunity to reflect critically on how racial difference is constructed and maintained but as a source of humor and shared laughter. The inside joke encapsulates the affective pull of performance as a mode of doing friendship. When we moved from our discussion and analysis of the play to its performance, we did not opt for so-called colorblind casting, which evades the weight of embodied identity in shaping social meanings, the categories we carry that give form to the content of power's enforcement of division and dispossession. However, since all but one student in the class were Black men, and the small class size necessitated that each student perform multiple roles, we decided to volunteer for roles at random. It felt less necessary to make race manifest in a space where its arbitrary construction to enforce power was everywhere apparent. Reorienting ourselves in the classroom, casting aside chairs for a makeshift stage, opened up a place for play in our often more serious space of study; we gesticulated enthusiastically, modulated the affect and tone of our voices, jumped and swayed.

The white student comedically played an older Us who at one point belts out, exhorting the White Devils to show their cowardly faces, "Come out, White Devil!" (198). Just as this student nearly shouted, "White Devil," a guard walked by the classroom and, as the door was slightly ajar, peered into our performance with confused disdain. After he passed by, we burst out into uproarious and sustained laughter—and for the rest of the semester joked about how our class had been surveilled for starting a race war. Making visible the whiteness that enforces racial capitalism, "Come out, White Devil!" became a refrain for shorthanding our naming of institutional racism and the prison regime. Though our performance was playful, the relationships we built through collective study of struggle were deepened by the laughter we shared that day. While this felt knowledge cannot be quantified, the quality of attachments strengthens commitments to imagining and building another world.

Toward Abolitionist Intimacies

Through the lens of friendship, the abolitionist pedagogy articulated here posits the ethos and ethic of building life-affirming, community-based alternatives to a punitive society. Following Omi Osun Joni L. Jones's stunning insights on agency and improvisation in relationship to performance, we chart unpredictable constellations of being together that are both "relational (improvised) and body-centered (vulnerable)" (11). Just as Jones advocates for playfulness and joy as a necessary part of movement work, abolitionist pedagogy can employ the openness, courage, and vulnerability of working through concepts *in relation* as central strategies of collective knowledge production. Holding space for a particular kind of vulnerability in the classroom can challenge the carceral state's antisocial demands for an absence of critical and collective inquiry. The fugitive repertoire of laughter, then, provides a Trojan horse tactic for pursuing a critique of racial capitalism in prison education programs. The refusal of legibility to the state through the inside joke shields collective knowledge production from cooptation, defanging, or incorporation. This modality of relationship-building is relevant to educators and community organizers as well as programs like HBB that seek to build collective autonomy amid conditions of captive study. Abolitionist intimacies implore us to demand and live into the impossible, at the site of what is not yet known as we nurture it into existence.

We recognize that we are navigating a contested terrain—as prison abolitionists working within the system we seek to render obsolete. Yet, despite the state's attempt to sever collectivity, we live into the generative possibility of seeding abolition through fugitive repertoires of shared laughter and friendship. Against the systematic severing of connection and coalition, we recognize transformative relationships as central to dismantling a spiritually bankrupt society. With that, we plot; we study; we turn to fugitive repertoires for insurgent practices of safety, justice, and freedom; and we do our damnedest to be disloyal to the racial order, the rule of capital, and the project of the neoliberal university itself.

NOTES

1. In addition to teaching and learning with students at Norfolk City Jail, HBB hosts community letter-writing hours in order to build solidarity with incarcerated writers across the state of Virginia. We also run a mutual aid and bail fund and facilitate political education programming throughout the Tidewater region; see humanitiesbehindbars.org.

2. We recognize that outside participants do not operate "under conditions of capture," since unlike inside participants they can elect to leave the facility at any point during or after class.

WORKS CITED

Alexander, Patrick Elliot. "Education as Liberation: African American Literature and Abolition Pedagogy in the Sunbelt Prison Classroom." *South: A Scholarly Journal*, vol. 50, no. 1, fall 2017, pp. 9–21.

Anzaldúa, Gloria. *The Gloria Anzaldúa Reader*. Edited by AnaLouise Keating, Duke UP, 2009.

Berg, Allison, and Meredith Taylor. "Enacting Difference: Marita Bonner's *Purple Flower* and the Ambiguities of Race." *African American Review*, vol. 32, no. 3, 1998, pp. 469–80.

Bonner, Marita. *The Purple Flower. Black Female Playwrights: An Anthology of Plays before 1950*, edited by Kathy A. Perkins, Indiana UP, 1990, pp. 191–99.

Collins, Suzanne. *The Hunger Games*. Scholastic Press, 2008.

Condorelli, Celine. "The Company We Keep: A Conversation with Avery F. Gordon, Part One." *How to Work Together*, 2013, howtoworktogether.org/

think-tank/celine-condorelli-the-company-we-keep-a-conversation-with
-avery-f-gordon-part-one/.

———. "The Company We Keep: A Conversation with Avery F. Gordon, Part
Two." *How to Work Together*, 2013, howtoworktogether.org/think-tank/
celine-condorelli-the-company-she-keeps-a-conversation-with-avery-f
-gordon-part-two/.

Davis, Angela Y. *The Meaning of Freedom: And Other Difficult Dialogues*. City
Lights, 2012.

———. "Racialized Punishment and Prison Abolition." *The Angela Y. Davis
Reader*, edited by Joy James, Blackwell Publishers, 1998, pp. 96–107.

Du Bois, W. E. B. "Of Our Spiritual Strivings." *The Souls of Black Folk*.
W. W. Norton, 1999, pp. 9–16.

Gilmore, Ruth Wilson. *Golden Gulag: Prisons, Surplus, Crisis, and Opposition
in Globalizing California*. U of California P, 2007.

Gordon, Avery F. *Ghostly Matters: Haunting and the Sociological Imagination*.
U of Minnesota P, 1997.

Haraway, Donna J. *Staying with the Trouble: Making Kin in the Chthulucene*.
Duke UP, 2016.

Harkins, Gillian, and Erica Meiners. "Beyond Crisis: College in Prison
through the Abolition Undercommons." *Lateral*, no. 3, spring 2014, csa
lateral.org/issue/3/college-in-prison-abolition-undercommons-harkins
-meiners/.

Harney, Stefano, and Fred Moten. *The Undercommons: Fugitive Planning and
Black Study*. Automedia, 2013.

Jones, Omi Osun Joni L. *Theatrical Jazz: Performance, Àse, and the Power of
the Present Moment*. Ohio State UP, 2015.

Locke, Alain, editor. *The New Negro: An Interpretation*. Illustrated by Winold
Reiss, Albert and Charles Boni, 1925.

May, Lyle. "Breaking the Unwritten Rule of Prison; or, What Happens When
the Guards and Prison Staff Interact as Just Human Beings." *The Marshall
Project*, 30 Aug. 2018, themarshallproject.org/2018/08/30/breaking-the
-unwritten-rules-of-prison.

McDowell, Meghan G., and Alison Reed. " 'Can a Poem Stop a Jail from Being
Built?' On Fugitive Counter-ethics as Prison Pedagogy." *Prison Pedagogies: Learning and Teaching with Imprisoned Writers*, edited by Joe Lockard and Sherry Rankins-Robertson, Syracuse UP, 2018, pp. 148–67.

Melamed, Jodi. "Racial Capitalism." *Critical Ethnic Studies*, vol. 1, no. 1, 2015,
pp. 76–85.

Meyerhoff, Eli. *Beyond Education: Radical Studying for Another World*. U of
Minnesota P, 2019.

Montgomery, Nick, and Carla Bergman. *Joyful Militancy: Building Thriving
Resistance in Toxic Times*. AK Press, 2017.

Robinson, Cedric J. *Forgeries of Memory and Meaning: Blacks and the Regimes of Race in American Theater and Film before World War II.* U of North Carolina P, 2007.

Rodríguez, Dylan. "The Disorientation of the Teaching Act: Abolition as Pedagogical Position." *The Radical Teacher*, no. 88, 2010, pp. 7–19.

"Operating Procedure 135.2, Rules of Conduct Governing Employees' Relationships with Offenders." Virginia Department of Corrections, 1 Oct. 2019, vadoc.virginia.gov/files/operating-procedures/100/vadoc-op-135-2.pdf.

Siddiquee, Imran. "The Topics Dystopian Films Won't Touch." *The Atlantic*, 19 Nov. 2014, www.theatlantic.com/entertainment/archive/2014/11/the-topics-dystopian-films-wont-touch/382509/.

Varner, Deena. "A Communitas of Hustle and the Queer Logic of Inmate Sex (Anti) Work." *Frontiers: A Journal of Women Studies*, vol. 39, no. 3, 2018, pp. 208–40.

The Sacred Writing Circle: Pedagogical Challenges of Creative Writing and Teaching among Incarcerated Women

Anastazia Schmid

I write to record what others erase when I speak, to rewrite the stories others have miswritten about me, about you. To become more intimate with myself and you. To discover myself, to preserve myself, to make myself, to achieve self-autonomy. To dispel the myths that I am a mad prophet or suffering soul. To convince myself that I am worthy and that what I have to say is not a pile of shit. To show that I can and that I will write, never mind their admonitions to the contrary. And I will write about the unmentionables, never mind the outraged gasp of the censor and the audience.

—*Gloria Anzaldúa,*
"Speaking in Tongues: A Letter to Third World Women"

It is eight thirty on a Saturday night. I gather together a cadre of beautiful women the outside world condemns as broken, deviant, unintelligent. I call out the start of class and we convene in the cramped makeshift unit library to slice open our guts with the sword of our pens and and fling out our insides through the force of our words. The Sacred Writing Circle provides time and space for creative self-expression in a nonjudgmental, uncensored, safe collective of incarcerated women.

Here, both diversity and individuality are exemplified through the unity of lived experiences and collective struggles. Any and every walk of life has joined me in this eclectic literary journey. Breshawn, a one-year veteran of the class and my assistant, has had everything set up and ready to go for at least fifteen minutes; this is how she adores this time and space. Sonja just woke up and rolls in as a zombie with coffee and notebook in hand. Nikki is pissed that she had to leave her friends for a couple of hours to attend, even though she signed up for the class herself and never fails to be happy she came. Kathy has to leave for med-line and is upset she will miss more than half the class again. Jamila traded out her shift on suicide watch because she refuses to miss class. Sita shows up with food and drink she has prepared for all to share as we "share." Blu just flat out "isn't feeling it" and boisterously complains as she takes her seat.[1]

Tonight, I couldn't agree more. I've been writing and crying all day and I don't want to be here either, in more ways than one. I take a deep breath and tell myself what I have told countless women I've taught this class to over the years: these are the times we most need to show up. Every week we show up to this circle of nonjudgmental support and sharing for the time to honor ourselves and others in all our messy complexity and the space to formulate, articulate, and accentuate ourselves in words, written and spoken. Despite the trials and tribulations in my life, my own mind, my own circumstances, here I am once again. I show up as a living testament, practicing what I preach. I show up when everything in me resists what I know. I show up for myself because I am worth the effort of investing in and investigating myself, sharing my varied forms of written expression. I show up to show others the way.

Tonight, we take turns drawing blind contours of one another and then write a line about what we see in each person, combining our sentences into a single text that does not differentiate one person from another. We read aloud our stream of consciousness about the faces around the table:

Shy, unsure quiet beauty, do not be afraid to shine—dazzle in the uncomfortable, there is so much more than meets the eye. Mischievous child the fun-loving trickster playing peek-a-boo behind those eyes inviting everyone to play in the lightness of the heart. Nervous, fidgety, wonder what we may think—do your thoughts show? Will I be accepted as I am? Yes! There is no judgment here in the safety of those who share your experience. Rebel no mask or façade can hide, find comfort in the perfectly imperfect beauty of the moment, glorying in your own skin. Trying to be everywhere but where you are—be still—model for a moment, there is an ocean of wonder to be found within. Here and now.

(Schmid, personal journal, 4 Feb. 2017)

I have been in this same space, at this same time, for four of my eighteen years of incarceration. I am an activist and an artist, a spoken word poet and a writer, a graduate independent scholar, and now a mentor and peer facilitator inside a maximum security prison on a housing unit designated as a "behavior modification program."[2] I teach creative writing in a class designed to meet the needs of women who happen to be incarcerated and for whom other teaching methods and the system have failed. The faces around the table have changed over time, but the soul and lifeblood of this circle remain the same.

I have been a writer for as long as I was able to formulate words. Free association writing has been my own mode of self-inquiry and healing for most of my life. Particularly since becoming incarcerated, I have spent immeasurable hours alone with my notebook and pen scribing in this fashion, unlocking answers for myself and my life. Although I have been a teacher in many areas throughout my life, I never made a conscious plan to teach others to write, and it never really occurred to me that this practice was a tool I could teach others until several women started to notice me sitting and writing, day after day, week after week in my own corner of space, or were participants in other writing groups alongside me and heard the feedback I provided for others' writing. I was already a mentor inside the prison and countless women came to me daily for practical and emotional advice. One Saturday night, as I sat and wrote, a few women asked if they could join me, and I obliged. All they asked was what I was always writing and why. Not really knowing how to answer their questions, I simply started reading them what I had been writing. They expressed a desire to "learn to write like that" and asked if they could write with me, if I would "show them how." I said all they had to do was write, not worrying about what or how, just writing whatever came to mind. I told them I would give them a single word and that's where they would start—that it didn't matter what happened, or didn't happen, from there. The task was to let go with that one word, wherever it might take them, and just keep going until nothing else came out.

I spent five solid hours with those women that night, writing, reading, and sharing. Something magical happened. Women who had never written anything found a way inside themselves to release the good, the bad, and the ugly. They found the courage to share their innermost thoughts, ideas, wants, and needs, their fears and tragedies, their hopes and dreams. They found strength with one another, gaining power through sharing their words. Some found a type of poetic talent they hadn't known they possessed. They found a love for words. We all found inspiration in each other's words. We wrote and shared until the dayroom closed. They asked me if we could do it again, every Saturday night. In that moment, unplanned, with no set direction or objective, the Sacred Writing Circle was born. A need was being met in a way that was contradictory to everything else that was being taught inside this place, and it was generating real healing and change. Word of mouth spread like a grass fire through the prison, and soon more and more women of all different backgrounds came to take a seat at the table. Over the years, the Sacred Writing Circle has included women of color, immigrants, LGBTQ+ and gender non-conforming women, women with nontraditional religious and spiritual beliefs, women of mixed educational and socioeconomic backgrounds, young women, elderly women, able-bodied women, and disabled women. Despite perceived difference, each group found the commonality that binds us all in this circle. No one was ever turned away, and anyone was welcome to come and go of their own volition. Some came for a short period of time, and others remained long term. The group has never failed to be a melting pot of diversity, empowerment, and healing.

Our lived experience provides a level of mutual understanding between incarcerated women stemming from a background of trauma, abuse, and multiple forms of violence, marginalization, and oppression, as well as the commonality of shared carceral experience. On the subject of mutual understanding, lived experience, and diversity, one Sacred Writing Circle participant, Dianna, stated, "When you hear how others write, it opened my mind to not be so judgmental. They've gone through the same things you have."

Addressing the issues of writing the personal and traumatic, Amy Hodges Hamilton reflects on female literary rhetoricians such as Virginia Woolf and Hélène Cixous, concurring that writing enables us to reclaim the female voice. Spaces and places of shared experiences of oppression are often overlooked and discounted by outsiders, and particularly in academic settings, our words are further silenced and disregarded. Yet beyond lived experiences illustrated through these negative frameworks lies the internal possession of inherent talents and creative expression and the tenacious spirit that thrives despite external circumstance: a sense of purpose and being that transcends oppression, which then seeks to uplift and empower others of similar circumstance—as one participant's writing so eloquently illustrates:

> Screaming in my mind, a repeat, backwards in time, pitching whispers to my ears, clogged vessels of the overlapping years, moments of agony where I'd rather be dead, I hear the lost words that you said, but never said, the voice is gone but your presence is still present, even if only in the tween places, in between one heart beat to the next, flames inside my soul that reach out and spread in a fiery blaze, glazed over darkness that lights up the most hidden parts, the corners where creativity is found, and where you'll always be, a piece of you, always with me.

These individual and collective polarities gave birth to the Sacred Writing Circle. Because of and despite the fact that traditional teaching methods in prison fail us, writing in a common collective is a more effective and democratic option for incarcerated women. For one, the class itself is voluntary, framed as self-help rather than classroom instruction. Unlike the large majority of the activities that are approved for incarcerated people, the Sacred Writing Circle isn't required for any program, and there are no system-dictated incentives for taking the class. The prison world that surrounds our circle revolves around efforts to earn "good time credit" or "packet certificates," things that supposedly attest to "rehabilitation" through systemic endeavors, but the benefits and allure of writing offer an alternative kind of "credit." When "credit" for completion is solely personal, the rewards are both internal empowerment and external resistance. When a person is in class because they want to be in this class, and they gain whatever they say they gain, they have a brief reprieve from the system of credit and debit of experience that organizes and confines progress inside this system.

Jointly, these components work to abolish, defeat, and write in defiance of violent institutions. The goals and organization of this class constitute what Sujani K. Reddy describes as "deschooling as an abolitionist practice." Reddy characterizes the ways school curricula and higher academia continuously reproduce brutality in myriad forms against Indigenous and other marginalized groups as part of the relationship between education and settler colonialism. Exploring the ways marginalized people can expand their knowledge beyond institutions of capitalist imperialism, Reddy includes the ongoing struggle of "the imprisoned whose quest for knowledge is self-led and oriented toward collective liberation." Reddy challenges us to begin "to think about who we understand as having knowledge, and how we come to learn not simply skills that will lead to resources within a capitalist system but also ways of knowing that are inherently oppositional to that system" (131). This class is by, for, and about women incarcerated in the prison-industrial complex and their own lived experiences, as they choose to express them, for their own means and ends in collaboration with others who desire to do the same. In this sense, writing and sharing through the spoken word, in any form or fashion, is knowledge for the oppressed—and knowledge against oppressive systems—used for empowerment and transformational healing, a way to learn and grow beyond violence, oppression, and exploitation. This essay takes as a subject of exploration and analysis the ways many formal education practices in prison fail us and the use of pedagogical strategies as larger forms of resistance. Incarcerated women in the Sacred Writing Circle learn that they are their own teachers and judges, that there is wisdom in their lived experience; and this knowledge has value and purpose beyond the hegemony of the carceral state. By identifying the shortcomings and systematic injustice of existing hegemonic approaches, I hope to explore how classes like the Sacred Writing Circle prove to be effective and liberating for students within the system and beyond the classroom.

Epistemic Violence and Injustice within Prison Educational Programs

This article does not intend to diminish educational programming in prisons. I am an advocate of education in all circumstances, particularly for people who are marginalized and oppressed, because both low-level and higher education provide limited opportunity and choice, which is a better alternative than what incarcerated people are usually entitled to: no opportunity or choice.

Education in prison is often promoted as a means of achieving "rehabilitation" and as an effective way to decrease recidivism. As Michael Sutcliffe explains, rehabilitation rhetoric follows a model in which "[b]roken, illiterate prisoners will be taught how to think, learn, and problem solve; they will be 'saved' through education" (175). Framing programs in a similar fashion to behavior modification or even religious conversion presumes the incarcerated student to be intellectually, academically, or morally deficient. For example, lack of education among incarcerated people is often viewed as a personal deficiency stemming from a lack of interest or personal motivation rather than an external problem stemming from unequal distribution of opportunity and resources. The fallacy of "opportunity equality" parallels the fallacy of "rehabilitation" in that neither exists within or for populations that the law and language have purposely marginalized or in realms where capitalist means of exploitation (in this context, "educational opportunities") are the vectors that maintain class privilege.

Beyond lack of access to robust and consistent higher education, additional restrictive policies and practices ensue within individual educational programs inside prisons. In the pursuit of knowledge and education, certain groups are denied access to sources of knowledge as well as the ability to be regarded as a knower, leading inevitably to systematic epistemic injustice and epistemic violence. Epistemic injustice inflicts harm by marginalizing individuals and groups by regulating the production, acquisition, distribution, and possession of knowledge and in assessing the credibility of testimony (Schmid 2). Miranda Fricker asserts that negative stereotypes about specific social identities reflect "a special kind of injustice [that] occurs when a hearer gives a speaker less credibility owing to prejudicial attributions of insincerity, irrationality, and incompetence." There are specific policies and attitudes inherent in the criminal justice system that systematically deny incarcerated and formerly incarcerated people the right to knowledge while disregarding and devaluing their testimony. A pragmatic, justice-oriented pedagogical approach would work to recognize how the lived experiences of epistemic injustice affect relationships among students, instructors, and course materials.

Further forms of epistemic injustice and violence occur when policies and practices deny access to either formal or informal education or educational resources. This dynamic includes restrictions placed on incarcerated people wishing to disseminate their own knowledge in both written and creative forms and prohibitions on incarcerated scholars educating or assisting fellow incarcerated people. Knowledge and the sharing and distribution of knowledge are seen as threats to the safety and security of the institution because through knowledge and awareness comes the potential for empowerment—personal and collective—and hence the potential for organizing and demanding legal rights, including improved conditions and treatment. In other words, access to information and resources enables people to challenge oppressive conditions and practices. Because knowledge that is truly rehabilitative empowers people, uplifts them, and may provide viable means of sustaining life beyond or outside of the system, institutions like our current system of incarceration, which is founded and sustained on violence and information suppression, are deeply threatened by the kind of education and access that the Sacred Writing Circle provides.

Beyond the epistemic violence limiting educational opportunities for incarcerated people, even system-approved external educators with the best intentions face exploitation and censorship at the hands of carceral institutions and sometimes in concert with them. By working in conjunction with the carceral system itself and a particular institution's educational policies, outside educators assist in dictating what and how incarcerated students learn, the forms knowledge takes (both in distribution and production), and who and what is considered a credible source or a possessor of knowledge. In order to even enter a prison, outside educators must, of course, work within the parameters set by the prison system. However, all too often those parameters are not questioned or challenged. Rote and often fallacious assumptions are made that all or most people in prison are uneducated, ignorant, and unmotivated; lack original ideas, expertise, and professional experience; only need or want the "basics"; are incapable of collegiate work or professionalism; or are in some way inherently different from and inferior to people in the outside world. Each of these false stereotypes has been projected onto me by outside educators, including those who considered themselves liberal or radical, at one time or another during my incarceration.

Even dazzling success in these educational programs may work against students. The education received while a person is incarcerated is given full credit for a person's "rehabilitation," thereby both proving that the system works and assuming credit for whatever admirable or redemptive qualities can be gleaned from that person—as if there were no knowledge, skills, talents, or any admirable or redemptive qualities within that person or inherent to that person before the saving grace of the prison and the educational opportunities provided to them while they were there. Students may be denied ownership of their talent and even of their work. I know of many cases when outside educators or prison administrators or employees have wantonly taken the ideas, work, research, and designs of their incarcerated students and claimed them as their own, giving little or no credit to the originators of that knowledge.

Censorship further hinders incarcerated scholars from working as reliable creators of knowledge. Topics of academic inquiry, research, and writing, more often than not, are required to appear nonthreatening and to avoid expressions of nonconformist political, religious, or cultural views. Thus, even the realities of one's own life, personal beliefs, and experiences may be off-limits as topics for academic exploration. This type of censorship—whether imposed internally or externally—shuts down opportunities for academic discourse and critical inquiry into topics relevant to one's own lived experience and depletes areas of personal enhancement and exploration specifically relevant to incarcerated women.

Perhaps the most obvious (at least to the affected person) form of direct harm is enacted when some aspect of an incarcerated person's knowledge is used against them, subjecting them to myriad forms of violence or punitive sanctions. In my experience, the decision by incarcerated people to silence their own voices is most frequently an act of self-protection and self-preservation similar to the phenomenon described by Kristie Dotson as "testimonial smothering" (244). Indeed, silence may be the only right that can be somewhat maintained in the academic sphere, in that it ensures epistemic safety in some regards.

Incarcerated women, many of whom harbor histories of abuse and trauma prior to incarceration, face retraumatization by the epistemic injustice inherent in incarceration. Traumatic histories coupled with fear of judgment, negative retribution, and potential violence cause incarcerated students to remain guarded and silenced, which eliminates the opportunity for real change, growth, and healing. In this way, programs like the Sacred Writing Circle can be a part of a larger goal of all activism and educational programs in the interest of personal recovery and the realization of true epistemic justice.

The limiting, exclusionary, and exploitative practices that can characterize carceral education programs further reinforce hegemonic systems while solidifying negative stereotypes and perpetuating multiple forms of epistemic injustice. In the name of rehabilitation, the methods of control and the lattices of power sustain retraumatization and, ultimately, recidivism. In order for education in the carceral state to truly be rehabilitative, there must be space for and inclusion of knowledge in all forms, from all people, above, beyond, and outside of hegemonic power structures in ways that do not reinforce, solidify, or otherwise uphold those systems. Despite the repercussions I have been forced to endure for writing and using my voice, I work with my students because I know firsthand both the personal detriment of remaining silent and the transformative power of the word and its ability to heal, collectively and individually. By seeking practices that address and resist the enforcement of epistemic violence, my pedagogy seeks to approach recovery rather than system-sanctioned "rehabilitation."

Empowerment and the Healing Pedagogy of the Sacred Writing Circle

To write and speak one's personal truth in the presence of a safe, supportive community is to become empowered. In this context, incarcerated women are validated in their personhood and lived experience and, through this process of writing and sharing, purging and releasing, essentially become their own therapists. A safe environment that validates the personal and believes testimony expands healing in both private and public dimensions, as an internal process within the individual and an external process through communal sharing of truth-telling. When conducted in this way, programs such as the Sacred Writing Circle can begin to transform communities.

In *Trauma and Recovery*, Judith Lewis Herman writes, "The core experiences of psychological trauma are disempowerment and disconnection from others. Recovery, therefore, is based upon the empowerment of the survivor and the creation of new connections. Recovery can take place only within the context of relationships; it cannot occur in isolation" (133). The Sacred Writing Circle incorporates these concepts of storytelling, empowerment, and connection and creates possibilities for communal relationship.

In relation to trauma and healing, telling one's story is not only a necessary means to self-validation and self-knowledge; it is an imperative for survival. Dori Laub articulates this need in reference to forms of "witness" with survivors of the Holocaust, stating, "There is, in each survivor, an imperative need to *tell* and thus to come to *know* one's story, unimpeded by ghosts from the past against which one has to protect oneself. One has to know one's buried truth in order to be able to live one's life." In the absence of outlets to articulate and validate traumatic experience, silence becomes an inescapable oppression and quotidian recurrence of internal harm. As Laub proclaims, "The 'not telling' of the story serves as a perpetuation of its tyranny. . . . The longer the story remains untold, the more distorted it becomes in the survivor's conception of it, so much so that the survivor doubts the reality of the actual events" (64).

Through the process of teaching writing to and *by* incarcerated people, transformational healing occurs in both individuals and the group as a whole. The Sacred Writing Circle provides the opportunity to learn to write in a unique way that eliminates rules, expectations, judgment, negative critique, forced production, and required "sharing." Because it is led by a facilitator who participates fully in the process and the experience (carceral, traumatic, and otherwise), group members more easily find freedom of expression, thought, and feeling—and thereby expansion of the mind.

Carly, a participant who took the class multiple times, examines the importance of recognizing trauma, which is embedded in the Sacred Writing Circle experience:

The class was wonderful. It helped me write about stuff I didn't think I'd ever be able to put on paper, to speak about our inner thoughts. Its comfortable talking about topics that someone else incarcerated can relate to, that a volunteer [or staff] can't relate to . . . we could say whatever we felt without any repercussions. Sometimes people just need to release on paper, just journaling. I get it.

Commenting about finding release in prison through writing, Carly stated, "We have to take control of our own lives and not allow others to control our being."

My course description is loose—somewhat vague on purpose—and I follow no set curriculum. The "W" word itself—*writing*—can be intimidating to many women in this environment. As a result, this class is not formatted like other prison classes, nor does it follow a systematic or traditional pedagogic protocol. What works is loosely repeated; what doesn't work is discarded. This format has supported substantial growth and change, both in the class itself and in the participants. I have found that true teaching occurs in the uncertainty and vulnerability of the unplanned. A "teacher's" openness and willingness to be a participant and an active learner from her students breaks down barriers through the removal of traditional classroom hierarchy and authoritative separation between teacher and student. At the end of every class, each participant writes in the others' notebooks about what they will take away from the class and what they have learned from each participant. One such entry in my notebook stated, "Well I tell ya I have learned some things about me thanks to you and being in this class. I didn't really know I could write different styles and it's so cool. You're a good observer and I think it makes you a good teacher. I know that I can only improve with the things I learned. I never really liked writing, but I truly do. I have embraced it." Topics, language, personal beliefs, and experiences considered taboo in other settings are acceptable. Sharing is encouraged but not required. Nothing is asked of the participants that I am not also doing right along with them. Flaws, imperfections, and the unknown are welcome here. The rules and styles of writing do not apply: grammar, spelling, punctuation, sentence structure, and the like are irrelevant. Educational backgrounds and "literacy" levels do not matter in this class. One of my bilingual participants, for whom English is a second language, was excited that she learned to write in English during the class.

Formality and the rigidity of rules stifle creativity and openness, particularly in oppressive environments. This absence of authoritarian power relationships is crucial to fostering freedom of expression and fearless self-inquiry because this classroom may be the only space where the participants have any semblance of freedom. The class process works precisely because there is a lack of expectation or prerequisite. If a person can move a writing utensil across a page and form some semblance of words, and has a desire to express themselves, they are welcome to attend. At its most basic, the group's guidelines are as follows:

No judgment, of ourselves or others, in our writing, our words, our expressions, or otherwise.

No apologies: we say whatever we want to say, however we want or need to say it. It doesn't matter where you go or how you get there; just move the pen across the page however it will.

Just write. I give a place to start for those who find a blank page intimidating, but there is no requirement regarding what or how a person writes from that point.

There is no "right way" to do it.

Write until the time allotted expires or the thoughts run out, whichever the case may be.

When the writing ends, sharing begins. Each woman is provided the opportunity to hold the floor with all others' undivided attention as she reads aloud what she has written (if she so chooses).

We listen intently, then take turns providing positive feedback. We share how we relate to the piece, what parts spoke to us and why. We interject what wasn't said but was evident, what the writer may wish to further explore.

We congratulate the reader and thank her for bravely sharing herself and her experiences.

I typically structure the class in six-to-eight-week blocks that participants are free to repeat as many times as they like or to step out of at any time.

We are all teachers teaching one another through our own words and our own experiences. We are our own teachers when we find strength and healing in writing, reading, and speaking our own words, in our own way, because we choose it for ourselves. Discussing the benefits of the group and why this writing style and class format worked for her, Dianna stated that the Writing Circle

> inspired me to keep writing, [from] different perspectives. [The class] made me feel I'm not alone. Learning how to write makes me feel. I can just give [feelings] away and don't have to worry about it anymore, it's very healing. . . . Writing Circle brought out a side of me I didn't know. I didn't know I could write. I felt like I could get my emotions out. It was like, an outlet [because] it's free. You can freely do it with how you feel. You go with your emotions, nothing's right or wrong. You're just putting it on paper, no one's judging you. At first I was shy to read aloud because I didn't think my writing was good enough. It wasn't about whose was good or not. It was about letting it out and how you felt afterward. It felt good. I left behind what I was writing about.

I am eternally grateful to the women of the Sacred Writing Circle. They are physical reminders of what matters and why I do what I do, week after week, year after year, in this place. They are mirrors of myself and the world at large. We are sacred, "set apart for, and dedicated to, some person, place, purpose, sentiment, etc." rather than to a god ("Sacred"). We are a circle, "a group of people bound together by a common interest" ("Circle"). Together, set apart, we write and speak. Together, we transcend, transform, empower, and collectively heal through the power of written and spoken words. I am not so much a writing teacher as I am a tour guide, leading other women into themselves, and into the truth that lies within them, through the medium of writing.

A circle has no beginning and no ending. Whether a woman's writing journey ends or begins with the Sacred Writing Circle, a sacred space is found for transformational healing. We have all been irrevocably changed by the experience, empowered to break the silence, self-imposed and externally forced, to write and speak our truth in fury and fancy, to testify to the unspeakable and scream the rebel war cry against all odds of oppression. Learning, growing, healing, and changing one letter at a time, in the breath of voice distinctly our own.

Defying all rules, among beatific insurgents, I pick up my pen and write. Bear witness to the power of our words.

fits like a news feed   was one thing we ever did **TOGETHER** show off   the feeling stays
keep your cool—rage against risk taker   scents of substance facing the world pop-artist
          cry like a baby instantly see—listen up   not your visible scars   the new intensity
what's inside is everything   your edge obsession with strong inspiring waiting to happen
                              here's why . . .
          TELL it   say goodbye to everything   last look bottoms up
nobody gets out alive   Turn-key   learn from failure   life is a sport   build up a tolerance
life after death you don't realize you want   Spoon-fed very unlikely place
          in writing—throw fade
     revealing the light turn up the **LOVE** make them count such dishevelment and confusion
                    three burning questions to the flow sexier with intense sex
                    a deeper connection to it—match-maker moves that stop you
dare to ask supernatural thriller   how I saved making the jump
          what I love reimaging the iconic on hold giving you someone   4 ½ hours
one of them is to prove wrong
     pouring your heart and soul into your out there to the imagination always dreamed of catching the **FIGHT**
keep it together story time   your mouth   **SURVIVES**
what lies beneath this way out teardrop lounge
          most wanted:
                    by the barrel ways to **LIVE**   made herstory.

NOTES

1. Names of writing circle participants have been changed throughout the essay.

2. I taught the class described in this essay at the Indiana Women's Prison through the Purposeful Living Unit Serves (PLUS) program, circa 2013–17. I have also led this type of group or class informally at multiple locations. At the time of this writing, I am located at the Madison Correctional Facility, a minimum security prison that lacks comparable programming. Several women who participated in the class have also been transferred to this facility, and some were interviewed about the class for this essay.

WORKS CITED

"Circle." *Webster's New World College Dictionary*, Houghton Mifflin Harcourt, 2014. *YourDictionary*, yourdictionary.com/circle.

Dotson, Kristie. "Tracking Epistemic Violence, Tracking Practice of Silencing." *Hypatia*, vol. 26, no. 2, spring 2011, pp. 236–57.

Fricker, Miranda. *Epistemic Injustice: Power and the Ethics of Knowing. Oxford Scholarship Online*, September 2007, https://doi.org/10.1093/acprof:oso/9780198237907.001.0001.

Hamilton, Amy Hodges. "First Responders: A Pedagogy for Writing and Reading Trauma." *Critical Trauma Studies: Understanding Violence, Conflict, and Memory in Everyday Life*, edited by Monica J. Casper and Eric Wertheimer, New York UP, 2016, pp. 179–204.

Herman, Judith Lewis. *Trauma and Recovery*. Basic Books, 1992.

Laub, Dori. "Truth and Testimony: The Process and the Struggle." *American Imago*, vol. 48, no. 1, spring 1991, pp. 75–91.

Reddy, Sujani K. "We Don't Need No Education: Deschooling as an Abolitionist Practice." *Abolishing Carceral Society: Abolition: A Journal of Insurgent Politics*, Common Notions, 2018, pp. 124–33.

"Sacred." *Webster's New World College Dictionary*, Houghton Mifflin Harcourt, 2014. *YourDictionary*, yourdictionary.com/sacred.

Schmid, Anastazia. Personal journal. 2017. Manuscript.

———. "Shattering the Illusion of the Convict Race: Epistemic Injustice/Violence in Media Representation of Incarcerated and Formerly Incarcerated People, and a Radical Challenge to Epistemic Privilege." 2019.

Sutcliffe, Michael. "All Our Community's Voices: Unteaching the Prison Literacy Complex." *Abolishing Carceral Society: Abolition: A Journal of Insurgent Politics*. Common Notions, 2018, pp. 171–91.

Of Toothbrushes, Bread, and Beanstalks: Freedom and Kinship Inside

Ann E. Green, Richard Sean Gross, and Rachel Swenarton

I (Ann) met Richard Sean Gross in a maximum security prison in Pennsylvania. Those of us who were from "outside," our word for "not incarcerated," were inside on this day for a celebration of the twentieth anniversary of the Inside-Out Prison Exchange Program, where instructors are trained to bring traditional college students inside a jail or prison to have class with people experiencing incarceration, or "inside" students. Lori Pompa, one of the founders of Inside-Out, describes it as a space where "the process of investigation and discovery is both communal and collaborative" ("One Brick" 132). We enter the jail[1] with a notion of cultural humility, and we bring both groups together to study the material of the course, which may or may not have to do with mass incarceration. (Inside-Out courses take place internationally and across disciplines.)

To get to the auditorium, we processed through metal detectors, were patted down, and were escorted by corrections officers down a long corridor. Cell blocks connected to the corridor at right angles. On the left side of the hallway were exits for small yards. The layout was familiar to me, since I had been trained for Inside-Out in this facility. The prison, over a hundred years old, was dilapidated. The state had almost completed a newer prison, but it had undergone several delays and increased costs. Meanwhile, the older prison continued with minimal maintenance. The auditorium resembled a high school multipurpose room left untouched since the 1970s. A colleague introduced me to Richard[2]—who goes by "Rich"—over cake after a day of conversations about mass incarceration. (The cake is an important detail: dessert, let alone a choice of desserts, would not have been provided in the absence of a special occasion with outside guests.) Rich, I soon discovered, was, like me, from small-town Pennsylvania. While in my experience you can never not be aware you are in prison when you are in prison, Rich felt as familiar to me as the guys I had gone to high school with, and we started to exchange letters.

Inside-Out courses are considered immersion service-learning courses because students encounter the "other" directly in the other's space. Critics rightly argue that service-learning done poorly can reinforce ideas about racism and poverty and fail to address structural inequality or promote social change (Green, " 'But You Aren't White,' " "Difficult Stories," and "Service-Learning"; Mitchell; Pompa, "Service-Learning"). Tania Mitchell argues that "critical service-learning," service-learning that critiques systems of power and goes beyond "helping," is one way to undo the hierarchy in the service-learning paradigm where the university is always perceived as "helping" the community, often through a white, middle-class lens. Mitchell articulates three different qualities of critical service-learning: participants work to address systemic injustice, develop "authentic relationships," and seek to redistribute power (50). This essay in turn asks *how* or perhaps *if* "authentic relationships" are possible across the walls that separate those of us who are outside from those of us who are inside. How can we tell stories to one another that we will hear? Tyrone Werts, a pardoned lifer who now works for the Inside-Out program (see Werts, "Reflections"), points out that the walls are designed to keep the average citizen out as well as keep the incarcerated in ("Tyrone Werts" 13:10–15). If the average person knew about the conditions in prisons and jails, perhaps we would move more easily toward radical reform or abolition of the existing criminal justice system.

In *Barking to the Choir: The Power of Radical Kinship*, Gregory Boyle argues that the most important thing we can do for "the other" is provide the service of radical listening (see also Browning; O'Reilley). By entering into prisons and jails with no desire to fix, offering only our presence, we can shift something in structures of oppression. Pompa, writing about Inside-Out, also calls for the need for mutuality and dialogue in the setting of a prison but emphasizes as well that those of us who teach and learn inside prisons and jails walk a fine line.

While many of us would answer the prison abolitionist Angela Y. Davis's question, "Are prisons obsolete?" with a resounding "yes"; while many of us are involved in the movement to end death by incarceration or abolish the death penalty; while many of us are interested in mutuality and dialogue; when we are teaching and learning inside, we must abide by the rules of the institution. To violate these rules risks not only personal consequences, like being banned from that facility, but also bans for the program. For example, outside students could be asked to testify in an inside student's trial or be charged for bringing in contraband. Consequences for inside students could be much more severe and include removal from the course, administrative segregation (solitary confinement), or even a delay in their parole. The rules for instructors of Inside-Out are somewhat different but are still restrictive. I am available for all students, inside and out, as a potential reference. I have, in fact, written letters for students who are eligible for parole or who are seeking commutation. In one case, I testified at a juvenile lifer's resentencing. Teaching in prison stretches the typical college professor's skill set.

The rules are byzantine and are often enforced arbitrarily. When we discuss the rules with colleagues, they often ask why: Why are hoodies not allowed? or the colors blue and white? or gum? While sometimes we have answers (blue and white are the colors of the incarcerated's T-shirts in Philadelphia jails), sometimes the answer is simply, "It's prison." The struggle exists on multiple levels, however. While the prison has detailed rules that we must follow, so does Inside-Out. To maintain the program inside a jail or prison, where we could be banned without warning or recourse, we also require all inside and outside students to agree to no contact after the course.

The "no contact" rule is a challenging one and is controversial within the Inside-Out program itself. Why, some of us ask, in a program that is designed to humanize folks behind the walls, do we insist on no contact before and after the course? In a system like prison, even the perception of violating the rules can result in disciplinary action against incarcerated people, and prisons are particularly sensitive about any relationship that could jeopardize security. In keeping with prison rules and in order to keep a program like Inside-Out viable, the "no contact" rule preserves the semi-anonymity of all participants (established by the use of first names only within the program) except for the instructors. Clear boundaries are designed to protect both inside and outside students and are for the greater good of the program.[3] So, while the walls of prison keep citizens out and people experiencing incarceration in, the rules of Inside-Out provide another level of separation that continues after the program ends.

Rich and Rachel, inside and outside students respectively, were not in the same class and have never met in person, by correspondence, or in any capacity except in reading drafts of this paper. Our collaboration has been kept within the rules of Inside-Out. Yet we have cooperated to demonstrate a collective voice that replicates the experience of Inside-Out. The work of building community is a song sung by a chorus, not a soloist. As a teacher of writing, I often encourage students to break familiar rules of writing—the seven-sentence paragraph, the five-paragraph essay. In crafting this essay with Rich and Rachel, we acknowledged how the rules of incarceration shape what we can write and say. By presenting our voices collectively, we hope the reader feels some of the tensions we encounter regularly as we teach and learn inside.

Getting into Jail: Ann

Teaching the Inside-Out course means holding space for students from both inside and outside prison to engage in collaborative meaning-making in an environment that is inherently unequal.[4] Each time I enter a jail or prison, I become queasy from processing in, the requirements of entering a jail. When I dress in the morning, I put on prison-friendly clothing: loose pants (but not too loose; very loose clothing can be used to smuggle contraband) and a shirt with sleeves, in an appropriate color. I make sure to eat something that will sustain me for three hours and to get hydrated. Before entering the visitor's room, I empty my pockets, remove my earrings, leave my keys, sunglasses, cell phone, and cash in the car, and, after a wait that can vary from five minutes to half an hour, walk through a metal detector and get patted down. I cannot bring in an Advil or a piece of gum or a bottle of water, and my prescription migraine medicine stays at the front gate with the corrections officers (COs). Two tampons or sanitary napkins are allowed. Students and I put them in the pockets of our jeans. Underwire bras are not allowed, but I talk with women COs to see how high the jail turns up its metal detector, and generally I wear mine in. Occasionally an outside student will send me a frantic text about her underwire before we leave for jail; this is not the typical teaching situation. If the COs are particularly strict on any given day, I cannot wear a sweater or a scarf. In order to process in, we must meet the requirements of the officers at the entrance, and these officers change from week to week. In the visiting room, we observe family members turned away for jeans with too many holes or a blue dress. Signs warn that a visit will be canceled if children are not "under control." Our two-and-a-half-hour class period with the men is twice as long as their weekly family visits.

While we are inside, we are subject to the same restrictions as our inside classmates. We process through a series of gates and sally ports; we are escorted to our classroom, often a room that is typically used for religious services and still littered with biblical tracts; to use the restroom, we must be escorted by a guard; if other men speak to us in the hallway, they are silenced by the COs and told to move along. Prisons, in my experience, are mostly loud; our classroom may have a window to a hallway but no outside windows. When I am bringing fifteen to seventeen traditional-age college students inside a prison, I am vigilant, trying to anticipate a CO's objection: no hoodies or shirts with words that could be misinterpreted, like *escape* (the name of a campus retreat) or *security*.

Students and colleagues often ask if I am scared to go "inside," and I always answer no, but that is not entirely true. I am not scared of the men I meet who are incarcerated, which is, I think, the question people want to ask. The men in our class are mostly not convicted but are awaiting trial. Often, given the rules of the parole system (another story entirely), they have violated parole. Like all people, men behind bars are a mix of good and bad, brilliant and not, angry and sad and happy. Some of the men whom I consider friends and colleagues are serving life sentences. The men in our classes in the Philadelphia jails typically have had six months of good behavior: no fights, no write-ups, no contraband. In other words, they have been able to live within the rules of incarceration and work to maintain their humanity.

What terrifies me about going inside is how quickly the system de-humanizes and isolates even visitors. The COs often come from the same neighborhoods as the men they police, and they too are working-class or lower-middle-class. They choose careers as COs for the same reason that many of the men inside choose to sell drugs: they have families and bills and need health care. While some COs create obstacles for the incarcer-ated men, others embrace the idea of rehabilitation and treat the men with fairness. They too are a mix of good and bad, brilliant and not, an-gry, sad, and happy. The hidden curriculum of prison comes from this combination of people who are trying to live within rules that often seem capricious, can be enforced arbitrarily, and are designed not for rehabili-tation but for punishment. The stated rules of Inside-Out are designed to keep the outside and inside students "safe" from violating these rules:

> No outside student may bring anything in to give to an inside stu-dent, no matter how small or seemingly insignificant, including such things as articles, pens, paper, and the like (not to mention books—institutions have strict policies about the process by which books are brought inside).
> No inside student may give anything to an outside student.
> (*Inside-Out* 32)

As the teacher in jail, I bring in large, clear plastic bags filled with books, notebooks, handouts, pens, Post-it notes, and markers for the in-side students. Most facilities let the inside students keep their notebooks, though not the pens. This works well until a cell is "tossed" (literally, the person's possessions are tossed around the cell during searches for contraband),[5] and then the man's possessions might disappear while he himself disappears to administrative segregation (solitary confinement, or "the hole") to wait for an internal disciplinary process. Typically, I ask the institution for a tour of the prison about halfway through the course, and they are willing to show the outside students around. The inside students meet us after the tour, and we tell them what we saw: often a meal tray, a workplace, sometimes the health center and a social worker's office. Often we look in on a block and see the tiers of cells and the common area. Sometimes we see a recreation area or the prison library, but we rarely see an individual cell.

After the tour, the inside students help us process what we saw. They tell us how long it takes to get an appointment at the health center; what the meals taste like; and how they make chichi, a prison meal, with ramen noodles, crushed Doritos, and other purchases from the commissary. Typically, we then hand out "Slick and the Beanstalk," by Judee Norton. This short piece of creative nonfiction tells how Norton subverted the rules of working in a prison kitchen by stealing a bean and growing it in a milk carton in her cell window in a manner reminiscent of a grade school project. While she has carefully considered the rules she is violating, starting with stealing the bean, she is not sure what rule might prohibit her from keeping a sprout on the windowsill. When she is discovered, her infraction is defined as "altering food" (173).

"Slick" makes visible the inflexible rules of prison, which inside and outside students proceed to unpack together. Reading the piece out loud after the tour of the prison helps us think about what the rules mean—not only their intention but also their effect. During one discussion of "Slick," we learned that our inside classmate kept a contraband toothbrush. The prison-issued toothbrush was cheap and fragile, designed for short-term use. The inside student described how the bristles fell out and mentioned that he had obtained his own toothbrush. Inside-Out's confidentiality rule facilitates such honest exchange by stipulating that what is said in the classroom stays in the classroom: stories cannot be shared in ways that would identify the speaker or discussed among the students outside class.

Responding to "Slick": Rich

For many years I noticed that I kept losing weight while kitchen workers that I knew kept gaining. I had been so proud to get a library job, but now that job seemed to be missing something. The food I ate did as well—it seemed to be missing any flavor whatsoever. One day, after a breakfast of grits and bread, I postulated that it might have been an optical illusion. My friends thought I was crazy until I explained: "It looked like food, and it felt like we were eating. However, I didn't taste anything, and I am still hungry, which makes me wonder if we actually ate anything at all."

Suddenly, none of us were sure if we had even been fed. We speculated on how advanced and affordable holograms might have become during our time away. All I knew for sure was that they weren't letting us back in line for seconds.

Eventually, I took the plunge and transferred to a kitchen job. Assigned to the serving line, I discovered a whole new world on the other side of the tray slot. It was considered a bad day if the workers had to eat the same thing they were serving. Most days we were treated to a "worker's meal," which often included real cheese, toppings for the pizza, icing for the cake, and salads with more than three ingredients. Things like Swiss cheese, grated cheese, tuna, and warm, fresh-baked apple pie were common in this exclusive diner's club. Those poor bastards in general population had no idea that edible, tasty food was being devoured right before their arrival. These items just never found their way onto a tray and out that slot. Only those with a "kitchen connection" even knew about these delicacies.

Needless to say, my weight shot right back up, but all was not perfect in the kitchen. The corrections officer who supervised the preparation and serving of the worker meal wanted to wait until ten thirty to serve it. He waited until all workers had arrived—and there were some who showed up at the last minute because no work was immediately expected of them. Some people didn't seem to do anything but steal food.

My problem was that the sergeant of the block I was serving wanted us to start serving at ten thirty so he could feed his block and do nothing for an hour until count time, after which he would have another hour to do nothing while waiting for count to clear.

Good for him, but not for me. I wanted time to enjoy my worker meal before we served. We could not eat while serving, and afterward we were expected to clean up and return to the block for count. Cleaning up was important. The roaches in that kitchen were as large as the mice, and both were well fed because many people didn't care about cleaning anything. I feared that if the roaches got much bigger, they might seize control of the institution, and that wouldn't be any good for anybody.

I tried forcing down the worker meal quickly, but that took all of the enjoyment out of it. It also created a choking hazard, as they didn't serve a beverage with the worker meal. I just don't eat as fast as most guys. Growing up, my mom always yelled at me for eating fast; now the Department of Corrections yells at me for eating too slow. Story of my life.

I tried to delay the start of serving, but that only got me in trouble. I was expected to be at my station when staff was ready to serve.

The boss yelled at me, "We start serving at ten thirty!"

"What time is the worker meal?"

"Ten thirty," he bellowed.

I looked up at him, expecting him to now understand the conundrum I was experiencing. Surely he would realize that I couldn't be in two places at the same time. That I deserved a meal and time to eat it.

Nothing. Didn't bat an eyelash. Refused to make eye contact. May as well have been a six-foot, three-hundred-pound block of stone. I knew then that my days in the kitchen were numbered. He may have known earlier. It wasn't long before I caught a write-up for trying to sneak food back to my cell.

"It was my worker meal," I protested to the hearing examiner.

"Did they say you could take it?"

Deflated, dejected, defeated, I answered him honestly. "No."

Finding Freedom: Rachel

A few months ago, I was handing out paper lunch bags filled with syringes and giving people HIV and hepatitis C tests in a small back room of an office in downtown Anchorage. Every day, I would meet with people in the most confined space that fire regulations would allow, where they would often admit to being in the most trapped place they had yet come to in their life journey. More often than not, these brief interactions between two strangers would give way to a moment of the purest freedom I have known.

This is the beauty of holding sacred space. For the purpose of this essay, let's understand *sacred* as describing an authentic, truth-telling, snot-dripping, "No, that is not a dumb question" place of curiosity and bravery. These spaces, it turns out, are created by nothing more than radical and intent listening. In my experience, these sacred spaces yield tears, guttural exhalations, connection, validation, and vulnerable sharing for speaker and listener. I've come to understand these moments as freedom.

The hardest part of creating these sacred spaces is that they are not all dimly lit churches or quiet beaches. They are harsh, sometimes awkward, and come unexpectedly—so you'd better grab them by the tail when you feel them. I began to understand this during my Inside-Out class.

It seems a bit contradictory to find a dimension of freedom in situations like relationship and confinement—conditions we associate with attachment and entrapment. It seems contradictory that having a structured and prompted conversation with a stranger can be the purest form of independence or autonomy. Yet the experience of studying in a prison has proved to me that entering intentional relationships without the desire to judge or change, wishing instead simply to hear and be curious, grants us the freedom to authentically be ourselves. Emotional and spiritual freedom comes from intentional relationships built on showing up and making connections.

But what if we are not capable of connecting? What if, after most of a person's physical and civil liberties have been stripped away, an institution attempts to strip away the freedom to have an authentic and trusting connection with another person?

After a few classes, I began to pick up on the idea that the issue most inside students had with the rules was not in the rules themselves. Most of the men understood the need to have limitations, as it was a prison, and as safety needed to be the priority. The issues were hidden in the arbitrary manner in which the regulations were enforced, the refusal to explain them, and the ever-present inconsistency. In other words, the relationships between the rule-enforcers and the rule-followers were not ones of truth and curiosity.

I have never worked or lived in a prison, so I cannot imagine the specific and immense stresses and concerns for safety and dignity that prison life creates. But while working in a syringe exchange, I have spent my day with populations that pose a risk for danger, and I have been threatened and challenged because of the rules that I have had to enforce. I have also had a lot of success on the days when I could muster the energy and patience to look someone in the eye and say, "Yes, I see this. . . . And I'm so sorry for how bad it hurts."

As David Foster Wallace suggests in "This Is Water," real freedom might not be the freedom to *do* but rather the freedom to exercise control over how we think and what we choose to think about. This is the sort of freedom that is not a right or privilege granted to us by our great country or social norms but is an intrinsic principle of *being*.

Relationships without understanding and respect are not relationships of authenticity and truth. A life without authentic relationships lacks a dimension of freedom that might just be necessary for being truly alive. I have come to understand that there are many ways a person can be denied this sort of emotional and spiritual freedom. I first thought those ways were unique to the prison system. I then learned they could include opioid addiction and exposure to trauma. Even my own personal experiences of self-doubt, internalized homophobia, and cultural ignorance have denied me authentic relationships along with the clarity, courage, and freedom those might yield.

I now accept that there are perhaps millions of institutional, structural, and personal demons that will deny the people of this world their freedom to authentically be. This is why, since sitting in a plastic folding chair under the fluorescent light of the jail, I cannot do anything but continue to look for sacred spaces. The lessons of Inside-Out transcended the details of structural injustice and regional nuances in writing style. My overwhelming understanding from Inside-Out is that if I want to contribute to radical and lasting change, I cannot do anything before I show up and be still. My journey to try and become an ally, a friend, or even a better human being is a journey that begins in silence. Entering the conversation, the news article, or even the voting polls is not the same as entering the room and holding sacred space with the person you are speaking with.

In "Messenger," Mary Oliver writes, "Let me / keep my mind on what matters, / which is my work, / which is mostly standing still and learning to be astonished." Perhaps then, it is true that we need to be taught to be still. We need to be taught to react with slowness and curiosity rather than the popular method of quick reactions and drawing on our own knowledge. There are so many ways to define freedom, and some of them contradict one another. Indeed, some of my freest moments are structured interactions with strangers whose faces blur more every day. I suppose all I can do is recommend pausing the search in the mountains and cathedrals, and looking for freedom in the person you are speaking with, or perhaps even within the place where you feel most trapped.

Baking Bread: Ann

When Rachel served as a Jesuit volunteer in Alaska, we texted and e-mailed occasionally. For a young woman from the Jersey shore to head to Alaska and participate in needle exchange was a huge leap. I worried about how isolating Alaska in winter would be for a person who was used to the beach. And then Rachel started baking bread. As she writes in "Let It Rise,"

> The knead isn't the hard part of bread baking. The hard part is in the patience of the rise. When you're in a moment of chaos, the least intuitive thing to do is rest. Yet sometimes after we feel conflicted, the most productive thing to do is silence our own thoughts for a while.

Relationships with people experiencing incarceration often involve the rest, the pause, the giving up on what you can't control and pushing for what you can. Following the rules means waiting for the long intervals between letters that are sent to Florida for processing before being scanned and sent to the recipient in prison. Following the rules has meant leaving out many of the more challenging and difficult stories that cannot find their way into print without endangering the program. Men disappear from class for the hole, for court, for health care, for release. While we hope the absences are "see you laters" and not "goodbyes," we also hope that the men we have grown to love are going home, but we do not know. Like so much else, life is brief and temporary, but when we can, we get to the kitchen and bake something good to share with someone else.

NOTES

1. *Jail* and *prison* are used interchangeably in this piece, though technically, jails hold people who are waiting for trial and sentencing, and prisons hold those who are sentenced and serving their time.

2. Elizabeth Linehan, a philosopher, professor, and volunteer in the Alternatives to Violence program at SCI Phoenix, and I have taught Inside-Out together for five semesters in four different jails in the Philadelphia jail system. It was her brilliant idea to incorporate "Slick" into our course.

3. From *The Inside-Out Prison Exchange Program Instructor's Manual*: "Individual interests and needs are secondary to the larger goal, that of making change through educating ourselves and one another about the problems and possibilities of our country's system of crime and justice. Hopefully, individual change forged through this process moves out into wider circles in our own lives and in the life of our society" (39).

4. We use the terms *inside* and *outside* to distinguish between the two groups of Saint Joseph's students enrolled in my course. After the course, the inside students become SJU alums.

5. According to a former inside student, Sergio Hyland, "Any number of guards storm into the chosen cell and strip the prisoner naked, forcing him/her to expose the most private regions of their body, in order to be searched for contraband. It's extremely invasive and humiliating—which is the purpose. It sends the message that a person in prison isn't a human; they aren't even a prisoner. They're property; owned and operated by the state. And one good look àt the guards' attire lets the prisoner know that any resistance will be met with extreme violent force." Hyland was incarcerated for twenty-one years, including five years in solitary confinement, and was released in 2022.

WORKS CITED

Boyle, Gregory. *Barking to the Choir: The Power of Radical Kinship*. Simon and Schuster, 2017.

Browning, Sharon. "Author: Sharon Browning." *Just Listening . . . for the Common Good*, 2021, justlistening.net/author/sharonbrowning/.

Green, Ann E. "'But You Aren't White': Racial Perceptions and Service-Learning." *Michigan Journal of Community Service-Learning*, vol. 8, no. 1, 2001, pp. 18–26.

———. "Difficult Stories: Service-Learning, Race, Class, and Whiteness." *College Composition and Communication*, vol. 56, no. 2, 2003, pp. 276–301.

———. "Service-Learning and Discernment: Reality Working through Resistance." *The Jesuit Tradition and Rhetorical Studies: Looking Backward, Looking Forward*, edited by Cinthia Gannet and John Brereton, Fordham UP, 2016, pp. 360–69.

Hyland, Sergio. E-mail to Ann E. Green. 29 Dec. 2022.

The Inside-Out Prison Exchange Program Instructor's Manual. Temple University, April 2011.

Mitchell, Tania. "Traditional vs. Critical Service-Learning: Engaging the Literature to Differentiate the Two Models." *Michigan Journal of Community Service Learning*, vol. 14, no. 2, spring 2008, pp. 50–65.

Norton, Judee. "Slick and the Beanstalk." *Wall Tappings: An International Anthology of Women's Prison Writings, 200 to the Present*, edited by Judith Scheffler, Feminist Press, 2002, pp. 169–74.

Oliver, Mary. "Messenger." *Thirst*. Beacon Press, 2006, p. 1.

O'Reilley, Mary Rose. *Radical Presence: Teaching as Contemplative Practice*. Heinemann, 1998.

Pompa, Lori. "One Brick at a Time: The Power and Possibility of Dialogue across the Prison Wall." *The Prison Journal*, vol. 93, no. 2, 2013, pp. 127–34.

———. "Service-Learning as Crucible: Reflections on Immersion, Context, Power, and Transformation." *Michigan Journal of Community Service-Learning*, fall 2002, pp. 67–76.

Swenarton, Rachel. "Let It Rise." *Ignatian Solidarity Network*, 23 Jan. 2018, ignatiansolidarity.net/blog/2018/01/23/let-it-rise/.

Wallace, David Foster. "This Is Water." 2005. *Farnam Street*, 2022, fs.blog/2012/04/david-foster-wallace-this-is-water/.

Werts, Tyrone. "Reflections on the Inside-Out Prison Exchange Program." *The Prison Journal*, vol. 93, no. 2, 2013, pp. 135–38, https://doi.org/10.1177/0032885512472483.

———. "Tyrone Werts." *A Peace of My Mind*, hosted by John Noltner, 24 Dec. 2021, apomm.net/2016/03/23/tyrone-werts/.

Relational Methodologies and Decolonial Outcomes for the Prison Writing Classroom

Anna Plemons

I had been teaching narrative nonfiction at New Folsom prison for a handful of years before I read Shawn Wilson's work and came to understand the deep potential of the writing classroom to function as a space wherein writers could actively support their families, loved ones, and communities outside the prison. Once I did, a flood of stories confirming that idea came rushing in. There was the story of the incarcerated dad washing his clothes in the small metal sink basin in his cell, mentally preparing for his visit with his son the next day—scrubbing and mulling over how to counsel a young son with autism who was being picked on at school. There was also the story of another incarcerated father, talking on the community phone in the cellblock, vetting the pimply teen who wanted to take his daughter to prom—facing away from the line of other men waiting to place a call, shifting his weight and wishing he could have conducted his interrogation from his couch, flanked by a rifle and a Rottweiler. And then there was the story of a dad who had doubled his sales on the street so that his son could go to the private preschool uptown.

I have also read an untold number of essays by incarcerated women, many of whom have kids and who keep the faces of their children in mind as they arm themselves with pens and pencils to face memories of addiction, pain, and violence caused and endured. There have also been stories of sons and daughters trying to write themselves back into the fabrics of their families. An incarcerated grandfather, who was working on his associate's degree, once wrote a piece of fiction that he hoped would introduce his grandchildren to some key pieces of African American history. These stories unravel the trope of the hardened criminal—that one-dimensional character, completely disconnected from society, who endlessly walks the yard, waiting out their just punishment for acts of lawbreaking done wantonly and without cause or context, looking to be rescued by a writing teacher who will transform them back into a moral and intellectual being.

It is precisely because these stories disrupt stale images of incarcerated people that I share them here. In this essay, I will share a methodology that I have been using in my teaching practice at New Folsom—not as a prescriptive remedy but as one of many possible options for prison scholar-teachers interested in delinking (Mignolo) their teaching practices from unintentionally colonial teaching and research logics. Using decolonial and Indigenous theory, I will argue that the literary classroom can be framed as a space where participants are re-membered as integral parts of communities outside the prison (Ngũgĩ). This significant shift away from individual reformation resituates incarcerated students as active co-laborers in the broader work of social justice, rather than passive recipients of literary-based behavioral interventions. A discussion of the methodology is followed by a few examples of what a literary classroom oriented around relationality might look like.

The Need for a Socially Just Intervention

A host of other scholars have already laid out a compelling case for why mass incarceration is a social justice issue (see Alexander; *Thirteenth*; Gilmore; Stevenson). And if that is true, then a teacherly engagement with the US prison requires a methodology that is itself socially just, meaning that it forwards fair and just relationships between incarcerated people and the larger society. Of course, a socially just classroom teaching practice will not "solve the problem of mass incarceration." That larger project, as Daniel Karpowitz has pointed out, "can only be addressed by putting fewer people in prison and for less time; by making our economy less punitive; and by eliminating the stark racial disparities that mar all aspects of American inequality and especially criminal justice" (25). With that said, the overwhelming scale and complexity represented by the crisis of mass incarceration does not excuse scholar-teachers from a clear-eyed assessment of the problematic ideologies and logics that continue to inform and animate much of prison pedagogy.

When I think about Audre Lorde's question regarding whether or not the master's house can be dismantled using the master's tools, I think of the antiquated image of the morally superior and intellectually pedigreed teacher working tirelessly to transform the wide-eyed and grateful pupils at the outposts of the empire. And while we expect that our field has moved past such clearly colonizing postures on campus, the context of the prison classroom often pulls otherwise progressive educators back into pedagogical practices and postures at odds with their own good intentions. In identifying the residual reverberations of colonial ideology, Walter Mignolo observes that such salvation rhetorics are very much still with us. The vocabulary of *conversion* has simply been replaced by updated terms like *development* (Mignolo xxiv). Nonetheless, the transformational project is intact, having shape-shifted from a spiritual to an economic form (Plemons, *Beyond Progress*).

This explains how prison scholar-teachers get caught perpetuating ideologies in their prison teaching that they critique when working outside the prison. Often, the need for funding compels prison scholar-teachers to produce evidence of personal development for incarcerated students, evidence that they are not required to produce for their students on campus. Such evidence comes primarily through autobiographical narratives that describe individual transformation. The formula looks like this: "I was born; I had problems; I made the wrong choices; I was apprehended by the police; I was incarcerated; I found God [or writing] and He [it] helped me. And . . . my life is now on a better track" (Meiners 139).[1] The thought that faculty members on college campuses would have to demonstrate that their students were morally bankrupt before taking their specific class and that the course definitively reoriented a student's moral compass is laughable. Nonetheless, prison scholar-teachers are regularly asked, and often willingly produce, this type of evidence when they teach in prison. Such methodologies do not forward fair and just relationships between incarcerated people and the larger society. Rather, they often have the opposite effect by authorizing a perpetual focus on the perceived moral deficits of incarcerated students. Harvard's treatment of Michelle Jones offers a raw example of how this works. In Jones's case, administrators at Harvard overturned her acceptance into a doctoral program in response to concerns that she had "played down her crime in the application process" and that her status as a formerly incarcerated person would "cause a backlash among rejected applicants, conservative news outlets or parents of students" (Hager). In the end, Jones accepted admission to a doctoral program in American Studies at New York University.

Suggesting a shift away from a focus on transformational narratives does not mean that incarcerated students should be censored for writing about their educational journeys but rather that such narratives need not be the end goal of the course (Plemons, *Beyond Progress*). Admittedly, the circulation of such texts is partially explained by incarcerated students' consistent interest in writing them. For many incarcerated students, writing their educational salvation narrative is an important part of coming back into integrity with their own selves. Making a choice to turn to anything positive in prison is difficult, and I deeply respect anyone who makes such a personal change. What is problematic, however, is the way that such narratives become a qualitative currency of sorts for prison scholar-teachers as they describe and justify their work inside. This genre of writing can be meaningful or cathartic for its authors, but when it is commodified and used as evidence by scholar-teachers, it perpetuates a colonizing focus on the individual that hobbles the broader emancipatory aims of prison education.

In its quantitative form, developmental data tends to focus on a reduction in recidivism. Reducing the number of people who return through the revolving door of prison is important, of course. However, recidivism as a primary measure is problematic (see Castro and Brawn; Gottschalk; Plemons, *Beyond Progress*). As Robert Scott has pointed out, recidivism is one of the few prison education metrics that fits "positivism's narrow horizon of testable and measurable results" (441). Fusing the notion of development with data that simply tabulates who gets out and stays out forecloses a host of important conversations about what counts as progress for an incarcerated person and what value they may already have, or be interested in adding, in communities that are important to them both inside and outside the prison. Here I am thinking of the many incarcerated people I have met who are serving life sentences without the possibility of parole. If an educational program is required to measure a reduction in recidivism, it will naturally exclude students who are doing important community-oriented work but who cannot possibly contribute to that metric.

A narrow obsession with development—either through individual narratives or recidivism data—is out of step with the critically informed solidarity that inspires many educators to teach inside. A clear-eyed assessment of the default settings of prison education suggests that scholar-teachers yet struggle to align social justice intentions with teaching and research practices that are themselves socially just. In the following section, I name some of the scholars whose work has been important to me as I have grappled with the disconnections between the types of knowledge authorized by the academy and the relational reality that is always already part of the classroom at New Folsom (see Waters). I also provide a relational methodology for prison-scholar teachers adapted from the work of Margaret Kovach.

Re-membering: Toward Relational Pedagogies

Ngũgĩ wa Thiong'o uses the term *re-member* to describe the work of re-connecting what legacies of colonialization have so violently torn apart. The image of putting back together things that have been unnaturally separated resonates with the best of what prison education attempts to do. Incarceration, by design, deeply separates people from the land, from each other, and from themselves. Marty Williams says it this way: "This place is about isolation. It is about closure of the heart and the mind and the spirit. And the worst thing about this place is that it is what it is. It's doing its job, which is to keep us contained. That's it. It serves no other purpose but containment" (*At Night I Fly*). In response to this profound separation, prison scholar-teachers can work to create methodologies for the prison classroom that directly work against such separation by dispensing with narrow individual narratives that obscure incarcerated students' relationships with communities outside the prison and by challenging deficit ideologies predicated on the idea that incarcerated students lack the intrinsic motivations and tools for educational and community engagement.

While the work of global decolonial scholars establishes the call for what needs to be done (see Ndlovu-Gatsheni and Zondi; Mignolo), the work of Indigenous scholars such as Wilson and Kovach provides concrete structures for creating and sustaining methodologies that make space for incarcerated students to re-member themselves as valuable contributors to communities that are important to them. Before continuing, it is important here to acknowledge that, as a white woman with over two decades of formal schooling in the West, I come to Indigenous thought as an outsider. I worry for good reason about issues of misuse, appropriation, and a general flattening of Indigenous theory. Nonetheless, I also agree with Zoe Todd that in the academy there is a "continued, collective reticence to address its own racist and colonist roots, and the debt to Indigenous thinkers in a meaningful and structural way" (10). So, while recognizing my complicity in the systems that Todd critiques, I also want to acknowledge my debt to Indigenous scholars (see Arola and Arola; Cordova; Deloria; Haas; Hampton; King et al.; Maracle; Mihesuah and Wilson; Smith; Wilson) by pointing to the ways that Indigenous thought can inform a methodology for the prison classroom that pushes back against deeply held Western notions of the primacy of the individual (see Plemons, *Beyond Progress*).

Wilson suggests that the goal of research—and, I would add, teaching—should be the "strengthening of relationships and the bridging of distance" (11). As I mentioned earlier, reading Wilson's work brought on the flood of stories that confirmed that many of the incarcerated writers I had been working with were already working hard to stay connected to the world outside the walls. Once the principle of relationality was at the fore, it suddenly seemed to me that relational bridging work was a reasonable goal for the prison classroom. As I have discussed elsewhere, Kovach's work provided some clear guidelines for how to build the type of respectful, reciprocal, and relational methodology that Wilson described. Kovach's methodology is predicated on an Indigenous epistemology, and I, as a white scholar, cannot and would not claim that knowledge. I do see, though, that an adaptation of Kovach's methodology can guide prison scholar-teachers as they work to develop pedagogies for teaching and methodologies for research that disrupt default colonial postures between teachers and students.[2]

This five-part methodology asks prison scholar-teachers to consider "the colonial legacies that inspired and sustain prison education; their personal motivations; the cultural assets and articulated needs of incarcerated students; and the connections incarcerated students have to communities outside the prison" (Plemons, "Something"). Each part of the relational methodology laid out below is important and connects to the others. For example, understanding one's relationship with dominant knowledge structures is important preparation for teaching inside, but it does not supersede the equally important labor of understanding one's personal motivations for such work. Beyond understanding context and motivation, a relational methodology also requires that scholar-teachers work with incarcerated people at each stage of a project and respect the sovereignty of the group should it be determined that the project becomes undesirable, unproductive, or even dangerous to incarcerated students.[3]

Decolonial intention and ethic: Researchers are committed to examining how both individuals and groups have been affected by and complicit in colonial legacies. Furthermore, they are committed to asking questions that challenge the Western knowledge systems that define what is real and how we know it to be such (see Haas).

Researcher preparation: Researchers are committed to exploring their own relationships to the research or project, finding and making sense of the memories and stories that inform their motivation for the work (see Hampton).

Community accountability: The research project responds to the articulated needs and desires of the community, evolves in response to community feedback, and is terminated when or if the community decides that the project is at odds with its health and sovereignty (see Wilson).

Reciprocity / community benefit: The research project respects participants as already valuable members of their respective communities and directly works to support community members in those existing roles. Benefits to the community, generated primarily by the community members themselves, are part of the clearly articulated outcomes of the research project (see Wilson).

Knowledge gathering / meaning-making: The types of knowledge gathered though the project and the meanings that are constructed about that knowledge privilege the community over the individual as the unit of analysis, balance a need for data with a respect for participants' desire to protect sacred or private knowledge, and directly include the community in the process of meaning-making and subsequent distribution of knowledge (see Kovach).[4]

The ways of knowing and ways of being suggested in this methodology take practice. Attempting to use a relational methodology to generate and carry out a classroom project does not inoculate prison-scholars from slipping back into the colonizing patterns of thinking and acting that have marked prison education. In short, this methodology does not purport to fix one's teaching in five "easy" steps. And, of course, many a new unforeseen crisis has developed at the hands of well-intentioned but hasty helpers. Kristin L. Arola and Adam Arola address such dangers in their essay on assemblage: "Even if our objective is to create in such a way as to open up new worlds of possibility in response to a confrontation with problems that we presently lack the resources to resolve, we still must be cautious that our employment of and engagement with the world do not unconsciously repeat and reinforce the world from which we are attempting to find lines of flight" (219). With that said, the following section provides some concrete examples of what a relational methodology might aim for and what it might look like in practice. In the next section, I describe the work of Michael Owens, the Family Arts program, and the creation of the workbook *Together We Can* at New Folsom Prison. None of these examples is intended to be prescriptive. My intention is to suggest that even as scholar-teachers acknowledge the immensity of the crisis of mass incarceration, the implementation of a relational methodology (by nature of how it works) will have a limited, local context and a protracted timeline. In this way, the structures of a relational methodology chafe against Western project deadlines and mechanisms for data collection.

Making Space for Self-Cultivated Justice

What I hope the relational methodology outlined above suggests is that individual educational narratives need not be the end goal of prison education but are rather a chapter in a long, long book. In other places, I have written about Spoon Jackson and the way that his individual educational narrative both reinforces and complicates the genre ("Literacy," *Beyond Progress*). The life and work of Michael Owens offer another example of someone who has moved through the role of student on his way to inhabiting the roles of teacher and community asset. In his coauthored article "Seen but Not Heard: Personal Narratives of Systemic Failure within the School-to-Prison Pipeline," Owens writes about his formal and informal educational journey:

> The school system failed me, but education was still a major factor in my evolution. I earned my G.E.D. while in Folsom State Prison at the age of 22. Soon after, I discovered the true power of education through the writings of Langston Hughes, Richard Wright, Stokely Carmichael, and Amiri Baraka. These black men spoke directly to my experience as a young black man in America. They were putting words to the inexpressible despair I was feeling. For the first time in my life, I did not feel alone in my pain. Every chance I had, I read the works of authors like these. I clung to them, not only because they shared my pain, but also because they spoke of reasons to hope.
>
> They taught me that I could, and should, struggle to create a better world than the one into which I was born. They taught me that it was my responsibility to search out the truth of who and why I was. The monster I had allowed myself to become was not an inevitability — just a tragedy. These men taught me I would have to fight for my humanity, and then fight again to have it recognized. They taught me that even a man convicted of murder and sentenced to life without the possibility of parole can redeem himself if he is willing to do the work of self-cultivated justice. (Jones et al. 65)

It is clear in this narrative that Owens was already motivated and capable of making change in his life. The opportunity for education and access to key writers supported the work he was already interested in doing. And when Owens speaks about "do[ing] the work of self-cultivated justice," he is describing a concrete engagement with the world (Jones et al. 66). In 2010, I had the chance to work with Owens to establish an Arts in Corrections (AIC) writers' workshop, which he capably co-led with another incarcerated writer. His strong and patient leadership in that group created a space for a handful of committed students to hone their craft. Through AIC, Owens also built a working relationship with the Sacramento Poetry Center, which provided some mentorship and support as Owens continued to write. Then, in 2017, Owens published *The Way Back*, a collection of his poetry. The book release celebration at the Sacramento Poetry Center included a reading by his wife and a second reading by a close friend. Owens is currently working on a facilitator's manual that can be used by teachers outside looking to engage young writers in the community. In Owens's story, the outsiders (prison scholar-teachers and other advocates) play a supporting role, making space where they can for Owens to do the work of re-membering himself as an asset to his community. In this way, Owens's story provides a timely example of what classroom work oriented toward strengthening relationships and bridging distances might aim for.

In my own teaching practice, Wilson's call and the methodology for prison-scholars adapted from Kovach led to the creation of the Family Arts (FA) program in 2017. An ongoing project sponsored by an Arts in Corrections grant, FA seeks to use classroom arts instruction to tangibly strengthen and support the relationships incarcerated people have with their families, defining *family* in broad terms. Specifically, FA views program participants as arts mentors in their respective families and functionally supports participants in that role by providing them with direct instruction, curricular materials that they can edit and circulate with some autonomy, mechanisms (including postage) for instigating a creative exchange with their family members, opportunities to mail home fine arts projects, and opportunities for the public performance or display of their work.

The creative writing branch of the program is made up of a twenty-four-part curriculum whose lessons address principles of writing practice and introduce students to writers whose work reflects those principles. The content of the lessons strategically works to privilege the voices of writers less likely to show up in a public school curriculum. To that end, the curriculum showcases the work of writers of color who describe and exemplify the principles of practice discussed in the series. Through the program, incarcerated writers, musicians, and visual artists simultaneously inhabit the roles of student and teacher and have reported that the program provides them opportunities to support the personal, academic, and creative goals of people important to them on the outside (Plemons, *Beyond Progress*).

In 2018, AIC creative writing and visual arts classes at New Folsom collaborated with Aaché Howard McDaniel, a student at Washington State University, and me to create *Together We Can*, a drawing and writing journal for children. The book is intended to be used as an arts-based interactive tool for incarcerated people to use when meeting with children in the visiting room (it can also be mailed home in cases where visits are not possible). The book was the first AIC project to fully utilize the relational methodology described in this essay. Because the methodology requires that the knowledge-making processes be collective, once the books were in distribution, Aaché and I returned to the prison to listen to participants talk about how they were using the materials. One participant thanked Aaché for including her own story in the book and reported that when he had read it to his young daughter she had responded repeatedly, "That is how I feel." He said that his daughter had never talked with him about her feelings regarding his incarceration and that he was deeply grateful to have provided an opportunity for her to open her heart and to have been there to comfort her.

"Looking over This Fence"

I am not naive enough to believe that children's journals alone can stem the tide of intergenerational incarceration. I am also not naive enough to believe that recidivism statistics alone tell a story worth repeating. Engaging with the crisis of mass incarceration requires a broad and nuanced calculus and the involvement of a wide host of relations, of which scholar-teachers are only a part. Prison scholar-teachers play an important role in this process, and the methodologies we use in constructing our classrooms matter. V. F. Cordova says that "present actions are like layers of snow added to a snowball—the shape of the present outer layer determines the future shape of the whole" (175). If we want prison education to reflect fair and just relationships between incarcerated people and the community outside the walls, then we will have to find ways to create that possibility through our present actions. One piece of that complex puzzle can be addressed by listening to what incarcerated people say about why they come to class and working, in concrete ways, to support their articulated desire to be re-membered.

In discussing his experiences with an Arts in Correction / Dell'Arte theater workshop, an incarcerated participant named Eric says it this way: "Life goes on out there. I'm looking over this fence right now. I'm trying to get back home and begin my life with my grandson." Alexander, a classmate of Eric's, adds, "We are trying our best to put back. We have something to give back" (DeSoto). Being re-membered is not the only reason incarcerated students come to class. Nonetheless, it is a reason that comes up often and, as such, is a productive articulation around which to imagine future methodological options for teaching literature and writing in prison.

NOTES

1. See Plemons, "Beyond Progress," for a more fully articulated discussion of the problematic nature of salvation narratives.

2. The adaptation of Kovach is further discussed in Plemons, "Beyond Progress" and *Beyond Progress*. As I see it, part of disrupting Western ways of approaching research is a purposeful pushing back against the teleological assumption that each conversation we start in the public record needs to be a node on a progressive plane along which we are endlessly chasing the newest or latest idea. I agree with Frankie Condon, who in *I Hope I Join the Band: Narrative, Affiliation, and Antiracist Rhetoric* notes that we seem "doomed to loop endlessly and helplessly through the same tired actions and reactions, claims and counterclaims, raising the same questions over and over and moving restlessly away from them before we've lived and lain with them, feeling the contours of the space, time, and perspectival horizons they might open for us" (12). My intention in this essay is to broaden the conversation about relationality in the prison classroom while also slowing it down. That work necessarily involves the decolonial choice to honor the work of Indigenous scholars like Kovach by acknowledging and circulating their contributions across publications rather than obscuring their work by "moving forward" to the next new thing.

3. On this point, it is important to note how little those of us who come and go through the front gate understand prison politics. In a scene from *At Night I Fly*, Jack, who is white, discusses the reasons he does not plan to acknowledge his Black classmates on the yard despite the mutual respect and friendship that have developed in the class (Jack does eventually publicly acknowledge his classmates, but it takes almost ten years for him to decide to take that risk). The film provides an unprecedented window into, and therefore rich examples from, the Arts in Corrections program at New Folsom prison. See Plemons, "Something" and *Beyond Progress*, for a deeper elaboration of key scenes in the film.

4. Originally published in Plemons, *Beyond Progress* 102.

WORKS CITED

Alexander, Michelle. *The New Jim Crow: Mass Incarceration in the Age of Colorblindness*. The New Press, 2010.

Arola, Kristin L., and Adam Arola. "An Ethics of Assemblage: Creative Repetition and the 'Electric Pow Wow.'" *Assembling Composition*, edited by

Kathleen Blake Yancy and Stephen McElroy, Conference on College Composition and Communication, 2017, pp. 204–21.

At Night I Fly. Directed by Michael Wenzer, Story AB, 2011.

Castro, Erin, and Michael Brawn. "Critiquing Critical Pedagogies inside the Prison Classroom: A Dialogue between Student and Teacher." *Harvard Educational Review*, vol. 87, no. 1, 2017, pp. 99–121.

Condon, Frankie. *I Hope I Join the Band: Narrative, Affiliation, and Antiracist Rhetoric.* Utah State UP, 2012.

Cordova, V. F. *How It Is: The Native American Philosophy of V. F. Cordova.* Edited by Kathleen Dean Moore, et al., U of Arizona P, 2007.

Deloria, Jr., Vine. *The Vine Deloria, Jr., Reader.* Edited by Barbara Deloria et al., Fulcrum Publishing, 1999.

DeSoto, Malcolm. "Arts in Pelican Bay State Prison." *Vimeo,* uploaded by Dell'Arte, 25 Aug. 2018, vimeo.com/287110304.

Gilmore, Ruth Wilson. *Golden Gulag: Prisons, Surplus, Crisis, and Opposition in Globalizing California.* U of California P, 2007.

Gottschalk, Marie. *Caught: The Prison State and the Lockdown of American Politics.* Princeton UP, 2015.

Haas, Angela. "Race, Rhetoric, and Technology: A Case Study of Decolonial Technical Communication Theory, Methodology, and Pedagogy." *Journal of Business and Technical Communication*, vol. 26, 2012, pp. 277–310.

Hager, E. "From Prison to Ph.D.: The Redemption and Rejection of Michelle Jones." *The New York Times*, 13 Sept. 2017, www.nytimes.com/2017/09/13/us/harvard-nyu-prison-michelle-jones.html.

Hampton, Eber. "Memory Comes before Knowledge: Research May Improve If Researchers Remember Their Motives." *Canadian Journal of Native Education*, vol. 21, 1995, pp. 46–54.

Jones, Kalinda, et al. "Seen but Not Heard: Personal Narratives of Systemic Failure within the School-to-Prison Pipeline." *Taboo: The Journal of Culture and Education*, vol. 17, no. 4, 2018, pp. 49–68.

Karpowitz, Daniel. *College in Prison: Reading in the Age of Mass Incarceration.* Rutgers UP, 2017.

King, Lisa, et al., editors. *Survivance, Sovereignty, and Story: Teaching American Indian Rhetorics.* Utah State UP, 2015.

Kovach, Margaret. *Indigenous Methodologies: Characteristics, Conversations, and Contexts.* U of Toronto P, 2009.

Lockard, Joe, and Sherry Rankins-Robertson, editors. *Prison Pedagogies: Learning and Teaching with Imprisoned Writers.* Syracuse UP, 2018.

Lorde, Audre. "The Master's Tools Will Never Dismantle the Master's House." *Sister Outsider: Essays and Speeches*, by Lorde, Crossing Press, 1984, pp. 110–14.

Maracle, Lee. *Oratory: Coming to Theory.* Gallerie Publications, 1990.

Meiners, Erica R. *Right to Be Hostile: Schools, Prisons, and the Making of Public Enemies.* Routledge, 2007.

Mignolo, Walter. *The Darker Side of Western Modernity: Global Futures, Decolonial Options.* Duke UP, 2011.

Mihesuah, Devon Abbott, and Angela Cavender Wilson, editors. *Indigenizing the Academy: Transforming Scholarship and Empowering Communities.* U of Nebraska P, 2004.

Ndlovu-Gatsheni, Sabelo, and Siphamandla Zondi. *Decolonizing the University, Knowledge Systems and Disciplines in Africa.* Carolina Academic Press, 2016.

Ngũgĩ wa Thiong'o. *Re-membering Africa.* East African Educational Publishers Ltd., 2009.

Owens, Michael. *The Way Back.* Random Lane Press, 2017.

Plemons, Anna. "Beyond Progress: Indigenous Scholars, Relational Methodologies, and Decolonial Options for the Prison Classroom." *Critical Perspectives on Teaching in Prison: Students and Instructors on Pedagogy Behind the Walls,* edited by Rebecca Ginsburg, Routledge, 2019, pp. 80–91.

———. *Beyond Progress in the Prison Classroom: Options and Opportunities.* National Council of Teachers of English, 2019.

———. "Literacy as an Act of Creative Resistance: Joining the Work of Incarcerated Teaching Artists at a Maximum-Security Prison." *Community Literacy Journal,* vol. 7, no. 2, 2013, pp. 39–52.

———. "Something Other Than Progress: Indigenous Methodologies and Higher Education in Prison." Lockard and Rankins-Robertson, pp. 88–108.

Scott, Robert. "Using Critical Pedagogy to Connect Prison Education and Prison Abolitionism." *Saint Louis University Public Law Review,* vol. 33, no. 2, 2014, pp. 401–14.

Smith, Linda Tuhiwai. *Decolonizing Methodologies.* 2nd ed., Zed Books, 2012.

Stevenson, Bryan. *Just Mercy: A Story of Justice and Redemption.* Spiegel and Grau, 2015.

Thirteenth. Directed by Ava DuVernay, *Netflix,* 7 Oct. 2016.

Todd, Zoe. "An Indigenous Feminist's Take on the Ontological Turn: 'Ontology' Is Just Another Word for Colonialism." *Journal of Historical Sociology,* vol. 29, no. 1, 2016: pp. 4–22.

Waters, Anne, editor. *American Indian Thought.* Blackwell Publishing, 2004.

Wilson, Shawn. *Research Is Ceremony.* Fernwood Publishing, 2008.

The Brain Is Wider than the Sky
David Bennett and Courtney Rein

There are two constants in prison that defy incarceration: the view of the sky and the ability to freely use one's brain. Emily Dickinson invokes both in her poem "The Brain—is wider than the Sky—." Like Dickinson, we believe in the inherent power of the brain; there is nothing on the planet that can contain or otherwise restrict it. Many incarcerated people can attest to the experience of the brain vividly transporting them back to the past or propelling them forward into an imagination of the future. But the brain in custody is at a loss in the immediate present, in the "now." That is where we believe structured education has a place: in giving the individual a fighting chance, both in prison and in the broader society. Yet common approaches to teaching in prison classrooms often resemble a journey into an unknown wilderness without a GPS or a planned route. The prison setting is a stir-crazy world filled with rules—overt and unspoken—and navigating it can be as dangerous as traversing a minefield. Many obstacles interfere with the academic success of students in custody: lack of self-confidence, academic challenges, prison politics, learning differences, institutional lockdowns and quarantines, physical and mental health struggles, cellmate dynamics, legal issues, and family problems. Imprisoned students are often juggling several such difficulties during a single semester. Thus, one challenge of prison education is the creation of engaging and democratic classrooms where students are willing—and able—to complete the courses in which they enroll, semester after semester. Yet the willingness and ability of students on the inside to be educated is no different than that of the average student in society. When we begin to talk about pedagogy in the prison setting, one thing has to be clear: incarcerated people are still human beings. As Bruce Michaels, an incarcerated "peer-to-peer educator," puts it, "The biggest thing I think outside educators miss when teaching prisoners is the commonality we all share, teachers and students alike: we all want to function with purpose" (Davis and Michaels 154). With this in mind, we are offering a road map for establishing an educational partnership that is mutually liberating for students and educators.

Though the offering of higher education within a prison setting is not a groundbreaking event in our current era, it is still somewhat revolutionary in that it is frowned upon by many in society. We frequently encounter prison administrators and other staff members who oppose free college education for currently incarcerated people. By default, there is a natural chasm between the jailers and the many "freedom fighter"–minded educators who imagine themselves taking the prison by storm in an attempt to liberate the minds (if not the bodies) of citizens in custody. However well-intentioned each individual instructor in this liberating force may be, outside educators have to be careful not to impose a predetermined outlook upon their students. Along these lines, the prison educator and professor Robert Scott warns, "If we are determined to have liberatory pedagogy in prison, it will have to proceed in an undeterministic manner. That means abandoning vanguardist proselytizing for the left, and being open to the possibility that the most important lesson from a college course can be in the dynamics of interaction between the classroom participants" (26). Even as teachers oppose the dominant beliefs and hierarchies of prison life, they must not swoop in and dominate the classroom with their own evangelizing ideas about salvation through their particular flavor of education. Scott notes the danger of treating "prison as a hostile wilderness that can be conquered or liberated by outsiders" (25). The antidote to such a colonizing approach lies in collaboration between outside educators and inside students to co-create the prison classroom as a democratic space of education. In the ideal classroom setting, students are empowered to work together to set classroom norms and standards and, in more advanced classes, to take part in developing the curriculum. This collective responsibility and investment boosts students' self-esteem, thus laying the groundwork for a more constructive classroom experience for all course participants.

Outside educators have a responsibility to be aware of the diversity of their students and their distinct needs and may need to embrace new pedagogical ideologies and techniques in order to meet those needs. Another Prison University Project (PUP) student at San Quentin State Prison shares his view: "Things are shifting in education—it used to be they [educators] only taught about Christopher Columbus, but now it's way left. I think it should be more in the middle." Riddle-Terrell's comment indicates a tension that educators inside prisons must address. A curriculum that moves beyond the traditional, white-dominated canon—without limiting itself to the politics of the left—allows students and teachers to be exposed to a more diverse range of thoughts, opinions, and styles. But it is not enough to diversify the curriculum; a prison classroom contains a wide range of learning styles and educational histories, and teachers have to be open to challenging themselves to engage with them. Educators need to question some of the traditional teaching forms with which they are familiar and comfortable, like lectures, teacher-centered discourse, and a "sage on the stage" method of pedagogy. Simone Davis, a coordinator of the Walls to Bridges program in Ontario, writes, "The educators who use more non-traditional teaching techniques, coupled with personal interactions that lead to quality relationships based in trust and integrity, usually do better than traditional educators" (Davis and Michaels 154). We, as members of the PUP community at San Quentin, here discuss what constitutes effective nontraditional teaching techniques and why they are so essential.

The first pedagogical order of business lies in recognizing that's there a pecking order in prison: it's key to establish respect from the onset, for respect is premium. Respect can be both tangible and intangible at the same time; though it is not heard, smelled, or touched, it can definitely be perceived, and perception is everything. Respect gives birth to trust, which opens students up to considering what outside teachers have to offer. As Odell Hodges, a PUP student at San Quentin State Prison, notes, "Teaching shouldn't seem like a strict duty, but you do have to have control." In line with Hodges's observation, we view teaching in prison as work that does not require superhuman, awe-inspiring action; to the contrary, all that is necessary is for outside educators to set a tone of mutual respect with the learning community from the moment class starts through the creation of an equitable classroom, conversations that allow for respectful disagreement, and content that invites students into those conversations.

At its best, a prison classroom has the capacity to undercut the isolation and damaging hierarchies of incarcerated life, to offer not just a space of education but an experience of momentary liberation. One PUP student reports, "When I get engaged in something, even though we're in prison, when we're debating and discussing and conversating, in those moments, I wasn't tripping the prison experience; it wasn't until I stepped outside the classroom that I remembered where I was." Hodges describes the beginnings of a more permanent liberation from a limiting set of beliefs—in this case, about sexuality—after reading James Baldwin's novel *Giovanni's Room*: "[Reading and discussing] *Giovanni's Room* gave me flexibility in understanding this different experience, to understand that gay people are people, too. They have to put on different shoes than I have to every day. It gave me a better outlook on all people. . . . It was very liberating; I don't have [to view people through] preconceived judgments anymore."

As these students attest, a classroom space can offer the chance to interact in powerful ways with ideas and with other human beings; the challenge is to foster the genuine co-creation of that space. The very act of imagining an ideal classroom must be collaborative, with students leading the way in naming the norms and practices they need most to succeed. Outside instructors may come in with notions about respect, participation, and effort, but they must defer to what students name as their own needs; otherwise, the classroom approximates or replicates the power structure of the prison, with—in the worst case—teachers standing in for correctional officers and classroom "guidelines" echoing the regulations and mandates of the prison institution. The first act of instruction must be to help students exercise their own agency, to combat the inherent disenfranchisement of incarceration by giving them the power to design a classroom dynamic based primarily on their input.

In our experience, the norms that students envision are both idealistic and practical, and they better reflect student needs than the expectations of even the most well-intentioned (and experienced) instructors. The following examples of student-generated norms speak to the idealized community students want to create, from logistics to interpersonal relationships to methods of teaching and learning. When students request of one another, "Try to be on time" and "Stay until the end of class," it is with personal knowledge of obstacles like prison lines (for chow, medical, packages), checkpoints, and prison geography. When they name the need for equity, for just practices of listening and speaking, they are naming—and creating—a form of respect that differs from the respect that governs interactions on the yard or in other prison spaces. Student expectations have included "Give one another a chance to speak or share; step back as often as you step forward" and "Give constructive criticism; and don't take things personally (especially the constructive criticism!)." These are radically different ways of interacting than are found elsewhere in most prisons, where vulnerability equals weakness and "taking things personally" is a way of maintaining your status and safety.

Perhaps most important, student-generated norms allow the classroom to be a space of aspiration rather than judgment and punishment. The classroom can become a place to name and practice students' desires to inhabit lives of their own best designs—for example, through norms like "Understand that people have different ways of listening and comprehending"; "Be aware of your bias"; "No judgments"; and "Be your brother's keeper." These guidelines rebel against a prison system that relies heavily on stereotypes and bias (for example, housing assignments and other racially divided prison spaces), where one system governs all (whether food or schedules or twice-daily mandatory counts), and where every citizen in custody is serving out a term based on the judgment of society. And it is worth noting that students are more reliable than outside instructors at anticipating possible pitfalls with reminders like "Don't come to class smelling like 'OOH-WEE!'" and "Try to get to the point, if you can." Whenever possible, it is essential that students be the authors of their own experience and choose what they want their classroom environment to be.

As noted earlier, the demographics of a prison classroom offer remarkable diversity: a class meeting can include participants ranging from nineteen-year-olds who are just starting a first sentence to sixty-five-year-old lifers who have endured decades of isolation at multiple institutions. Additionally, the range of ethnicities and racial backgrounds spans every group one might find in the United States, even as Black and brown students are heavily overrepresented. Taking into account as well differences in class, culture, and school experience, it can be difficult to choose texts that challenge and engage all students. There are many ways to lose your audience (e.g., "We're reading Foucault again?"), and sometimes curricular choices reflect outside instructors' preconceptions (e.g., choosing only Black authors, or only contemporary authors, or only authors whose work draws on themes and experiences related to incarceration). Students on the inside deserve the same range of topics, themes, and authors as students in any other academic setting. That said, choosing texts that grip students helps them stay invested and keeps them feeling confident and engaged. Our appendix contains a few examples of texts that have ranked as "greatest hits" in PUP classes, including allegories, like Plato's ancient but relevant "The Allegory of the Cave" and Ursula K. Le Guin's dystopian "The Ones Who Walk Away from Omelas"; a modern critique of standard English by Vershawn Ashanti Young; historical texts that challenge the status quo (Friedan; King; Malcolm X); and humor pieces that blend levity with compassion (Vowell; Sedaris). We have paired our examples with brief reflections on what makes them effective and powerful tools for reading, discussion, and writing.

Our strategies for establishing democratic classrooms align with Scott's assertion that "[a] radical transformation of the system will not come in the form of an answer from the outside, but from *mutual exchange and problem solving in such a way that new coalitions can form*" (27). For all parties involved, it is important to recognize the power of collaboration. At PUP, curriculum has evolved in ways that reflect the interests and needs of the student population. When we imagine an even more democratic classroom, we think about students actively joining with instructors to generate topics, find readings, and set curricula. In the past two years, PUP has created teaching assistant positions, empowering students to offer formal support to their peers and to give invaluable feedback to instructors. It is our hope that we can amplify these democratic processes, inventing a new kind of college experience where students work alongside instructors and where co-learning is one of the foundations of the community. As Vivian Nixon, a cofounder of the Education from the Inside Out Coalition, writes, "[Incarcerated people] have been among those who have taught with the most dedication, the most compassion, and the greatest results" (qtd. in Davis and Michaels 149). This truth underscores our vision of an ideal classroom: a learning community where students are not just invited but also empowered to shape their experience, and where teachers—both incarcerated and free—can liberate one another from the mental shackles of preconceived notions about what education is and should be.

WORKS CITED

Davis, Simone Weil, and Bruce Michaels. "Ripping Off Some Room for People to 'Breathe Together': Peer-to-Peer Education in Prison." *Beyond Mass Incarceration: Crisis and Critique in North American Penal Systems*, special issue of *Social Justice*, vol. 42, no. 2, 2015, pp. 146–58.

Friedan, Betty. "Statement of Purpose." National Organization for Women, 1966.

Hodges, Odell. Interview. 13 Aug. 2018.

King, Martin Luther, Jr. "Letter from Birmingham City Jail." *A Testament of Hope: The Essential Writings and Speeches*, by King, edited by James Melvin Washington, HarperCollins Publishers, 1991, pp. 289–302.

Le Guin, Ursula K. "The Ones Who Walk Away from Omelas." *The Wind's Twelve Quarters: Stories*, by Le Guin, Harper Perennial, 2004, pp. 277–86.

Malcolm X and Alex Haley. *The Autobiography of Malcolm X: As Told to Alex Haley*. 1966. Ballantine, 1987.

Plato. "The Allegory of the Cave." Translated by Shawn Eyer, Plumbstone Books, 2016, scholar.harvard.edu/files/seyer/files/plato_republic_514b -518d_allegory-of-the-cave.pdf.

Scott, Robert. "Distinguishing Radical Teaching from Merely Having Intense Experiences While Teaching in Prison." *The Radical Teacher*, no. 95, spring 2013, pp. 22–32.

Sedaris, David. *Me Talk Pretty One Day.* Little, Brown, 2000.

Vowell, Sarah. "Shooting Dad." *Take the Cannoli: Stories from the New World,* by Vowell, Simon and Schuster, 2000, pp. 15–24.

Young, Vershawn Ashanti. "Should Writers Use They Own English?" *Iowa Journal of Cultural Studies,* vol. 12, no. 1, 2010, pp. 110–17.

APPENDIX

The readings below come from the syllabus for a composition class taught at San Quentin State Prison. They are examples of texts that support the ideas and practices discussed in this chapter.

Plato, "The Allegory of the Cave"

Plato's allegory is set in an imaginary space that offers no single reader an inside track to understanding through their own background. The strangeness of Plato's conceit, of a person forcibly liberated after being born into incarceration, offers multiple avenues for interpretation. The text demands that students perform initial decoding at the literal level before they can enter into the next stage of analysis. This skill—of reading on multiple levels—is one of the foundations of critical thinking. Plato's allegory demands a philosophical mode of inquiry, one that invites connection to many individual perspectives without privileging any one over another; it is also an invitation to engage with ancient ideas that connect to modern experience. One of the challenges in prison education can be making historical knowledge seem relevant; the figures in Plato's allegory enable reflection on enduring topics like groupthink, misconception, and revelation (e.g. spiritual, intellectual, scientific). The allegorical nature of the cave inhabitants' imprisonment offers a point of overlap with incarcerated students' experience, but that detail is merely a starting point for discussions. In addition, this piece pairs well with any number of other readings (e.g., "Mecca" [Malcolm X 201–14]) as a way to practice generating conversation across texts.

Ursula K. Le Guin, "The Ones Who Walk Away from Omelas"

Another allegory, this dystopian story offers opportunities to investigate social systems and values. Without advocating any identifiable ideological stance, the story invites readers to reflect on where they stand with regard to the systems they inhabit. This apolitical strategy leaves it to readers to consider what it might take to change the system of oppression and inhumanity that defines the crux of the narrative.

Vershawn Ashanti Young, "Should Writers Use They Own English?"

This article directly addresses the rules of academia, their sources, and their limitations and, in a bold shift from most academic writing, is written in Black

Vernacular English. Especially valuable for incarcerated students who may feel marginalized or tentative if their educational background has given rise to non-standard English forms, Young's article invites his readers into his debate with standard-English advocate Stanley Fish, empowering students to reflect on their own histories and assumptions about language and power. In its language and its argument, the article opens a space for a greater range of speakers and readers, debunking the myth of academia as a place that is hostile toward anyone who does not—or does not always—speak or write in standard English. Using a range of nonstandard linguistic forms and powerful rhetorical techniques, Young demands space in the academy for nonstandard English writers.

Betty Friedan, The National Organization for Women's 1966 "Statement of Purpose"

This statement of ideology establishes a context for discussing political movements and assertions of empowerment and introduces a feminist perspective (often absent from the daily lives of incarcerated men). It also allows readers to explore the role of intersectionality in establishing an ideological statement as part of a social movement.

Martin Luther King, Jr., "Letter from Birmingham City Jail"

The context of King's writing of this letter—from solitary confinement in jail, on scraps of paper and in the margins of a newspaper, with myriad allusions drawn entirely from memory—is inspiring for any incarcerated thinker. King's position is complex: as a leading Black voice who offers spiritual guidance, he also reveals the hypocrisy of the dominant Judeo-Christian spiritual community and supposedly supportive "white moderates." Steeped in historical, moral, literary, and rhetorical power, King's letter reflects one remarkable man's response to the surreal feeling of having multiple freedoms removed and provides a model of the reflection that is possible while confined.

Sarah Vowell, "Shooting Dad" David Sedaris, *Me Talk Pretty One Day*

These writers conjure humor and irony to get at serious issues, including ideological differences within a family, homophobia, and power differentials between teachers and students. They offer alternatives to the earnestness and humorlessness that can characterize academic writing and discourse. Levity, like nonstandard English, seems to be anathema within the academy, and yet its power is clear: it can allow writers deeper access to incendiary topics, it can defuse some of the more dangerous emotions, and it embraces a wider audience than most academic writing. Especially in a prison, the academic setting can be relentlessly serious, because the stakes are so high. Humor can bring welcome relief and even make schoolwork itself more palatable.

Meteorite
Elizabeth Hawes

What helps and what hinders incarcerated writers?

Specific rules are unique to every institution, but the overall writing challenges of the incarcerated are universal. Issues of privacy and vulnerability, lack of space (both physical and reflective), lack of access to information and opportunities, expense and timelines, and the location where we are locked up affect and often impede our work. Of course, there also many resources that help and are useful to an imprisoned writer. Access to books, classes, and outside writers, teachers, and artists; notification of competitions and places to submit our work; and in-house and community readings all open up and encourage possibility. As someone who has been imprisoned for a decade, I share in this essay my prison experience, as well as some of my previous work,[1] and offer suggestions to improve the conditions of writing for the incarcerated storytellers, poets, and historians of the future.

Privacy and Vulnerability

The lack of privacy is staggering. I think back to being a teen, mortified if I ran into anyone I knew when my mom had an economy-sized box of maxi pads in the shopping cart. If you have a drop of self-consciousness left, prison will be daily humiliation. Everything we receive and carry is in clear plastic bags or loosely woven knit bags. Anyone can see what books or bra you've picked up at the property window or how many ramens you purchased from canteen. Everyone sees and comments on everyone else's business. Anyone on the wing floor can hear your phone conversation no matter how personal. Anyone can hear who passed away or who is sleeping in your bed, how your child did on a math test or what your mom thinks of your new boyfriend. A request for a divorce, or a revelation to your husband that you have cancer, happens with an audience of twelve to fourteen people.

In the computer lab, we can set up a home folder to leave our writing projects in, but nothing is private. Any staff member can go in at any time to see what you are working on, what you wrote. Our history is not private either. Not only are "true crime" television programs that constantly broadcast sensationalized versions of people's wrongdoings and trial outcomes available to everyone in the institution, but we can be easily looked up on the Department of Corrections website by nosy people on the outside informing nosy people on the inside. We live open, and hence vulnerable, lives.

Excerpt from "Edify"

Today is Friday. The lockdown began on Monday. On Wednesday, everyone in the unit was strip-searched and marched over to another building for five hours while guards gutted our rooms. They also brought in drug-sniffing dogs. On previous lock-ins, room shakedowns had not been a problem; dogs sniffed and guards left things respectfully intact. This time, upon my return, the room was in shambles. My clean clothes were now mixed in with worn clothes that had been in a dirty laundry bag and hurled across the now sheetless bed. There were punctures in the mattress from dogs' teeth or claws (I'm not sure which) and bite marks on my bed linens ("linens" mean ill-fitting, bleach-smelling cotton sheets and two thin, synthetic blue blankets). All my papers were in piles, and all my mail—including my legal paperwork, which had been in an envelope marked "attorney-client/private"—was out and had been gone through. My books were scattered; my holy books lay helter-skelter. We are fed this falsehood of "You matter." But the truth is it's all about control. The system matters. Not health. Not education. Not well-being. Not even recidivism. The system is protected by the system. Writing about staff or unpleasant conflicts within the institution can get us a quick ticket to segregation. There is vulnerability due to who we are as prisoners.   (Hawes, "Edify")

"Exposure"

Every time imprisoned people submit their writing into the public sphere, they are subjecting themselves to an audience who can easily look them up and be told a prosecutor's version of a story (true or untrue) about their conviction. This is in opposition to all they need and desire: to put the past behind them, to lie low and quietly merge back into society, and to reconnect with those they love in fresh circumstances. (Hawes, "Exposure")

Writing as a prisoner ties one's name to the label of felon. A prisoner must ask, Am I willing to put myself out there? To possibly be talked about (again)? To be judged (again)? And, more importantly, is this story/play/poem/idea worth my vulnerability? Will people listen or judge? While all artists/writers question the value of their work and wonder who is viewing it and how it is being perceived, a prisoner who is an artist or who writes always carries the added burden of having to apologize for their past. Or for a piece of their past, or for one afternoon of their past, or for one minute of their past.

I often feel that mass incarceration is war and I'm a reporter on the front line. I don't want to be here, but I am here surrounded by struggle, vulnerability, anger, grief, and confusion. I listen and ask questions that sometimes I wish I hadn't because often the story behind the time is long, sad, and painful. I keep asking because every person is important and deserves to tell their story. It empowers people to be heard and to become visible. And that is why it is worth the risk for me to elbow my way into the written conversation of the world beyond the wall.

Space

We have three drawers to put all our belongings in: a drawer for food that we buy off of canteen, a drawer for all our paperwork, and a drawer for clothes. At any time of the day, we can be asked to do a two-bin compliance. That means we have to fit everything we own into two plastic containers, the equivalent of four and a half cubic feet of space or two milk crates. Whatever doesn't fit we have to throw out or send out. There are about five people in the institution that can fit all their things into two bins. We are allowed to buy electronics, like a hot pot, a hair dryer, an alarm clock, or a hair straightener. We can buy typewriters. There are yarn and beads to pack if you are a crafter. God help you if you bought a lot of snacks. It is always a losing situation. But that is not the worst thing about condensing all your (few) possessions, about having only one drawer allowed for paperwork. The worst thing as a writer is not being able to save things that would be helpful in future work: the reference paper where I cited all the sources perfectly, lists of books not yet read and authors loved, scraps of phrasing and quotes, those delicious bits of verse or dialogue jotted down while watching TV or overheard in the lunch-room, those facts odd or important scrawled on the backs of envelopes:

> The Native population in the state of Minnesota is four percent.
> The Native population in the women's Shakopee prison is twenty-six percent.
> Irish soda bread = 1 lb of flour, 1 t of baking soda, 1 t of salt, 3 1/4 C of buttermilk.
> *Susurrus* means a whispering or rustling sound.

I cannot save those random, beautiful words that I know will be useful or helpful, eventually. Like *funambulist*. Or *honey mustard poi sticker poet*.

I wish I could keep the scholastic materials about different ways to organize stories in a chapbook, or my poems about flowers.

But I've been locked up for over fourteen years. I send a box of paperwork and books home about three times a year. This pains me more than I could tell you.

We are allowed ten books. If you could choose ten books, what would they be? I have no favorite books in my possession. No *Velveteen Rabbit* or Masha Gessen. No Lucia Berlin or David McCullough. I keep reference books and holy books, as they are the most useful.

Aside from the cramped physical space, there is also a lack of quiet, reflective space in prison. I never realized the extent to which we were being continually bombarded with announcements until I took up a meditation practice. I was hoping to have a window of fifteen to twenty minutes of quiet. According to everything I've read, the best time to meditate is early in the morning—setting receptivity for the day. This did not work because of relentless announcements and noise. After trying unsuccessfully to meditate at a multitude of a.m.'s and p.m.'s, I now practice sitting after 9:45 p.m., after the last voice comes over the loudspeaker.

It's not just the overhead broadcasts. We have one to two hall phones in every wing. That's one or two phones for twelve to fourteen people, depending on your hall. Thanks to this phone, I know far more about everyone than I want to know. There is a continual hall or phone conversation from 6:30 a.m. to 9:25 p.m., the times we are allowed out of our rooms.

I don't have a roommate because I've been here for a minute, but about seventy-five percent of the general population does. They live in wing lounges of four to six people or in doubles with two people in a room. It is not natural to sleep in a room with a bunch of people you don't know—or don't know well. We are constantly around others. We eat in a large, loud cafeteria. We attend activities that we've signed up for, such as gym, library, or church, that usually involve the same women that we've worked with all day. The only quiet, reflective space for most people is the shower. And that is used by twelve to fourteen people too, so you had better be quick.

It can be difficult to find quiet time to gather thoughts, to not be distracted and write. I know there are distractions everywhere, but in prison we can never get away from the chaos or volume with a walk in the park or a bubble bath. We are stuck in a soup of noise.

Lack of Access

In prison, we have no Internet access and are often unaware of opportunities to submit our work. I know there are many publications and venues out there; I just can't reach them. Many of the publications that are looking for work only accept online submissions. We are unable to send a PDF. Similarly, we are unable to comply with many publishers' submission entry rules because of prison policies; for example, we are not allowed stamps (we buy envelopes that get stamped in the mailroom) and thus cannot submit a self-addressed envelope along with our work—meaning we cannot get work back or receive feedback (when offered).

Cut off from information or the capacity to do research, we seek answers aloud in the computer lab. It is easy to distinguish the writers from the women who are studying for their GED; you can tell by the questions they ask. The women who are studying for their GEDs ask about fractions or pronouns. The writers ask for information they need for stories, information not found in a dictionary. Without looking up from their computers, women start calling out answers.

"Who is the Hindu goddess of war?"
"Are you talking about the blue goddess with all the arms? Vishnu, maybe?"
"Brahma."
"No, that's a creator, not a destroyer."
"I think the blue one is love and sex."
"Of course you'd know that."
"It's Shiva. She is a destroyer and that would be war."

"Who was a pinup girl in World War II?"
"Betty Grable; she had great legs."
"Jayne Mansfield."
"Rita Hayworth."

"How about Hedy Lamarr? I just saw a documentary on her on PBS; she was brilliant."

"Farrah Fawcett."

"Shut up."

"Marlene Dietrich."

"Wasn't she German? Why would our soldiers want a pinup of a German to help them through the war?"

"I don't know. I saw her on that old 'Vogue' video of Madonna's."

We are our own *Google*.

We are unable to translate any of our words into another language on our computers. For whatever reason, I always seem to need some foreign-sounding dialogue in my work, and this is very frustrating. *Mais nous ne devons pas céder à la frustration.*

We must not give in to frustration.

There are encyclopedias in the library—two sets, actually. But here's the catch: the library is open Monday to Friday with times determined by our last names (A through K or L through Z) or by where we work (food services workers: 4:00–4:30 p.m.), which can present a challenge depending on schedule. Or it can be closed. The librarian (surprise) is very pro-reading. She does a million things for the women here with little fanfare. One of those things is taking book requests for books not found in our library. Super nice. But, like everything within the Department of Corrections, it's a slow process. To get a book this way, we fill out a request form for the wanted book. You can request up to two books. Slips have to be in by Wednesday, because it is on Thursdays that the librarian makes the trip. The book may or may not be helpful, because you were unable to look at it before you borrowed it. You have one week to pick it up and two weeks to read or use it.

In the same area as the computer lab, there is an office support program in full swing where women are learning office and computer skills. The woman in charge of this program is very nice and (surprise) pro-writing. But there are always staffing shortages, bringing frequent cancellations of lab time. As I write this, the computer lab has been closed since mid-December. It is now the first week of March. I'm allowed to type with the office support class thanks to the kindness of the office support teacher. We have to sign up several days beforehand; we can't just drop in and finish a project because our schedule opens up. There is also a problem of printing. We are allowed to print things, but not a lot of things. As a writer who generally works on large projects, I am constantly printing smidgens of pieces (double-sided) until I can get my whole project in hand. They don't mind a four-page paper. They do mind a seventy-page play.

Expense and Timelines

For most people here, twenty-five cents is an hour of work. What seems inexpensive to a free person is pricey to the incarcerated. But while there are expenses associated with writing—namely, paper, mailing, copies, and occasionally phone calls—the bigger problem is timelines. If I get wind of an opportunity to submit my writing (or need to submit some legal work) and I need it copied, here is the process:

> Requests for photocopies must be accompanied by a completed, signed voucher. Photocopies cost 25 cents per page. Offenders requesting copies of their own personal documents must attach the document to the voucher. Offenders requesting copies of library materials must note that the request is from a library item and include the full title and appropriate page numbers. All completed, signed vouchers should be sent to finance. Vouchers are processed at Faribault while the copies are made at Shakopee after the money is withdrawn. Therefore, there will likely be some lag time between when you are charged and when you receive your copies. The typical turnaround time is 7–10 days.
>
> (Minnesota Correctional Facility-Shakopee)

Because the process for obtaining anything—a book, a copy, a space in the computer lab—is so slow, it is difficult (and stressful) to meet last-minute submission deadlines. You have to be very organized and have a good idea of what you want to write and how you want to write it. The person who runs the mailroom says that in the near future we will have all our mail sent to an off-grounds mailing site, where it will be copied, and then the copies will be given to us. I have a friend in a prison in Wisconsin that uses this system, and it takes two weeks for him to get a letter.

Our mailroom people work Monday to Friday. This means we receive mail Tuesdays to Saturdays, and we have to mail things by Thursday night if they are to go out that week. All books sent in must be sent directly from the place of purchase. We have thirty days to get a receipt or have to send books back, throw them out, or donate them to Goodwill.

Whenever I submit writing, I always add my husband's phone number and e-mail address as a second contact, but not everyone has the ability to get or pass along a message in this way.

With attention, all these hurdles can be overcome. We can figure a way around these difficulties because, even though our government and the DOC specialize in isolation and separation and do not recognize interconnection, writers are the most imaginative, creative people on earth. As the ultimate creators, we are able to identify a hardship, propose solutions, gather support, and implement a plan.

Let's look at what works.

Minnesota Prison Writing Workshop

In Minnesota, we have the Minnesota Prison Writing Workshop (MPWW). This organization, created by the wonderful Jen Bowen Hicks, brings in quarterly writing classes given by brilliant writers and educators. I have taken everything from Lyric Poetry to Flash Fiction, from Novels to Stories of Our Ancestors. I am a much stronger writer because of these classes.

MPWW provides writing mentors who act as editors or private tutors for anyone who has completed a class and is interested. It is because of my mentors that I have had success in state and national competitions and have been published. I am dazzled by my mentor. He continually sends me samples of writing that reflect my work and gives me creative suggestions on how to improve the format of a piece or tighten or expand a narrative where it would be fitting to do so.

MPWW answers to a spectrum of needs. Occasionally, they offer weekend workshops with several instructors who give an all-day sample class. These Saturday seminars encourage people who might otherwise be intimidated to begin a writing practice. MPWW has also started writing collectives for serious writers. These collectives bring hard-core writers together to talk and get feedback on their projects. The collectives can do whatever writing-based activity they decide on as a group: ours chose to do workshopping. Our collective meets on the first Sunday of the month and currently has six members. We love it.

It is through MPWW that we hear of writing competitions and opportunities. The program has an annual reading at Hamline University every fall that features work from all of the locations at which they teach, bringing our writing to a larger audience. At the readings, MPWW passes out postcards that the audience members can use to respond to our work in real time. This postcard feedback is so lovely because you actually feel heard and appreciated and encouraged even as you sit alone in your small manila room. Jen and her posse have changed my world in prison.

Art Exposure

Because we're sensory-deprived, another important element of wholeness and creativity is exposure to the arts in the form of outside speakers, theater, and music. For example, there is a theater group called Ten Thousand Things that performs here a few times a year. Most of their work is a new take on the classics. Their performances are well received. A friend of mine (mid-thirties, high school graduate) told me that she had never seen a play before but now loved theater and hoped to see more when she was released. Prior to incarceration, I had worked as an actor for twenty-five years. I was shocked to learn that an adult had never seen a play. But my friend's comment showed me the transformative effect that exposure to music and performance could have and how the experience helped people connect and learn and get their heads out of prison for a few hours.

Readings

The writers here really enjoy sharing their work. Whether that sharing takes place within our writing groups or reaches the public, it empowers people. I have often witnessed the healing power of sharing stories. There was a woman who wrote about the first time that she was molested and whispered afterward, *I've never told anyone that before.* Another writer shared with us her childhood experiences with an empty-shelved kitchen, and a poet, writing about drunken brutal beatings, somehow found freedom from smothered, painful silence. In-house readings given by both prisoners and outside readers are valuable. An outside reader might be an author of a book attending a book club meeting or someone lecturing about Emily Dickinson and her work and handing out a few copies of her poems. People here appreciate learning something new. People here like to have conversations about things other than prison. People here like to feel smart.

Education

Classes on writing, history, literature, and sociology help people expand their views and communicate articulately. To learn one's history helps one form a positive identity. To know that other people survived hardship helps us know that we too can survive.

Felon. Failure. Mother without custodial rights. Perpetrator. Addict. Victim. Being a student or a writer gives a new identity other than *prisoner.*

Book access is also helpful. Books on craft, books on diversity, work by other prisoners, and, oddly enough, books of poetry are favored. I was surprised to learn how many of my fellow prisoners love poetry. They love to read it and to write it. The two most popular classes are always on poetry and memoir. Poems help people express emotion in a safe place. I have seen the most stoic people cry and laugh on paper. I have listened to stories of severe trauma read by quiet people who I never knew were in so much pain. Memoir allows people to heal. Writing your story gives you power in a place where you have little.

Places to Submit

Notification of different writing contests or places that are looking for stories or poems is always appreciated. We love it when journals and forums specifically invite incarcerated writers and make it easy for us to submit pieces (longer lead times before deadlines, mailed submissions, contacting us with responses). To have work chosen by people outside prison brings a sense of belonging and acceptance. It tells us what we write matters and that what we have to contribute is important to the world.

Suggestions

Long before *Google* and sites like it, there was a 411 information phone line. I would like to see the development of regional centers that writers in prison could call for assistance in preparing and submitting their work. The phones could be answered by people who would look up the information needed for a story or other project. Longer answers or more extensive research could be faxed to the prison, where it could be put in a prisoner's mail. These centers could be places to send pieces for submission, to be scanned and sent online or faxed and mailed. Perhaps if the submitted pieces required a self-addressed stamped envelope, a grant or funding source could provide those stamped envelopes, allowing us to get our work back after it was sent out. If there is particular need in a local area—like no access or minimal access to typewriters or computers in a prison—the regional centers could look at those needs and accommodate them. These centers could inform writing outlets about this new service so that publishers could reach out to the centers when seeking stories or new contributors.

At the very least, more sets of encyclopedias would be very helpful to writers. Perhaps they could be digital sets not linked to the Internet but searchable from prison. In areas where writing programs are scarce, writing teachers could record video lessons for a correspondence class and review faxed assignments. The class could come together with a reading at the end of the quarter whose theme most people would feel comfortable sharing with peers, like stories about pets or poems about grandparents. It would be an excellent way to celebrate the students' work with minimal staffing requirements.

Writing

In geology, a meteorite is described as a chunk of material that plunges into the earth's atmosphere, survives passage, and reaches the ground. It is not seen as beautiful, but is the most valuable rock on the planet. Prisoners are meteorites and have a lot to teach the world.

James Michener's novel *Hawaii* shows a large, burly boat captain, Hoxworth, bullying a scrawny, journaling missionary who is advocating for Chinese immigrants. The missionary tells Hoxworth that he should be fearful of him and all the missionaries. Hoxworth asks why.

> Because missionaries have one terrible power. They write. They are the conscience of the Pacific.

Like the missionaries, imprisoned writers have purpose. We listen. We notice. We care. We write.

Writing sustains many incarcerated people by helping us explore what is immediate and document visible moments of an often invisible group of people. This community, the prison community, cries out to be noticed. Writing works as a safe and brave space where people can express and release their pain. Writing allows people to experience freedom and creativity within a small, condensed, and controlled environment. In digging out a space in which to be, we elbow our way into the conversation. By remembering the truth about the ground we walk, we find our voice. Writing heals our past and imagines new beginnings. I identify as a writer. Writing is what keeps me alive in prison, and I am not the only one who feels this way. Writing is about connection and commonality. For me, it is a way to remember things that I'm starting to forget. For everyone, it is a way to say, *Look at me; my story has value. I have value.*

We listen. We notice. We care. We write.

To all the writers and educators out there who help us do that, thank you.

NOTE

1. These works are available online as readings with transcripts ("Kirya Traber"; "Mahogany L. Browne").

WORKS CITED

Hawes, Elizabeth. "Edify." 2017.

———. "Exposure." 2018.

"Kirya Traber Reading 'Edify' by Elizabeth Hawes." *YouTube*, uploaded by PEN America, youtube.com/watch?v=sL9uadYFfxw.

"Mahogany L. Browne Reading 'Exposure' by Elizabeth Hawes." *YouTube*, uploaded by PEN America, youtube.com/watch?v=qThkY2euqvE.

Michener, James A. *Hawaii*. Random House, 1959.

Minnesota Correctional Facility-Shakopee. "Requesting Photocopies." 31 Jan. 2019. Memo.

Shakespeare with Survivors: Learning from Incarcerated Women in the Me Too Era

Jenna Dreier

The fact that prison arts programs for women in the United States have routinely involved the study of Shakespeare raises a familiar question for feminist scholars, artists, and educators: how can Shakespeare's plays, written for an all-male stage and with limited women's roles, ever be harnessed to promote the interests of women? In the wake of the Me Too movement in 2017,[1] the question of how the study and practice of Shakespeare can serve the interests of women has grown to include a heightened attention to the prevalence of domestic and sexual violence in the plays. In response to Me Too, feminist scholars have begun to investigate the ethics of negotiating that violence both in performance and in the classroom. For some feminist artists and educators, the episodes of abuse or sexual violence in Shakespeare have increasingly been taken up as tools for illuminating the structures of patriarchal power or for jumpstarting important conversations about consent.[2] Yet they are not the first to consider Shakespeare through the lens of abuse. For decades, women's prison performance programs have opted to stage plays like *The Taming of the Shrew* specifically because they deal with instances of domestic abuse—a topic that far too many women who are incarcerated are profoundly familiar with. Therefore, as I will argue, scholars and artists who aim to develop a new ethics for teaching and performing Shakespeare in the era of Me Too ought to look to these performances by women who are incarcerated—which were specifically adapted for ensembles and audiences that included survivors of abuse, given that the majority of incarcerated women in the United States are victims of abuse—as models for that new ethics (Alexander 13).

In this essay, I draw from firsthand research on one of the newest prison Shakespeare programs for women, as well as the oldest, in order to demonstrate what incarcerated women have to teach outside scholars, educators, artists, and facilitators about navigating issues of sexual or domestic violence in Shakespeare. I take as my starting point the work of Jean Trounstine, a trailblazer in the prison arts world and the facilitator of the original Shakespeare Behind Bars (SBB) program, which operated from 1988 to 1996 at the Framingham women's prison.[3] Drawing on interviews with Trounstine and access to her performance archives, I situate SBB performance practices in relation to the more recent work of the Detroit Public Theatre's Shakespeare in Prison (SIP) program for women. My research on SIP is based primarily on interviews with alumnae of the program and with the lead facilitator, Frannie Shepherd-Bates. By investigating how the open secret of abuse has informed performances of Shakespeare in women's prisons, and specifically each group's approach to adapting *The Taming of the Shrew*, I trace the shifts in feminist philosophies for empowering incarcerated women over the span of almost thirty years. These comparative case studies reveal a dramatic shift in prison pedagogy for women from one focused on product (SBB) to one focused on process (SIP)—a participant-driven shift that is worthy of consideration in the development of a new ethics for appropriating Shakespeare in the Me Too era.

The Open Secret of Abuse

In this essay, I use the term *open secret* to refer to a truth that is widely known but not openly acknowledged or discussed by those who are directly involved or affected. In the case of abuse in women's prisons, it is widely known that a majority of the women incarcerated in the United States are victims of domestic abuse or sexual violence. Browse through any recent volume—scholarly or otherwise—on the subject of women's prisons, and you will be met with two essential statistics. The first is that there has been an exponential (seven hundred percent) increase in the number of women incarcerated in US prisons since the 1980s—more than double the rate of increase in incarcerated men ("Incarcerated Women"). The second is that an obscene number of the women incarcerated in this country—the most recent estimates put this figure at over ninety percent—have experienced sexual or domestic abuse (Alexander 12). These facts are not secrets. They have been publicly stated by activists, scholars, and politicians, and those who currently reside or work in women's prisons in the United States consider them basic knowledge. And yet the intimate details of this reality often remain under wraps. Incarcerated women are typically fully aware of the fact that the majority of the women in their community have experienced abuse, and in some cases are aware of the specific past traumas that others have suffered, but they are simultaneously aware that social norms insist that this information should never be openly acknowledged. These histories of abuse therefore function as an open secret.

Jean Trounstine's Shakespeare Behind Bars

The open secret of abuse in women's prisons is not a recent phenomenon, yet I found marked differences in the ways women's prison ensembles engaged with members' histories of abuse across a span of approximately thirty years when dealing with *The Taming of the Shrew*. In my interviews with Trounstine, I learned that the participants in her program included women with personal histories of abuse and that these histories impacted the ensemble's artistic decisions in a variety of ways. For instance, the initial choice to study *The Taming of the Shrew* stemmed from the relevance of the domestic violence that it depicts.[4] Yet Trounstine's philosophy as a director was to "treat [the women] as professionals," an approach that encouraged the women in her program to channel those experiences into their work but not to unpack their personal traumas in rehearsal. As Trounstine described it to me, this philosophy grew out of her earlier work teaching writing in prison, and she noted that her students "would bring pieces to the class that were very emotionally connected to them and they would start to cry as they were reading the piece." This practice indicated to her that women "deal with their emotions" and are "therapized." What these women lacked, she felt, were opportunities to learn to work through their emotions on their own in order to maintain a professional standard. "What they don't have often," she noted, "is the kind of thing that men get a lot, which is that no matter what you're feeling, no matter what you're going through, you have to do your job; you have to rise to the occasion." She went on to clarify that this suppression of emotions can be traumatic for men in its own way, but that she felt that this unwavering professionalism was an essential skill for "women of [her] generation," as "it's hard to learn . . . but it's what kept a lot of women from success in the past because we came in with our emotional card." So Trounstine would tell her ensemble that she expected them to be professionals and that, "we're going to do this experience together, we're going to put [our trauma and emotions] in our work, we're going to put it in our characters, but we're going to be professional artisans together." In these remarks, Trounstine references the fact that her philosophy is representative of her own generation of feminist performance practices. Based on her commentary, this philosophy valued the development of professionalism above all else, or, to use my terminology, one that prized product over process.

Trounstine's dedication to creating professional performances rather than providing a therapeutic experience was further borne out in our discussion of the group's 1992 production of *The Taming of the Shrew*, an adaptation they retitled *Rapshrew*. The work reappropriated the term *shrew* as a badge of honor worn by a rap ensemble of six women called the Shrews, who serve as a chorus. As described by Amy Scott-Douglass, the Shrews "reappear [throughout the play], like a Chorus led by Medea, bound to undermine any trace of sexism that might exist in Shakespeare's play" (87). Yet the adaptation still struggled to reconcile that feminist vision with the misogynistic thrust of the play, ultimately shying away from engaging with the primary factor in choosing the play: the role of abuse in Katarina and Petruchio's relationship.

As I learned from both a video recording of the performance and my interview with Trounstine, the production reframed the conflict between Katarina (whom they call Kate) and Petruchio (renamed Truck-T) not as a relationship in which a man uses physical and verbal abuse to tame his new wife but as an understandable conflict between partners with competing needs. In place of the famous submission speech, Kate instead reaches the epiphany that Truck-T has been socialized in such a way that he "needs to be right" and that this is his weakness. This epiphany occurs when Kate submits to Petruchio's assertion that they are looking at the moon rather than the sun and sees that by doing so she can "make him happy" and change his behavior. After he warns her, "Whatever I say goes or you go back to the house," she signals her willingness to go along with this, saying, "Let it be the moon or the sun or whatever, you can call the shots." To my fascination, the group hung representations of both the sun and moon on the wall above the actors during this scene, which injected an ambiguity into the scene about who was correct and, by extension, about whether Petruchio's test should be read as an episode of his abusive control or more simply of stubborn disagreement. In Trounstine's words, when Kate sees how pleased Truck-T is when she plays along, she recognizes that "she can play to his weakness without giving up her power" and that in making this recognition Kate is telling the other women in the audience that "this is what we need to do." At the end of the play, Kate delivers a speech in which she further explains the moral of the adaptation to the audience: "He has a need to be a right. I have a need to be right. We all have a need to be right. My sister has a need for attention. I have a need for attention. We all have a need for attention. We have to recognize needs in one another. I guess what I'm trying to say is that it takes two to make a thing go right." Although the performance did not address how Kate's choice to play along and let Truck-T "be right" was not itself a submission to his control, this closing speech, written by the actor herself, opts to present Kate and Truck-T as equally flawed and equally responsible for the events that have occurred. Since, according to Trounstine, the actor who delivered these lines in the video also composed them, it appears that the actor had a considerable amount of agency in devising this interpretation, and it is notable that she arguably choses to try to ignore the abusive nature of the relationship. In doing so, the actor choses not to portray Kate as victim.

Yet the adaptation did not ignore the abusive dynamic altogether. Although much of the most overt abuse in the original play—such as the scene in which Petruchio starves Katarina—was cut, the production included one clear representation of domestic abuse in which Truck-T briefly holds Kate in a rear chokehold to demonstrate his physical control over her (while telling her that she will be his wife). When I asked Trounstine about the motivation behind that choice and whether any of the women had expressed concern about depicting domestic violence in prison, she explained that she had personally wanted to include that moment, and that she wanted it to be followed by a scene in which Kate would be "even angrier," but that the actor playing Kate had struggled to achieve that anger. According to Trounstine, "It was hard for her to be quite as angry as . . . I thought she should be there, and that's her own personal thing. It's easy for her to be abused, but it was hard for her to be as forceful to him." When discussing what was "easy for her" and "hard for her" in this statement, Trounstine was referencing the actor's talent for acting the part of an abused women or an angry woman convincingly rather than analyzing the actor's emotional state when performing a scene that involved physical abuse. Here, Trounstine demonstrates that her philosophy indeed emphasized the importance of crafting a professional-grade performance.[5]

The Detroit Public Theatre's Shakespeare in Prison

Fast-forward almost thirty years to 2015, and another ensemble of incarcerated women was preparing a production of *Taming*, but this time the priorities were almost entirely reversed. The Detroit Public Theatre's Shakespeare in Prison program, led by Shepherd-Bates, has been operating at the Women's Huron Valley Correctional Facility since 2012. In my interviews with Shepherd-Bates and with recent alumnae of the program, I learned that the first priority in SIP has always been the emotional safety of the ensemble and their audiences and that the quality of the final performance is of far less concern. In the case of *Taming*, the desire to protect women in the ensemble led the group to dramatically alter their interpretation of the play to the point that Kate was not to be understood as a victim of domestic abuse; instead, the play was "about finding balance in communication in relationships" because the "abuse was equal" and Kate was the one who "started this." As Shepherd-Bates explained, the ensemble reached this interpretation by imagining that Kate had previously treated the men in the play with cruelty and that "none of them know how to handle it until Petruchio" shows that he is "just better at giving back to her what she's giving to everybody else." There is a clear parallel between this interpretation and the one offered by the actor who played Kate at Framingham in 1992, in that these women have insisted on not depicting Kate as a victim. In this more recent case, the SIP ensemble avoids emphasizing Kate's victimhood by instead imagining her as an equal match for Petruchio.

Initially surprised by her ensemble's insistence on this interpretation, Shepherd-Bates did not learn until several years later that the group made this decision in order to protect a couple of women in the ensemble who "simply could not be in the play if we had lingered too much on the abuse." In other words, several women in the ensemble struggled with the discussions about abuse that were prompted by this play, to the point that they were on the verge of leaving the program. To address their discomfort, the ensemble decided among themselves that they would not play Petruchio as an abuser and instead would play him as "a guy who just knows how to play her game." An alumna of the program later expanded on the ensemble's approach to interpreting Petruchio, saying:

> That play was strange for us because we were dealing with a lot of women that had been assaulted and victims of domestic violence, so we wanted to do it in a way that they would feel safe. So we had to really kind of figure out how to come at that role [of Petruchio]. So we ended up playing it different than what I had thought we would . . . we kind of played it in a way where like Katarina was in love with him and kind of had met her match, not necessarily that he dominated her.

As this participant indicates, the ensemble's choice to try to avoid the abuse and to de-emphasize Katarina's status as a victim was directly informed by the fact that the emotional safety of their fellow ensemble members was the higher priority. When I asked Shepherd-Bates how this interpretation had been achieved in performance, she explained that the ensemble chose to emphasize the intellectual conflict between the characters and avoided any references to physical conflict. The one exception she could think of was that in their adaptation Katarina "got thrown off a horse, and [Petruchio] was indifferent and not very helpful," but she went on to reaffirm that "there was never any kind of physical abuse shown on stage about that."

In this particular instance, select members of the ensemble had been aware of the specific traumas that fellow ensemble members had experienced and chose to alter the entire performance in order to protect and include those women. Yet it seems that the ensemble had not yet reached a point where these lived traumas were spoken aloud and acknowledged in the rehearsal space by those who had experienced them, since the facilitators remained unaware. By the following year, that dynamic had begun to change.[6] In recognizing that they had avoided the hard conversations about domestic abuse with *Taming*, the group made the collective decision to return to that subject matter the following year by staging a performance of *Othello*. This time, the ensemble began to have open discussions about abuse. Some asked why Desdemona and Emilia stayed in their abusive relationships, and others explained from personal experience that "when you've got hands around your neck, you're not thinking about fighting back, you're thinking about *surviving*." As Shepherd-Bates recounted, this was a moment in which the women who could not understand Emilia and Desdemona heard "women whom they knew to be intelligent and strong and talented and warm and wonderful and not that much different from themselves, talk[ing] about their experience being victims, [which] gave them much more empathy and gave them a different view [on the play]." Here I want to suggest that the ensemble began to break the boundary of the open secret by acknowledging these personal histories and how they informed possible readings of the play.

Even as they achieved this open dialogue together, the women still found it important to continue to take precautions to ensure the safety of their ensemble and their audience. One of these precautions was to avoid having the new male facilitator read the role of Othello. As Shepherd-Bates noted, it was that very facilitator who first asked her, "Do you think maybe I should not read Othello? Like ever?" When Shepherd-Bates brought that question to the group, the ensemble agreed that he should not read Othello, and instead he often read Desdemona's lines during rehearsals. A second precaution was to stage Othello's murder of Desdemona behind a curtain in order to protect the audience, because, in the words of an alumna, "We knew that [the domestic violence content] would affect a lot of our audience as well." The same alumna also indicated that the ensemble's investment in protecting their audience from triggering content was not limited solely to victims of abuse but extended to women haunted by the trauma of committing such an act. In her words, "We were hesitant to show [Desdemona's killing] onstage, because obviously we are dealing with women that are there for murder."

Learning from Incarcerated Women

In reading these performances through the lens of the open secret of abuse, artists and educators stand to learn a myriad of valuable lessons from women who are incarcerated. In both programs, the actors demonstrated the importance of avoiding portrayals of women who are defined by victimhood. We also learn from the contrast between the two programs, which reflects a shift in feminist philosophies for empowering incarcerated women. The SIP ensemble's dedication to protecting incarcerated women from reliving traumatic experiences—as victims, perpetrators, or both—was strikingly different from the approach of Trounstine and her ensemble a few decades before. In Trounstine's work with incarcerated women in the late 1980s and early 1990s, the open secret of abuse actively informed the rehearsal space, but for reasons including the emphasis on product (or the crafting of a professional performance), that open secret remained firmly intact. By contrast, in the more recent programming offered by the Detroit Public Theatre, the emphasis on process (which involved trust-building exercises, group bonding, and a commitment to maintaining emotional safety) worked to acknowledge—and perhaps to begin to dismantle—the open secret of abuse by allowing some of these past traumas to become *spoken* traumas. A shared element of both programs was a recognition of the personal traumas that women in the ensembles had more than likely experienced, which in many cases would have involved sexual or domestic abuse. Yet a consequential difference was whether women used their performance group as a therapeutic space in which the particularities of those traumas were shared, processed, or otherwise openly acknowledged. The SIP program's eventual success in dismantling the open secret of abuse demonstrates the value of their model, which is almost entirely participant-driven. It is a model that puts the emotional safety of the ensemble and audience first, valuing it far above the scholarly merit of the ensemble's interpretation or the quality of the final performance.[7] Only after establishing safety in this way were these women eventually able to create a space where they could acknowledge the open secret of abuse; thereafter, the ensemble continued to prioritize that emotional safety in their choices in staging as well as in their general rehearsal practices.

This shift from prioritizing product to prioritizing process correlates to larger social shifts in our understanding of trauma and to the dramatic shift in the public recognition and validation of women's experiences of harassment and sexual assault that was ushered in by the Me Too movement—another moment in which we as a society heard stories from women we "knew to be intelligent and strong and talented and warm and wonderful and not that much different from [our]selves" that fundamentally changed our understanding. And it is in the wake of the lessons of Me Too that scholars, teachers, artists, and facilitators should be particularly keen to learn from incarcerated women as we develop new ethics for navigating the incidents of sexual and domestic abuse in Shakespeare and in literature more generally.

NOTES

1. In 2006, Tarana Burke began using the phrase "me too" in her activism supporting survivors of sexual assault. Ten years later, following the published allegations against the Hollywood heavyweight Harvey Weinstein, "Me Too" became the slogan of a national movement to combat sexual violence against women when the actor Alyssa Milano tweeted, "If you've been sexually harassed or sexually assaulted write 'me too' as a reply to this tweet" ("#MeToo").

2. In a recent article in *Electric Literature*, Laura Kolb attends to how theatrical performances of Shakespeare have begun to reflect the concerns of the Me Too movement by drawing a correlation between the growing anger over issues of sexual harassment and the "uptick in productions of *Measure for Measure*, a play in which a woman gets so angry at male desires and male behaviors that she tells her brother she will 'pray a thousand prayers' for his death." In April 2019, I participated in a seminar at the Shakespeare Association of America, titled #OpenSecrets, which both fueled the inquiry I offer in this essay and offered me the opportunity to engage with feminist Shakespeareans who are actively investigating these questions.

3. Trounstine's program for women preceded Curt Tofteland's program for men, which shares the same name. With its 1988 start date, Trounstine's program is considered the first prison Shakespeare program launched in the United States. Tofteland launched his Shakespeare Behind Bars program at the Luther Luckett Correctional Facility for men in 1995. Familiarity with Tofteland's program has been bolstered dramatically by the award-winning documentary *Shakespeare Behind Bars*, which chronicles the group's 2003 season and performance of *The Tempest*.

4. The choice to perform *Shrew* was by no means a given because it belongs to Shakespeare's canon. Despite the program name Shakespeare Behind Bars, Trounstine's approach was actually quite distinct from that of more recent prison Shakespeare programs for women in that she did not work exclusively with Shakespeare. Instead, the group's performance history included just one other

Shakespeare play—*The Merchant of Venice*—which was its first, in 1988. The group then moved on to Aristophanes's *Lysistrata* (1989); Clifford Odets's *Waiting for Lefty* (1990); a theatrical adaptation of *The Scarlet Letter* (1991); *Rapshrew* (1992); Josefina Lopez's *Simply Maria* (1993); an adaptation of Jean Giraudoux's *The Madwoman of Chaillot*, retitled *Madwomen of the Modular* (1994); and Joseph Kesselring's *Arsenic and Old Lace* (1995).

5. While Trounstine's dedication to helping these women craft high-quality performances stands in stark contrast to the therapeutic motivations of Frannie Shepherd-Bates in her more recent work with Shakespeare in Prison, I want to stress that there were certainly moments of emotional spontaneity in SBB's history. For example, Trounstine herself has written, "One of the most striking moments in our *Rapshrew* had occurred when we invited the families of cast members to a Sunday show. After our traditional talkback at the end of each production, the actors spontaneously took the microphones and turned to their mothers and grandmothers who were in the audience, singing, 'I remember Mama in a special way.' The space, already sanctified through all of the energy and love exuded in the performance, now led the women into church songs. Tears flowed as they connected with their loved ones" (Trounstine, "Revisiting Sacred Spaces," 241).

6. As part of her commitment to helping her ensemble build enough trust and unity to have these difficult conversations, Shepherd-Bates also relies on a variety of Augusto Boal's Theatre of the Oppressed exercises. For example, Shepherd-Bates describes her fondness for the "Blind Cars" exercise in the SIP blog as follows: "In this exercise, one person 'drives' another, who closes her eyes and works to trust the driver and follow nonverbal commands. It tends to be fun and terrifying at the same time, as the driver has a lot of responsibility, and the car is very vulnerable. There is always a mix of feelings about whether it's more comfortable to be the car or the driver. It builds trust within the ensemble while simultaneously helping us learn about our own vulnerabilities and the importance of both supporting and leaning on each other in our work" ("Season Seven").

7. Even in doing so, the ensemble still achieves beautiful performance moments. I witnessed a striking example in their 2018 performance of Shakespeare's *Macbeth*. Because the actor playing Lady Macbeth struggled to memorize her lines, the ensemble elected to have one of the male facilitators follow her during the sleepwalking scene so that he could drop lines to her. Because this facilitator was playing the role of Duncan in the performance, the choice created a moving effect in which Lady Macbeth appears haunted by the ghost of Duncan as she laments, "Who would have thought the old man to have had so much blood in him?" (Shakespeare, *Macbeth*, 5.1.34–35)

WORKS CITED

Alexander, Michelle. "Standing without Sweet Company." *Inside This Place, Not of It: Narratives from Women's Prisons*, edited by Robin Levi and Ayelet Waldman, Voice of Witness, 2017, pp. 11–14.

Boal, Augusto. *Theater of the Oppressed*. Theatre Communications Group, 1993.

Greenblatt, Stephen, et al., editors. *The Norton Shakespeare*. 3rd ed., W. W. Norton, 2015.

"Incarcerated Women and Girls." *The Sentencing Project*, 10 May 2018, sentencingproject.org/publications/incarcerated-women-and-girls/.

Kolb, Laura. "The Very Modern Anger of Shakespeare's Women: What *Measure for Measure* Means to Us in 2019." *Electric Literature*, 6 Feb. 2019, electricliterature.com/the-very-modern-anger-of-shakespeares-women/.

Macbeth. Directed by Frannie Shepherd-Bates, Shakespeare in Prison program, 19 June 2018, Women's Huron Valley Correctional Facility.

"#MeToo: A Timeline of Events." *Chicago Tribune*, 2 May 2019, chicagotribune .com/lifestyles/ct-me-too-timeline-20171208-htmlstory.html.

OpenSecrets Seminar, Shakespeare Association of America, 19 Apr. 2019, Renaissance Washington Hotel, Washington, DC.

Rapshrew. Directed by Jean Trounstine, Shakespeare Behind Bars, 1992, Framingham Women's Prison. VHS recording of live performance.

Scott-Douglass, Amy. *Shakespeare Inside: The Bard behind Bars*. Continuum, 2007. Shakespeare NOW!

Shakespeare, William. *Macbeth*. Greenblatt et al., pp. 1017–69.

———. *The Taming of the Shrew*. Greenblatt et al., pp. 343–414.

Shakespeare Behind Bars. Directed by Hank Rogerson, Philomath Films, 2005.

Shakespeare in Prison alumnae. Personal interviews. August 2018

Shepherd-Bates, Frannie. Personal interview. 20 June 2018.

———. "Season Seven: Week 4." *Shakespeare in Prison Blog: Updates from the Women's Ensemble*, Detroit Public Theatre, 4 Oct. 2017, www.detroit publictheatre.org/blog?offset=1508854134437.

Trounstine, Jean. Personal interview. 17–18 July 2018.

———. "Revisiting Sacred Spaces." *Performing New Lives: Prison Theatre*, edited by Jonathan Shailor, Jessica Kingsley Publishers, 2011, pp. 231–46.

Playwriting across the Walls as Abolitionist Practice

Rivka Eckert

It is in the depths of North Country winter when I print out the final drafts of playscripts and seal each inside a manila envelope bearing the SUNY Potsdam academic crest. I handwrite the address of each institution across the envelope's front under the playwrights' names followed by the department identification number, or DIN, that trails them through the prison system and will continue to shadow them upon their release. Thinking of the bureaucratic and institutional navigations that the Plays Across the Walls (PATW) project demanded, I place seven envelopes, one for each playwright, into the outgoing mail slot. This final action, a thank-you note to the playwrights and a clean copy of their final script, cuts through all the walls in a way that only art can.

The North Country region spans from the New York state border with Canada to the Erie Canal and from the edge of Lake Champlain to the shores of Lake Ontario. This largely rural and impoverished area (nearly twenty-eight percent of residents in St. Lawrence County live below the poverty line) has experienced a population drop as industry and opportunity call people elsewhere. While the upstate New York population shrinks as people move downstate toward Albany and New York City, prisons have moved into the North Country. According to the Brookings Institution, in the late 1980s and early 1990s, when Riverview Correctional Facility and Ogdensburg Correctional Facility were built, nearly thirty percent of new residents in the region were prisoners (Pendall 1).

Prison is one industry that assures stability and reliable economic support in the rural United States. There are two prison hubs within the Northern New York region, Clinton and Watertown, which account for eleven prisons. A regional backlash occurred when the then governor Andrew Cuomo announced his intention to shutter three correctional facilities, according to North Country Public Radio (Mann). Senator Patty

Ritchie's "Protect Our Prisons" petition, which has more than 6,200 constituent signatures, is only one example of this backlash and speaks to the region's acceptance of and dependence upon prisons.

The United States incarcerates more people than any other country in the world; in fact, every US state incarcerates more people per capita than any independent democracy on the globe (Widra and Herring). While figures from 2020 show the incarceration rate at the lowest levels since 1995, there are currently 1.4 million people in America's state and federal prisons (Carson). According to Emily Widra and Tiana Herring's research with Prison Policy Initiative, "[S]tates like New York and Massachusetts appear progressive in their incarceration rates compared to states like Louisiana, but compared to the rest of the world, every U.S. state relies too heavily on prisons and jails to respond to crime." Those people, and their connection to their communities, are some of the strongest motivators for my prison-based theater work.

In *The New Jim Crow: Mass Incarceration in the Age of Colorblindness*, Michelle Alexander writes that "criminals are the one social group in America that nearly everyone—across political, racial, and class boundaries—feels free to hate" (228). Alexander lays out the historical and political framework for the criminal (in)justice system and the prison system as race-making institutions, illustrating the culture of white supremacy embedded in US society. The prison-industrial complex is defined by the national abolitionist grassroots organization Critical Resistance as a term that describes "the overlapping interests of government and industry that use surveillance, policing, and imprisonment as solutions to economic, social and political problems" (49). In order to change this culture, representation and perception must be addressed.

In the past ten years, there has been marked awareness and a shifting societal perception around the role of the prison in the US criminal (in)justice system. In 2017, the American Civil Liberties Union reported that ninety-one percent of Americans support criminal justice reform. Recent social justice movements like #DefundThePolice, #CopsOffCampus, and #8CantWait show a rapid development in the public's willingness to consider alternatives to current carceral systems. While political will and public sentiment around punishment and incarceration may ebb and flow, there have been no major interventions in the prison-industrial complex, most likely because of its ability to make money. David Shapiro, writing for the ACLU National Prison Project, details the economic advantage of prisons to large corporations, listing the nearly $3 billion in revenue to the largest private prison companies in 2010 (5). Private for-profit prisons and their contractors—in fact, entire economies—are dependent upon mass incarceration, and little is being done to change that.

There is no ethical engagement with the carceral state beyond the advocacy for abolition. From this standpoint, I offer an abolitionist and community cultural development (CCD) theater-making model that addresses the challenges of finding partnership with the New York State Department of Corrections and Community Supervision (DOCCS) by looking at the 2018 PATW project. The PATW Festival began as a ten-week writing workshop with seven men incarcerated at Riverview Correctional Facility in Ogdensburg, New York, and culminated in performances by students and actors from SUNY Potsdam and St. Lawrence County Correctional Facility. In codifying this methodology, I present the impacts, challenges, and guidelines for extending plays written within the prison context to larger communities. In offering my learning around abolition and CCD, I situate playwriting and theater as a challenging site in which to reclaim space for civic discourse around mass incarceration.

What Is Meant by *Abolition*?

The term *prison abolitionism* speaks to a political vision that works toward the elimination of the use of prisons as a form of legal punishment while creating lasting alternatives to punishment and imprisonment. While the abolitionist position allows for reformist steps (like the preservation of life reform, i.e., advocating for the end of the death penalty; or quality of life reform, i.e., better opportunities for education, art, therapy, etc.; see Critical Resistance), in general, as Dylan Rodríguez notes in *Radical Teacher*, "the rise of the prison industrial complex is in part a direct outcome of the liberal-progressive 'prison reform' successes of the 1970s" (10). As such, all advocates of prison abolition see reform efforts, if pursued at all, as functioning in dialectic with abolitionist aims. From this angle, abolitionist pedagogy must walk the fine line between, on the one hand, affirming the systemically harmed humanity of incarcerated people and radically changing policies and procedures within the criminal (in)justice system and, on the other, upholding the demand for the holistic dismantling of the prison-industrial complex. Thus, in order to advance the cause of prison abolition, prison educators, and prison-based artists such as myself, must work in a way that does not support the aims of the carceral state.

The scholar Ruth Wilson Gilmore cites the activism and movement around Black Lives Matter for pushing the cultural imagination toward an acceptance of ideas around abolition. Gilmore argues that through the use of protest, media campaigns, and activism to open up conversations that question the role of the police state, "Black Lives Matter has got people thinking about and using the word 'abolition.'" Dovetailing with Gilmore's stance on the opening of the cultural imagination, the abolitionist and educator Mariame Kaba describes "abolition [as] a theory of change, it's a theory of social life. It's about making things." Kaba's discussion of abolition as being about presence, not absence, means that strategies around abolition must include the presence of collective action to create care networks that uplift culture and creative expression and a plan for forming structures that address harm and hold people accountable, creating conditions that decrease the demand for police and public surveillance. Abolition is not simply about the destruction of the prison state.

The critical prison studies scholar Joy James, in the introduction of *The New Abolitionists: (Neo)Slave Narratives and Contemporary Prison Writings*, distinguishes between three categories of abolitionist neoslave narratives: those of the master state (or state as master); those of the non-incarcerated abolitionist and advocate; and those of the prisoner slave (xxiii). I find this framework incredibly important, as my proximity to the crisis of mass incarceration must be labeled appropriately. As a non-incarcerated abolitionist, I can only speak credibly by virtue of the insight bestowed upon me by those who are incarcerated and of the work of other abolitionists. Based on this wisdom, and the 2018 PATW project, I offer the following as a guiding framework from which to build an abolitionist artistic practice. As I understand them, artistic practices make visible that which society has disappeared, celebrate and encourage freedom, actively resist capitalism, and are grounded in theories of change.

Make Visible What Society Disappears

Within this abolitionist framework, CCD grows like a spring bud upon a tree branch. CCD is the naming of a system of practices used by community organizers and artists rooted in the creation of culturally responsive art. As Arlene Goldbard writes, in *New Creative Community: The Art of Cultural Development*, "[T]he work is grounded in social critique and social imagination" (1). If theater-making allows for spaces of collective imagining—toward a future that does not rely on the prison-industrial complex—then the potential power of the artist as an "agent of transformation" must be recognized (16). I don't use *transformation* here in the rehabilitative sense, although it is so often used as a measurement of success for programming in prisons. I use this term in recognition of the artist's capacity to create transformation. This means that the artist develops facility in creating multidirectional cultural dialogue through theater that "cultivat[es] a mutuality of knowledge and respect" (Gold-bard 109). Sometimes this is called building cultural capital.

Part of the success of the PATW project meant leading the exchange with great generosity, which Simone Weil Davis writes about in *Razor Wire Women: Prisoners, Activists, Scholars, and Artists*. The exchange of generosity, in this project, included my giving time without compensation, giving feedback meant to empower and inspire, and applying for and finding funding for purchasing books and supplies. I received generosity through the trust granted me as a director to safeguard the only copy of a handwritten script, to work with the fresh worlds of the plays, and to present the playwrights' visions wholly. Davis calls these contraband exchanges "empathetic negotiations" or "multidirectional empathy," with recognition that this connection, and the courage that is required to share artistry, requires both great generosity and gratitude. This reframing, Davis says, can move "from thinking of education as part of a gift economy, rather than as cultural capital; we can go further and think of it as *contraband*" (218). DOCCS, while they have strict rules against contraband, missed that in these plays whole worlds, characters, and visions crossed the razor-wired boundaries.

Another necessary element is, of course, institutional cooperation. All collaboration and agreement must be determined by people, the power brokers who represent institutions but are decidedly not them. I find even the phrase *institutional cooperation* to be misleading, as institutions and corporations are not people (in spite of what the United States Supreme Court decided with the 2010 Citizens United ruling) and therefore cannot act as partners. The larger the institutional structure, the more difficult it becomes to navigate the relationship-building that is critical in moving a project from idea to implementation. I would not categorize my negotiations with the power brokers who represented either the correctional facility or the academic institution as being full of generosity and gratitude.

The prison's default position is *no*. As a place built on safety and security—principles emphasized through exerted control—there is little reward for the risk of openness to change, or for generosity and gratitude. The existing social capital runs along defined hegemonic power lines. COs (corrections officers) trust COs. Administrators trust administrators. Politicians trust each other. No one trusts the incarcerated.

I came flush against this mentality as I went through the Institutional Review Board (IRB) process at my university. Prior to my research proposal, research in prisons was not reviewable. I had to leverage social capital to advocate for a change in my university's bylaws around research in prison. This meant that I developed a proposal over a year out from the project's start date and submitted it to the IRB for initial review. I then met with the IRB and with the college's provost and president to discuss and explain the benefits and challenges of conducting research at correctional facilities. After the bylaws were changed, the IRB asked that I obtain research approval letters from the highest-ranking officials in the New York State DOCCS (State Commissioner Anthony J. Annucci) and from the St. Lawrence County Correctional Facility Administrator (Peggy Harper). I also was asked to locate justice representatives who were formerly incarcerated, or formerly justice-involved, who could review the research proposals.

The rigid power hierarchy of the DOCCS creates a communication dynamic that complicates its ability to partner. Within this paramilitary structure, I found little flexibility or acceptance of more equitable models of partnership. By being forced to decide the assessment metric almost a year in advance of the project start date and without knowing the actors and playwrights I would be working with, I felt strained to create specific and relevant questions to assess the project. That noted, I created an audience survey that asked for audiences to provide feedback around what it meant to watch the plays. I had already received approval from my project partners (the men in Riverview's drama group, volunteer service coordinators at the Riverview prison and the St. Lawrence jail, the jail administrator, and the prison superintendent) at the facilities in which the data collection would take place—people with whom I had established social capital. Because of the difficulty of navigating large institutional bureaucracies, it took over nine months for my proposal to make its way to Commissioner Annucci's desk. Prisons are meant to divide communities, to hide and render invisible the people behind the walls. When the director of program planning, research, and evaluation finally did review the document, the only communication I received was a denial letter stating that the DOCCS had contracts with other researchers who were looking at questions of efficacy and influence, which they believed would address the impact of other types of programming. The DOCCS and the university are uncomfortable partners within a CCD methodology. Institutional partners can grant or deny access and can coordinate but are challenged by concepts of cooperation and collaboration.

Cooperation and collaboration, as bonding social capital, flourish in direct exchange related to theater-making. Stephani Etheridge Woodson, in her book *Theatre for Youth Third Space: Performance, Democracy and Community Cultural Development*, defines collaboration as shared authority and risk-taking, where partners influence each other's mission, and participants set goals and conduct evaluation together (169). Collaboration like this, between artists within and without the walls, is not what is supposed to happen in prisons.

This generous human exchange can be deemed contraband. Treacy Ziegler, writing on the hindrance of kindness in prison communities in "The Incarceration of Kindness," reasons that this type of exchange "is hindered because prison creates a single identity for the prisoners and then institutionalizes hate for that single identity of inmate. How does this institutionalized hate make kindness suspect between individuals, thus making kindness/lack of kindness not a function of an individual, but of a system?" (11). If the prison situates identity in such a way that kindness, generosity, and gratitude are suspect, then building collaborative exchange between inside and outside artists acts as an abolitionist practice.

One of the questions that plagues my experience crossing prison walls and endeavoring in theater practices with those who are incarcerated remains around the ethics of short-term collaborative exchange. Both inside and outside artists relish the creative process and learn from one another. But when the project ends, so does the connection. While this often happens organically on the outside, the prison's firm boundaries at the points of physical contact and correspondence make the cleaving a different experience for prison-based arts projects. This is perhaps most glaringly obvious at the end of a play or performance, when the cast party that would be typical outside prison walls, usually a jovial affair with lots of hugs and handshakes, is replaced with increased CO surveillance as project participants shuffle their feet and try to find words to fill in the places where in normal situations a hug or high five would exist.

Celebrate and Encourage Freedom

Framing freedom as a guideline for work inside a prison is an excellent way to have one's volunteer status revoked, but I draw a distinction between freedom and emancipation. Emancipation is liberation from state control. Freedom is an inside job. James speaks to this inner journey: "Freedom is an ontological status—only the individual or collective—and perhaps a god—can create freedom" (xxiii). Within this understanding, freedom is to be celebrated and encouraged.

The freedom to choose to participate, or to be able to say no, is a step toward dismantling systems of forced involvement. The continual punishment of required participation in programming is described in "The Attica Liberation Faction Manifesto of Demands": "The programs which we are submitted to under the façade of rehabilitation are relative to the ancient stupidity of pouring water on a drowning man, inasmuch as we are treated for our hostilities by our program administrators with their hostility as medication." The ability to say no to participation, even if only in a small way, cultivates a sense of freedom and agency. PATW started with ten playwrights. Seven playwrights completed plays. I celebrate the others too. Their ability to say for themselves, "This isn't for me right now," or "This isn't how I want to spend my time," is a radical expression.

No artistic program can actually free or emancipate people, but such programs offer the opportunity to engage with freedom. Playwriting is the ultimate practice of freedom in that it allows the playwright a chance to create and control a complete world. Within this world, and in the process of creating this world, playwrights experiment with what it means to express identity and culture, create meaning, and find resolution. Many students at first seemed to find a compulsion to speak to narratives that seem expected by the state. These types of narratives around recovery, or confession, became more complex as playwrights went through rewrite after rewrite. A prison sentence is only one part of the playwrights' lives, and the next chapter is open. In imagining together, the playwrights make their futures and their art free.

Actively Resist Racial Capitalism

Prisons are inseparable from a long history of large-scale racist state violence. In this regard, at its historical roots, the abolition of slavery was one very visible display of resistance to the racist foundations of capitalism in the United States. Since the nation's formation, racial capitalism played a key role in creating the circumstances that led to slavery. As Alexander articulates, "African Americans repeatedly have been controlled through institutions such as slavery and Jim Crow, which appear to die, but then are reborn in new form, tailored to the needs and constraints of the time" (21). This institutionalization of racialized social control and economic exploitation, and Black people's collective struggle against being used as free or cheap labor, did not end with the 1863 Emancipation Proclamation, as the Black Codes, convict leasing system, peonage system, sharecropping, and prison-industrial complex have made evident over the past century and a half. In questioning these continued practices of slavery—while understanding that slavery has been the foundation of the US economy—we can begin to dismantle a democracy that has been built upon oppression and reimagine the project of democracy anew. Preceding Alexander's thinking on the through line of economic prosperity built on the backs of Black workers, the former political prisoner and longtime prison abolitionist scholar and activist Angela Davis writes, "The challenge of the twenty-first century is not to demand equal opportunity to participate in the machinery of oppression. Rather, it is to identify and dismantle those structures in which racism continues to be embedded. This is the only way that the promise of freedom can be extended to masses of people" (*Abolition Democracy* 29). Sounding the call for abolition extends to all systems where oppression and racism are exercised.

In a small but calculated way, the PATW project actively worked in awareness of this racial-historical context to oppose the oppressive forces of capitalism. There were no costs associated with being an audience member at any of the performances. There were no costs to playwright participation. I leveraged the university's resources to level the costs of notebooks, marketing materials, printing, and transportation. The university production was livestreamed in order to make it accessible to those with limited geographic access or means of travel. Our stripped-down aesthetic, in which the actors performed in street clothes, using scripts on music stands and no props, invited the audience to engage their collective imagination. The playwrights' words stood on their own—without any of the production shine that money could buy. And within the collective imagination, the audience experienced some of the promise of freedom that only the connection of storyteller to audience can grant.

Grounding PATW in Theories of Change

Assessment and evaluation define both how change happens and why. Woodson suggests using graphic mapping to characterize the change environment as either emergent, transformative, or projectable (196). By developing a theory of change in this tangible manner, project planners can assure that growth and change are intentional, documented, and implemented.

Particularly within an abolitionist mindset, it is critical to ask questions around what exactly is being abolished: What systems, practices, or institutions are being ended? What assessment protocols can be established to hold participants and artists accountable? How specifically is change measured?

While an abolitionist theater project and correctional facilities may seem odd bedfellows, to say the least, a number of goals found smooth alignment. PATW project goals focused on building cultural capital, creating social bonds, and empowering participants as agents capable of reclaiming narratives around incarceration. By grounding assessment in Reeler's Projectable Change Theory, as outlined by Woodson, I focused primarily on evaluating outcomes as they related to reclaiming narratives around incarceration. Woodson describes Reeler's projectable change environments as fitting best inside "highly organized systems in which partners have clear visions of their needs, desired outcomes, and causal pathways to success" (195). As mentioned earlier, the highly organized systems of prison and academic institutions made evaluation difficult but not impossible.

The mixed ensemble (university students and incarcerated actors) performed the plays at St. Lawrence County Correctional Facility. University students performed at SUNY Potsdam's Performing Arts Center and at Riverview Correctional Facility. Seventy-six people from audiences at the county correctional facility and the university performances completed voluntary surveys about the impact of the plays. There were two significant findings that came from this data: first, eighty-nine percent of audience members reported thinking about the lives and history of the people who wrote the plays—men who are incarcerated; and, second, eighty-eight percent of audience members reported considering new issues or points of view.

An overwhelming majority of audience members reported spending time thinking about the life of the playwright and considering new perspectives or futures. The importance of the experience of shared humanity cannot be overstated. Many audience members wrote of this experience on their surveys, stating that the performance "makes me think about the talent wasted behind bars" and that they "felt connected to [the performers'] stories/life." While I recognize that "thinking about" and "considering" are only the first steps toward tangible change, I document them as progress because I see such evidence of raising consciousness as a crucial precursor to the work of social transformation, including the project of prison abolition.

In this regard, an entirely appropriate question to ask, knowing that PATW has the ability to change audience perception around artists who are incarcerated, is, What happens next? Projectable change demands continuing the "if then" growth pattern: if audience ideologies or perceptions are shifting to include a more expansive and humanizing view of those behind bars, then how can this experience be spread? How can we work more closely in line with abolitionist demands, like those released during the 2018 national prison strike (Jailhouse Lawyers), the manifesto from the Attica uprising, or Angela Davis's concept of an abolition democracy that calls for the abolition of institutions that advance the dominance of any one group and collectively imagines the democracy to come (*Abolition Democracy* 19)?

The Battle against Institutional Control

Within the prison or university context, institutional bureaucracy shapes the ability to measure and identify outcomes. The PATW project brought out provocative questions for me around the ability to partner with institutions within a CCD model. For instance, I wondered: does the hierarchical power structure of institutions, like prisons, contribute to seeing collaboration as a threat to stability? If so, what would it take to frame instability as growth? If, as Kaba suggests, we "have to transform the relationships that we have with each other so we can really create new forms of safety and justice in our communities," then what would it take to see using collaborative art-making practices as beneficial to a reimagining a shared future that includes all of us?

The playwrights and theatermakers inside Riverview Correctional Facility are constantly convincing me to push and dream bigger. PATW came from a desire, spoken by the men inside, that their art would not get trapped behind the walls. When I first started facilitating drama inside, I was careful to keep the stakes low—in-class performances, previously staged work, and so on—but, as trust, generosity, and creative capital have grown with the ensemble members, I have the audacity and the encouragement to dream and question. What would it mean to launch a festival in which the men could perform in front of the community—not inviting the community in but inviting the men out? How can the arts be truly free? How exactly can freedom be assessed?

I am motivated by these stronger, more complex questions. In *Are Prisons Obsolete?*, Angela Davis describes the prison as both present and absent from our own lives and seemingly beyond the scope of societal criticism. Davis writes, "People tend to take prisons for granted. It is difficult to imagine life without them. At the same time, there is reluctance to face the realities hidden within them . . . To think about this simultaneous presence and absence is to begin to acknowledge the part played by ideology in shaping the way we interact with social surroundings" (15). Prisons have not always been a part of the community, and they do not have to be a part of our future. It is the abolitionist artists' mission to remain dedicated to creating, in both process and product, art that sounds a call for humanism. In making visible the humanity of folks held in prisons by giving a platform through PATW performances, we demand presence. We demand recognition of the lives held behind prison walls. We demand that these lives be respected for their worth and value.

WORKS CITED

Alexander, Michelle. *The New Jim Crow: Mass Incarceration in the Age of Colorblindness*. New Press, 2010.

American Civil Liberties Union. "91% of Americans Support Criminal Justice Reform, ACLU Polling Finds." *ACLU*, 16 Nov. 2017, aclu.org/press -releases/91-percent-americans-support-criminal-justice-reform-aclu -polling-finds.

"The Attica Liberation Faction Manifesto of Demands." *Race and Class*, vol. 53, no. 2, Oct. 2011, pp. 28–35, https://doi.org/10.1177/0306396811414338.

Carson, E. Ann. "Prisoners in 2020 — Statistical Tables." US Department of Justice, Dec. 2021, bjs.ojp.gov/content/pub/pdf/p20st.pdf.

Critical Resistance Abolition Toolkit Workgroup. *The CR Abolition Organizing Toolkit*. Critical Resistance, 2004, criticalresistance.org/wp-content/ uploads/2012/06/CR-Abolitionist-Toolkit-online.pdf.

Davis, Angela Y. *Abolition Democracy: Beyond Empire, Prisons, and Torture*. Seven Stories Press, 2005.

———. *Are Prisons Obsolete?* Seven Stories Press, 2003.

Davis, Simone Weil. "Inside-Out: The Reaches and Limits of a Prison Program." *Razor Wire Women: Prisoners, Activists, Scholars, and Artists*, edited by Jodie Michelle Lawston and Ashley Lucas, State U of New York P, 2011, pp. 203–24.

Gilmore, Ruth Wilson. "Prisons and Class Warfare: An Interview with Ruth Wilson Gilmore." Conducted by Clément Petitjean, *Verso Books*, 2 Aug. 2018, versobooks.com/blogs/3954-prisons-and-class-warfare-an-interview -with-ruth-wilson-gilmore.

Goldbard, Arlene. *New Creative Community: The Art of Cultural Development*. New Village Press, 2006.

Jailhouse Lawyers Speak — #ShutEmDown 2022. "Press Release: National Prison Strike August 21–September 9th, 2018." *Twitter*, 24 Apr. 2018, twitter.com/JailLawSpeak/status/988771668670799872?lang=en.

James, Joy. *The New Abolitionists: (Neo)Slave Narratives and Contemporary Prison Writings*. State U of New York P, 2005.

Kaba, Mariame. "Towards the Horizon of Abolition." Interviewed by John Duda, *The Next System Project*, 17 Nov. 2017, thenextsystem.org/learn/ stories/towards-horizon-abolition-conversation-mariame-kaba.

Mann, Brian. "Gov. Cuomo Wants to Close Three More State Prisons." *North Country Public Radio*, 18 Feb. 2019, northcountrypublicradio.org/news/

story/38068/20190218/gov-cuomo-wants-to-close-three-more-ny-state
-prisons.

Pendall, Rolf. "Upstate New York's Population Plateau: The Third Slowest Growing 'State.'" Brookings Institution, 1 Aug. 2003, brookings.edu/research/upstate-new-yorks-population-plateau-the-third-slowest-growing-state/.

Ritchie, Patty. "Ritchie: More than 6,200 Have Signed Petition to 'Protect Our Prisons'—Have You?" *The New York State Senate*, 14 Mar. 2019, www.nysenate.gov/newsroom/press-releases/patty-ritchie/ritchie-more-6200-have-signed-petition-protect-our-prisons.

Rodríguez, Dylan. "The Disorientation of the Teaching Act: Abolition as Pedagogical Position." *The Radical Teacher*, no. 88, 2010, pp. 7–19. *JSTOR*, www.jstor.org/stable/10.5406/radicalteacher.1.88.0007.

Shapiro, David. "Banking on Bondage: Private Prisons and Mass Incarceration." American Civil Liberties Union, 2 Nov. 2011, aclu.org/banking-bondage-private-prisons-and-mass-incarceration.

Widra, Emily, and Tiana Herring. "States of Incarceration: The Global Context." *Prison Policy Initiative*, Sept. 2021, prisonpolicy.org/global/2021.html.

Woodson, Stephani Etheridge. *Theatre for Youth Third Space: Performance, Democracy and Community Cultural Development*. Intellect Press, 2015.

Ziegler, Treacy. "The Incarceration of Kindness." *Anthurium*, vol. 15, no. 2, 2019, https://doi.org/10.33596/anth.392.

Cracks in the Glass Ceiling
C. Fausto Cabrera

Except for the chicken-wire windows and rusted iron bars, it could have been a classroom anywhere: three rows of rectangular tables with two chairs at each, a Smartboard, bookshelves lining the outer walls, a few computer stations under large square windows. This room was designated for higher education. The sets of outdated textbooks, preapproved, represented a complete associate of arts degree program in Stillwater Prison.

With a few elective classes under my belt, I looked forward to Psychology 101 the most. A "prison intellectual" progresses through a litany of self-help and psychology titles reinforcing the idea that education is the answer; it can save, empower, and rehabilitate. The chatter settled. We'd spent the customary time on signing the Department of Corrections (DOC) paperwork laying out the rules, which were really just more threats. I had plucked the textbook from the shelf weeks earlier and now sat squirming in my seat. The professor's authentic quirk of unkempt grey hair, thick-framed glasses, and tweed jacket told me this class shouldn't disappoint.

He began, "My name is Professor [so and so]. I want you to know how proud of you I am for being in this classroom tonight, for taking steps to better yourselves despite your circumstance. I have no intention of making it difficult. Everyone is going to receive an A." "Oh, it's a reverse grading system," I thought, looking down at his syllabus. I flipped it over, seeing a single side of chapter headings no more elaborate than the table of contents.

"All I ask," he continued, "is that you participate in the class discussions. We'll begin with the given chapter, but if we end up talking politics or current events, so be it!" That's it? What about tests or quizzes? He said there'd be a few we'd go over as a class. "I'm just so proud of you guys for being here!"

There was a collective glee. I scanned the room, my face drooping from disappointment, but what did it matter? I wondered what he imagined this prison to be like for us. Did he assume we had to tape magazines to our waists as protection, carry crude shanks around the unit with our heads on a swivel? Proud of us for just being here . . . instead of drinking hooch made in a toilet, slapping cards on a table, or gangbanging? Had he watched the absurdly stereotypical episodes of *Lockup* for research so he would be able to empathize and relate, drawing the conclusion that we have limited capacity? Was this pity masquerading as pride?

DOC programming is set in a certain language of self-help. Once you know the expected terms, it's easy to become an avatar of reform, because you know what's being asked of you, regardless of your level of sincerity. True enlightenment isn't necessary. After every class or completed program we receive the same printed certificate to add to a file. It became about collecting symbols of change rather than chasing growth.

The singular prison narrative is that of a law-abiding phoenix rising from the ashes of a villainous criminal—like it's merely a choice between good and evil. Once you see the light, learn your lesson, and obtain the correcting skill sets, then you are reformed—but only once you are released from prison. This is not to say the system isn't effective in the hands of the well-intentioned, which implies the credit is due to the system. Surviving the conditions of a harsh place doesn't make you a better person. It only makes you stronger—but not necessarily accountable.

Now, I don't know the business of colleges or how an accredited institution could offer classes for ten dollars, but I do know that given the Republican pendulum budget swing, the AA program survived staffed solely by volunteer professors for a while. I cringe when I hear people criticize funding prison college programs as offering an "unfair" advantage over already privileged kids. It's hard to imagine that people are mad they have to pay tuition while criminals get courses for free, as if education were some sort of reward for bad behavior rather than the logical step toward rehabilitation.

It took me over ten years to earn my two-year degree. A heightened security mentality and underfunding severely affected the availability of classes. It always seemed like we were in the middle of a professional compromise. On the one hand, professors dealt with the lack of updated materials and Internet access, limited typing availability, and inadequate contact with students. But on the other hand, they were always met by a room full of invigorated students who knew the value of the experience and the opportunity before them. We were undistracted and engaged. This was our chance to show family, friends, and staff that we weren't giving up on ourselves. For some, it was a chance to stay involved in teaching their kids. We never considered college as a natural step. Most participants barely had a GED. The pursuit of a degree was about more than grades or receiving a certificate; education is a restoration of dignity.

We are all encased in metaphorical glass, made of the standards and expectations we inherit from parents, family, neighborhoods, and socialization in general. Outsiders can't always appreciate different perspectives, and it's difficult to translate what happens to the psyche when you see the world through the dirty windows of an adverse childhood. In some places, kids go off to college after high school and are allowed to "find" themselves through experimentation. In other places, guns, drugs, and funerals are as natural as sports and music. Once you figure out that these are experiences that are meant to be examined, challenged, or broken, you start to see the cracks in the glass that surrounds you. Most often, it takes exceptional people to recognize you are on a precipice of discovery and just need a little help to have a breakout moment.

Minnesota Prison Writing Workshop and Stillwater Writers' Collective

I walked into the education director's office with a notebook full of ideas, hopes, and concerns for the future of the degree program. Pat had invited Jen, the founder of the Minnesota Prison Writing Workshop (MPWW), and Deb, our matriarch and newest MPWW staff member, for a closed meeting to discuss the coming year. I sat among this circle of professionals glowing in a beam of importance, honored to be there and proud that the effort was being officially legitimized. The hours flew by while we ironed out schedules, logistics, recruiting, future classes, expectations, and potential problems.

At that point, I wouldn't have called myself a writer, but I knew I could manage the Stillwater Writers' Collective (SWC). I'd been an active member of the Restorative Justice Council and was an institutional representative to the prison administration and lead facilitator of the Long-Term Offender Group. My desk was in the art department, on the other side of Pat's office wall. From that desk, I had run the art program for the better part of a decade. I managed the budget, wrote the curriculum, taught new students, processed paperwork from the annual art sales, and produced art for various functions and charitable events. It was beginning to feel like too much of a job that was stealing my creative verve. I needed a new outlet, and writing was it. With access to my own computer and a supportive platform, I could manage the SWC even though I wasn't yet confident as a writer. There were so many validating moments during the meeting that I wish I could have crystallized.

It was a rare look behind a curtain I could only have imagined as an outsider. Jen warned me about what it would cost to take on the bulk of administrative duties and how it could make my individual writing suffer. Deb added that there was a danger of creating a cult of personality and exercising too much control over the collective. I looked down, flipping through my notes; then, with another topic on the tip of my tongue, I was jarred by the anger in a man's voice. "Hey! Come on. Let's go! It's count time." Leaning through a door down a short hallway was a guy in a uniform and a utility belt, who came to return me to my cage. Scrambling to collect my papers and grateful for that experience, I couldn't quite find the words to express myself. So I simply extended my hand to shake their hands, looked them in their eyes, and thanked them. This would have been such a simple and straightforward gesture anywhere else, but in prison, it was fraught with anxiety and stigma. Staff and inmates should never touch. That handshake defied boundaries just as my presence at that meeting had. None of them hesitated, including Pat. I could have gone to segregation for that, but I'd long since realized that there is a difference between morality and policy and that it's my responsibility to decide what to live by.

There is nothing more empowering than responsibility. To have a purpose that extends beyond personal goals and ambitions can define people and create community. Some see it through parenting and some through developing a business or championing a cause, while many understand it through the sacrifice of working a nine-to-five job. In that meeting we took on the task of fostering the idea that everyone was entitled to a voice and that fine-tuning one's voice was a responsibility. Being heard initiates the charge of having something to say, and taking hold of one's narrative is an absolute necessity for imprisoned writers.

We didn't know how big MPWW would become, so Zeke Caligiuri and I established the SWC independently and operated through a board of directors, a handful of Deb's initial students. We thought it was important to promote writing without a classroom under the premise that writing could be empowering through independent will. Each of us created a brochure that focused on a specific genre, outlining the basics of getting started, and made them available through our section in the library. We finalized a mission statement and developed a brochure to introduce the purpose and function of the collective. We offered peer mentoring and sponsored activities, like guest speaker events, readings, writer's forums, and workshops, and set out to foster a strong writing community. MPWW was growing exponentially, so our first duty was to accommodate the writing community's needs.

No Rest for the Wicked

There were records to keep, sign-up sheets to create, classrooms to set up, and participation lists to develop so participants could get passes. We started closing out workshops with public readings for the internal population in the higher education room, which meant creating invitations and guest lists, designing programs, setting up and tearing down the room, dealing with complications, and making decisions on the fly. Taking the initiative felt like my responsibility, especially since Zeke, the original inspiration for the writing class, was not able to participate. I took on the bulk of the duties, mainly as a function of my controlling nature, but also because there were tasks that needed attending to. I wasn't reading as much as I should have been, and my writing suffered, but we were building a new culture centered around literature. It was an honor to be so involved in creating a system that helped develop the talents of others. It was akin to what I'd felt in the art department. There was an extrapolated effect to seeing the successes of the guys growing in their craft, but there were still only a handful of guys really focused. We needed to fill these classes with new blood.

Writing is a tough sell in prison: the requirements include vulnerability, exposure, probing reflection, and a ton of reading. There is limited access to research and computers, no front-end gratification, and no possible way to half-ass or fake this—writing is hard work. Oh, and there are no certificates. I worked to recruit solid men who I knew had something to say. Recruits risked the stigma of selling out or dry snitching about details better left unrecorded. There is a rite of passage that is the outlaw's privilege; certain experiences can never translate to the uninitiated. Our stories are too often told through shaded and cracked lenses, including police reports, false testimony given in exchange for deals, vindictive prosecution, academic takes by criminologists with no firsthand knowledge, crime dramas (*CSI, NCIS, Law and Order*), sensationalized versions of the worst elements of crime and punishment (*Another 48, Lockdown, Locked Up, Cops*)—and then there are the entertainers perpetuating a street lifestyle we are paying the price for while they cash the checks. I understood the need to fill the void of our perspective. Silence is the language of the marginalized.

I had to find ways to balance the scales. How could I inspire guys to write if it wouldn't immediately change how we are viewed or treated? I waged war on a cosmic plane, trying to see decades into the future, while creating short-term, almost myopic incentives. To fill classes, I called in some favors, came out of my athletic retirement to play flag football and basketball, bartered property, dabbled in the black markets, and even blackmailed some of my brothers, all for the greater good, hoping to create an honorable roster of convicts weaponizing writing as resistance. There were so many good dudes around me with experiences lying dormant under the soot of poor decisions. It saddened me to know that these stories, the ones truly worth telling, might perish in the dignity found in forgetting. I finally came to accept that these classes weren't for everyone.

I took every MPWW workshop offered (sci-fi and fantasy, screenplay, oral storytelling, fiction, whatever) and encouraged the board members of the collective to do the same. It was our duty to protect the program by keeping workshops filled with participants. Most of them weren't interested in exploring outside their chosen genre, but I absorbed all I could. I was spreading myself thin between the collective, facilitating Long-Term Offender Group, and managing the art department. But the workload became a reason to wake up. Something new, challenging, or enriching always lay on the horizon. This was the epitome of living a creative lifestyle. Sure, I was exhausted, but I was so grateful for the opportunities to be involved in something I loved.

The Potency of Craft

As I began to grasp the mechanics of craft, I saw how much writing had affected my view of the world and my place within it. It also bled into the structures of the other groups I was participating in and strengthened the formats of the programs I influenced. There seemed to be this powerful thread of owning one's narrative throughout all these rehabilitative efforts.

In the Long-Term Offender Group, we met every other Tuesday for a few hours in a group of seventeen to twenty inmates and four staff members for a year. Julie, a former correctional officer turned case manager, developed a platform guided by these terrible packets written in the vernacular of an outsider. It was as if a person who'd never done drugs or taken a sip of alcohol had written a rehab program about embracing change. In the beginning everyone sat in a circle in their best reformed inmate personas saying what they thought the staff wanted to hear. In the personal essay and memoir workshops, I had learned how important transparency was to establishing trust with the audience, so I figured we didn't have the time for the class to evolve organically. A few sessions in, at the right moments I'd divulge something darkly personal or typically contradicting. One time, I said, "You might see me stumbling in the unit, drunk dialing an old girlfriend with three peppermints in my mouth, stinking of hooch. That doesn't negate the investments I've made unless I get caught." Julie would scoff. The guys who knew me knew I was being honest, and a collective laugh eased the tension. Vulnerability drove conversations about things we'd never have considered talking about, like bouts of depression, propensities to self-medicate, and the alienation of our beloveds. There's no growth in the absence of honesty, which begins with self. In a room full of the forsaken, if we couldn't be transparent enough to see the cracks in each other, how could we possibly contribute? Those shared emotional truths were what created the bonds.

The significant change came with the biography assignment, which required us to explore our lives from childhood into incarceration in detail, with the option to present. The process allowed us to push through different layers of perspective that humanized everyone in the group at a point when we could learn from each other the most. One year, nearly everyone shared their story. Some were excruciatingly mundane, inappropriate at stages, or flat-out false, but none failed to affect my perception of the person courageous enough to share. Nothing compares to hearing a person's story in their own voice. The first time I shared my story publicly was as a cautionary tale at a prerelease class. I walked into a room of rambunctious short-timers on their third day of getting "talked at." They were treating the prerelease coordinator like an elementary school substitute teacher. I thought I might have to fight one of them if they didn't show me the respect I felt I deserved. The coordinator introduced me and an eerie silence fell. Some of the more disruptive guys hung their heads in between making sober eye contact. I could feel the weight of my sentences upon them as they shuddered at the possibility of spending decades in this place. If we aren't mining the stories we have buried, how can we expect to find any semblance of correction?

Through the MPWW readings we were starting to be heard, even if it was only by staff members and fellow inmates. We wanted to broaden the scope. We figured that by building a bridge to Victim Services we might be able to spotlight the possibilities of using creative writing to expand into established programs like Restorative Justice (which had similarly partnered with our long-term offender group). We designed a workshop with MPWW using a restorative justice approach, honoring the perspectives that system refers to as victim, community, and offender. For ten weeks, we explored the ripple effect of our crimes using the craft of different creative writing genres and techniques. One guy personified his victim's father as he was called to identify his only son's body. Another spoke indifferently in a poem about a bullet that had done so much damage. Another man got a second chance to say what he wished he could have said at his trial twenty years earlier.

Works were selected to represent the range of perspectives at the evening reading. The participants sat in a curved row around the podium at the front of a room full of DOC staff members and personally invited inmates. The DOC commissioner was in attendance, along with the head of the DOC's restorative justice program from the central office. The head of Victim Services, our initial guest of honor, did not attend.

I read a piece about my aunt Kathy's continued support since the passing of my mother when I was twelve years old. I was doing fine until I looked up and made eye contact with Deb, our writing matriarch, and saw tears flowing down her face, more in maternal pride than in pity. I lost it as well, barely making it through the crescendo, where I tried to acknowledge that my aunt was still proud of me despite how far I'd fallen. It was the most unexpected experience I'd ever seen: a room of thugs pouring their hearts out, emotions bursting around the room, boxes of tissue passed throughout the rows of a little less than a hundred people. Julie, the Long-Term Offender Group facilitator, participated in the workshop and was the other staff member to join the SWC. She read a short essay about her greatest shame, breaking down the barrier between staff and inmate as a way to hold herself accountable, just as she'd always held us to higher standards. We found a way to quantify remorse through creative writing. It felt like a degree of dignity was restored.

MPWW provided nothing short of an underground MFA program. Through the strength of their growing members and resources, the program expanded beyond our wildest expectations. They began an extensive mentoring program that linked prison writers with working professionals and started an annual internal literary journal for which inmates serve as the editorial board. They hold annual broadside contests, sponsor guest visits by major literary figures, have placed gumball machines dispensing student poetry around the Twin Cities, and host an annual reading of selected student work at Hamline University every fall. An authentic writing community emerged, and the concept of refining one's voice deepened through publishing opportunities across the country.

We were poets, the antithesis of tough guys, thieves, and murderers. With our senses heightened, we found a need to make sense out of our senseless surroundings. We became obsessed with examining the boundaries as cracks in our glass ceilings to cut ourselves upon. It became a movement. We had a responsibility to confront the stigmas, stereotypes, and harsh realities of the forsaken without excuse or absolution. This is what prison reform would look like in an age when the refined inmate perspective is necessary to create a more effective system.

I recall an early workshop when a big, burly bear of a man sat in the hot seat, unable to respond to a class critique as we chopped up his story. The guidelines were great: start positive, use open-ended statements and questions, redirect back to craft, and, most importantly, remember that the critique is about the work, not the writer. There is a responsibility in listening. For the rest of us that day, responsible listening meant presenting an honest reaction while finding something significant to offer the writer. For that writer, responsible listening meant learning how to receive criticism and to take or leave pertinent information in order to make the work better. His face was beet red, and as he squirmed in his seat, sweating defensively, I remember thinking how uncomfortable growth can be. I chuckled under my breath knowing that, as writers, our skins would thicken.

In a culture of violence, any confrontation leads down a dark road. But in the right hands, under correcting circumstances, we learned how to appreciate the perspectives of others for the greater good. Through the craft of writing we figured out how to disassociate the process from personal emotion. Writing was making us better people.

Before I became a writer, I would see a guy and judge his character based on a flimsy facade—his looks or my assumptions about his crime or background. Through characterization, I saw how flat first impressions could be. Everyone is walking a plotline, connected to secondary characters, defined in backstory scenes adding layers of unknown depth. As a writer, I could no longer be so stern toward people. How could I expect any benefit of the doubt from society under the brand of "murderer" when I was quick to categorize and condemn those around me? Writing classes, like literature, should lead to empathy. Writing enabled us to understand that humanity lies within the complexity of experience, coupled with a willingness to break the silences.

These workshops fueled my wonder and broadened my language. There was so much craft to consider everywhere. I watched TV thinking about the cinematography, the writers, the producers, and the choices that the director didn't make. There's always so much more to consider, and asking questions was keeping me engaged beyond anything I'd known before.

Writing as a Revolutionary Act

I think about the cracks in the glass ceiling in specific terms at a precipice of criminal justice reform and feel like I should be fighting harder to be heard. Then I think about my own worst enemy and how I define success from a prison cell, knowing that whatever I do will never be enough to save my brothers destined to die in prison for what they did as stupid kids. I know that whatever I publish or produce will be only a fraction of what's needed to turn the tide. I think about the gatekeepers who have the power to create opportunities for those brought up in adverse conditions, molded by imprisonment, who have put themselves together from shattered lives despite the callous system that only seemed to spend money on punishment when it was too late. I consider how James Baldwin felt knocking on the door of a white world, wondering who was looking through the peephole and what was taking them so long in answering. I think about the political statement it makes when a work is published by a marginalized person. I thought Zeke's debut memoir, *This Is Where I Am* (Caligiuri), was going to win the Minnesota Book Award and make a bold statement that would knock down the doors for all of us incarcerated writers. When it didn't, my despair that the world was not quite ready to make that statement fell crushingly upon me and that glass ceiling was reinforced. I was still grateful for his nomination and figured the door had at least opened, even if the chain was still on.

I can't say literature is an answer to injustice any more than it was an answer to Baldwin's blackness or his sexuality; rather, it is an absolute necessity. Acceptance within the arts is a show of cultural recognition. Inmates around the world are being heard in literary circles, as are the formerly incarcerated. The SWC is playing a part in this war, gaining ground through publications. Yet there is a paradox at play. Becoming the person the system expects weakens you within the environment they have created. I liken it to domesticating an animal and then returning it to the wild, forever changed and alienated. We were empowered by these writing classes that gave us a voice, a presence, and restored humanity, but we are not allowed to address the conditions of our prisons.

I am many symbols. To society, I am the problem. To inmates, I'm one of them, an advocate and (I hope) a role model of uncompromising balance and integrity. To corrections officers, I am the inverse, a manipulator playing a game and waiting for my opportunity to strike. To MPWW professors and support staff members, I am a cipher who can unlock inmates' potential. However, even now, after all I've accomplished, I'm still viewed with skepticism by some education and library workers who are held hostage by security mentalities. I am an amalgamation of all these groups, philosophies, and successful programs, along with the dark experiences of subversive cultures and convict living. No matter what I achieve, while I'm still incarcerated, I'm treated like just another inmate, because that's how corrections is designed.

I'm now in the Rush City facility, a security-minded place that's indifferent to my intentions to influence my community in any positive manner. This education director has iced MPWW out for whatever personal reason he's harboring, which has paradoxically liberated me from communal responsibility. Focused on my individual work, I am steadily building publishing credits with independent momentum thanks to the tools Deb and Jen have gifted me throughout the years. But there is a darkness that still grows inside me every day that I spend in a cell. It's the same darkness present in our political landscape, spiraling back through the Civil War: a darkness that differentiates and separates. It's a darkness parents hide from their kids for as long as they can, the same darkness I see suppressed in the eyes of the guards who lock my door. It's a messy darkness that I didn't know how to deal with before that rippled out of me into a complicated circumstance that hurt so many people and that I am now trying to be accountable for. I went before a judge and was condemned to receive a prison sentence for more years than I had been alive. Through literature and writing, I gained the means to write my own prison sentence, and it's imperative that I be heard.

WORK CITED

Caligiuri, Zeke. *This Is Where I Am.* U of Minnesota P, 2016.

Rethinking the Hero Narrative of Critical Pedagogy: Teaching Creative Writing with and for Women at the County Jail

Molly Dooley Appel and Shannon Frey

"I am a mother of two girls." "I write poetry." "I'm only here for another week." These responses were a few of the statements women in a creative writing class at the county jail shared with us when they introduced themselves. They each chose certain aspects of their lives to represent themselves to us, the teachers and outsiders. None of the participants responded by stating their crimes or their jail sentences; it was clear that they saw themselves as, and wanted us to know them as, people whose lives went beyond the particular classroom context in which we met them.

Identity and representation of identity are central issues to education, influencing how teaching and learning occur and are perceived. In both scholarly and practitioner conversations, the roles of teacher and student are often clearly defined and a person is generally represented as one or the other. These boundaries and their hierarchies tend to be exacerbated within carceral settings. In such settings, the roles of both "expert" and "student" are often driven by hero narratives: narratives that position teachers as heroes and students as individuals overcoming tremendous odds through a transformational yet deeply hierarchical relationship (Newkirk 130–52). Paulo Freire's framework of critical pedagogy provides a prominent critique of such traditional teaching methods and roles and has proven influential for contemporary prison classroom initiatives. The premise of Freire's ideas rests on freedom. However, when it is summarily prescribed as a model for prison classrooms, Freire's ideas can result in a reification of the hero narrative in which the educator assumes the identity of the rescuer and the student is viewed as someone transformed by their rescuer.[1]

This essay addresses the ways in which we developed a feminist pedagogy of human dignity by allowing the women in our creative writing class to pursue an agenda of their choice rather than a prescribed route to freedom. The team-teaching approach we took enabled us to reflect on and evaluate our teaching methods as well as the possibilities and limits of critical pedagogies. When researchers and teachers enter correctional spaces as outsiders, their work is often framed within a heroic view of transformation. However, when the students' insider perspectives are privileged, this heroic view reveals itself to be prescriptive and limiting rather than liberating. In order to facilitate something closer to a liberating space with and for the women of our class, we needed to reject the hero narrative of applied models of critical pedagogy and adopt a pedagogical model grounded in listening. Our work highlights the ubiquity of the hero narrative within correctional educational spaces and encourages us to interrogate the role of the hero narrative in the more traditional educational spaces in which we work.

The Hero of the Humanities Classroom

The sharp distinction between expert and learner is deeply ingrained in education. A prominent example is the Freirean critique of traditional teaching methods and promotion of his model of critical pedagogy. Freire decries the "banking method" of education as a form of suppression in which an educator provides information to the learners without opportunity for discussion or analysis. Ultimately, Freire's hope for educators is that they develop a relationship with learners and guide them through the process of critical thinking, teaching them how to educate themselves and not be forced into perpetual reliance on others to provide ways to think about the world (*Pedagogy of Freedom*, 102–03). Freire assumes that as people increasingly understand the world and their context through engagement in critical dialogue, they learn to read and name the world, and their newfound knowledge will spur them to action, specifically action that leads toward liberation from their oppressors (*Pedagogy of the Oppressed*, 87–89). Although Freire's goal as an educator was liberatory, knowledge generally flowed in his model from the teacher to the students. The teacher had the power to awaken the desire for freedom and a different life for the students. Educators might learn different methods and relevant ways of teaching from those in their class, but the general idea expressed is that they come into class with an awareness of how students' lives can be improved, and that students will experience that benefit, including some personal transformation, if they follow the teachers' expertise.

For many scholars working on jail and prison education, the goal of the educational programs is the transformation of the participants. For example, Irene Baird, a well-known prison educator, described the process of teaching one of her classes, commenting, "[M]arginalized women, using the writing of established female authors of similar race, class and experience, take action on themselves, on their liberation through critical reflection and creative self-expression. Both methods, ultimately, help the learners find a 'voice', shattering what Freire describes as the 'culture of silence' of the oppressed" ("Imprisoned Bodies" 3). While her efforts are laudable and may ultimately benefit the women in her class, the emphasis is on the teacher providing the means for students to have the experience necessary to transform, to find their voice. Baird also notes that the ten weeks she spends in class with her students are not long enough to accommodate the full "liberatory learning process" (6). It seems that the process depends upon expert guidance, a single figure of (heroic) authority, in order to come to fruition. This outlook is evident in many publications about education for incarcerated women (see Baird, "Evolution"; Boudin; Hamilton; Rose).

The imagined pathway to transformation exemplified by Baird reflects a broader reliance on human capital theory as a basis for justifying correctional education efforts. The prevalence of research embracing human capital ideology, which emphasizes skill and knowledge development for the purpose of economic gain, demonstrates the pervasive nature of this philosophy within adult education. Human capital theory claims that "more educated workers will always be more productive than their less educated counterparts" (Baptiste 189). The emphasis on using education to change criminal behavior, reduce recidivism, and support an individual's integration into mainstream society reflects the values espoused by human capital theorists. In reality, no standardized methods exist for molding people, including incarcerated students, into model citizens, but many scholars and educators seem to seek a path to realizing this goal (Druine and Wildemeersch). The concept of transformation is prominent in adult education literature, including education in prisons and jails. The stated goal in numerous prison education articles is for the educational programs to reduce recidivism (see Esperian; Jacobi; Rose; Torre and Fine). Classes are valued for their potential usefulness to society, and the general view of successful education for incarcerated women is that it should benefit all society, not only the women in the class.

Within this utilitarian framework, the "expertise" of the teacher goes beyond knowledge-based benchmarks of productive citizenship to the very capacity to identify populations as "at risk." This power takes on troubling connotations when understood in terms of Newkirk's description of the heroic narrative in education: the hero becomes the one who decides who is in need of their heroism. These narratives usually follow a pattern in which someone is mislabeled or misunderstood, a teacher realizes and addresses the problem, the student responds to the teacher's kindness and changes, others see the difference, and no one involved is ever the same again (Newkirk 140). The representation of the teacher or expert as the rescuer of their hapless students has been circulated in American society through popular culture, including films such as *The Miracle Worker* (1962), *Stand and Deliver* (1988), and *Dangerous Minds* (1995). These narratives, which Newkirk describes as iterations of the "archetypal American story," emphasize that without the teacher, the learners could never have accomplished their achievements; thus, their victories are the triumph of the heroic pedagogue (Newkirk 142). Following this predictable narrative pattern places the audience in the position of the expert, able to correctly speculate about what comes next, and affirms their shared identity as someone outside the sphere of need expressed in the narrative. The familiarity of these narratives causes prime audiences—including academics—to more readily accept stories of education that conform to these themes. Thus, not only does the hero narrative establish the very educational dynamic it seeks to solve, it obliges scholars and educators to conform to its patterns in order for their work to be recognizable as transformative education.

Transforming the Narrative of Transformation

When Shannon first spearheaded the class in the county jail, she and her first co-teacher envisioned the class as an opportunity to provide basic literacy skills for incarcerated women, including reading, writing, parenting, and other topics of interest to women joining the class. However, when they asked the class what they were interested in learning, to their surprise, everyone wanted to learn about creative writing. They were further surprised when their assumptions about a basic literacy skills class did not conform to the class needs. Everyone had obtained at least a GED diploma, most had finished high school, and some had completed college courses or degrees. When Molly joined Shannon as her co-teacher, the class had evolved to focus on creative writing.

In co-teaching the class, we realized that we had come with many assumptions about our students, most of them based on publications we had read about prison and jail populations. None of the women in our class needed basic literacy skills, but they still wanted to come to class and learn something, even if their chosen topic was not in our original plan. Creative writing was not a subject that either of us had experience teaching or doing, and it was also clear that some of the class members had more knowledge and experience about certain aspects of creative writing than we did. As we continued to share the class space and material with our students, the role of teacher became further complicated: though we were recognized as subject "authorities" in this space based on our levels of education and our positions as outsiders, it was clear that everyone in the class knew more about the jail system than we did.

Over the course of our class, we had to acknowledge and jettison the hero narrative of critical pedagogy that we had inadvertently brought to our writers. The women involved in the creative writing class had not necessarily come to class to learn critical thinking in a Freirian way or even to seek solutions to their problems. They had other classes that focused on this, and many of them had heard the same information innumerable times. Based on the women's accounts, other programming available to them seemed to follow a more typical narrative, advocating for participant change as participants realized their power over their own decisions. These programs are undoubtedly well-intentioned and may have been helpful to many people, but they stood in contrast to the environment the women seemed to want for their creative writing class: one in which they were free to assert and express their own competence within their present, incarcerated conditions.

Although the class included many creative writing activities, it crucially became a space where the participants could escape some of the pressure to change. We worked to create a place where the women could simply be their human selves and find a respite from the jail's emphasis on becoming someone different. For example, attendance was entirely voluntary, and consequently the class participants varied from week to week, although a core group of students consistently attended. When selecting materials for the class, we often purposely avoided subjects that might raise unwanted memories of abuse or hardship. One class session was centered on watching fifteen minutes of a movie every week, then participating in a writing activity based on the movie and exploring supplemental related information.[2] Other lessons included reading articles from *The Onion* and then writing our own satirical headlines, writing a scene with a major plot twist after reading an O. Henry story, and writing haiku and other poetry. If, during the class, participants wanted to reflect on their past or to discuss how they wanted to change their lives, we supported their decision to do so. If they wanted to invent a lewd or comical story that flew in the face of traditional moral values and make us all laugh, we encouraged this as well.

We also provided dialogue journals in which participants could write anything they chose throughout the week (e.g., responding to a writing prompt, journaling about life, writing about their past, or creating their own stories or poems). They gave us their journals at the beginning of class, and we provided written feedback at the end of class based on their preferences, which meant anything from offering our recommendations for their continued writing to responding to their personal stories in ways that validated their humanity. The students did not always choose to write in the journals, and we never required it. It was clear that the students' main purpose in coming was not to become better writers, as some of them consistently attended class but seldom wrote in their journals between classes. They seemed to enjoy having a weekly opportunity to laugh and joke and make up funny stories without fear of being ridiculed or censored.

Who is the hero in this narrative? If the hero is the problem-solver, one who causes others to transform, then a hero was absent from our class. The class participants' lives were full of complications both in and out of jail, and hearing their stories raises many questions about the ways jails are organized and the broader system of incarceration. These issues are massive and certainly not solvable by any one person. The students do not leave class with their problems solved, nor do they seem to expect that outcome. Creating a small space in which the participants had some say in what they did for one hour inside their highly regimented environment allowed for some moments of freedom and pleasure in their lives. In this space, we did not ask them to change their identity or become something different from who they were. They could acknowledge or hide their identities as they wished and to any extent that was helpful for them. If a student found enjoyment in communicating her identity as a mother, we welcomed her conversation and writings about her children. If she found such associations painful or distressing, then she was free to choose to focus on another aspect of her life or to invent an imaginary story far from her reality. In the space of the classroom, she was free to have any identity that brought her the pleasure that was the most helpful for her life.

Few published research studies related to writing programs and incarcerated women allow their research participants simply to be. Like the hero narrative that has the capacity to code others as "in need of heroism," such studies code their participants through an identity marked, a priori, as "criminal"; the goal of such studies, in turn, is for the women to be transformed into "not criminal." Tobi Jacobi sums up this position, although she does not endorse it, stating that "[w]riting workshops can provide incarcerated writers with motivation to improve literacy skills and self-confidence through creative expression and participation in a community of women that moves beyond crime as identity" (Jacobi 55). This perception of women as moving between the categories of criminal and not criminal ignores the women's humanity, which is far more complex than their criminal record. The women we knew were mothers, girlfriends, nurses, poets, wives, caretakers, artists . . . the list goes on, and these aspects of their lives are thickly and deeply layered. Such approaches to the incarcerated classroom flatten a person's identity into "drug addict" or "thief" in order to remove that very label through a transformative hero narrative. Most troublingly, they suggest that incarcerated women require fundamental change without seeing who they fundamentally are.

If the notion of transformation is associated with positive change, one must ask whose point of view determines it to be positive.[3] Returning to Freire's ideas, critical consciousness-raising is considered to be an unequivocally helpful turn of events for those who become aware. However, there were several situations in which raising consciousness would not have benefited our class participants. At one point during the class, the students related an incident that had occurred in their cellblock and that seemed unjust to them. Our first response as teachers was to wonder if we could assist in writing a petition to the jail warden regarding the situation. However, the students quickly explained that any protests on their part, even if formally expressed, could result in their punishment, including possible time in isolation. We have no way of knowing how accurate their perceptions were, but what mattered was that they felt powerless in the situation. Raising consciousness might end in greater restrictions instead of greater freedom, especially in the extremely rigid jail environment. For these women, becoming more aware merely emphasized their lack of power without providing an avenue for action.

A final example highlights the way in which critical pedagogy itself can become a hero narrative rather than pathway to self-realization. When a teacher centralizes consciousness-raising, rather than centralizing dialogue within and among students, they are illustrating what Freire himself called the "narration sickness" of a banking model of education. Freire writes:

> A careful analysis of the teacher-student relationship at any level, inside or outside the school, reveals its fundamentally *narrative* character. This relationship involves a narrating subject (the teacher) and patient, listening objects (the students). The contents, whether values or empirical dimensions of reality, tend in the process of being narrated to become lifeless and petrified. Education is suffering from narration sickness. (*Pedagogy of the Oppressed* 71)

The phrase "Education is suffering from narration sickness" introduces a connection between narrative form and the vertical hierarchy of liberal societal values seen in human capital theory: the desired qualities of educability, of learning, come down to a student's ability and willingness to receive that narrative as a "banking deposit." Irrespective of whether or not such a pedagogy is actually effective in achieving its intention, Freire's analogy stages the harm produced by an education that is built on instrumentalization without recognition and the harm of the transformational hero narrative in correctional spaces.

Listening as an Act of Teaching

The reality is that, as educators, our control over someone else's life is largely imaginary; the only guaranteed transformation is to be found within ourselves. Considering the idea of education as a transforming agent, Beth Daniell comments that "the only change pedagogy can promise [is] . . . the transformation of the teacher" (183). There is no guarantee that educators' efforts can or should change the students, but in the process, the teacher may become different in response to the situation. Indeed, as we have worked with women at the jail, we have been profoundly changed. Much of the difference has come from listening, especially from listening to people whose voices we had never heard before. As Daniell indicates, listening made the distance between us, as the instructors, and our students much smaller: "If we don't listen, the gaps get larger. If we don't listen, we don't have to grapple with the issue. We don't have to look at our own role. We don't have to decide, consciously and self-consciously" (182).

The fundamental practice of listening actually returns us to the original notion within Freire's practice of critical pedagogy. In the Portuguese text, when Freire discusses the fundamentally narrative character of education, he clearly links it to narrative that is made by a monological speaker: "Quanto mais analisamos as relações educador-educandos na escola, em qualquer de seus níveis (ou fora dela), parece que mais nos podemos convencer de que essas relações apresentam um caráter especial e marcante—o de serem relações fundamentalmente narradoras, dissertadoras" ("A careful analysis of the teacher-student relationship at any level, inside or outside the school, reveals its fundamentally narrative character"; *Pedagogia* 79; *Pedagogy of the Oppressed* 71).[4] Further, his assertion that "education is suffering from narration sickness" is followed in the Portuguese with an antidote for this banking sickness, not included in the translation published as *Pedagogy of the Oppressed*: "A tônica da educação é preponderantemente esta—narrar, sempre narrar" ("the antidote to this education is preponderantly to narrate—always to narrate"; *Pedagogia* 79; our trans.). If we situate this antidote within Freire's commitment to learning as dialogue, we see that for Freire, it is possible for narration to be both the sickness (as monologue) and the antidote (as dialogue). This linkage helps us better understand how an educational space of storytelling, seen dialogically, can represent an alternative form of pedagogy that has the potential to interrupt the instrumentalization of a hero narrative.

Because the hero narrative has a distinctly patriarchal undertone, it has been all the more urgent that we rethink our own identities as educators in a prison space for women. Feminist scholars and writers have defined powerful frameworks for creating educational-creative spaces that are pleasurable and transformational through the validation of lived experience and identity. These frameworks creating a feminist space of dignity are founded on polyphony (versus a monologic hero narrative) and on listening.

For instance, Gloria Anzaldúa's notions of writing and identity formation in the transformative space of *nepantla*, defined below, articulate a way for teachers to rethink the role of "expert" and orient learning as "coming to know the other / not coming to take her" (*Interviews* 45). Anzaldúa's processes of identity formation envision emotional and intellectual "wounds"—such as the experience of being in jail—as something that enables "a tolerance for contradictions, a tolerance for ambiguity" (*Borderlands* 101). In other words, trauma does not have to be coded as a problem to be "fixed" by an external force—as it is in a hero narrative—but is rather a crucially generative moment for consciousness building. In her characteristic mixture of Spanish, English, and Nahuatl, Anzaldúa writes that

> [e]ste choque [a violently disruptive event] shifts us to nepantla, a psychological, liminal space between the way things had been and an unknown future. Nepantla is the space in-between, the locus and sign of transition. In nepantla we realize that realities clash, authority figures of the various groups demand contradictory commitments, and we and others have failed living up to idealized goals. (*Light in the Dark* 17)

How might teachers help establish and sustain an educational space that acknowledges, and even celebrates, contradictions, failures, and transitions? This form of consciousness-raising cannot be developed by teachers taking on the role of expert. Rather, it suggests that in order to detach ourselves from hero narratives of the jail writing classroom, we need to foreground listening.

Listening as a pedagogical practice can be understood through Kelly Oliver's evocative notion of witnessing as response-ability and address-ability. Oliver argues that "[o]nly a response that opens rather than closes the possibility of response is a responsible response" (108). Similarly, Anzaldúa observes that "[t]he ability to respond is what is meant by responsibility" (*Borderlands* 42). In other words, scholars and educators in correctional spaces must, above all, remain "self-vigilant" in listening to and for silences and absent voices "in which we are implicated and through which we are responsible to each other" (Oliver 133).

Finding a Voice in the Correctional Classroom

Transformation of one's consciousness or skills, particularly in a setting of incarceration, is often hailed as a political act. This notion of political action, which permeates jail settings, is put into practice through a predominantly masculine hero narrative that neatly divides the roles of "expert" and "learners." In this way, it ultimately supports the model of identity (that of being a productive citizen) sought by human capital theory. Yet if a woman is constantly battered by pressure to undergo such a transformation, is not her assertion of her own value and efficacy a political act? In order for a moment of empowerment to garner political recognition, must it be oriented away from the experiences of the present? We maintain that, to the extent that our creative writing class created an opportunity for these women to affirm and express their own competence, it fostered a feminist political community. As the educator Cathy Davidson wrote in an online discussion on student-centered learning, "By finding a voice, one does not need to be told to question power. By feeling empowered, one begins to question power." Our writers corrected their own correctional setting by asserting a safe space in which to be their layered, complex selves, insofar as the course was ultimately sanctioned by the jail authorities.

At the same time, we also remain wary of asserting our own hero narrative. We are keenly aware that we have excluded details and unintentionally omitted important elements in the interest of maintaining the present scope of this essay. More important, we recognize a danger in memorializing the women of our class, of assigning them an identity and a role in our narrative, by writing about them in a fixed manner or by writing as if the situations we describe are static. The identities of both educators and learners in the situations we have described are fluid and do not belong neatly in one category. We continue to grapple with the complications and confusions associated with our class at the jail and are learning to approach our work without a packaged conclusion that we can tidily present to our readers as a familiar and validating trophy. Doing so would troublingly echo the ways in which the transformational hero narrative of critical pedagogy ultimately negates the consciousness, and the modes of transformation, that incarcerated learners already embody.

Nevertheless, we believe that our experiences have broader implications for all academics. They invite us to reflect on how our institutions of education, including our norms related to scholarship, enact pedagogical objectification by conforming, even inadvertently, to the tropes of a hero narrative. How do we prescribe learning identities to our students in the spaces of our instruction that place us in the position of rescuer? Our class revealed that whenever we either objectified or validated these women's lived identities as learner-experts, we were, in turn, objectifying or validating ourselves.

NOTES

1. See, for example, Castro and Brawn on the complications of Freirian student-teacher relationships within the constraints of carceral settings.

2. For example, one session involved watching *Mighty Macs* (2011), a film about a women's college basketball team in the 1970s. We also discussed the implementation of Title IX.

3. Contesting the idea of transformation as unequivocally positive, Beth Daniell states, "*Transformation* is typically a God-term, indicating a change the speaker approves of. More negative terms—degradation, erosion, brainwashing—are used for changes the speaker disapproves of" (177).

4. Our analysis of the Portuguese line focuses on Freire's separate emphasis of the term *dissertadoras*, whose connotations include "lecturing" and "speaking" specifically.

WORKS CITED

Anzaldúa, Gloria. *Borderlands / La Frontera: The New Mestiza.* 4th ed., Aunt Lute Books, 2012.

———. *Interviews/Entrevistas.* Edited by AnaLouise Keating, Psychology Press, 2000.

———. *Light in the Dark / Luz en lo Oscuro: Rewriting Identity, Spirituality, Reality.* Edited by AnaLouise Keating, Duke UP, 2015.

Baird, Irene. "Evolution of Activists: Prison Women's Writings as Change Agent for Their Communities." *2001 Conference Proceedings*, New Prairie Press, 2001, newprairiepress.org/aerc/2001/.

———. "Imprisoned Bodies—Free Minds: Incarcerated Women and Liberatory Learning." *1997 Conference Proceedings*, New Prairie Press, 1997, newprairiepress.org/aerc/1997/.

Baptiste, Ian. "Educating Lone Wolves: Pedagogical Implications of Human Capital Theory." *Adult Education Quarterly*, vol. 51, no. 3, May 2001, p. 184.

Boudin, Kathy. "Critical Thinking in a Basic Literacy Program: A Problem-Solving Model in Corrections Education." *Journal of Correctional Education*, vol. 46, no. 4, 1995, pp. 141–45.

Castro, Erin L., and Michael Brawn. "Critiquing Critical Pedagogies inside the Prison Classroom: A Dialogue between Student and Teacher." *Harvard Educational Review*, vol. 87, no. 1, 2017, pp. 99–121.

Daniell, Beth. "A Pedagogy of Listening: A Response to Kristie Fleckenstein." *Journal of Advanced Composition*, vol. 22, no. 1, Jan. 2002, pp. 176–84.

Davidson, Cathy. "By Feeling Empowered, One Empowers Others." Comment in "Peer Mentoring and Student-Centered Learning Discussion," *HASTAC*, 21 Sept. 2015, www.hastac.org/initiatives/hastac-scholars/scholars-forums/peer-mentoring-and-student-centered-learning-discussion.

Druine, Nathalie, and Danny Wildemeersch. "The Vocational Turn in Adult Literacy Education and the Impact of the International Adult Literacy Survey." *International Review of Education*, vol. 46, no. 5, Sept. 2000, pp. 391–405.

Esperian, John H. "The Effect of Prison Education Programs on Recidivism." *Journal of Correctional Education*, vol. 61, no. 4, 2010, pp. 316–34.

Freire, Paulo. *Pedagogia do Oprimido*. Paz e Terra, 2011.

———. *Pedagogy of Freedom: Ethics, Democracy, and Civic Courage*. Translated by Patrick Clarke, Rowman and Littlefield, 1998.

———. *Pedagogy of the Oppressed*. Translated by Myra Bergman Ramos, 6th ed., Continuum, 1970.

Hamilton, Kendra. "Education behind Bars: Marymount Manhattan College Teams with Volunteers to Keep College Hopes Alive for Incarcerated Women." *Black Issues in Higher Education*, vol. 22, no. 1, Feb. 2005, pp. 30–34.

Jacobi, Tobi. "Writing Workshops as Alternative Literacy Education for Incarcerated Women." *Corrections Today*, vol. 71, no. 1, 2009, pp. 52–53.

Newkirk, Thomas. "The Narrative Roots of the Case Study." *Methods and Methodology in Composition Research*, Southern Illinois UP, 1992, pp. 130–52.

Oliver, Kelly. *Witnessing: Beyond Recognition*. U of Minnesota P, 2001.

Rose, Chris. "Women's Participation in Prison Education: What We Know and What We Don't Know." *Journal of Correctional Education*, vol. 55, no. 1, 2004, pp. 78–100.

Torre, María Elena, and Michelle Fine. "Bar None: Extending Affirmative Action to Higher Education in Prison." *Journal of Social Issues*, vol. 61, Aug. 2005, pp. 569–94.

Spanish Co-instruction in Prison: A Dialogue on Language, Identity, and Pedagogy

Paméla Cappas-Toro, Antonio Rosa, and Ken Smith

This essay is the result of a three-year-long process of collaborative instruction at the Community Education Project (CEP), Stetson University's higher-education-in-prison (HEP) program, located at the Tomoka Correctional Institution (CI) in Daytona, Florida. As incarcerated and nonincarcerated teachers and researchers of second language acquisition, our subjectivities within the prison and the power dynamics embedded inside and beyond these walls have resulted in confrontation with the various institutional barriers that have challenged our teaching and learning experiences since we first began offering Spanish classes at Tomoka CI in 2016. Given the distinct vantage points from which we teach, think, and write about the purpose and value of Spanish language instruction in carceral spaces, we present this essay as a dialogue between the three of us as co-instructors. This format best allows our readers to engage in our collective classroom experiences while still permitting each writer to voice their distinct relationships to institutional power, privilege, and knowledge. Moreover, because we recognize that identities are "relational and contingent rather than permanently fixed," we do not wish to obscure the challenges and the uneven processes of becoming language teachers in prison (Giles and Middleton 36).

We are convinced that incarcerated students', educators', and researchers' voices are crucial for second language acquisition and for scholarship in the emerging HEP field. We view the dynamics of the carceral language classroom as a "product of a long history of political struggle and oppression that made the emergence of particular language practices possible" (Flores and Rosa 148). Therefore, we hope that this dialogue is the beginning of an overdue conversation about how linguistic segregation in prisons impacts educators, both incarcerated and otherwise, and that it suggests a model, though an imperfect one to be sure, that centers and respects the knowledge and skills of incarcerated people to create language learning spaces on the inside.

Background

Paméla

When I started at Tomoka CI, I had three years of experience designing and implementing an English as a Second Language (ESL) program with the Education Justice Project at the University of Illinois, where I trained incarcerated students to become ESL instructors. The prison we teach in now is very different from the one where I previously taught in Illinois. Perhaps most notably, there is no community college at Tomoka CI, and in fact, there is only one community college in the entire state offering college credits through the Second Chance Pell Program. All the college-in-prison programming at Tomoka CI is a result of our collective work building CEP together. In Florida, I have relied on the experience and knowledge of incarcerated students to determine how to approach language instruction. I'm interested in knowing what made you both decide to teach Spanish with me.

Ken

Correctional education adheres to deficit models that concentrate on what's wrong or missing in inmates. In this way, it is similar to a colonizer that "sees the world and its problems, classifies people, and projects into what is good for them" (Mignolo 2). For an incarcerated student seeking to obtain their GED, the only courses available in preparation are English and math. All other topics are considered nonessential and are left out of the curriculum. Education in carceral spaces becomes a site for normalizing a discourse where incarcerated people are considered inherently deficient and therefore undeserving of widening their scope of education. Additionally, individuals with a life sentence, or a term of years that is a de facto life sentence, are often denied the ability to pursue a high school diploma.

Correctional institutions' discursive practices construct subject positions that attach to an incarcerated person's identity. Such discourses seek to produce "docile bodies" that can be "subjected, used, transformed and improved" by categorizing and naming them (Foucault 136). Incarcerated instructors that teach in correctional educational departments in Florida are labeled Inmate Teaching Assistants (ITAs) by the institution. This marker implies that there is a nonincarcerated teacher in a position of power who is assisted by an ITA. While there is a nonincarcerated person in an administrative position, in actuality, the instruction of students and all the responsibilities incumbent on the station fall upon the ITA. Chris Barker and Emma A. Jane state that "[l]anguage is the means and medium through which we form knowledge about ourselves and the social world" (85). Assigning a label—such as ITA—makes it impossible for the incarcerated instructor to see themselves fully as a teacher. Co-teaching Spanish seemed a way to directly address the deficiencies in the corrections education model.

Antonio

I see service to the non-English-speaking community inside these fences as the greatest justification for teaching Spanish. This view comes from my experience as a certified law clerk at a prison law library where, prior to my being hired, the legal needs of this community were completely ignored. There was nobody in the federally mandated prison law library capable of helping non-English-speaking users read correspondence from their public defenders, file administrative and judicial appeals, answer divorce or child custody pleadings, or understand deportation proceedings and possible defenses. The absence of Spanish-speaking law clerks stemmed partly from statewide policy disqualifying most Latinos from working in law libraries because of confirmed or suspected membership in gangs, officially known as security threat groups (Sanchez 1675).[1] For the incarcerated Latino population, this a social justice issue regarding access to the institutions that directly impact their lives.

My work as a certified law clerk and Spanish teacher has convinced me that the teaching of Spanish inside Florida prisons can help provide the Latino population better access to powerful institutions, like courts (state, federal, and immigration), and departments within the prison (medical, dental, mental health, classification, and property), from which they are excluded by the language barrier. The classroom can be constructively utilized for language acquisition while the rest of the prison serves as a site for "conversing with real people in real situations in the target language" (Carney 231). Being of service to the non-English-speaking community benefits Spanish learners by giving them the social capital necessary for meaningful interactions (Swain and Deters 282). Not understanding Spanish serves as a symbolic marker of difference that is removed when nonnative Spanish speakers learn the language to improve the lived experiences of this marginalized community (Ebacher 398; Olinger et al. 80). The interaction with native Spanish speakers outside the classroom provides opportunities to further the learning of Spanish beyond what is taught in a textbook (Carney 231) and to "(re)construct" identities (Swain and Deters 824). As such, second language acquisition serves as a way for learners to reconstitute themselves as more than simply prisoners but as members of a community. Identities formed through entering a new language community have the potential to make life in prison more meaningful and productive.

Positionalities

Paméla

When I first approached you both about teaching Spanish, I imagined that transitioning into that role would present challenges for you. I acknowledge we have had different experiences being recognized as instructors. When I enter the prison, it is only for a few hours at a time. I am a Puerto Rican woman with a PhD and institutional affiliation through a university that is highly regarded in our community. I have felt respected by incarcerated students as an expert figure as a Spanish professor, even when they may not have appreciated a particular lesson plan or pedagogical choice. Our positionalities in carceral classroom spaces produce unique responses, challenges, and transformations—both positive and negative—for ourselves as well as for our students. Could you explain your process of becoming a co-teacher in the prison?

Ken

At first, I felt hesitant to teach, since I was aware of the social structure of a prison and the ways perceptions of power can affect relationships between groups. In prison, it's easy to be stigmatized as the "police" or a "snitch" when one assumes a role that can be perceived as authoritative (Drew et al. 33). This was a real worry for me because I am a white, nonnative speaker who is not fully fluent in the Spanish language, so the reason I am a co-teacher could be unclear to the other students. My acceptance of the role was based on two reasons: first, you and the professors of CEP had, in previous classes, implemented practices in which teachers and students acted as a collaborative learning community. This atmosphere made my transition from student to instructor less conspicuous, since most learners were accustomed to their knowledge being valued. Second, the sense of personal worth and pride that was created in me when you showed that you had enough confidence in me as a person to carry out that type of responsibility demanded that I act.

Even still, during our first classes, I did not identify as a language teacher. I felt like a teacher in name only. That specific designation was placed upon me by my peers more than it came from the inside. Being addressed by you as co-teacher caused the students to do likewise, which made me see myself in a new light. Dennis J. Sumara and Rebecca Luce-Kapler spoke of this effect, arguing that "[a] sense of personal identity cannot be subtracted from a sense of communal identity; the sense of self alters as social relations and situations change" (69). That moment of self-identifying as a teacher came when you, as the result of a clerical error in the prison, could not attend class for two weeks and Antonio and I were left to teach the classes without the support your presence gave. Your confidence in us to continue the class without you was, for me, the defining moment in which I first adopted that identity. Of the challenges we faced at that point, understanding the goals you set for each class was the most difficult, considering the fact that communication from you during this time was accomplished through sticky notes passed to us by other CEP professors.

Antonio

Over the course of three summer Spanish language workshops, my sense of feeling like a teacher progressed in direct relation to my increasing classroom participation and professionalization as a teacher. In the 2016 workshop, my role was that of a tutor with limited responsibilities. On account of my native fluency in Spanish, my role was to serve as a resource to individuals needing help with pronunciation or completion of exercises. Sometimes, I would role-play Spanish conversations with you so that students could hear the language. Since I was not a teacher, I was not required to create lesson plans or present material to the class. This limited role in the classroom did not allow me to feel like a teacher. Yet acting as a tutor still demanded that I respect personal boundaries and observe other norms of prison culture.

When my classroom role expanded to co-teacher in the 2017 workshop, I began to feel like an instructor because of my newly acquired responsibilities: preparing lessons and presenting course material before the entire class. You socialized me into the classroom by telling the students that I would be a teacher and by treating me as one in front of them (Block 865). But although I was considered a teacher by my co-teachers and students, and even performed as such by preparing and presenting lessons, I did not always feel like one because of my lack of pedagogical training and "teaching manner" (Sumara and Luce-Kepler 80). The wide range of teaching techniques you used made me more conscious of my limited abilities. While I explained points of grammar in ways that you and Ken did not, my teaching sessions were often bogged down by requests for further explanation. I would feel relief when my sessions were over. When I did feel like a teacher, it was often in the classroom and not when lesson-planning in the dormitory.[2] My ambivalence about being a teacher inside and outside the classroom is consistent with Emily K. Asencio and Peter J. Burke's discussion of how "reflected appraisals" are internalized when they differ from one's self-view (177).[3] Since my limited teaching ability did not allow me to see myself as a teacher, I could not internalize my peers' "reflected appraisal" that I was, in fact, a teacher.

Following the 2017 workshop, I worked to redress my lack of pedagogical training by studying your loaned copy of James Lee and Bill VanPatten's *Making Communicative Language Teaching Happen* and reading several articles on second language acquisition (SLA) theory. When the 2018 workshop came around, I felt a confidence that was lacking in previous workshops. The SLA theory and communicative language teaching methodologies at my disposal enriched my observation sessions, enabling me to identify the pedagogical tools that you and Ken used in your instruction. I then wielded a variety of teaching techniques like Total Physical Response (TPR), conversation, information-based tasks, and auditory exercises.[4] This knowledge gave me the sense that I had somehow crossed some threshold, that I was now an insider (Benedict 231).

Environment

Paméla

I knew there would be pedagogical changes in how I approach teaching in the prison classroom. We lacked material resources, and in the beginning we didn't even have a classroom, let alone a language lab, online platforms, or Spanish language tutors to help students further their language acquisition outside the classroom. While I recognized that the culture of the prison would not permit me to assign students to practice Spanish with native speakers on the compound, what I did not anticipate is that Antonio would face pushback in becoming a Spanish teacher from other Latinos in the prison. Would you mind discussing the resistance you faced?

Antonio

Teaching Spanish to non-Latinos within the prison led to some pushback from a native Spanish speaker in my dormitory. He was opposed to having the language taught to those he considered "outsiders." For him, Spanish use served as both a symbolic marker of difference and a means of resisting unwanted surveillance of his private conversations by prison staff and other prisoners.[5] I was inadvertently undermining his resistance by inviting others into our linguistic community. One participatory goal of SLA argues that "developing the ability to communicate through the language" is part of the process of becoming a "member of a community" (Swain and Deters 823). Although knowledge of Spanish does not necessarily grant entry into the Latino community in prison, it does remove a major obstacle to legitimate peripheral participation within the Spanish-speaking community (Swain and Deters 824).

While having a third party listen in on a conversation may seem innocent or trivial in noncarceral contexts, prison surveillance and punishment of private speech gives rise to prison culture's preoccupation with "informers" (Kilgore 60). The Florida Administrative Code constrains conversational practices by outlining at least eleven rules of prohibited conduct dealing with speech. Spanish-speaking prisoners find a measure of privacy and safety in outsider ignorance of Spanish. Prison staff will often disrupt conversations in Spanish with an order to use English; refusal to comply is processed as "disobeying a verbal order" (Florida).[6] The use of Spanish or code-switching therefore serves as a form of resistance to surveillance in that it reclaims a space for conversational privacy that this environment is designed to deny. It is for this reason that some Spanish speakers feel strongly against teaching monolingual Anglophones how to speak Spanish. I answered criticism about teaching Spanish by diverting attention from myself to the institution offering the Spanish language workshop. The point was that CEP students would learn Spanish whether I taught them or not.

Analysis

Paméla

Teaching in the prison is distinct from teaching on the main campus because of the many restrictions we face. Erin Castro and Michael Brawn explain that "[t]he process of intellectual collaboration can be frustrating because there never seems to be enough time to think and process together, exchange ideas, and productively trouble the politics [and access] of information" (115–16). I often felt rushed in our efforts to communicate, especially given the obligations of instructors to be cognizant of many issues that do not cross our minds on our main campus, most notably security regulations that we must follow. Even given these limitations, do you feel as if we were able to create a collaborative co-teaching model?

Antonio

I would say that our collaboration has been unevenly successful. As far as co-instruction and co-observation, the 2018 workshop was a huge success when compared to 2017. However, we were still unable to meet for syllabus construction, lesson-planning, and reflection following the classes. This inability to meet forced you to construct the curriculum on your own and apportion to each of us material to cover. Our agency was limited to determining how we would cover our respective portions of the day's lesson. Our co-teaching efforts can be more properly described as a division of labor rather than a collaborative project where the ideas of each were taken into account in the construction of the course.

The biggest obstacle to collaboration and my personal development as a Spanish teacher has to be the lack of opportunities for formalized pedagogical training. Ken and I were unable to meet with you for training purposes because of your responsibilities at Stetson and our program's inability to obtain approval for resource room hours. We had to work within the already approved evening classroom hours, which were twice a week from 6:00 to 9:00 p.m. I therefore co-taught the 2017 Spanish workshop without any second language acquisition preparation. I read Lee and VanPatten's *Making Communicative Language Teaching Happen* outside the classroom but did not have the opportunity to discuss any of the material with you. In the six months leading up to the 2018 workshop, I studied and became familiar with some of the theories and teaching methods highlighted in the work. However, up to that moment, I did not have the opportunity to implement any of these lessons learned into practical language exercises.

Insights

Paméla

As you know, there were numerous institutional challenges we faced in becoming a credit-bearing program in a part of the country with very few college-in-prison projects and at an institution that had not historically offered incarcerated people these educational opportunities. We also faced unexpected barriers such as the organization that refused to recognize you two as coauthors for a conference paper we wrote together because of your inability to pay a $250 registration fee. Given the many challenges you have faced as educators and researchers, why have you decided to continue teaching and writing about language instruction?

Antonio

I believe that my positionality as a former traditional college student, prisoner, teacher, and researcher gives me a unique view on the intersections of prison culture and higher education in prison (Scott 27). Any HEP program must balance two different and often contradictory cultures, the outside culture—including the university and wider society—and the inside prison culture (Wright 31). In 2005, Randall Wright described the carceral classroom as a sort of borderland where "teachers experience the collision of cultures and the deeply embedded assumptions in them" (36–37). This collision is not exclusive to professors teaching inside the prison. I experienced the same conflict when I had to negotiate the prisoner and teacher identities while co-teaching the Spanish workshop.

As a stakeholder in the nascent literature on HEP, I have the potential to provide perspectives obscured or overlooked by administrators concerned with presenting their prisons in the best light and professors who unwittingly "perpetuate societal beliefs about who deserves quality educational opportunities and who does not" (Castro and Gould 3). Angel E. Sanchez, a former prisoner in Florida and current law student, agrees when he writes, "[C]ontributions by those directly impacted safeguard the body of knowledge from what Professor Alan Freeman calls the 'perpetrator perspective' and from the paternalistic we-know-best attitude described in Professor Derrick Bell's writings" (1654). Knowledge creation by prisoners remedies the "epistemic silences" of a devalued population (Mignolo 4). Finally, knowledge produced by researchers in my position can help challenge "the discursive practices which shape . . . the world of learning in the classroom" (Grundy 39).

Collaborative research is a valuable tool for identity construction, alternative use of carceral spaces, and knowledge production. My involvement as a co-teacher has allowed me to become a researcher of SLA theory within these spaces (Benedict 234). These experiences have been shared at various academic conferences. My research has transformed my bunk from a place where I sleep and the state confirms that I am still in its custody to a space where I read and write academic papers. Remarkably, a place intended for my warehousing and "doing time" is used to enter into academic discourses on SLA theory and teaching languages in carceral spaces. When I am critically engaging with research articles or writing my own papers, I do not feel like a warehoused prisoner but like a researcher with valuable knowledge to contribute to scholarly discourses (Benedict 231).

Ken

When CEP professors recognized me as a co-teacher in a beginning Spanish class, and I eventually adopted this identity myself, I felt a sense of self-worth that was not present before. Teaching allowed me to participate, through the education process, in other people's lives. This helped me shatter a cultural myth that I was fully invested in: that an incarcerated individual cannot be productive. Further, this experience was transformative not only for me but also for other students as they became involved in the collaborative effort as well, supporting the idea that the "restorative quality of prison education is magnified when students learn through peer instruction, as they witness fellow prisoners entrusted by an outside academic institution to become educators" (Drew et al. 32).

Looking at a range of HEP programs' publicized goals, Alexandra Cavallaro found that the majority of these programs emphasized their ability to lower recidivism, save taxpayers money, and rehabilitate students through education (7). The spirit of these types of restrictive policies is expressed by many HEP programs. As Castro explains, "When the purpose of higher education in prison contexts are anchored in a rationale of recidivism, a vision for the educative possibilities within carceral spaces can become constrained" (Castro et al. 16). Programs that fail to see incarcerated students in the same light as nonincarcerated students, as people with dreams and a multiplicity of expectations that can be fulfilled through education, are following the model practiced by the correctional educational department. Not all HEP programs adhere to such restrictive models, however; some instead seek to offer an education that is inclusive as well as liberating.

Moreover, Castro and Mary Gould argue that positioning CIP in this fashion is problematic, as it misrepresents and limits the value of higher education in prison to the public (5). I agree with Castro and Gould but feel that we need to go a step further by acknowledging how HEP programs that champion restrictive policies affect incarcerated people's view of higher education in prison. It is critical that an incarcerated person, whose entire daily regimen is dictated and imposed upon them by a penal institution, not have their educational goals dictated and imposed upon them too.

NOTES

1. When this policy went into effect, I was listed as a member of a security threat group but was allowed to continue in my position as law clerk because the service I was providing to the large Latino community at the prison was highly valued. I served as a law clerk for three years before burning out and quitting because of the heavy workload.

2. Stewart's study of the negotiation of multiple identities by Black students at a predominantly white liberal arts college discusses the acceptance of "multiple facets of identity . . . in certain environments perceived as nurturing and supportive" (200–01). Sumara and Luce-Kepler discuss identity conflict when preteaching and lived-teaching identities are not yet woven together (80). These studies have helped me understand how identities must be integrated and how they can be experienced differently according to the situational or environmental context.

3. Asencio and Burke define self-view as identity and reflected appraisals as the "perceived views of others" (164).

4. "TPR in its simplest terms refers to learners carrying out the actions commanded by the instructor. The instructor first performs the actions while learners listen and watch. Then the learners perform the same actions with the instructor" (Lee and VanPatten 41).

5. McDowell and Reed discuss using "coded language" to "strategically hide and to reveal radical critique" from guards who supervised their writing program within a jail (159).

6. Orders that prisoners use English when in the presence of staff members reinforce restrictions on Spanish use in public schools. For a discussion on the effect of policy on Spanish use in the classroom see García (67). Prohibiting Spanish speaking in prison "mirrors disempowering relations" experienced in society (Roberts Auerbach 16).

WORKS CITED

Asencio, Emily K., and Peter J. Burke. "Does Incarceration Change the Criminal Identity? A Synthesis of Labeling and Identity Theory Perspectives on Identity Change." *Sociological Perspectives*, vol. 54, no. 2, June 2011, pp. 163–82.

Barker, Chris, and Emma A. Jane. *Culture Studies: Theory and Practice.* 5th ed., SAGE Publications, 2016.

Benedict, Kimberley. "Writing-about-Writing Pedagogies in Prison." Lockard and Rankins-Robertson, pp. 224–45.

Block, David. "The Rise of Identity in SLA Research, Post Firth and Wagner (1997)." *Modern Language Journal*, vol. 91, no. 1, 2007, pp. 863–76.

Carney, Terri M. "How Service-Learning in Spanish Speaks to the Crisis in the Humanities." *Hispania*, vol. 96, no. 2, 2013, pp. 229–37.

Castro, Erin L., and Michael Brawn. "Critiquing Critical Pedagogies inside the Prison Classroom: A Dialogue between Student and Teacher." *Harvard Educational Review*, vol. 87, no. 1, 2017, pp. 99–121.

Castro, Erin L., and Mary R. Gould. "What Is Higher Education in Prison? Introduction to Radical Departures: Ruminations on the Purposes of Higher Education in Prison." *Critical Education*, vol. 9, no. 10, 2018, pp. 1–15.

Castro, Erin L., et al. "Higher Education in an Era of Mass Incarceration: Possibility under Constraint." *Journal of Critical Scholarship on Higher Education and Student Affairs*, vol. 1, no. 1, 2015, pp. 13–31.

Cavallaro, Alexandra. "Making Citizens behind Bars (and the Stories We Tell about It): Queering Approaches to Prison Literacy Programs." *Literacy in Composition Studies*, vol. 7, no. 1, 2019, pp. 1–21.

Drew, Jenifer D., et al. "Community Colleges and Spanish Language Instruction: Peer Pedagogy in Prison." *New Directions for Community Colleges*, vol. 2015, no. 170, summer 2015, pp. 31–40.

Ebacher, Colleen. "Taking Spanish into the Community: A Novice's Guide to Service-Learning." *Hispania*, vol. 96, no. 2, 2013, pp. 397–408.

Flores, Nelson, and Jonathan Rosa. "Bringing Race into Second Language Acquisition." *The Modern Language Journal*, vol. 103, 2019, pp. 145–51.

Florida Department of State. Rule 33-601.314. *Florida Administrative Code and Florida Administrative Register*, 18 Jan. 2021.

Foucault, Michel. *Discipline and Punish: The Birth of the Prison*. Translated by Alan Sheridan, Pantheon Books, 1977.

García, Ofelia. "U.S. Spanish and Education: Global and Local Intersections." *American Educational Research Association*, vol. 38, no. 1, 2014, pp. 58–80.

Giles, Judy, and Tim Middleton. *Studying Culture*. 2nd ed., Blackwell Publishing, 2008.

Grundy, Shirley. "Challenging and Changing: Communicative Competence and the Classroom." *Encyclopedia of Language and Education*, edited by Bronwyn Davies and David Corson, Kluwer Academic Publishers, 1997. 8 vols.

Kilgore, James. "Bringing Freire behind the Walls: The Perils and Pluses of Critical Pedagogy in Prison Education." *Radical Teacher*, vol. 90, no. 1, 2011, pp. 57–66.

Lee, James F., and Bill VanPatten. *Making Communicative Language Teaching Happen*. 2nd ed., McGraw Hill, 2003.

Lockard, Joe, and Sherry Rankins-Robertson, editors. *Prison Pedagogies: Learning and Teaching with Imprisoned Writers*. Syracuse UP, 2018.

McDowell, Meghan G., and Alison Reed. "'Can a Poem Stop a Jail from Being Built?': On Fugitive Counter-Ethics as Prison Pedagogy." Lockard and Rankins-Robertson, pp. 148–67.

Mignolo, Walter D. "Epistemic Disobedience, Independent Thought and Decolonial Freedom." *Theory, Culture and Society*, vol. 26, nos. 7–8, 2009, pp. 1–23.

Olinger, Andrea, et al. "Prisoners Teaching ESL: A Learning Community among 'Language Partners.'" *Teaching English in the Two-Year College*, vol. 40, no. 1, 2012, pp. 68–83.

Roberts Auerbach, Elsa. "Reexamining English Only in the ESL Classroom." *TESOL Quarterly*, vol. 27, no. 1, 1993, pp. 9–32.

Sanchez, Angel E. "In Spite of Prison." *Harvard Law Review*, vol. 132, 2019, pp. 1650–83.

Scott, Robert. "Distinguishing Radical Teaching from Merely Having Intense Experiences While Teaching in Prison." *Radical Teacher*, vol. 95, no. 1, 2013, pp. 22–32.

Stewart, Dafina Lazarus. "Being All of Me: Black Students Negotiating Multiple Identities." *Journal of Higher Education*, vol. 79, no. 2, 2008, pp. 183–207.

Sumara, Dennis J., and Rebecca Luce-Kepler. "(Un)Becoming a Teacher: Negotiating Identities While Learning to Teach." *Canadian Society for the Study of Education*, vol. 21, no. 1, 1996, pp. 65–83.

Swain, Merrill, and Ping Deters. "'New' Mainstream SLA Theory: Expanded and Enriched." *Modern Language Journal*, vol. 91, 2007, pp. 820–36.

Wright, Randall. "Going to Teach in Prisons: Culture Shock." *Journal of Correctional Education*, vol. 56, no. 1, 2005, pp. 19–38.

Poetic Difference: How Emplaced Writing Influences Lives in Prison

Seth Michelson

In October 2015, I began teaching poetry workshops in the most restrictive maximum security detention center in the United States for undocumented, unaccompanied youth. In that facility, the children, ages thirteen to seventeen, are housed in isolation cells, and life is difficult, a fact that is documented in multiple reports citing serious concerns over self-harm and suicide.[1] A federal lawsuit was even filed against the detention center in October 2017, reporting "unconstitutional conditions that shock the conscience, including violence by staff, abusive and excessive use of seclusion and restraints, and the denial of necessary mental health care" ("Doe" 1), among other allegations. Such information bears immediate pedagogical mention because teaching is always emplaced. It depends upon the specificities of the site, meaning both the space and its people.

Through and against the specificities of the institution, the young poets and I met for weekly poetry workshops in Spanish. Like the scholar of higher education in prison (HEP) Patrick W. Berry, I understood from the start that "literacy is situated and contextual" (3), so I developed a site-specific pedagogy capable of welcoming and nurturing all the writers in our collective, whether able to read or otherwise. My aim with this essay is therefore twofold. I will elucidate how and why we engaged in collaborative poetry writing under a particular configuration of maximum security restrictions, and I will aim for that elucidation of pedagogy and practice to serve as a template for readers to consider in relation to their own carceral teaching. In this manner, we may continue to grow networks of artists, teachers, students, and others inside and outside of prisons, jails, and detention centers who are collectively striving to influence—if not eradicate—conditions of captivity in the United States.

Methodologically, my pedagogy pivots upon a practice of empathic listening to difference through poetry. First and foremost, this importantly positions poetry as activity, which imbues the workshop with a thrumming vitality. For us, workshop is action. We are constantly listening to, discussing, and writing poetry, and through it, we paradoxically cohere through our differences into a collective of poets. I pointedly emphasize this identitarian shift by insisting in workshop that we identify first as poets, thereby disrupting oppressive and discriminatory discourses that would otherwise seek to identify the poets first as "prisoners," "criminals," "aliens," or "illegals." More than semantic play, this gesture is metonymic of my methodology. Poetry is our purpose and process for coming together, and this makes the workshop both locus and method. We, as poets, assemble regularly in a shared space for poetry. Through our poetry, we listen empathically to our differences, which we celebrate rather than punish, and in this manner, we influence conditions of possibility for incarcerated life.

In poetically creating space for difference, we are daring to destabilize the familiar, fixed, and enforced. We are shifting perspectives from punishment to possibility. Through workshop, we reveal limits and containments while also imagining them otherwise. Moreover, at least for the duration of workshop, we can create alternative, life-affirming ways of being, and this is more than linguistic and imagined. In the most basic sense, while writing in workshop no one is engaging in self-harm or suicide attempts. We are countering self-destruction by each affirming our lives while also forging new affinities and solidarities with one another. With each poem written, we come to understand more ardently how "a poem [is] that very thing that teaches the heart, [that] invents the heart" (Derrida 231). It is continuously reconstitutive, and it is group actuation through recalibration by differences. As such, our practice countervails normative thanatopolitical and necropolitical carceral logics, giving rise to modes of survival through poetry.

Dreaming America: An Apologia

Here, I focus exclusively on my workshops in the aforementioned facility, despite having done work with poetry with imprisoned people at multiple maximum security facilities across the country over the past twenty years. I have chosen this focus for many reasons. First, it offers a limit-test to my pedagogy. As of the writing of this essay, the maximum security juvenile detention center I have mentioned has been identified as the most severe of its category. Besides the documented concerns over abuse, there are concerns about due process. Labeled by the state as maximum security stateless prisoners and thus lacking constitutional protections, such as the right to legal counsel, the incarcerated children exist in a liminal space within the U.S. carceral system. Consequently, their precarity is as juridically extreme as any we might consider within this book.

A second benefit to readers of my site-specific focus is the resulting rhetorical cohesion of my explanation of my pedagogy. Limiting my focus to a single site allows me to render in detail the conditions of its workshops and the poetic activity tailored specifically for them so that readers can better apprehend my schematic and adapt it to their own carceral teaching. My approach recognizes Ramón Grosfoguel's admonition that "[m]igrants do not arrive in an empty or neutral space" (607). I understand the same to be true of imprisoned people, as well as of writers arriving to a workshop. And in this juvenile detention center, the poets are all three. We must therefore negotiate our shared space of the workshop as an ever-shifting amalgam of people grappling with migration, imprisonment, and shared poetry writing, and that intersectional complexity directly influences my pedagogical preparation and activity. Like the HEP scholar Erin Castro, I strive toward an "emplaced praxis that accounts for the situatedness and lived realities of participants, the construction of educational space, and negotiations of power and ethics in the prison classroom" (Castro and Brawn 102). I acknowledge, too, that such work is fraught with many irresolvable tensions, including those due to my privilege compared to my fellow poets (McQuaide). I likewise concede that carceral teaching cannot be fully realized (Thomas). Such is the difficulty of our work.

To engage that difficulty, I prioritize the local as a powerful, if paradoxical, means to explore the plurality of phenomenological possibilities intrinsic to empathic listening to difference. Such work is challenging under any conditions, let alone under maximum security restrictions. It requires not only courage, creativity, and focus to contemplate multiple, competing, and often unfamiliar locales, interests, and perspectives, but also a willingness to abandon habitual ways of being. This is no small sacrifice for imprisoned people. The familiarity and control of their habits are sometimes their only grounds for agency, self-determination, and self-soothing. Yet they consistently take the risk, joining our workshop and writing poetry. It is as if they have always already understood, like the cultural psychiatrist Laurence Kirmayer, that a "close approximation to another's feelings requires imaginatively reconstructing and inhabiting some portion of their world—which of necessity means bracketing off or decentering from our own habitual stance" (461). Such is our practice in workshop, wherein we decenter ourselves from habit, whether personal or carceral, to embrace a plurality of possibility through poetry.

Consequently, we can conceive alternative ways of being, each in ourselves and together in common, thereby disturbing the very grounds of carceral logics of captivity and isolation.

Third, my focus on these workshops grants me the opportunity to reflect in writing on my most recent sustained experience with carceral teaching under maximum security restrictions. After three years of collaboration, I can say with confidence that these young poets count among the finest incarcerated writers with whom I have ever worked. Thousands of copies of their bilingual anthology of poetry, *Dreaming America: Voices of Undocumented Youth in Maximum-Security Detention* (Michelson), have been sold, and the book is being taught in high schools, colleges, and universities across the United States and beyond, and in fields as diverse as literary studies, critical legal studies, Latin American studies, and poverty studies. It has been turned into original music by two composers and into plays by theater groups on each coast of the United States. I also have been invited to give talks on it across the United States, Mexico, Argentina, and Uruguay and in multiple television, radio, and newspaper interviews.[2]

I attribute *Dreaming America*'s wide appeal to the power of its poetry, which connects its authors deeply with readers beyond the detention center and opens their lives in isolation to the world. Through poetry, these children return to presence within and beyond the detention center and contribute in their own words to ongoing transnational debates on migration, incarceration, and belonging, from which migrating people themselves are too often conspicuously absent. The diversity of their book also helps disallow dangerous narratives about migrating or incarcerated people, such as the exceptionalizing templates of the good immigrant and the good prisoner. Likewise, the agonies and failures in the book counter hyperbolic rhetorics of hope, particularly those in prison studies that frame "literacy as . . . a magical actor capable of transcending social, material, and economic problems" (Berry 4–5). Instead, these poems illustrate the complexity, enormity, and ferocity of a carceral system that no poetry could dismantle.

Nevertheless we write. We write against the despair and violence of this particular space and its aegis, and we write to convoke a newfound poetic community of subsistence within it. That community is not defined by detention, punishment, or rehabilitation. Rather it celebrates the poets' creativity, vitality, and agency, however besieged.

Crucially, too, we also commodify our poetry. That is, all proceeds from the sale of *Dreaming America* go to a legal defense fund for the incarcerated children, and that procurement of legal aid is quite possibly the most radical and transformative aspect of our project. When representing themselves in federal immigration court, undocumented children in maximum security detention in the United States win only about six percent of their cases. In contrast, they win around seventy percent of their cases when represented by legal counsel (Cruz). Thus *Dreaming America* comprises a unique model for publishing: incarcerated people can enact their freedom by retaining attorneys through poetry writing.

Spatial Politics: An Argument for Preparedness

Long before entering any prison or detention center to initiate a workshop, I work to understand the site both locally and systemically. For example, before meeting a single child in this detention center, I learned from staff members that the children range in age from thirteen to seventeen, possess on average a second-grade education, are in many cases illiterate, and hail from a diversity of Hispanophone countries of origins. I then researched such information more broadly, seeking intersectional discourses on migration. I studied geographically specific pathways and processes of migration, including comparative legal scholarship, narratives in the Latin American tradition of testimonio, and studies of race, gender, sexuality, state violence, and poverty. I also learned as much as possible about this specific facility and the children's various, individual routes to it, as well as the structure of their days once here and the specific possibilities to come.

I understand, too, that much information about the place and its people is withheld from me by institutional policy. Yet even this awareness of absent information, of my enforced ignorance, is helpful. It guides me to understand better the boundaries and possibilities of our workshop. That absent information paradoxically reminds me of the continuous violence, both experienced and possible, that structures space and therefore daily life for the children. It compels me, too, to reflect metacritically on how I as lead poet might at times unintentionally and perhaps inevitably act as an agent of state power and not a facilitator of its questioning. Quite perilously, without careful planning and practice, the "teacher [in prison too often] becomes mapped onto the role of the prison guard instead of the dialogic facilitator" (Castro and Brawn 101). This is more than a pedagogical failure; it actively hurts students. As the HEP scholar Rebecca Ginsburg notes, "[W]hen prison educators become stand-ins for correctional officers, college-in-prison reinforces the regression of incarceration" (2). To try to eschew such pitfalls, I enact my pedagogy of emplaced, empathic poetry writing, though I simultaneously know that poetry writing cannot unmake structural racism or systemic economic injustice.

Nevertheless, good and meaningful work in prison is possible. While I certainly agree with Castro and Brawn that "the development and potential of [incarcerated] students . . . are always thwarted by the brute contours of institutionalized confinement" (118), I also believe like Berry that prisons "are sites in which powerful words and creative expression are produced" (5). This is true, for example, of our workshop. It reveals how "educational programming [in prison] at its best creates spaces of humanity and dignity that invite incarcerated scholars to breathe, build community with one another, and to produce and create" (Ginsburg 5). To maximize that possibility, I therefore refine my emplaced pedagogy continuously. The more I learn about the institution and its people, the better I can develop the pedagogy and its resulting workshops.

Hence, I not only read an interdisciplinary array of pertinent scholarship but also strive to learn each child's specificities. Of note, they can shift daily; I am always seeking information on who is hungry, exhausted, medicated or unmedicated, and able or unable to write and read. I also listen to every detail from them about their countries and cultures of origin, their languages, and their stories of migration and detention. I likewise listen for variations on such information from the institution's representatives. It is critical to engage with everyone inside the facility. I deeply value my interactions with the poets in workshop, and I also value my interactions with the administrators, corrections officers, therapists, social workers, clergy members, and anyone else that I encounter in each facility. These perspectives help me to create better, more informed workshops and to maintain safe and sustainable relationships with the host institution.

Similarly, I have learned never to presuppose anything about anyone in prison, including the staff, and I account for this, too, in my pedagogy. More precisely, I am committed to involving everyone present in the room during a workshop. Everyone participates in the writing process by listening empathically. And if staff members move from listening to partaking in workshops, then I thank them. I also immediately and explicitly thank the incarcerated poets on these occasions for their generosity of spirit, since staff participation can introduce tangents or distractions. I celebrate this inclusion as a testament to the incarcerated poets' hospitality and as a marker of their willingness to engage difficulty and complexity. I also use it as an opportunity to reinforce the poets' growing sense of their solidarity and strength in community and their individual resilience through creativity and poise.

All this helps foster the conditions of a workshop that aims to privilege and recuperate the agency of the incarcerated children, however ephemerally. The children's positive responses to these conditions in writing and conversation indicate to me that they find them helpful and affirming. I therefore welcome opportunities to integrate staff members into our workshops, whether in the form of a corrections officer's offhand comment on a poem or that of a social worker's willingness to scribe for an illiterate poet. In one especially wonderful case, a senior administrator in the juvenile facility was so enthused by our workshops as to participate on an almost weekly basis, sitting in during the free-writing portion of our sessions and always joining us at the end for the poets' reading of their new work. These interactions built enduring, positive connections between the children and the administrator, helping everyone involved to better navigate their interactions in the carceral space beyond workshop.

We must acknowledge here, too, that these are anecdotal glimpses of some of the successes of workshops at the interpersonal level within a carceral regime that systematically perpetuates institutionalized violence, oppression, racism, and despair. That is, by design, the US carceral system neither seeks nor nurtures rich ontological and sociopolitical experiences for imprisoned people. Instead, it perpetuates a foundational, endemic racism, mobilizing a white supremacist, colonial logic in the service of political economy.[3] This system stands in stark contradistinction to the aegis of our poetry workshops. Rather than celebrating difference to create informed and supportive communities through a poetics of empathic listening, the carceral system aims bluntly and brutally to homogenize, anonymize, and mute its pathologized people. As the critical prison studies scholar and former political prisoner Angela Y. Davis explains, "[P]risons do not disappear problems, they disappear human beings" (2), and I would add that such disappearances are quite lucrative.

Furthermore, as the civil rights lawyer and scholar Michelle Alexander notes, "No other country in the world imprisons so many of its racial or ethnic minorities" (6). The poets in my workshops number among the more than 34,000 immigrants who are detained daily in the United States, most of whom hail from Mexico, El Salvador, Honduras, and Guatemala ("Fact Sheet"). Many of the facilities housing these people are private; the two largest private prison corporations, the GEO Group and Corrections Corporation of America, received $184 million and $135 million, respectively, from the federal government during fiscal year 2017 ("Detention"). The Federal Bureau of Prisons tells us that "Hispanic" people, who constitute 18% of the US population (Flores 2), make up 32.2% of the national prison population ("Inmate Ethnicity"). Targeted with even more frequency, "Black" people, who compose 12.6% of the US population, constitute 38.1% of the prison population ("ACS"). As a result, Black and brown people are disproportionately excluded from the national body politic.[4]

This "racial capital" is worth billions of dollars to the domestic economy. For example, in Virginia, where these children are incarcerated, the most recently available operating budgets for the state department of corrections are around $1.17 billion for fiscal year 2016 and $1.13 billion for fiscal year 2015 ("Management"). Such is the immensity of the institutional power oppressing imprisoned people, including those featured in *Dreaming America*.

Democratic Hospitality: Poetry in Action

What are the avenues for engaging with a problem that remains intentionally occluded? One answer is to work from within, and poetry offers an available means of doing this. In the broadest terms, as the Salvadoran poet Roque Dalton explains, "[P]oetry, like bread, is for everyone" (39). Believing similarly, I exhort incarcerated people to write. Through writing we examine carcerality from within, thus making meaningful discoveries through poetry that are shared by the collective of the workshop. We do this in many ways, beginning with the very conception of writing, which for us is broad and multiple. That is, we certainly write poetry individually, but we also write in pairs, in small groups, and all together. We also write in silence and we write to music, which—due to carceral restrictions— means that we write to music produced using our voices, hands, and feet. We also write within and across genres, and we write whether literate or not.

We also read a radical diversity of authors, with whom we write dialogically. For example, after reading from the "Letter from Birmingham City Jail" and "I Have a Dream" by Martin Luther King, Jr. (289–302, 217– 20), the poets respond intertextually with their own thoughts and dreams, creating poems like "I have a dream . . ." (Michelson 104) and "To Have a Dream," whose author writes, "I dream of discovering a world where nothing would matter more than what you carry within" (80). Likewise, we respond to poetry by the Peruvian poet César Vallejo, who in 1921 was incarcerated for suspect, political reasons, much like many of the poets in workshop. His poem "The Black Heralds" includes the refrain "There are blows in life so powerful . . . I don't know!" (24–25), prompting workshop writers to release their own ineffable suffering, as evident in poems like "Blows in Life" (Michelson 58) and "Loneliness" (60). Similarly, we write poetry after reading investigative journalism about the labor politics exploiting undocumented people in California farming. A poignant example of the resulting poems is "From the Earth" (24), which follows in its entirety.

> From the earth grew a fruit
> so delicious
> I paused to wonder,
> Who harvested this fruit?

Other genres that have especially inspired our poets include decolonial historiography, testimonio, origin stories, and flash fiction, and it bears mention that none of my intended texts have ever been censored by the facility. Writers with whom the poets have particularly enjoyed dialoging include Sappho, Nezahualcoyotl, Dante, Nancy Morejón, Li Po, Marge Piercy, and Amiri Baraka, to name but a few. These transhistorical and transcultural literary exchanges open new possibilities for workshop participants, who explore hybridity, polyvocality, and resiliency. Importantly, too, their poetry, with its complex plurality of voices, disrupts the essentialist, univocal rhetoric of the carceral system.

To further enact that empowering, disruptive plurality, we conclude each workshop with the poets reading their new work aloud to the group. The aim is to celebrate and learn from the courage, ingenuity, and resiliency of each poet in daring to express not only suffering, fear, and rage from life in isolation but also love, hope, and beauty. We acknowledge each poet's humanity by listening to and witnessing their experiences. It is empowering to be heard and witnessed in one's struggle, and all the more so when living in enforced isolation. We strive to build a supportive network of writers, both in the flesh and on the page. We continuously trace intertextual similarities and dissimilarities between the many texts, whether ours or others', fortifying and extending our solidarities as a rich and diverse community of writers. And there again shines the pedagogical importance of empathic listening: it binds us.

Such is the affective force of emplaced poetry. As the literary theorist Laurent Dubreuil explains in his book on poetry and cognitive science, poetry encourages "self-relation to our own emotions through empathy and memory [and this] blurs the lines of what *I* once felt. . . . The verses we know *implant* in us memories of affects and passions that we can recognize as being ours, as part of our life history—even if they have been in fact delivered by verbal artifacts" (88). In other words, in workshop we create verbal artifacts, and their consequent affects circulate both within and beyond the conditions of their creation. They bring us more deeply into communion with ourselves and with one another. Those affective valences go on to resound in a readership as exponentially extensive as the network of distribution of the verse. I therefore always include pathways to publication for incarcerated poets in my pedagogy, believing the affect of their verbal artifacts to be ontologically and sociopolitically crucial.

Practice Makes Possible: Notes toward a Preliminary Conclusion

Our workshop is action. It empowers agency, however fraught, limited, and transitory. In workshop we listen empathically to difference through poetry, believing with Kirmayer that "[e]mpathy combined with knowledge of the causes of suffering leads to compassion" (460). Thus a pedagogy of empathic listening to difference aspires ultimately to create compassion within and across our many overlapping communities. The depth of the compassion correlates to the poets' ability to manipulate the tropes and figures of poetry. Through them, the poets can conjure and communicate affect in ways capable of connecting and transforming worlds. As the cultural theorist Lauren Berlant explains, "public spheres are affect worlds at least as much as they are effects of rationality and rationalization" (451). Accordingly, poets can influence any community's conditions of possibility. More pointedly, poets in enforced isolation can propound a more deeply moral hospitality than that of the state, welcoming otherness and honoring difference rather than fearing and punishing it. Here again Kirmayer is helpful, explaining that "[t]o lead to compassionate action, empathy must be coupled to moral commitments, and translated in action, guided by detailed knowledge of specific pragmatic social and cultural contexts" (461). This is precisely the power of a pedagogy of empathic listening to difference through poetry. Or, as one child explains far more beautifully,

> Poetry is a form of explaining your feelings to
> yourself, someone else, or many others, a way
> of freeing yourself from the chains that tie you
> to harsh reality. Poetry is also a kind of description
> that defines who you are and who you will become in life.
>   (Michelson 40)

NOTES

1. Articles on this subject abound. Most succinctly, a recent and comprehensive transnational study of the impact of detention on immigrant detainees by psychologists "demonstrated severe mental health consequences amongst detainees across a wide range of settings and jurisdictions" (von Werthern 1; see also Knadler; Sanchez; Habib; Liebelson).

2. To date, copies of *Dreaming America* have been shipped not only across the hemispheric Americas but also across Europe, Africa, and Asia. Such travel is no small achievement in the light of the fact that its authors live in isolation cells in the United States. It also signals the important breadth of the networks of its readership.

3. For a helpful understanding of the historicity of the US carceral system, including its inception in white supremacist logics and violence, please see the introduction and first chapter of Dylan Rodríguez's *Forced Passages*. For insights into white supremacist logics of carceral power in relation to Chicanx people in particular and Latinx people in general, see Ben Olguín's *La Pinta*.

4. For a deeper theorization of internal exclusions, including helpful historicizations of notions of the ban and the banned, see Giorgio Agamben's *Homo Sacer* and *Remnants of Auschwitz*. For an intersectional feminist reading of exclusion as constitutive, see Sina Kramer's *Excluded Within*.

WORKS CITED

"ACS Demographic and Housing Estimates: 2012–2016 American Community Survey 5-Year Estimates." United States Census Bureau, census.gov/programs-surveys/acs/technical-documentation/table-and-geography-changes/2016/5-year.html.

Agamben, Giorgio. *Homo Sacer: Sovereign Power and Bare Life*. Translated by Daniel Heller-Roazen, Stanford UP, 1998.

———. *Remnants of Auschwitz: The Witness and the Archive*. Translated by Daniel Heller-Roazen, Zone Books, 2002.

Alexander, Michelle. *The New Jim Crow: Mass Incarceration in the Age of Colorblindness*. New Press, 2010.

Berlant, Lauren. "Critical Inquiry, Affirmative Culture." *Critical Inquiry*, vol. 30, no. 2, 2004, pp. 445–51.

Berry, Patrick W. *Doing Time, Writing Lives: Refiguring Literacy and Higher Education in Prison*. Southern Illinois UP, 2018.

Castro, Erin L., and Michael Brawn. "Critiquing Critical Pedagogies inside the Prison Classroom: A Dialogue between Student and Teacher." *Harvard Educational Review*, vol. 87, no. 1, 2017, pp. 99–121.

Cruz, Tanishka. "Immigration + Cville: An Educational Panel." 4 June 2018, Building Goodness Foundation, Charlottesville, VA. Presentation.

Dalton, Roque. *Poemas clandestinos / Clandestine Poems*. Translated by Jack Hirschman, Curbstone Press, 1990.

Davis, Angela. "Masked Racism: Reflections on the Prison Industrial Complex." *Colorlines*. 10 Sept. 1998.

Derrida, Jacques. "Che cos'è la poesia?" Translated by Peggy Kamuf. *A Derrida Reader: Between the Blinds*, edited by Kamuf, Columbia UP, 1991, pp. 234–37.

"Detention by the Numbers." *Freedom for Immigrants*, 2018, freedomfor immigrants.org/detention-statistics/.

"Doe v. Shenandoah Valley Juvenile Center Commission." 5:17CV00097. United States District Court, 4 Oct. 2017.

Dubreuil, Laurent. *Poetry and Mind: Tractatus Poetico-Philosophicus*. Fordham UP, 2018.

"Fact Sheet: DHS FY 2017 Budget." United States Department of Homeland Security, 9 Feb. 2016, dhs.gov/news/2016/02/09/fact-sheet-dhs-fy-2017 -budget.

Flores, Antonio. "How the US Hispanic Population Is Changing." Pew Research Center, 18 Sept. 2017.

Ginsburg, Rebecca, editor. *Critical Perspectives on Teaching in Prison: Students and Instructors on Pedagogy behind the Wall*. Routledge, 2019.

Grosfoguel, Ramón. "Latin@s and the Decolonization of the US Empire in the 21st Century." *Social Science Information*, vol. 47, no. 4, 2008, pp. 605–22.

Habib, Yamily. "Suicide and Despair: The Reality of Young Immigrants in Detention Centers." *Al Día*, 11 Sept. 2018.

"Inmate Ethnicity." Federal Bureau of Prisons, bop.gov/about/statistics/statis tics_inmate_ethnicity.jsp. Accessed 29 Sept. 2018.

King, Martin Luther, Jr. *A Testament of Hope: The Essential Writings and Speeches*. Edited by James Melvin Washington, HarperCollins Publishers, 1991.

Kirmayer, Laurence. "Empathy and Alterity in Cultural Psychiatry." *Ethos*, vol. 36, no. 4, 2008, pp. 457–74.

Knadler, Jessie. "Inhumane Conditions Alleged at Juvenile Detention Center Near Staunton." *WMRA*, 13 Dec. 2017, www.wmra.org/wmra-news/2017 -12-13/inhumane-conditions-alleged-at-juvenile-detention-center-near -staunton.

Kramer, Sina. *Excluded Within: The (Un)Intelligibility of Radical Political Actors*. Oxford UP, 2017.

Liebelson, Dana. "In Detention, Troubling Cases of Self-Harm among Migrant Youth." *HuffPost*, 3 Aug. 2018.

"Management Information Summary Annual Report for the Fiscal Year Ending June 30, 2016." Virginia Department of Corrections, 2016, vadoc.vir ginia.gov/media/1205/vadoc-financial-annual-mis-report-2016.pdf.

McQuaide, Stacy Bell. "Go Hard: Bringing Privilege-Industry Pedagogies into a College Writing Classroom in Prison." Ginsburg, pp. 102–11.

Michelson, Seth, editor. *Dreaming America: Voices of Undocumented Youth in Maximum-Security Detention.* Settlement House, 2017.

Olguín, Ben. *La Pinta: Chicana/o Prisoner Literature, Culture, and Politics.* U of Texas P, 2010.

Rodríguez, Dylan. *Forced Passages: Imprisoned Radical Intellectuals and the U.S. Prison Regime.* U of Minnesota P, 2006.

Sanchez, Melissa, et al. "As Months Pass in Chicago Shelters, Immigrant Children Contemplate Escape, Even Suicide." *ProPublica*, 6 Sept. 2018, www.propublica.org/article/chicago-immigrant-shelters-heartland-internal-documents.

Thomas, Jim. "Ironies of Prison Education." *Schooling in a "Total Institution": Critical Perspectives on Prison Education*, edited by Howard S. Davidson, Praeger, 1995, pp. 25–41.

Vallejo, César. *The Complete Poetry: A Bilingual Edition.* Translated by Clayton Eshleman, U of California P, 2007.

Werthern, M. von, et al. "The Impact of Immigration Detention on Mental Health: A Systematic Review." *BMC Psychiatry*, vol. 18, no. 1, 2018, p. 382.

Unsettling Literacy: Querying the Rhetorics of Transformation

Anne Dalke

Since I was a child, books have helped me understand the world I live in and served as entry into other, much larger ones. Learning to rewrite the stories of my time and place—learning to be present and active in shifting their form—came later. As a college English professor, I explored alternative pedagogies and co-constructed dialogues in which participants laid their different perspectives alongside one another, new stories emerging in the process. Working collectively and co-creatively to challenge existing structures, sharing those creations with others in writing, became my political work.

Now, as a volunteer writing tutor for Inside-Out college courses in Philadelphia jails and Pennsylvania prisons, I work with incarcerated scholars for whom reading has not often been an easy pleasure, writing not a common means of reflection. My hope when I first entered a prison classroom was that, in offering the skills of reading and writing to my students inside, I might create what Asao Inoue describes as spaces of "feedback or dialogue," where "the student's own urge to communicate and identify with others" could be directed into finding "freedom and power through writing" (300). I wanted to offer my students what Frederick Douglass promised in his famous claim that learning to read and write "had roused my soul to eternal wakefulness. Freedom now appeared, to disappear no more forever" (55).

Douglass's celebration of the liberatory effects of education is one of many in a lineage of declarations written from slavery and prison cells. Reading while incarcerated, Malcolm X reported that "I never had been so truly free in my life" (70). Much current writing by incarcerated scholars and their teachers testifies similarly to the transformative effects of prison education. The Inside-Out Prison Exchange Program claims a "pedagogy of transformation" (Davis and Roswell). A recent *Critical Edu-*

cation special series, *Radical Departures: Ruminations on the Purposes of Higher Education in Prison*, is filled with titles promising "elevating connection" (Evans) and "transformation" (Heider), sounding "liberatory possibilities" (McCorkel and DeFina), and offering practices for "liberating humanity" (Heppard). A recent *Twitter* chat discusses the "transformative opportunity that is post-secondary education in prison" (College and Community Fellowship).

Education for Liberation is also the title of a book by the American Enterprise Institute about the return of incarcerated individuals to society "as productive and law-abiding citizens" (Robinson and Smith). It is that last turn which concerns me here and provokes the interrogation that follows of the claims—now common on both right and left—about the liberatory potential of prison education. What kind of freedom is being referenced here? Becoming "lettered" in prison may prepare students to fill roles in stratified, normalizing institutions. It may give them increased leeway in living their lives, perhaps offering radical possibilities. It may open their consciousness to the width and density of the structures in which they are entrapped. It may also offer them ways to negotiate, if not to escape, those networks.

This essay works the tension between these four linked outcomes of "learning our letters": as training "good workers for a problematic system" (Cohen), as "an emancipating skill" (Ryden 9), as raising awareness of the extent of structures within which we all operate, and as learning what choices can be made and how to shift the shape of those systems. The latter option will receive most of my attention here.

I am accompanied in this interrogation by the "rough consensus" of the "rowdy corpus" that is critical prison studies, or CPS (Seigel 124, 136). This includes celebration of "a coalition-built learning environment" that intervenes temporarily in "the institutional power dynamics" that govern "lives behind bars" (P. Alexander 16, 12). Aiming to undermine the educational deprivation, social isolation, asymmetrical power dynamics, and logic of human disappearance of everyday prison life, these scholar-activists also issue powerful cautions about the ways in which "the teaching act is constituted by the technologies of the prison regime," compelling "students and teachers to examine how deeply engaged they are in the violent common sense of the prison" (Rodríguez 3, 5). Some CPS scholars believe that it is not possible to "liberate" the "abject identity category" of prisoner, impossible to achieve, in prison, the transformation promised by critical pedagogy (Ginsberg 66). I situate myself somewhat differently, grounded not in a conviction of "power disparities between instructors and students" (Ginsberg 64) but rather in an awareness of the multilayered complexities and possibilities of a particularly constrained and conflicted site. My account is less about fixed positions of power than about the subversion possible amid its complicated interactions.

Querying the Myth of Literacy

Education-as-liberation must take into account students' incarceration, which may feel "free" in relationship to the backgrounds that led them to jail. Incarcerated students often speak of their fear of being released, including a woman "from a years-ago class, headed back out with no home, no idea where her son—labeled schizophrenic—is, last she knew on the streets, and who says out loud with almost a sense of just speaking her interior: you know, we all have one more crime in us" (Cohen and Dalke, 63). An essay cowritten by incarcerated students describes "a cellmate who believed that he was much more 'free' in prison. . . . [A] great many persons who engage in adult criminal behavior once lived in abject poverty, frequently were victims of physical or emotional abuse and chronic neglect, and were exposed to a variety of other painful experiences as children" (Ahmed 73). Compared to the neighborhood, prison can seem a site of safety.

Education-as-liberation must also take into account the relationship of the classroom to the prison that surrounds it. Malakki, an incarcerated student, explains that when an outside educator appears in a classroom setting in prison, "a special place comes into existence that allows us to be a different us than the cell, chow hall, yard, and dayrooms . . . . the place where you have your class becomes defined and sanctioned by the group as a sort of sacred space" (18).

Education-as-liberation must take into account, too, the current myth of what prison education can accomplish, promising a conception of "transformation" that it may well not be able to deliver. As Kirk Branch explains, the concept of literacy "has the fantasy of emancipation built into it. . . . It narrates personal, social, and cultural development. Like requited love in a romance novel, literacy signals movement into social and personal fulfillment . . .'the literacy myth' . . . is associated with the triumph of light over darkness, of liberalism, democracy, and of universal unbridled progress" (29–30). In the prison classes where I now tutor, literacy often looks to me less like transformation than like a punch in the gut. Taught by professors of political science and criminal justice, these courses introduce incarcerated students to troubling analyses of their own situations. Such "newfound consciousness" can be very difficult to assimilate. James Davis is explicit about the ways in which his education does "not translate to freedom. . . . [B]eing educated in prison . . . helps me understand the extent to which I am unfree. . . . higher education comes at a cost . . . [allowing] me to recognize the primary trauma of capture and incarceration . . . prison . . . has not ceased to be the site of my confinement" (2, 11).

Liberation by education is hard won and can begin in anguish, as Douglass testified long ago: "[L]earning to read had been a curse rather than a blessing. . . . It opened my eyes to the horrible pit, but to no ladder upon which to get out. . . . this ever-lasting thinking of my condition . . . tormented me" (55). Wendy Ryden claims that the "liberatory effects" of Douglass's education were "intrinsically connected to the conflicted conditions" under which they were acquired (15–16). Following her line of thinking, I suggest that it is precisely because the prison classroom is a space of such constraint and conflict that it can become a site of such promise.

Reading and Rewriting the Classroom

I began the spring 2019 semester inspired by Fred Moten's wonderful "Anassignment Letters," in which he refuses to assign his students "rule-based," "isolating and alienating" activities, directing them away from the "organizing safety . . . of having been told what to do rather than the complexity and danger, but also fun and pleasure . . . of paying attention to process . . . in . . . the commonality of listening to . . . and thinking in the world with other people . . . an open form of scholarship" (234–35). I recognize, in Moten's celebration of collaborative study as inherently unpredictable and uncontrollable, the primary reason I enjoy classroom interchange. Because shared work is emergent, all about what is not yet known, it has always been, for me, the site of real learning and a springboard for further action. I assign texts and set the stage for their discussion, never knowing what will be said or how it will interact with what else is offered.

Such open forms of scholarship offer especially useful models for the group of high-achieving college students in the prison classroom I cohost each Wednesday afternoon, who may learn there to attend less to the promotion of individual distinction, more to the practice of thinking in common with others. Moten's exhortation works well, too, in guiding their classmates, incarcerated scholars eager to discuss their own cases at the expense of hearing others or to the neglect of larger issues raised thereby. Central to the learning of all the students is balancing the telling of "one's own unique story" with the insistence that thinking must be shared (Moten 234).

Prodded by our inside students, who find the writing of their outside classmates lacking in energy and personality, I convince my co-teachers to invite a different sort of student essays than those tightly argued to reach clear conclusions, which we'd collected by the handful the year before. In search of messier, more "heart-full" work, we agree on weekly writing "anassignments" to be shared among inside and outside students: journal reflections, responsive to texts and to one another, which will build up to final cowritten projects.

The outcomes of our approach are, predictably, messy, in large part because of the complicated, constrained conditions under which the incarcerated students live and work. The week before the midsemester paper is due, one of them says that he hasn't yet begun working on the assignment, which he finds too exploratory and open-ended. He explains that, because he's incarcerated, he has become a rule-follower. If I tell him what to do, he will do it, but he's been indoctrinated: he cannot move until he's told to. As Davis says, "carceral logics" make "conformity a requirement" (9). I tell my student that much more privileged students, used to succeeding at the tasks set before them, are also well socialized into being compliant. His outside classmates are afraid to break the rules too; their desire to succeed has generated multiple anxious questions about what is wanted in each of their assignments.

However, the capacity and the freedom to take risks is allotted differentially here (Dalke). The same incarcerated student registers his emerging awareness of the extensive historical structure of systemic injustice within which his individual experience takes place. He is shaken by reading Michelle Alexander's *The New Jim Crow*, which argues that even if the prison-industrial complex could be abolished, it would be replaced by another form of institutionalized racism. The student tries to reckon with the implications of this claim. Within the terms of the racial caste system, which continues to discriminate so unremittingly against poor Black men, he might well be said to be rightly incarcerated—although he did not commit the crime for which he is doing time.

The student says that he is hopeful—that's "just [his] DNA"—but that Alexander's book "really forced [him] to take a knee." His striking language suggests a response that is not submissive but resistant and disruptive of the larger dynamics of a system constructed explicitly for the management of America's "disposable populations" (Hill 123). As a player in the National Football League, Colin Kaepernick famously knelt during the national anthem to protest police brutality and racial inequality. How might one "take a knee" inside a prison?

A few weeks after our class ends, this student's conviction will be overturned, and he will be released from prison. In the meantime, he requests that we give him rules to follow. That doing so is a means of survival is made clear both in his experience and in the 1998 novel with which our course begins: Walter Mosley's *Always Outnumbered, Always Outgunned*. The book opens with Socrates Fortlow's release after serving twenty-seven years for murdering two people and raping one of them: "And then there was three convicts I killed . . . And then there was all the men I brutalized and molested, robbed and threatened. I either committed a crime or had a crime done to me every day I was in jail" (122).

Over a number of months (and pages), Socrates comes to recognize that, while he thought he was rebelling against the system, he was actually playing by a set of rules designed to constrain him and his mates: "I thought I knew what I was doin' but I was just workin' for the man made the rules. Killing my own people was just part'a the rules. Makin' myself a jailbird was just what they wanted" (164). Davis offers an excellent gloss here: "violence can feel like liberation." As a "temporary remedy," however, it is really "a mechanism of disempowerment" (10).

An incarcerated student who has spent ninety percent of his life in prison says that it was a mistake to assign Mosley's novel because it tells a story about another time, when inmate-on-inmate violence was sanctioned by correctional officers; it gives outside students the wrong idea about what prisons are like today. One of his classmates counters that Socrates's experiences still recur periodically around the state and that even in a less violent setting the racism ingrained in prison culture creates mental, emotional, and spiritual oppression. The examples in Mosley's novel, he argues, will impress that fact on outside readers. Is it better to start this class with a dated example in order to call attention immediately to the abuses of the system or to present an apparently more compassionate model that could mislead outside students into thinking that the overall system is "working"? How might our syllabus give those students a fuller picture?

The prison classroom both holds a space for this conversation and provides witness to it. Struck by the acuity of the analysis—a Foucauldian account of discipline gone underground, of manipulation shifting from physical to mental—I am heartened by this pedagogical debate between incarcerated students about how best to educate their classmates. They are both reading and rewriting the classroom and, with it, interpretations that may well guide the activism of their classmates for years to come.

Shifting the Contours of the System

More than thirty years ago, Paulo Freire argued that literacy is

> a form of cultural politics, a set of practices that either empowers or
> disempowers . . . according to whether it reproduces existing social
> formation or promotes emancipatory change. . . . [S]tudents have to
> become literate about their histories, experiences, and the culture
> of their immediate environments . . . . [T]hey must also appropriate
> those codes and cultures of the dominant spheres so they can tran-
> scend their own environments. There is often an enormous tension
> between these two dimensions of literacy.   (47)

There is also a third dimension, which interests me more: using all available codes to challenge the terms not just of one's own culture but also
of the dominant one. It's a tricky project, trying to guide students into
mastering a set of skills while simultaneously offering a critique of the
social power that holds them in place.

Douglass described the difficult circumstances under which he studied as giving him the impetus to learn to read: "I owe almost as much
to the bitter opposition of my master, as to the kindly aid of my mis-
tress. I acknowledge the benefit of both" (50). Kristin Bumiller makes a
similarly compelling argument about prison classrooms: that the restrictions there, which enable students to "observe the conditions that sustain institutional violence," make them sites par excellence for critical
thinking (181). Students in prison classes quickly learn to recognize the
"conditions of institutional power," "the boundlessness of institutional
control," and the instrumentality of "institutional power in knowledge
production" (182). Seeing "managerial practices . . . made visible, and
called into question," students inevitably observe "the complicity of the
Inside-Out program in the forms of institutional power against which it
imagines itself to be in opposition" (180–81).

Bumiller does not believe that observing such contradictions and
uncertainties changes "the institutional mandates of prisons or the academic conventions that define knowledge and learning" (186). It is my
experience, however, that being able to make such observations in the
context of reading and writing collectively and co-creatively actually has
the potential to challenge existing structures. I offer here an example of
such a practice, a recent classroom conversation in which my co-learners
reflected together about the systems in which we work and began to describe ways to shift and change them.

A man who has been incarcerated for over forty years asked the district attorney, who joined many of our class sessions that semester, to speak about proportionality of sentencing. The conversation (in which other class members participated, and which I reconstruct here from notes I took as it occurred) instantly went deep:

"If a man only has one life, how can he get two life sentences?"

"A lot of people think that this is an appropriate sentence, if two lives have been taken."

"But you could achieve the same goal without exaggerating the reality; if you want someone to die in prison, just calculate their estimated life span, and sentence them to that many years."

"If two people, from two different families, are killed, what do you think the families want? Can you see justice from their perspective: one life for each of the lives that was taken?"

"Rather than appealing to the darker side of a grieving person, your office can explain to the victims' families how they can get their pound of flesh from one life sentence. Should the New Zealand shooter, who killed fifty people, be given fifty life sentences?"

"We don't sell them on just outcomes. We have never had conversations with family members who asked us to go easy. Whether it's the city or the suburbs, there is a shared sense of what justice is. This is not a criminal justice issue; it's a cultural one."

"You say that families bring an 'eye-for-an-eye' mentality to the table, but the D.A. is not removed from this process. When you knock on the door, they assume that you are the prosecutor, there to get the harshest sentence possible. You can offer other alternatives. You can say, 'We can get justice without asking for multiple life sentences.' You can start to change the culture."

"I agree with what you say about their expectations of us. But our most difficult conversations are those when we don't think a crime merits a life sentence, when we are going to ask for less than the maximum penalty. Families of color have said to us, a thousand times, 'He was just another Black kid. You don't care about him.' You are asking a lot: for one leg of a stool to hold up the whole structure. It requires not just a change in the prosecutors, but a whole new way of thinking."

"My father was murdered. I was sent to the same prison as the man who killed him. We talked. Like me, he was a juvenile lifer. I looked at him. I empathized with him. I realized the system he was caught in. I understood what he did. I knew that he wasn't thinking when he did it. I hope that we both have opportunity to get out."

Following this conversation, the readers and writers of this prison classroom have continued to reflect on the arguments put forward and to interrogate their foundations. That work is enabled and enriched because the class fosters mixing not otherwise on offer. All of us are differently imbricated in the machinery of a cultural system that upholds the current prison-industrial complex. One of us is a prosecutor; many of us have been prosecuted; many others of us—though we too have made mistakes, some of them criminal (M. Alexander 215)—have evaded prosecution. The inside/out hybridity of classroom presence here is evocative of what Mary Louise Pratt calls a contact zone, "where cultures meet, clash, and grapple with each other, often in contexts of highly asymmetrical relations of power" (34). Reflecting together on structures—of the classroom, of the prison where that classroom is situated, and of the culture that keeps that prison in place—gives the topic of our discussions, and its implications for our own further action, a particular valence.

Such conversations take place in the company of seekers whose life experience and understandings of the world differ drastically from my own. In trying to understand what makes these discussions possible, and in trying to imagine how we might make more of this form of exchange available within the current system of discipline and punishment, I rely profoundly on the work of Dylan Rodríguez, who insists that "it is incumbent on the radical teacher to assess the density of her/his entanglement in this historically layered condition of violence," to acknowledge the ways in which "the relative order and peace of the classroom is perpetually reproduced by the systemic disorder and deep violence of the prison regime" (7).

I find an alternative to reproduction, and hope for intervention, in the work of la paperson, whose small book, *A Third University Is Possible*, makes a strong claim for the contingent agency possible in constrained, conflicted situations. The text describes a wide range of colonial schools throughout the world that "did not always produce the intended result" (xiii). Students in such schools, la paperson argues, were able to use their "structural agency" within the system to "subvert and reassemble its machinery"; "the very circuitry of systems meant to colonize" extends the possibilities for actively reinventing, reappropriating, and breaking down the system (xiii–xiv). Seeing "structure as a limited analytic about how power works" and "agency as a discourse occupied with individual freedom," la paperson focuses on a form of subversive action that "springs from assemblage" (60).

In developing these possibilities, la paperson contrasts "the first world university" (a "corporate academic enterprise . . . characterized by accumulation of prestige") with that of "the second world" (a liberal arts college that "seeks to challenge and provoke the critical consciousness of its students toward self-actualization" but "remains circumscribed within the ivory tower"). Within both first and second world universities, however, he claims that a "third world" is possible: one that teaches "first world curricula," offers "a second world critique," and equips "its students with skills toward the applied practice of decolonization" (36).

When I first read la paperson's imaginative tract, I laughed aloud. Receiving my PhD in a research I university, teaching for thirty-five years in a small liberal arts college, I well recognized the "hidden curriculum" and "academic accumulation" operating in both (42). But only when I moved from working in "the privilege industry" to volunteering in "the punishment industry" (McQuaide 102) did I begin to see ways in which a third university (or is it a fourth?) might be said to be emerging in the prison classroom communities in which I participate. No utopias, they reflect an insistent working within-and-through the structures available to us, in which "agential capacity" depends not on our (impossible) liberation from the system, but rather on our being part of it (la paperson 61). These communities are not in control, but are able to move and act to shift the system's contours.

NOTE

I thank the Inside-Out Prison Exchange Program, the Petey Greene Program, Emma Sindelar, Keith Reeves, Maggie O'Neill, Ed McCann, and the Chester and Swarthmore students in our class, as well as Jody Cohen, Alice Lesnick, and Joel Schlosser, who continue to help me better understand the political work we can do when we read and write together.

WORKS CITED

Ahmed, Reaz, et al. "Cons and Pros: Prison Education through the Eyes of the Prison Educated." *Review of Communication*, vol. 12, no. 1, 2019, pp. 69–76.

Alexander, Michelle. *The New Jim Crow: Mass Incarceration in the Age of Colorblindness*. New Press, 2010.

Alexander, Patrick. "Education as Liberation: African American Literature and Abolition Pedagogy in the Sunbelt Prison Classroom." *South: A Scholarly Journal*, vol. 50, no. 1, 2017, pp. 9–21.

Branch, Kirk. *Eyes on the Ought to Be: What We Teach about When We Teach about Literacy*. Hampton Press, 2007.

Bumiller, Kristin. "Transformative Learning in Prisons and Universities: Reflections on Homologies of Institutional Power." Davis and Roswell, pp. 177–86.

Cohen, Jeff. "Training Good Workers for a Problematic System." *Imagining Justice*, 22 Sept. 2014, imaginingjustice.org/blogs/training-good-workers -problematic-system/.

Cohen, Jody, and Anne Dalke. *Steal This Classroom: Teaching and Learning Unbound*. Punctum Books, 2020.

College and Community Fellowship (@ccf_ny) et al. #RestorePellChat Announcement. *Twitter*, 27 Mar. 2019, twitter.com/ccf_ny/status/11080505 00102942721.

Dalke, Anne. "A Force of Disruption: Refusing the Success/Failure Complex." *Failure Pedagogies: Systems, Risks, Futures*, edited by Allison Carr and Laura Micciche, Peter Lang, 2020.

Davis, James III. "Caught Somewhere Between." *Critical Education*, vol. 9, no. 15, 2018, pp. 2–12.

Davis, Simone Weil, and Barbara Sherr Roswell. *Turning Teaching Inside Out: A Pedagogy of Transformation for Community-Based Education*. Palgrave Macmillan, 2013.

Douglass, Frederick. *Narrative of the Life of Frederick Douglass, an American Slave, Written by Himself*. New American Library, 1968.

Evans, David. "The Elevating Connection of Higher Education in Prison: An Incarcerated Student's Perspective." *Critical Education*, vol. 9, no. 11, 2018, pp. 1–14.

Freire, Paulo, and Donald Macedo. *Literacy: Reading the Word and the World*. Bergin and Garvey, 1987.

Ginsberg, Raphael. "The Perils of Transformation Talk in Higher Education in Prison." Ginsburg, pp. 60–67.

Ginsburg, Rebecca, editor. *Critical Perspectives on Teaching in Prison: Students and Instructors on Pedagogy Behind the Walls*. Routledge, 2019.

Heider, Carmen, and Karen Lehman. "Education and Transformation: An Argument for College in Prison." *Critical Education*, vol. 9, no. 10, 2019, pp. 1–13.

Heppard, Brandyn. "The Art of Liberating Humanity." *Critical Education*, vol. 10, no. 3, 2019, pp. 2–10.

Hill, Marc Lamont. *Nobody: Casualties of America's War on the Vulnerable, from Ferguson to Flint and Beyond*. Atria Books, 2016.

Inoue, Asao. *Antiracist Writing Assessment Ecologies: Teaching and Assessing Writing for a Socially Just Future*. WAC Clearinghouse, 2015.

la paperson [K. Wayne Yang]. *A Third University Is Possible*. U of Minnesota P, 2017.

Malakki [Ralph Bolden]. "An Open Letter to Prison Educators." Ginsburg, pp. 17–18.

Malcolm X and Alex Haley. *The Autobiography of Malcolm X: As Told to Alex Haley*. Random House, 1965.

McCorkel, Jill, and Robert DeFina. "Beyond Recidivism: Identifying the Liberatory Possibilities of Prison Higher Education." *Critical Education*, vol. 9, no. 10, 2019, pp. 1–17.

McQuaide, Stacey Belle. "'Go Hard': Bringing Privilege-Industry Pedagogy College Writing Classroom in Prison." Ginsburg, pp. 102–11.

Mosley, Walter. *Always Outnumbered, Always Outgunned*. W. W. Norton, 1998.

Moten, Fred. *Stolen Life*. Duke UP, 2018.

Pratt, Mary Louise. "Arts of the Contact Zone." *Profession*, 1991, pp. 33–40.

Robinson, Gerald, and Elizabeth English Smith. *Education for Liberation: The Politics of Promise and Reform Inside and Beyond America's Prisons*. Rowman and Littlefield, 2018.

Rodríguez, Dylan. "The Disorientation of the Teaching Act: Abolition as a Pedagogical Position." *Radical Teacher*, vol. 88, no. 1, 2010, pp. 7–19.

Ryden, Wendy. "Conflicted Literacy: Frederick Douglass' Critical Model." *Journal of Basic Writing*, vol. 24, no. 1, 2005, pp. 4–23.

Seigel, Micol. "Critical Prison Studies: Review of a Field." *American Quarterly*, vol. 70, no. 1, 2018, pp. 123–37.

PART TWO
PRACTICES

Liberators in Theory, Collaborators in Deed: Navigating the Constraints of the Prison Classroom

R. Michael Gosselin

In February of 2017, *The New York Review of Books* published a highly favorable review by Jonathan Zimmerman, from the University of Pennsylvania, of recent books by prison educators, titled "Scholars behind Bars." "By any conceivable measure," Zimmerman writes, "the education that these inmates receive is vastly superior to the standard academic experience of the roughly 20 million undergraduates in the United States." Most people who teach college in prison would be surprised at such an assertion. But should we be? With the expansion of college prison programs, teaching narratives have proliferated to the point where they can almost be considered a new literary genre. Many of these narratives are written by educators who, struck by the passion and intelligence of their students, and wanting to advocate for prison reform in general, paint a picture of an ideal, romanticized learning environment, with perfectly engaged students, free and open discussions, and a pedagogy of liberation. The prison classroom has been called "a magical space," and it is—for teachers.

For students, the experience can be a lesson in disappointment, frustration, and control. A common complaint is that classes often begin late or end early, depriving students of instruction time. Other concerns include a dearth of research resources and an almost complete lack of choice in selecting courses. The students' grievances suggest that power in the prison classroom is wielded by two different institutions with seemingly opposite goals. Both, however, can limit agency and educational freedom, while instructors risk unwittingly playing a part in an authoritative regime that they believe themselves to be opposing.

"Why Are You Here?"

During my first night of class, after going over the syllabus, I said, "Are there any questions?" and a voice in the back immediately called out, "I have a question: Why are you here?" My quick response was, "I'm getting paid!" That turned out to be the best answer I could have given under the circumstances, but it was instinctual and only minimally true. The question still haunts me twelve years later. Certainly, as one of my colleagues once told me, my teaching has a "touch of the missionary" in it, and I realize how fortunate I am to be involved in one of the great social issues of our time, but I also can't overlook the moments of pedagogical euphoria that stay with me for days. In other words, my participation is not entirely altruistic.

The students are right to be suspicious; everyone seems to want something from them. As Michel Foucault wrote in *Discipline and Punish*, "The penality of detention seems to fabricate—hence no doubt its longevity—an enclosed, separated and useful illegality" (278). The prison industry is profitable. Incarcerated people fight forest fires, provide therapy for abused shelter dogs, and are a source of free labor for small communities all over the country. Attica Correctional Facility, where I have been teaching college-level courses, is a major employer in the region. Each week when I arrive, local restaurants are delivering dinner to the officers. The facility is like the medieval castle on the hill in terms of its civic and economic impact. It even looks like one.

There are less material uses for imprisoned people as well—some political, some moral, and some even pedagogical. Teaching in prison is seductive, allowing instructors to turn an often frustrating routine into an exploration of our deepest notions of education, freedom, service, and civic morality. There is a sudden realization, after only the first few minutes of entering the prison environment, that here are students who are vulnerable to—and equal to—our own powers and passions. The lightest rhetorical act hits a nerve. Lectures, long ago given up as rote exercises, touch people on the deepest levels of their current needs. In 1992, Stewart A. Dippel, of the University of the Ozarks, wrote about teaching in Attica:

> Having taught traditional college for sixteen years, as well as in prison for the past four years, I have reached the conclusion that, in many ways, the quality of higher education in prison far surpasses that on campuses. Student inmates read more, and they talk more about what they have read. They interact more with the reading, with each other, and with the professor. They work harder and complain less than traditional students. (61)

Dippel, like myself, was smitten, and everything he says is true. At Attica, students already possess superb critical thinking skills—which seem to make up the bulk of my teaching on the main campus. They read everything and read it well. For example, one showed interest when I brought up critical discourse analysis (CDA), which is "fundamentally interested in analyzing opaque as well as transparent structural relationships of dominance, discrimination, power and control when these are manifested in language" (Huckin et al. 107–08). I gave him a scholarly article on CDA, and he handed it back the following week. "It's just more textual analysis," he said, with a disappointed shrug.

Presumably, this student's own experiences with "structural relationships of dominance, discrimination, power and control" simply outmuscled anything I could show him. There is little to be done in that regard other than supplying grist for a well-functioning mill and introducing the notion that students' own knowledge and insights have already been codified and given fancy academic names like "CDA." It's exciting to realize that the students are intellectually equal to any text but sobering to think where those close reading skills came from; the difference between bare survival and graduate-level textual analysis is one of degree, not kind. But these descriptions of the students only speak to what they bring to college, not what college brings to them, which isn't as much as we like to think.

Peggy Rambach, in a 2013 article in the *Chronicle of Higher Education*, describes being in the prison classroom: "I'm bombarded with sensory information that I must instantly interpret and anticipate, responding to every individual in the room with respect, authority, sensitivity, intuition, and imagination, and wielding all of those things with the agility, stamina, and concentration of a martial artist." "When class is over"—there's the rub. After class, I get to leave the place, emotionally exhausted but intellectually and morally aroused and refreshed for another week on the main campus. The famous wall of the prison is made of pale-gray concrete, and it looks almost pure white in the glare of the floodlights, especially during a western New York blizzard. Those who come into contact with it cast their own emotional, moral, and political selves onto its face, and, like Ahab, "burst their hot heart's shell upon it" (Melville 186). It is at once a mirror and a massive tabula rasa.

Their Prison and Their Lives

It's hard to imagine any other prison having such a troubling relationship with the communities around it. When it was first proposed, almost a hundred years ago, Attica Correctional Facility was met with optimism. A story in the *New York Times* announced that the wall of the prison "will have a gap in the centre. Here, a fence will be erected. . . . There will be an unobstructed view from the street of the administration building and other structures" (Kavanaugh 125). The gap never materialized; the wall is total. The residents of the village were enthusiastic about having a prison in their community. In this regard, according to another article in the *Times*, "Locally there were certainly no need for riots to spur building activity" (Wilner 51). The 1971 uprising changed everything. A reporter for the *Times* visited the village about a week after the incident and found a town in shock (Schumach 26). The *Times* caught up with Attica again in 1991, reporting that "[e]ach Sept. 13, a priest celebrates a memorial service in front of the prison for the correction officers. Many relatives of those killed at Attica stay away. At the ceremony and in their lives, the fundamental issue that the town has to sort out is how to reconcile their prison with their lives" (Cohen 34). Twenty-five years later, they were still working on it; in 2016, the Batavia *Daily News* reported, "Friends, family, corrections officers from across the country and the public bowed their heads in remembrance for those lost in one of the most well-known prison riots in this country's history," and one officer at the prison—whose own father had been killed in the riot—was quoted as saying, "There is a state service because the officers and employees of Attica Prison carry out this very unique job[;] even though (the riot) was 45 years ago, they aren't going to get over it" (Diefenbach).

Immediately after the uprising, it was believed that most of the hostages had been killed by members of the uprising, a story promulgated by the state of New York, as detailed by Heather Ann Thompson in her book, *Blood in the Water: The Attica Prison Uprising of 1971 and Its Legacy*. Despite the ultimate revelation that all the victims were killed by officers and state troopers, the trauma to the community has not abated. Shortly after winning the Pulitzer Prize, Thompson gave a presentation at Genesee Community College. The lecture hall was overflowing. In the audience were former hostages and family members of the victims, and emotions were still running high. The prison itself contains a number of memorials, inside and out, and there is a yearly ceremony honoring the slain officers. The uprising means nothing to my students, other than the fact that they're in the hands of people who are still living it. Considering such deep-seated resentment, Zimmerman's declaration that the education imprisoned students receive is "vastly superior" to all other college students is not only wrong—it's potentially dangerous.

A Question of Ethos

The constraints on the prison classroom begin with the daily regimen of the facility. It's a place where anything can happen—or nothing. On any given night, the whole place could be on lockdown. "Getting in" is never a given, and it's not uncommon for a security issue to cost students an entire week of instruction.

The physical environment also offers challenges. At the end of one of my composition courses, one student wrote on his evaluation sheet, "Fix the lights so we don't have to learn in the dark. And get Mr. Gosselin a desk." The desk was not an issue for me—I always stand up during my classes—but the student was right about the lights. They had been expiring throughout the semester, one by one, until, come December, we were sitting in the glow of a single bulb. Another time, when I entered the room, the radiator was spouting steam, and there was a puddle of water in the middle of the floor. The first three students to show up immediately turned around, came back with a bucket and mop, and had the whole thing cleaned up in under a minute. Still another time, there had been a surprise inspection earlier in the day, and the classroom looked like a bomb had gone off. To me, these are inconveniences; to the students, they're an affront. One student, in a course review, opined that the conditions felt deliberate, as if, despite all their best efforts at success, they were being continuously reminded of their status. The state of the room, apparently, was a violation of their notions of what an educational environment should look like—an insult to their new role as college students.

Once, right in the middle of a lecture on citing sources, a student raised his hand and said, quite calmly, "Mister G., I have a question about ethos." Now, a question about ethos should not be unusual in a writing class, but I hadn't used the word once since the previous semester. To have it pop out of the underbrush at this point was startling. I lowered the strip of toilet paper I'd been using to clean the white board, and waited.

"You said that 'ethos' means 'good character.'"

"Yes. Partially."

"Well, given who we are," he continued, gesturing vaguely to the rest of the class, "why would anyone read anything we write?"

For postsecondary learners at Attica, being a college student becomes an identity—an ethos—and any reminder of their separation from their peers on the main campus can be painful. I found that out during my very first semester when they insisted on having spring break. To me, not having a desk or enough light was an inconvenience; to them, it was an existential threat.

The Wider Environment

Zimmerman's review makes another wrong assumption while celebrating the supposed paradise of the prison classroom. After the usual complaints about "trigger warnings and microaggressions and safe spaces," he writes:

> The comparison of the two kinds of discussion tells us a great deal, not just about the mind-deadening quality of prison life but also about the ways that elite campuses can dare constrain minds in the name of protecting them. . . . Many of the [imprisoned] students aren't young, and they have caused or witnessed physical injuries that most of our campus students can only imagine. They're not put off by controversy, and they never ask professors to shield them from it. One suspects that in many cases they get more out of college than their on-campus peers do, in part because the inmates aren't afraid to give—or receive—offense.

He concludes, "It is astonishing to think that prisoners could have, in effect, more freedom of speech than free citizens in many colleges. But in narrow matters of concern about offensive language, it might also be true." They "could" have more freedom, and it "might" be true, but they don't, and it's not. Undoubtedly, the classroom is itself a kind of "safe space" within the facility. "Your role of facilitator is key," writes Malakki (Ralph Bolden) in his "Open Letter to Prison Educators," but the notion of a perfect forum is overly romantic. Some subjects are expressly forbidden. In 2011, for instance, the Texas Civil Rights Project found that Texas banned reading material meant to "achieve the breakdown of prisons" and publications that are "detrimental to offenders' rehabilitation" (Watson et al.). Such strictures can serve the purpose of deputizing professors as defenders of the prison, thereby undermining their goal for teaching there in the first place.

One topic in particular that does not merit inclusion on the Texas Banned Book list is race. The racial disparity within the prison system is egregious. My students are well aware of this fact—I assume the rest of the prison population is as well—and tensions can be high. In fact, one of my students quite pointedly asked me to refrain from discussing racial issues, as such teacher-led discussions show a lack of awareness of the wider environemnt and might put some students in danger. And, a few semesters ago, another student wrote that during a lesson on Reconstruction in history class he had begun to worry about being targeted when class was over. This gives "safe space" a whole new meaning.

Instructors in college-in-prison programs simply have no way of knowing the level of tension inside their chosen facility. In my classroom, the rules of decorum are not only followed but closely monitored by the students themselves. Certainly, debates can be freewheeling, even raucous, sometimes causing an officer to stick his head into the room to check on the noise level. But they are also constrained by a formal, even archaic, graciousness. At such times, all I can do is watch as the argument becomes an intricate dance of intellectual and physical deference. What appears from my perspective to be a textbook example of intellectual exchange might actually be an attempt at diffusion. The racialized basis of incarceration in the United States—as chronicled by, for example, Michelle Alexander in *The New Jim Crow*, Khalil Gibran Muhammad in *The Condemnation of Blackness*, and Elizabeth Hinton in *From the War on Poverty to the War on Crime*—itself discourages attempts to address it in class. Whether through diktat or an overabundance of caution, the very topics most in need of discussion have been silenced.

Wrestling with the Syllabus

The syllabus for English 101 requires students to write a minimum of twenty pages, and one of the course learning outcomes reads: "Employ the stages of the writing process to produce and revise college level academic prose—to be assessed by measuring an informative or persuasive paper (3 pages minimum) against its rough draft (2 pages minimum)." Assigning a three-page paper "in Times New Roman 12-point font" is impossible when students are writing by hand, on differently sized notepads. And, without word processing, revising any paper is an onerous and time-consuming slog. Revision becomes a matter of economics as well. Paper and pens are not easy to come by—never mind Wite-Out—and the prices at commissary are high. In May 2018, Stephen Raher of the Prison Policy Initiative published a study entitled "The Company Store: A Deeper Look at Prison Commissaries," which lists average sales per category of goods in three states. In the category "mail and stationery," people in prison spent an annual average of $20 in Washington, $28 in Illinois, and $48 in Massachusetts. It's hard to know what incarcerated people earn throughout the country, but one of my students submitted a paper in the fall of 2018 claiming that prison wages could be as low as nine dollars every two weeks and only as high as thirty. Under these circumstances, demanding extensive revisions is not just impractical; it's immoral.

The English 101 syllabus also states that students must "incorporate relevant and appropriately documented research into their own essays" and that they are to receive "instruction by a college librarian in research methods, appropriate online databases, and documentation as they apply to a variety of papers and readings." In the prison, there is no research. The prison library is rudimentary and, I'm told, largely inaccessible. Computers are nonexistent. The students are not allowed access to college databases, and we are not allowed to bring in articles at their request. Everything comes from the professors, using material of our own choosing, which must be approved by the facility well in advance. Even then, course packets and textbooks can go missing or sit in mail rooms until the middle of the semester. Sometimes these restrictive circumstances can lead to unique research opportunities: one of my students performed a qualitative study on the effects of video games on violent behavior by interviewing the men in his company. Overall, however, they are a violation of both the course objectives and the very nature of free inquiry. Even worse, they can make the professor complicit in the carceral project.

Collaborators in Deed?

During a class on the short story, a student once asked, "Hey, professor, is it true that hyenas are unisex?" My immediate reaction was a kind of bemused shock. On reflection, though, I can understand: for the past few semesters, I had been the only source of information for him and the rest of his classmates. The lack of research opportunities is probably the greatest drawback of the prison classroom, and it problematizes the student-professor relationship. The situation is captured by Michael Brawn, an incarcerated student at the University of Illinois at Urbana-Champaign, in a 2015 article for the *Journal of Critical Scholarship on Higher Education and Student Affairs* entitled "Higher Education in an Era of Mass Incarceration: Possibility under Constraint." Brawn confesses to feeling a certain "tension" when he considers his role as an incarcerated student:

> When students are wholly reliant upon teachers for access to information, can the goals of critical pedagogy be achieved? After much reflection and study, I am now able to articulate some of this tension, which is that the central tenets of critical pedagogy are challenged in prison spaces because these classrooms are enwrapped within a network of power imbalance and control. . . . Information in prison is provided to us as it is deemed necessary by authorities in charge of the facility. (Castro et al. 21)

Information is also provided as it is deemed necessary by college professors and program administrators. "As one can imagine," Brawn concludes, "living in this kind of informational vacuum can be very frustrating. Unintentionally replicating this power dynamic in the classroom creates an oppressive space that works against the spirit of critical pedagogy" (21). One of my own students expressed frustration with the college's lack of response to inquiries he had submitted. To him, the administration's silence matched that of any other state-level actor in its implied disregard for people in prison. I wish I could say he was wrong, but there have been times when administrators have seemed to meet student complaints with the attitude, "They should consider themselves fortunate to be in the program. If they don't like it, they can always quit." Not once have I heard that said about students on the main campus.

Fortunately, though, my concern about being part of the system is not shared by the students. As my colleagues and I try to help them navigate the college environment, they help us navigate theirs. They translate "prison speak." They worry about how we're being treated by the facility. They're sympathetic to the difficulty we have with time constraints and censorship of material, and they appreciate our efforts. The student who wanted me to have a desk was genuinely concerned. The student who complained about shabby treatment at the hands of the administration wrote appreciatively about his professors and credited them for his continued participation in the program. Once, while I was showing a film in class, somebody wordlessly handed me a Jolly Rancher. And every week, when class is over, I get words of thanks, and somebody is bound to say, "Have a good week, professor, and drive safe."

In the words of James Baldwin, "The object of one's hatred is never, alas, conveniently outside but is seated in one's lap, stirring in one's bowels and dictating the beat of one's heart. And if one does not know this, one risks becoming an imitation—and, therefore, a continuation—of principles one imagines oneself to despise" (qtd. in Gates 87). How can this be avoided? Remain aware of motives. Make sure that program administrators are prison educators. Choose course load and reading materials carefully, with input from the students if possible. Instead of simply carrying existing courses into the prison, where they will be subject to the restrictions and circumstances of the facility, create prison-dedicated courses that will acknowledge both what cannot succeed there and what can only succeed there. Above all, change the public narrative to one that tells the real story of higher education in prison, from the restrictive venues to the modest, hard-fought successes. Otherwise, prison educators risk feeding the flames of exploitation and resentment that define our country's relationship with its incarcerated citizens—liberators in theory but collaborators in deed.

WORKS CITED

Alexander, Michelle. *The New Jim Crow: Mass Incarceration in the Age of Colorblindness.* New Press, 2010.

Castro, Erin, et al. "Higher Education in an Era of Mass Incarceration: Possibility under Constraint." *Journal of Critical Scholarship on Higher Education and Student Affairs*, vol. 1, no. 1, 2015, pp. 13–33.

Cohen, Noam S. "Attica Town Struggles to Forget 1971." *The New York Times*, 1 Sept. 1991, p. 34L.

Diefenbach, Mallory. "Honoring the Fallen; Memorial Service Held for Forty-Fifth Anniversary of Attica Prison Riots." *The Daily News*, 14 Sept. 2016.

Dippel, Stewart A. "The Attica Muse: Lessons from Prison." *The History Teacher*, vol. 26, no. 1, 1992, pp. 61–70.

Foucault, Michel. *Discipline and Punish: The Birth of the Prison.* Random House, 1979.

Gates, Henry Louis. *Loose Canons: Notes on the Culture Wars.* Oxford UP, 1992.

Hinton, Elizabeth. *From the War on Poverty to the War on Crime: The Making of Mass Incarceration in America.* Harvard UP, 2016.

Huckin, Thomas, et al. "Critical Discourse Analysis and Rhetoric and Composition." *College Composition and Communication*, vol. 64, no. 1, 2012, pp. 107–29.

Kavanaugh, Edward. "A Keyless Prison Is to Rise in Attica." *The New York Times*, 31 Mar. 1929, p. 125.

Malakki [Ralph Bolden]. "An Open Letter to Prison Educators." *Critical Perspectives on Teaching in Prison: Students and Instructors on Pedagogy Behind the Walls*, edited by Rebecca Ginsburg, Routledge, 2019, pp. 17–18.

Melville, Herman. *Moby Dick.* Penguin Books, 1955.

Muhammad, Khalil Gibran. *The Condemnation of Blackness: Race, Crime, and the Making of Modern Urban America.* Harvard UP, 2011.

Raher, Stephen. "The Company Store: A Deeper Look at Prison Commissaries." Prison Policy Initiative, May 2018, www.prisonpolicy.org/reports/commissary.html.

Rambach, Peggy. "Logged Off." *The Chronicle of Higher Education*, 9 Sept. 2013, chronicle.com/article/Captive-Audience/141375.

Schumach, Murray. "Students in Town of Attica Are Recovering from Shock." *The New York Times*, 24 Sept. 1971, p. 26.

Thompson, Heather Ann. *Blood in the Water: The Attica Prison Uprising of 1971 and Its Legacy.* Random House, 2016.

Watson, Maggie, et al. *Banned Books in the Texas Prison System: How the Texas Department of Criminal Justice Censors Books Sent to Prisoners.* Texas Civil Rights Project, 2011, prisonlegalnews.org/media/publications/texas_civil_rights_project_prison_book_censorship_report_2011.pdf.

Wilner, M. M. "New Attica Prison to Cost $12,000,000." *The New York Times*, 26 Jan. 1930, p. 51.

Zimmerman, Jonathan. "Scholars behind Bars." *The New York Review of Books*, 23 Feb. 2017, www.nybooks.com/articles/2017/02/23/scholars -behind-bars-college-prison.

Collaborating to Reimagine Knowledge Sharing in the Prison Classroom

James King and Amber Shields

When we enter a classroom, we carry our past with us. We come in as individuals shaped by our own experiences and by opinions that have been passed down to us and that we have formed over time. We come in with the label "teacher" or "student" and, especially by the time we are in higher education, with preconceived notions of the structure and power dynamics of a classroom that guide us through the space. For entering a classroom is walking into a space of time-honored power structures. There are rules and codes we follow in this space. Teachers pass on knowledge to students, who often take it and replicate it. In this structure, learning is a process of passing down not only information but also the rules and codes of the learning environment, which reflect, as the educator and education scholar Lisa Delpit describes it, a "culture of power" (282). This structure perpetuates itself as those students who thrive in this environment become teachers and pass on the same norms, canons, and power dynamics they were taught.

The implications of such asymmetries of power in the classroom are amplified in prison. The prison classroom carries within it not only the contexts of the educational institution but also the prison institution's unique contexts. Prisons take people from marginalized communities with limited access to certain opportunities and disenfranchise them even further through their explicit enforcement of a lack of rights. In the prison setting, the classroom's implementation of the educational institution's own history of marginalization is more severely felt. This marginalization is further exacerbated in the curriculum itself, which, based on passed-down canons, often upholds a nonmarginalized, Western, white male perspective as the accepted knowledge base. In this structure, success is defined by inclusion in or tolerance of the culture of power, leaving students who do not assimilate excluded.

Our classrooms and courses in the Prison University Project, a program offering an accredited associate of arts degree inside California's San Quentin State Prison, mirror the higher education institution from which students seek to obtain a recognized degree. A number of the volunteer teachers bring in this institutional context, since many teach in universities or are undertaking their graduate studies nearby. As a student teaching assistant and teacher respectively, we came together in one of these classes and began a conversation about not only what we were doing in the classroom but how we were doing it, asking, How are institutional power frameworks from educational institutions perpetuated and interpreted in these circumstances? What happens and what can be done when there is a disconnect in this relationship and the classroom material and structure do not necessarily take into consideration the needs of students who have not always been included in this framework?

By critically exploring writing and humanities courses in a higher-education-in-prison (HEP) program, in this essay we examine how higher education is delivered in the prison system. We study the enaction of power structures through classroom dynamics and curriculum and consider its effects on students. Amid the prison restrictions that everyone involved in HEP programs faces, we emphasize the specific structures and restrictions that are brought in and perpetuated by higher educational institutions. As nonincarcerated teachers and incarcerated students navigate these cultures of power within the prison setting, classroom dynamics and curriculum can reemphasize exclusion through subtle marginalization. Gaps in social and cultural relevance, and in understanding in teacher training and curriculum design, can result in not only the inability to meet student needs but also the continuation of harmful narratives, trauma, and power hierarchies. Social injustices can thus be reinforced even while attempts are being made to break them down.

As the HEP movement grows, we ask, How can we interrupt learning based on a culture of power and instead build a more reflective and inclusive classroom? Part of this reflection and revision should be a dialogue in which teachers and students participate as equal stakeholders to challenge classroom structures and canons. Contextualizing our own experiences with higher education in prison in the light of Abena Subira Mackall's argument that the HEP discussion should center on examining education as a democratizing tool and encouraging civic-minded citizenry, we question the ways in which this aim is thwarted by current classroom power structures and curriculum. We consider how targeted institutional support, classroom norms, and curriculum shifts might allow for a more democratically incorporated student both inside and outside the classroom. Our goal is to expose the replication of the culture of power from traditional educational institutions into prison institutions and overturn it by encouraging dialogue and democratic approaches in the classroom and curriculum.

Our essay first examines ways that power is enacted in the educational institution through classroom norms and curriculum, especially those centered on "canonical" texts. We then discuss ways to democratize power structures and promote student inclusion to implement change. By questioning the ways that cultures of power are introduced and replicated in the classroom to the benefit of some and the continued marginalization of others, and by seeking a collective reimagining of this dynamic, we look for new ways to promote greater social justice. We offer these ideas in relation to the larger current discussion of educational institution reform. We hope to join this crucial dialogue through our exploration of how the prison classroom, as a place of meeting of two rigid institutions, can be transformed into a space of innovation and social justice.

Reflecting on Our Classrooms

To transport the higher education system into prison is to introduce an institution that itself does not have the best track record in supporting diverse student populations. Educational institutions in the United States have traditionally perpetuated assimilation, colonization, and white supremacy rather than democracy. It is worth noting that while the US criminal justice system stresses individual accountability (and ignores the punishing effects of white supremacy), US higher education institutions stress individual merit (and assimilation into the paradigm of white supremacy) and have been a central site of reproducing white privilege through curriculum and pedagogy (Peters). In replicating this system within a specifically marginalized and disenfranchised population—incarcerated people—we must look at not only the benefits of education but also the potential harm of replicating some aspects of higher education's pedagogy and canon.

The classroom has always been both a place for learning and one of assimilation or marginalization. The classroom's rules and codes reflect those of the culture of power, and thus the power dynamic between teachers and students shifts depending on whether the student is already a part of or familiar with that culture. This is because, as Delpit examines, there are cultural structures at play that favor the implicit transfer of information between comembers in a group. Students who are members of the same ethnic or class group as the teacher have a far greater chance of avoiding the communication breakdown, and often subsequent punishment, that can happen in cross-cultural communication (58). The implicit message is that the marginalized students, not the classroom, must change.

This barrier to inclusion obstructs the practice of the classroom as a democratic space. As bell hooks explains, students who believe they are entering a "democratic" space in education are censored from voicing critique of "bourgeois class biases," as any questioning of this system is labeled as unpopular or troublesome (179). This censorship also extends to the students' bodies. In both prisons and classrooms, students are told when it is acceptable to speak, stand up, or leave. Of course, this is true of most settings that have social and cultural norms, but the prison classroom carries with it the added baggage of teachers and prison guards who often assert power in very similar ways. All too often, teachers replicate the pedagogical tactics that informed their learning in the classroom without realizing how such tactics mirror or even strengthen the ways that guards maintain power in the larger prison structure. College classes are often promoted as a privilege, an opportunity to leave the long hours of boredom, sprinkled with seemingly arbitrary violence, that characterize most prison yards and engage in learning. This in turn makes higher education valuable to the incarcerated student, not primarily because of the learning itself but because it offers a means of mental escape. Prison officials recognize this dynamic and then use it as a means of controlling incarcerated learners' behavior. Thus, the educator becomes a tool whereby the prison can assert even greater control over those people it is holding captive.

It is important when thinking of power dynamics in incarcerated classrooms to make a distinction between the different ways hierarchy is created in a learning environment. Teachers draw power from the positional authority granted them by the institution providing the education, the correctional institution allowing the class, and their knowledge of the proposed topic and their credentialed expertise. Some of these sources of authority are unavoidable whereas others are socially constructed; some help move the class and others cause harm. When teachers and students do not explicitly acknowledge and address these differences, power and privilege are allowed to work in ways that undermine some traditional objectives of higher education in prison, like teaching critical thinking and exploring agency.

These power dynamics are reinforced through the use of canons. Because participants in HEP programs are often taught by teachers working within educational institutions, the canons of particular fields are typically introduced. Most of these courses are introductory courses, giving students a glimpse of key texts and ideas in a field but not leading to more focused, higher-level courses that often serve as the places for canonic breaks in higher education. While there is a growing movement to include more diverse materials, many of the guiding principles and histories of various disciplines are based on these canons, so it is difficult to break from the desire and perceived need to share foundational classics. Promoting canons, however, constitutes a use of the culture of power that undermines students' expression of their own agency and desire to explore ideas that go beyond dominant perspectives.

Film studies, for example, a relatively new discipline, is already steeped in a tradition that endorses chosen directors—almost all white, Western men, with a few key (male) exceptions—as individually acting auteurs to serve as the base of study, though the work of these directors offers little diversity of subject matter or point of view. Style and artistic merit are most often put front and center while harmful themes are overlooked, as when D. W. Griffith's *The Birth of a Nation*, infamous for its incendiary racism, is canonized and taught for the sake of its narrative style and editing techniques. Having seen this film taught at San Quentin as a technical exemplar, I, James, reflected:

> It's jarring to be in a room full of people whose lives have been severely affected by the residual effects of slavery; people who are indeed still enslaved because of a constitutional amendment that says it is permissible to enslave people who have broken laws, as we are subjected to some of the most vile racist propaganda this country has produced, all under the auspices of the "value" of the art. What message does it send when artistic skill is considered important enough to potentially retraumatize people who only signed up to study film?

Determining on students' behalf that the perceived merits of a work outweigh the potential for harm highlights the students' lack of agency. Classifying the harmful text as beneficial may alienate students through the implication that the text is more valuable than they are.

Despite the double institutional layers that we need to work against in HEP programs, we also believe that the HEP classroom is a place for questioning the status quo and instituting change. We all carry multiple pasts with us into the classroom, but we carry with them multiple possibilities. In any class at any time, the roles are blurred. Teachers learn, students teach, and teachers rely upon students to help manage other students' behavior or to clarify a teaching point that they are having difficulty expressing. Looking forward, we want to lean into this learning capacity and the blurring of roles to consider how we can reposition and rediscover all of ourselves as learners who will dare to reimagine the classroom.

Reimagining Our Classrooms

We want to explore how the classroom can be, as Mackall suggests, a place that advances democratic values as opposed to power hierarchies. Mackall describes the prison classroom as ideally being able to offer "a distinct social environment . . . in which incarcerated men and women can work in diverse groups, develop self-esteem, practice empathetic perspective taking, and through this access to knowledge better understand themselves and their actions" and thus develop the skills for "active civic membership in a democratic society" (10). Such an environment is created in part by student interaction but also depends on reenvisioned and co-created teacher-student dynamics and curriculum in which learning and development are based on student contributions, interests, and needs. We believe that practicing democratic norms will better align with many of the stated values of higher education and produce graduates better equipped to critically assess their environments. While there is not one answer—as the diversity of people, programs, and institutions should not be confined to one vision—we want to share some of our reimaginings as part of a larger reenvisioning that we hope continues to grow.

Before we begin looking at our practices, we must assess our language. Throughout the first part of the essay, we used the words *teacher* and *student* to describe two key stakeholders in current classrooms. This labeling, however, fails to fully reflect the classroom's fluid learning environment and also creates a hierarchical binary from which we want to break away. In this part of the essay, we therefore use the terms *facilitator* and *participant* to describe these two stakeholders and their new positions in the classroom. Though a facilitator does have authority while facilitating, that authority is not as absolute as that of a "teacher." Facilitators listen, manage discussions, encourage dialogue, move the discussion between talking points, and remind participants of agreed-upon norms. *Participant* is a more neutral term than *student* and leaves room for all the ways people engage in the classroom.

The programs and institutions that directly or indirectly show up in these spaces are also participants in the journey of education. Although an individual facilitator or participant can create change, it is unfair and unsustainable to make progress contingent on any single person's actions. Unsupported change can be hard, especially when faced with factors like years of institutional conditioning, the transitory nature of facilitators and participants in mainly volunteer-taught HEP programs, and a lack of committed time and space to develop and implement these changes. The question, then, is how we can create program support and spaces to bring together different stakeholders so that no one is forced to dream and fight for that dream alone, but all can arrive and test out new visions through supported collaboration.

While the end goal is to create a different learning space for all stakeholders, the preparation for reimagining the classroom starts before we enter. In setting up preclass training and support systems, stakeholders must take into account the past, including the system relationships, trainings, and practices that facilitators and participants have already experienced. As explored in the first section of this essay, these include cultural codes shared between like groups, classroom power dynamics that put a facilitator in a position of constructed authority, prison power dynamics, and canonical emphasis that reflects the culture in power. Working to undo the mindsets and practices that are a result of these past conditionings requires facilitators and participants to independently examine their own experiences, mind frames, and biases as elements that shape the learning space and to put those reflections into action. In her book, *Culturally Responsive Teaching and the Brain: Promoting Authentic Engagement and Rigor Among Culturally and Linguistically Diverse Students*, the educator and national educational consultant Zaretta Hammond offers suggestions for facilitators, including building awareness of the different levels of culture and unpacking sociopolitical contexts, that can be used as a starting point in trainings prior to meetings between all facilitators and participants. Since we are suggesting that facilitators in incarcerated classrooms should avoid relying upon traditional classroom norms for exercising power, it is important that the supporting HEP program and educational institution offer a space for facilitators to learn and think through alternative classroom views. Trainings should include a focus on how facilitators can manage classes in ways that recognize all participants' input and agency and also share classroom authority.

This training will set the stage for a larger group reflection, and Hammond's recommendations for facilitators can also be applied here. Before a class starts, stakeholders, facilitators, participants, and program administrators should come together to consider the individual contributions and relationship dynamics that will shape the classroom. This is a time for facilitators to share about themselves, showing that they are not infallible beings and have their own experiences that they bring (and that bring them) to this particular setting. They might show participants that they are willing to earn the privilege of facilitating by explaining their experience with the topic at hand while also acknowledging that everything they say may or may not be correct. Facilitators can relate examples of mistakes that they have made in past classrooms and explain how participants have dealt with those mistakes in productive ways in order to model how current participants can do the same. By sharing in talking circles like these with participants before the class meetings begin, facilitators can show themselves as learners who are also on a journey, and participants can share their experiences in the classroom. We find that many of our participants have had negative classroom experiences and thus can enter into the HEP classroom with a wary attitude. While it may be difficult to acknowledge these histories before relationships are built, opening a space early on to discuss feelings and apprehensions about the class establishes the space and commitment for trust-building.

A frank discussion in which facilitators articulate their preferred teaching styles, participants share their preferred learning styles, and all stakeholders set class norms will help lay the foundation for a collaborative learning environment. Facilitators and participants will occasionally bring opposing norms to the table but may not be inclined to disrupt the implicit culture of power by expressing them. A learning environment that challenges hierarchies of power, however, will be informed by values the participants bring from outside the classroom. For example, unspoken boundaries are often very important to incarcerated participants. It may be considered the height of disrespect to impinge on another participant's "time" with the facilitator, and an interpolation that might not be read as impolite in a traditional classroom may be unacceptable in prison culture. It can also be important to establish protocols for conducting partnered or group work involving participants who may have had disagreements outside the classroom, so an honest exploration of how facilitators and participants might best navigate that scenario in the HEP classroom should be part of the discussion. All stakeholders have to collaborate to distinguish which cultural norms are acceptable and which are too restrictive in a learning environment.

In order to truly practice "culturally responsive teaching" that addresses differences such as varying social norms, Hammond recommends that facilitators not only reflect upon and incorporate into their lesson planning their own experiences and biases but also build an alliance between themselves and participants that reflects a mutual commitment to growth. In looking at the construction of this alliance, Hammond, borrowing from Edward Bordin's idea of a "therapeutic alliance," emphasizes the following three aspects as crucial for creating a viable and beneficiary relationship between parties:

> a shared understanding and agreement to tackle a specific goal;
>
> a shared understanding and agreement about the tasks necessary to reach the goal along with confidence that these activities will lead to progress; and
>
> a relational bond based on mutual trust that creates an emotional connection and sense of safety for the client in order to do the hard work necessary to reach the goal. (93)

These first two points can begin in preclass talking circles. The third point, however, requires a bit more finesse. Trust is tricky in HEP classrooms. First, we are often working with people whose trust has largely been betrayed and who therefore harbor wariness toward all institutions. Further, this same system thwarts the building of these bonds through strict impositions against overfamiliarity. Any "emotional connection" between facilitators and participants is frowned upon and may be punished, whereupon the participant bears most of the repercussions. While individual trust based on emotional or personal connections is a difficult negotiation in this particular setting, there is still the ability to build trust in the classroom space itself. Preclass talking circles and continued mutual respect and commitment to learning differences through the course gives mutual trust the space to grow, albeit in its own particular way influenced by institutional restrictions.

Establishing a safe space for trust creates the foundation for further work in building a classroom community. In *Teaching to Transgress*, hooks observes that a way to combat cultures of power is by "creating in classrooms learning communities where everyone's voice can be heard, their presence recognized and valued" (185). In this instance, we define "voice" or "presence" as inclusion of each stakeholder's perspective on class goals, learning styles, cultural norms, and input on curriculum, when applicable. This commitment to inclusion will likely uplift individual participants and also, according to hooks, "helps establish communal commitment to learning" (186). Further, it leads to the potential for bottom-up change by redefining the educational space and the allotment of power. By bringing together all parties in creating an environment that values all and is conducive to everybody's learning, we open the space for practicing democracy and social justice and realizing the greater learning potential for those traditionally disenfranchised.

We further see these preclass talking circles as a place to start to break from the canon. To be clear, we are not proposing a more inclusive canon or some other revision. Instead, we are reimagining a classroom that does not rely upon canons. Today's greater interaction with and access to learning about diverse experiences means we have the ability and responsibility to question the emphasis we place on texts that historically have been deemed essential to the process of becoming educated. In many instances, knowledge of the canon is a proxy for academic excellence. However, recognition and familiarity with a text does not necessarily constitute academic excellence, and, depending on how texts are presented, can instead lead to academic exclusion. Critical consideration of how a text was created, what it meant at its time of publication and what it means or does not mean now, and how those meanings affect participants not only demystifies the text but also pushes participants to pursue academic excellence through critical thinking and personal engagement.

In accredited classes that need to meet certain requirements, the facilitators can start these conversations by talking through goals and giving examples of some texts they plan on using or that participants have used in the past. This discourse might also include a pedagogical training from the supporting institution to give facilitators a chance to reflect on their own teaching practices and to give participants insight into those practices that will assist them in distinguishing between teaching and content. From there, all stakeholders can participate in a conversation about which curriculum could meet these goals while also reflecting the participants' own personal goals and interests. Creativity in the earliest stages of curriculum development, incorporating films, television shows, music, and even sporting events, increases the odds of locating the areas where the participants can best connect with the learning objectives (and reduces the chance that participants with fluency in any one discipline will dominate the discussion). Thus a potential "culture of power" classroom becomes one shaped by the learning of every stakeholder. In this way, the idea of a canon is broken as classes become goal-related and are continually reinvented depending on the class.

As dialogue between facilitators and participants about the course curriculum allows for a disruption of the canon and the power structures and negative learning experiences it can perpetuate, it also allows for participants to become greater stakeholders in their education through shared responsibility for the structure and material of the class. The facilitator, meanwhile, has a renewed commitment to looking at new ways to engage with the material and use it to reach academic excellence. We hope that a greater commitment to preclass talking circles between facilitators and participants will shift the power dynamics of the HEP classroom and create more of a sense of personal and community commitment and, along with that, participant retention.

It is advisable for facilitators to attend these preclass talking circles as open moderators, ready to learn from and listen to participants but also willing to step in to steer discussion. Rather than allow a simple transfer of the power typically held in a classroom by a facilitator to a few dominant participants, facilitators are responsible for setting a space in which all participants are given equal power to explore their individual potential in class. The moderation must also find the balance between participant interests and desires and the class's overall goals and commitment to academic excellence.

Reimagining a space first requires reflecting on the space we have. Part of this process is for individual as well as collective stakeholders to reflect on what they bring and why they are there. While personal reflection may lead to a change in individual behavior, to truly create change there must be a space to reimagine as a community. Coming together in preclass talking circles allows for conversations and reflections by all individuals involved and lays the foundations for trust and collaboration to create new materials and power-sharing codes that support learning for all.

While we believe there is a clear need to start to implement these ideas in all higher education, and especially in HEP programs, there is still the question of how exactly to go about this work in the day-to-day realities that facilitators and participants face. It would be amazing if we had the power to halt everything for a moment, take a look at our broken systems, and engage in these crucial dialogues for change before moving forward. However, systems are in place and running, and we keep running with them. As our attention is pulled in a million different directions by questions of funding, accreditation, student needs, teacher needs, and so forth, it is hard to stop and rebuild a system that is already entrenched. Despite the difficulties, we need to create the space to start to imagine change. We need to push ourselves as teachers and students and program administrators to move beyond these labels and come to dialogue together as facilitators, participants, and collaborators. We need to have these discussions regarding how, in our fight for greater democracy and larger social change, we can reexamine our own practices in the classroom and change this microenvironment as we look to influence the broader society.

We feel hopeful, though, as we see the beginnings of this work in the conversations we have, in the classrooms and workshops and trainings our program offers, and in the greater opportunities for gathering like the national academic conference Corrections, Reform, and Rehabilitation, held by the Prison University Project inside San Quentin State Prison in October 2018. At that conference, we were reminded that even though it often feels like we are working in a silo, focused on solutions for our own classrooms, others have similar questions and preoccupations and are struggling to find the place and support to make these changes. The community is hungry for this dialogue, and we have to continue to look for ways to make it an ongoing conversation beyond our own spheres of operation. Collaborating to reimagine knowledge sharing is a continual process that must have the ability to change as it responds to and is taught in new ways to particular classroom learning communities. Again, democratic dialogue and the presence of everyone's voice is essential as the diversity of people, programs, and institutions demand that the canon and classroom be reimagined, not just once but continually, for our individual and collective growth.

WORKS CITED

The Birth of a Nation. Directed and produced by D. W. Griffith, 1915.

Delpit, Lisa. "The Silenced Dialogue: Power and Pedagogy in Educating Other People's Children." *Harvard Educational Review*, vol. 58, no. 3, 1988, pp. 280–98.

Hammond, Zaretta. *Culturally Responsive Teaching and the Brain: Promoting Authentic Engagement and Rigor among Culturally and Linguistically Diverse Students.* Corwin, 2015.

hooks, bell. *Teaching to Transgress: Education as the Practice of Freedom.* Routledge, 1994.

Mackall, Abena Subira. "Promoting Informed Citizenship through Prison-Based Education." *Critical Education*, vol. 9, no. 13, 2018, https://doi.org/10.14288/ce.v9i13.186342.

Peters, Michael. "Why Is My Curriculum White?" *Educational Philosophy and Theory*, vol. 47, no. 7, 2015, pp. 641–46.

Disrupting the Time of Incarceration: Close Reading in a Justice-Oriented Prison Classroom

Rachel Boccio

At the time of this writing, 445 teenage boys occupy bare, echoing cinder-block cells at a correctional facility in Cheshire, Connecticut. Manson Youth Institution (MYI) is not a juvenile detention center; it is a maximum security state prison for young people (many unsentenced) who are charged, tried, or convicted in the adult criminal justice system. The boys incarcerated there—primarily poor, undereducated people of color—embody alarming but long-standing statistical realities. Though one of the wealthiest states in the country, Connecticut tolerates the largest racial disparity in its prison population (where Black youths are committed at fourteen times the rate of their white peers) and the highest academic achievement gap (a persistent, severe imbalance in the educational performance and attainment of students with lower socioeconomic status; see Love et al.; "Connecticut Profile"; "Every Child"). Not surprisingly, teens arriving at Manson—where enrollment in the high school program is compulsory—have histories of school truancy, failure, and expulsion; their average academic grade level equivalency is between fourth and fifth grade (see Connecticut, Department of Correction 8). A majority have learning disabilities, substance abuse problems, and behavioral conditions, including trauma-induced neurodevelopmental and psychiatric disorders (see Love et al.).

I taught English full-time (seven sections of reading, literature, and writing) at Manson Youth Institution for twenty years before accepting a faculty position in higher education. While I do not intend in this essay to gloss over difficulties with classroom management and instruction—which persisted to the end of my tenure—I do claim the prison classroom as a uniquely provocative space for resisting traditional relations of power (which persist in education to the especial detriment of underprivileged, low-performing students) and for eschewing educative practices that prioritize amassing information.[1] The pedagogical scene highlighted here—three days spent examining Mumia Abu-Jamal's memoir *Live from Death Row*—draws upon established foundations for social justice education and from a theory of close reading that articulates interactive and experimental aspects of the literary practice. This kind of close reading is a form of deep reading in that it provides "an array of sophisticated processes that propel comprehension," such as inferential reasoning, critical analysis, and reflection (Wolf and Barzillai 33). As such, I follow established practices for encouraging and supporting deep, critical reading, including teacher modeling of comprehension strategies, the use of graphic organizers, and opportunities for social learning.[2]

The students I taught are enrolled in a class called High School English 7; they are grouped by age, not ability. Of the fifteen students, five have taken English courses in their city high schools, and one progressed to the twelfth grade. Three students are only functionally literate, having not attended school routinely since the elementary grades. The remaining boys have common tales: in and out of towns and districts, semesters begun but not completed. In other words, the student body of High School 7 is representative of young people in mandated prison classrooms across the country. Some days the students arrive lethargic or angry, directing these emotions at me and at each other: they put their heads down, push papers off their desks, tell me "this" or "that" is "stupid." Yet they can be drawn out. Years of teaching incarcerated students compels me toward a pedagogy that recognizes their unique knowledge (even as they are, at times, surly teens) and involves students analyzing and disrupting the identities that structure our social worlds—whether around race, class, or civil status. Put another way, in the rigid, hierarchal, disciplinary space of prison, the only teaching that I have found to work is the kind that is forthright about the politics—both juridical and pedagogical—that shape the material conditions of learning.

What follows is an account of my time reading Abu-Jamal's *Live from Death Row* with this particular group of high schoolers. The experience, though specific, can address broader challenges of teaching complex literary texts to academically underprepared students in prison. My objectives, methods, and sequence are readily adaptable by social justice educators teaching incarcerated students in a variety of prison programs and with other primary texts.

Introducing the Literature

To effectively engage the students at Manson in thinking alongside me, I need to first convince them that the new direction we are about to take in a unit or course is worth their attention, interest, and sincere participation.

So, the afternoon before we are scheduled to begin *Live from Death Row*, I project onto the classroom wall Abu-Jamal's image as it appears on the cover of his book. The students are immediately attracted to the steely brown face—long dreadlocks partially shadowing a bearded front; intense, dark eyes. They wonder aloud, "What is his deal?" As they gaze and snicker, I pass around a paperback—my copy. At Manson, like many prison schools, there are scant funds for educational materials and few means of safeguarding property in inmate cells. For this reason, among others, I seldom assign reading or other assignments to be completed outside class, nor do I expect students to arrive with texts or writing implements. Instead, all instructional activities are undertaken together, usually with materials I've supplied.

Live from Death Row, first published in 1995, is a collection of vignettes, scathing political indictments of the US criminal justice system, written while Abu-Jamal was on death row in a Pennsylvania correctional facility—confined in a six-by-ten-foot cell for twenty-two hours a day. Each student takes the book in hand, flips through the pages, reads the back cover, checks for pictures and a table of contents, notes the publication date—all habits they have been encouraged, again and again, to adopt. As enthusiasm spreads, I select (appearing to do so at random) five students whom I know to have higher reading and critical thinking abilities; around these students I tell the others to coalesce (no more than three to a group). As clusters configure—within a cacophony of swapped seats, new grievances, and rising excitement—I pass out photocopies of the book's introduction, written by John Edgar Wideman. This we read together in round-robin fashion. Initially, I ask for volunteers, but I also walk around, highlighting short, easier passages on the pages of my reluctant readers: "Be ready to come in here," I say, and then call on them respectively. Wideman's brief essay provides the biographical and historical context of the book. It situates *Live from Death Row* in the American literary tradition of captivity generally and in the genre of prison writing specifically.

Next, I project a list of chapter titles, all evocatively named: "Blackmun Bows Out of the Death Game," "Manny's Attempted Suicide," "Expert Witness from Hell," "Two Bites of the Apple in Dixie," and more. Students deliberate over which vignette their group will analyze in the three classes that follow. They shout out suggestions, settling first on one and then abandoning it for another. To help them decide, I deliver worn photocopies of each title—yellowed, dog-eared pages beset with penciled marginalia (some inspired analysis, mostly lazy doodles). By the end of the afternoon, merely a run-up to our actual start, groups are formed, roles assigned, chapters selected. The students spend the last remaining minutes bombarding me with questions about Abu-Jamal: "Who did he kill?" "How long was he on death row?" "Where is he now?" "What else did he write?" They want more: images, details, stories. I tell them about different leftist political groups that continue to agitate for Abu-Jamal's release and about his consistent presence on a number of popular podcasts. I surprise them by playing an episode; Abu-Jamal's deep baritone fills the room:

> Days of chaos, nights of madness. . . . A bull is loose in a china shop, wrecking everything in reach. The world looks on with alarm and a sense, a growing sense, that the American empire is moving to its last days. . . . The world spins on the edge of madness, US empire, BEHOLD, empire of chaos. . . . From Imprisoned Nation, this is Mumia Abu-Jamal. (Abu-Jamal, "Days of Chaos")

It's a good start.

Day 1: Understanding the Text

While there are disparities among students in any learning environment, prison classrooms are exceptionally heterogeneous when it comes to intellectual aptitude, prior knowledge, and reading ability. Still, distances are bridgeable; emergent or struggling readers can engage with challenging texts (even readings that far exceed the instructional level) when they encounter those texts collaboratively. On the afternoon we begin *Live from Death Row*, students arrive at a room refashioned by five "literature circles" spread wide apart. On their desks are copies of the chosen vignettes that they will come to deeply know. Today's work, however, is strictly comprehension: by the end of the class, students will be able to read their vignette, define challenging vocabulary, answer recall questions accurately and thoroughly, and raise questions that direct and foster further dialogue.

They begin by skimming pages and choosing their sections; the "Day 1 Leader" (a role meant, plainly, to rotate) sees that everyone has a part. Students do not need to speak equally, but every student must lend their voice to the group read. As they skim and clamor for parts, I pass around a vocabulary T chart—a graphic designed to organize the acquisition of new words. The group reading "Philly Daze: An Impressionistic Memoir" (149–66) begins to underline: "eloquent," "internecine," "bona fide," "ranting," "interwove," "simulcasting," "whitenized," "impunity." These words are listed in the left-hand column; there is space for the students to add others. Later, they'll debate the meanings of these isolated terms, working together to incorporate the words into new written and spoken contexts, some of which they'll record on the right-hand side of the T chart.

Soon there is the familiar drone of parallel reading; circles tighten as students lean in. I do the same, interrupting groups at key moments in their respective texts. I ask one student to summarize what another has read; I am deliberate with my queries, eliciting basic recall from some and higher-level evaluation from others. I ask them to justify their thinking; I encourage debate, dissent, and dialogue. When each group finishes reading, they labor together to craft responses to written questions. For example, students reading "Teetering on the Brink between Life and Death" (3–18) are asked, Where is Abu-Jamal incarcerated? How, in his mind, is death row unlike other forms of imprisonment? What are the "rules and regulations" that order his day? Why are the imprisoned men allowed televisions but not typewriters? Who is McClesky? What facts did he bring before the US Supreme Court in 1987?

Social justice pedagogy is inquiry-based.[3] As the students engage with the text and with one another, questions emerge, which they write on the reverse side. The group working on "B-Block Days and Nightmares" (65–72) wonders, How did Abu-Jamal get an article in *The Nation*? Can we publish our writing? Is B Block worse than Seg at Manson? Why are the imprisoned men encouraged to watch so much TV? Why are the prison guards so racist? Why are they racist here? Are the guards all from the country and the imprisoned men all from the city? How did Abu-Jamal learn everything? How did he learn to talk like that? Where did he go to school? Turning, eventually, to me, they ask, "Would you read this chapter out loud? Would you say all those bad words?"

Day 2: Code-Switching

The "B Blockers," as they call themselves, are not the only students to perceive abrupt and adroit shifts in tone and language. *Live from Death Row* is a masterclass in rhetorical savvy; each vignette lays bare the complex institutional histories, legal structures, and psychological strategies—essentially the entire state-sanctioned apparatus—for obliterating the personhood of human beings on death row, for converting self-directed, vibrant Black men into "the best behaved and least disruptive of all inmates": tame zombies "possessing little or no psychological life" (5, 7). Yet at the same time Abu-Jamal upends this narrative in more than one way. First, his stories of excessive cruelty and bizarre ritual perform a kind of execution of the book's powerful class. The guards, wardens, police, and judges who people *Live from Death Row* are not people at all; they are flattened allegorical constructs, caricatures of dystopia. These brutal figures are ever predictable: from the dimwitted, provincial correction officers to the educated, prominent judges, they keep to script—a paramilitaristic prison code or a racist legal one. Against this static backdrop, Abu-Jamal shifts, chameleonlike. His speech assumes the vulgarity of the convict, the objectivity of the reporter, and the erudition of the philosopher. Within the space of short paragraphs, he oscillates between the profane and the poetic:

> Hey man—you smell that water?!?
> What the fuck??!
> Hey, dude, this shit smells like gasoline!
> Gagging and spitting . . . a day begins at Huntingdon gulag in central Pennsylvania. . . . "Water up! Water up!" chants fill the morning air, ricocheting like verbal bullets, echoing, careening from cell to cell. (50)

I ask students about code-switching: "What does it mean? When do we do it? Why is it advantageous?" I ask for volunteers; two spirited teens rise immediately. They perform "This is how we talk" and then "This is how we talk to you."

Once we have agreed upon a definition, I ask each group to find examples of code-switching in their selected sections. I provide a rubric to help guide students from identification to analysis. When readers of "Nightraiders Meet Rage" seem puzzled by the task, I read the vignette's opening sentences: "Prisons are repositories of rage, islands of socially acceptable hatreds, where worlds collide like subatomic particles seeking psychic release. Like Chairman Mao's proverbial spark, it takes little to start the blazes banked within repressive breasts" (37). "How does this language mark Abu-Jamal?" I ask. "What does it tell us about him?" Students comment that it demonstrates his sophisticated knowledge, his understanding of science and politics, his ability to think abstractly, to write lyrically. "But what is the effect?" I ask. Thus prompted, students arrive at a conclusion they will return to often: Abu-Jamal is "smarter," they say, than everyone in the book. He is "better" than they are, on heightened ground—morally, spiritually, intellectually. In the narrative's details, we see the guards holding him down, but in its language, he rises above.

The next paragraph brings a sudden shift in place and tone: "I thought about that spark one morning recently when I heard an eruption of violence that hit Huntingdon's B Block, snatching the writer from the false escape of dreams" (37). I ask the students to notice that now Abu-Jamal has shifted to reporting on events that have just occurred; together, we consider this shift. *Live from Death Row* exhibits many of the tropes and conventions of the prison narrative.[4] It is, on one level, preoccupied with informing sympathetic readers of conditions they would otherwise know little about; thus the author frequently assumes the role of chronicler. I ask students about that touch of intimacy, the image of the sleepy writer. It's a sweetness that both humanizes the condemned man and also intensifies the shock that immediately follows: " 'Oh! You like hurtin' people, huh?' Punches, grunts, thuds, and crunches echoed up the steel tiers, awakening the groggy into sudden alertness. 'Getta fuck offa that man!' 'Leave that man alone, you fat, racist pussy!' " (37). In these lines, students recognize Abu-Jamal's convict persona—the "gangsta thug," as they say, whose communication with cellmates, throughout the book, remains raw. Students are pleased by Abu-Jamal's range: the author who quotes Mao Zedong, Fyodor Dostoevsky, and Albert Camus, who refers to legal appeals as "Sisyphean battles" and calls their neighborhoods American Bantustans—is, in the man who grieves, "Yard in?! Shit, man, we-a just go out here," a faithful voice from within the story, justly able to tell it (4). Their reaction to Abu-Jamal's "prison-speak" offers the chance to discuss literary dialect more generally, in terms of its power to particularize but also to validate the geographic and social backgrounds of characters. And it is an occasion, too, to name the work we've been engaged in doing.

Day 3: Close Reading

For practical as well as pedagogical reasons, close reading thrives in the prison classroom. In the stripped-down, low-budget atmosphere of the carceral school, close reading benefits from a lack of material requirements. Moreover, because close reading, in its purest form, eschews the hierarchical and atomized focus on testing (the "right/wrong" of so much mandated prison education, including the GED preparatory courses), incarcerated students, in my experience, are drawn to close reading instruction. When taken seriously and deliberately, close reading forces upon the reader "an ongoing decision," described by Andrew DuBois as "how much, exactly, writing has to do with *our* being, how individually, humanly important reading really, ontologically, is" (16). For the author of *Live from Death Row*, "writing" (and reading, for that matter) has everything to do with "being"; it is an "ontological" labor, a strategy for becoming that necessitates, precisely because of its origin, an especial validation from the audience. We—as close, attuned, sympathetic readers—help reanimate Abu-Jamal and constitute the humanity of one who, in the author's words, "walks the razor's edge between half-life and certain death" (5). Seen in this light, reading is an intellectual labor with mighty ethical weight.

On the third day, students are tasked with selecting passages from their vignettes that they find poignant or moving and recognize as doing important critical work in the text. By way of example, I turn their attention to a subsection of the book's first chapter, a scene titled "Humiliation":

> What visitors do not see, prior to the visit, is a horrifying spectacle—the body-cavity strip search. Once the prisoner is naked, the visiting-room guard spits out a familiar cadence:
>> Open yer mouth.
>> Stick out your tongue.
>> You wear any dentures?
>> Lemme see both sides of your hands.
>> Pull your foreskin back.
>> Lift your sac.
>> Turn around.
>> Bend over.
>> Spread your cheeks.
>> Bottom yer feet.
>> Get dressed. (8–9)

A through line of *Live from Death Row*, connecting the book's examination of case law with its graphic scenes of violence, shame, and trauma, is the link (historical, psychological, and ideological) between modern practices of incarceration and US chattel slavery. The prison ritual described here does this work of transporting readers to the "horrifying spectacle" of the slave auction, where Black bodies, often naked, awaited inspection: teeth, hands, feet, mouth. In the prison and at the auction, the officer shouts and "spits" grotesque commands. He is the brute, dehumanized by the viciousness of his duty.

Students comb the vignettes, now heavily marked, for passages, arguing for the distinction of this one or that. When they settle on selections, I have each "Day 3 Recorder" type his chosen portion into a computer, which projects the text for the other students to see. The group that has been reading "Spirit Death" offers this paragraph for careful scrutiny:

> The most profound horror of prisons lives in the day-to-day banal occurrences that turn days into months, and months into years, and years into decades. Prison is a second-by-second assault on the soul, a day-to-day degradation of the self, an oppressive steel and brick umbrella that transforms seconds into hours and hours into days. While a person is locked away in distant netherworlds, time seems to stand still; but it doesn't, of course. . . . Times, temperaments, mores change, and the caged move to outdated rhythms. (53)

"Doing time" is a common phrase in the discourse of imprisoned communities, and its meanings are multiple. "Doing time" can refer to the duration of a sentence, the boundary of a "bid": five years, ten years, twenty. It can refer to one's psychological or emotional orientation to incarceration—the way in which an individual might "do time." An imprisoned person might, in other words, "do time" by maximizing programmatic opportunities: anger management, drug and alcohol treatment, vocational education, fatherhood and mentoring programs. For the imprisoned, time is measured in the certificates of completion that accumulate on cell walls. Others "do time" by battling—they rail against systems, guards, each other—and in so doing mark time as mounting disciplinary infractions, trips to solitary confinement, fresh scars. But "doing time" can also designate, as it does in Abu-Jamal's text, the punishing temporality that inheres to carceral life, that makes prison a condition of the mind. The time of prison obliterates the linearity—the sense of passing through a progression of sequential events—that organizes cognition, that provides for unified subjectivity. And this stasis—this circumstance of "time stand[ing] still"—is, for Abu-Jamal, the "profound horror," the "banal[ity]" of the evil of prison life: it is the "assault" on every "soul," the "degradation" of every "self," the "oppressi[on]" that succeeds, finally, in carrying out the true punishment of incarceration.

Though they are young and have not been imprisoned for long, the students at Manson—every one of them—recall men who have returned to their homes, apartment buildings, and neighborhoods after decades of confinement, men who "moved to outdated rhythms." They tell me about people who cannot use computers, who are suspicious of cell phones, who look in vain for comforting objects long out of fashion (an AM/FM radio, a phone booth, a VCR), who are afraid to step outside. A potent pessimism spreads through the room, prompting a short respite (a chance to swap happier memories of home and family) and then a return to the text. I ask students to look more closely at the passage to identify where Abu-Jamal is unsettling the "horror" of prison time. It is helpful to point them to words, expressions, grammatical marks, so I begin to highlight pieces that deserve attention. The phrase "but it doesn't, of course" points, on the one hand, to the dismal fact that time, in the free world, moves on—that "mores change." And yet, "but it doesn't, of course," also draws attention to the myriad ways Abu-Jamal, the writer, the fighter, the provocateur, stands within the temporal "horror" of Pennsylvania's death row and refuses to be undone by it, made a relic. I alert students to the forward-inclining temporal flow operating at the level of each sentence: "day-to-day," "days into months, and months into years, and years into decades," "second-by-second," "seconds into hours and hours into days." There is an urgency made palpable in the hyphens and repetitive prepositions that together push the next words onward, an insistence on forward momentum that is as much about writing as it is about surviving.

Social Justice as Praxis

Live from Death Row figures a critique of modern incarceration into a searing aesthetic form, one that challenges intellects and consciences. Still, this achievement in and of itself does not make the teaching of Abu-Jamal's book emancipatory. Paulo Freire, the Brazilian educator, philosopher, and author of the groundbreaking text *Pedagogy of the Oppressed*, is perhaps the starting point for theoretical discussions of social change through radical praxis. His approach is writ large over the three days of instruction presented in this essay, not necessarily in the learning activities (which are more conventional than revolutionary) but rather in the pedagogy's methodological foundations: Education in High School 7 is a humanizing vocation; it proceeds from collaborative decision making and from shared material struggle. This intellectual labor disrupts the time—the profound, banal horror—to which students are sentenced. In engaging their chosen vignettes—first comprehending, then questioning, finally analyzing, always close reading—the students join Abu-Jamal in resisting the temporal paralysis that marks their incarceration and also the "national paralysis" that, in the words of John Stephen Hartnett, "fuels the desperation, cynicism, and dropout mentality [which] leads to crime and violence" (3). These students form a community of learners struggling not merely to read in a sophisticated manner but to understand the effects of power and the social construction of identity—how it is, exactly, that their middle-class, white teacher came to be in charge, and how they (all poor, Black and brown) came to be her imprisoned pupils.

Questioning authority is the cornerstone of liberation praxis. What I hope comes through this essay is a ceding of at least some power on my part, with the intention that everyone contributes, everyone explores. Maurianne Adams describes it this way: "[T]he pedagogical choices we make as social justice educators are as important as the content we teach, so that *what* participants are learning and *how* they are learning are congruent" (28). Said another way, it is not enough that students acquire a particular way to read a certain transgressive text; rather, that reading must practice and perform the logic and values of that text. Hence, with respect to *Live from Death Row*, the students of High School 7 determine for themselves the vignettes to read and the passages that merit special attention. They labor to craft intelligent responses together, to make meaning as a cohesive, democratic group. They adhere to norms that are maintained by rotating student-leaders; they balance the emotional and cognitive components of their learning. And they openly query their instructor, insisting that she assume risks and feel out of place—as in the appeal that I "code-switch" using words of Abu-Jamal's more vulgar prose.

Freire saw social justice education as the means by which oppressed people are made conscious of the strategies underlying their subordination so as to become agents at the vanguard of social change. It is an exceptionally high bar, especially in the carceral space, where an innumerable myriad of protocols exist to eliminate free thinking, expression, and rebellion.[5] Yet this is why we are drawn to the teaching of writing and literature in prison. With these exceptional students, we strive to engage a pedagogy that destabilizes the architectures of oppression from within, that makes transformation a matter of praxis, and that affirms the wisdom of the marginalized in efforts to reconstitute the world. I began this essay by noting the gross structural inequalities that increase the likelihood that certain populations of young people will become incarcerated. The hope I bring to teaching in prison, and to teaching in this way, is that students trained in close reading and in collaborative inquiry will apply these analytical practices to their own lives so as to make sense of, and perhaps even work to repair, endemic social failures that weaken us all.

NOTES

1. For related studies demonstrating how cooperative, student-directed, non-lecture approaches to teaching benefit lower-achieving students within and

beyond the K–12 classroom, see Awang; Edelsky; Lee; Emerson and Taylor; and Slavich and Zimbardo.

2. For a fuller discussion, see Fisher et al.

3. For a fuller discussion, see Adams et al.

4. I find it useful to consider general commonalities among many works produced by imprisoned people over the course of the twentieth and twenty-first centuries. Having said this, I recognize the term *prison narrative* to be a highly contested one. Patrick Elliot Alexander, for example, avoids the designation (as do many critical prison theorists) because, as he explains, the "literary works commonly classified as 'prison writings' or 'prison narratives' were not conceived of as such by their authors" (14). Moreover, Alexander points out that *Live from Death Row* and many works like it are perhaps better understood as *antiprison* narratives (15). To be sure, categories suggested by Alexander and others (*antiprison narrative, prisoner abuse narrative, prison-abolition narrative*) allow for a more astute accounting of analyses made by imprisoned and formerly imprisoned writers, specifically of draconian state violence within carceral settings that reproduces historical forms of racialized exploitation and control. For more discussion of "prison writing" as a problematic broad categorical designation, see also Rodríguez 81–86.

5. For an analysis of a pragmatic praxis that tests the possibilities of maintaining radical urgency in restrictive institutional and curricular confines, see Boccio. For broader discussion of the "context-specific challenges" that undermine critical pedagogy in prison, see Castro and Brawn. As one remedy, these authors offer an "emplaced praxis" for nonincarcerated educators working within prison systems that acknowledges contradictions in authority while also engaging, as much as possible, critical emancipatory paradigms.

WORKS CITED

Abu-Jamal, Mumia. "Days of Chaos." *Prison Radio*, prisonradio.org. Accessed 2 Feb. 2018.

———. *Live from Death Row*. Perennial, 2002.

Adams, Maurianne. "Pedagogical Foundations for Social Justice Education." Adams et al., pp. 27–51.

Adams, Maurianne, et al., editors. *Teaching for Diversity and Social Justice*. 3rd ed., Routledge, 2016.

Alexander, Patrick Elliot. *From Slave Ship to Supermax: Mass Incarceration, Prisoner Abuse, and the New Neo-Slave Novel*. Temple UP, 2018.

Awang, Mariyamni. "Cooperative Learning in Reservoir Simulation Classes: Overcoming Disparate Entry Skills." *Journal of Science Education and Technology*, vol. 10, no. 2, 2016, pp. 220–26.

Boccio, Rachel. "Toward the Soul of a Transformational Praxis: Close Reading and the Liberationist Possibilities of Prison Education." *Pedagogy: Critical Approaches to Teaching Literature, Language, Composition, and Culture*, vol. 17, no. 3, 2017, pp. 423–49.

Castro, Erin L., and Michael Brawn. "Critiquing Critical Pedagogies inside the Prison Classroom: A Dialogue between Student and Teacher." *Harvard Educational Review*, vol. 87, no. 1, pp. 99–121.

Connecticut, Department of Correction, Unified School District #1. *Annual Performance Report, 2021–22*. Sept. 2022, portal.ct.gov/-/media/DOC/Pdf/USD1/USD1-Annual-Report-21_22.pdf.

"Connecticut Profile." *Prison Policy Initiative*, prisonpolicy.org/profiles/CT.html. Accessed Jan. 2019.

DuBois, Andrew. "Close Reading: An Introduction." *Close Reading: The Reader*, edited by Frank Lentricchia and DuBois, Duke UP, 2003, pp. 1–40.

Edelsky, Carole. "On Critical Whole Language Practice: Why, What, and a Bit of How." *Making Justice Our Project: Teachers Working toward Critical Whole Language Practice*, edited by Edelsky, National Council of Teachers of English, 1998, pp. 7–36.

Emerson, Tisha L. N., and Beck A. Taylor. "Comparing Student Achievement across Experimental and Lecture-Oriented Sections of a Principles of Microeconomics Course." *Southern Economic Journal*, vol. 70, no. 3, 2004, pp. 672–93.

Every Child Should Have a Chance to be Exceptional. Without Exception: A Plan to Close Connecticut's Achievement Gap. Connecticut Commission on Educational Achievement, portal.ct.gov/-/media/SDE/Press-Room/Files/CT_Commission_on_Ed_Achievement_Report.pdf. Accessed Jan. 2019.

Fisher, Douglass, et al. "Research into Practice: Reading for Details in Online and Printed Text: A Prerequisite for Deep Reading." *Middle School Journal*, vol. 42, no. 3, 2011, pp. 58–63.

Freire, Paulo. *Pedagogy of the Oppressed*. Translated by Myra Bergman Ramos, Penguin Books, 1993.

Hartnett, Stephen John. "Empowerment or Incarceration?: Reclaiming Hope and Justice from a Punishing Democracy." *Challenging the Prison-Industrial Complex: Activism, Arts, and Educational Alternatives*, edited by Hartnett, U of Illinois P, 2011, pp. 1–12.

Lee, Carol. "Culturally Responsive Pedagogy and Performance-Based Assessment." *The Journal of Negro Education*, vol. 67, 1998, pp. 268–79.

Love, Hanna, et al. "Data Snapshot of Youth Incarceration in Connecticut." Urban Institute, June 2017, urban.org/research/publication/data-snapshot-youth-incarceration-connecticut.

Rodríguez, Dylan. *Forced Passages: Imprisoned Radical Intellectuals and the U.S. Prison Regime*. U of Minnesota P, 2006.

Slavich, George M., and Philip G. Zimbardo. "Transformational Teaching: Theoretical Underpinnings, Basic Principles, and Core Methods." *Educational Psychology Review*, vol. 24, 2012, pp. 569–608.

Wolf, Maryann, and Mirit Barzillai. "The Importance of Deep Reading." *Educational Leadership*, vol. 66, no. 6, 2009, pp. 32–37.

Reading and Writing between the Devil and the Deep Blue: The Appalachian Prison Book Project

Katy Ryan, Valerie Surrett, and Rayna Momen

A book club meets every other week, year-round, inside a women's prison in West Virginia. For five years, we have gathered to discuss literature and to write. The book club is part of the Appalachian Prison Book Project (APBP), a nonprofit that mails free books to people incarcerated in six states and offers educational opportunities in and out of prison. APBP grew out of a graduate course on the literature of imprisonment and resistance taught by Katy Ryan at West Virginia University (WVU) in 2004. Since then, APBP has mailed over fifty thousand books, created book clubs in prisons, organized a symposium on educational justice and Appalachian prisons, financially supported credit-bearing college classes in prison, launched a campaign opposing exploitative tablet contracts, and engaged the public in conversations about policing, the justice system, prison conditions, reform, and abolition.

Like most prisons in our region, the ones in which we volunteer are built in remote rural areas, hidden in plain sight. Surrounded by mountains, the prisons are set back from main roads and camouflaged by woods and steep elevation changes. The landscapes magnify the harsh prison architecture, a stark juxtaposition of concrete and lush green. It is not uncommon to see deer grazing near barbed-wire fencing. The land also bears the scars of Appalachia's history of resource exploitation and environmental destruction. An out-of-use surface mining site visually cuts the prison property in half. Like so many in Appalachian communities, those incarcerated here worry about the impacts of mining on air and water quality.[1]

For a small state, West Virginia has a surprising number of federal prisons (six) and, per capita, more federal prison cells than any other state (Wagner). Most people are imprisoned far from home, and, since it is nearly impossible to travel to these locations by public transportation, family visits are rare.[2] Dense fog means we may not be allowed in; perimeters must be visible at all times. In the introduction to *Reading Is My Window: Books and the Art of Reading in Women's Prisons*, Megan Sweeney notes that her study does not include women in the Federal Bureau of Prisons. These prisons, she wrote, "present particularly difficult barriers to access" (9). Although we regularly encounter cancellations and lockdowns, the book club is, as far as we know, the longest-running book club in a women's federal prison in the country.

APBP book clubs typically consist of fifteen incarcerated members and four volunteers, mainly graduate students and faculty from the WVU English department. We have created book clubs at a women's multisecurity prison, a men's medium security prison, and a prison camp. While prison administration and supporters often cast the book club as corrective or rehabilitative therapy, we have never understood it as such, except to the extent that any learning community can be described in those terms. "We all need mitigation," as Bryan Stevenson writes in *Just Mercy* (201). Our intent has been to create a collaborative space for intellectual and creative growth in places predicated on isolation, deprivation, and degradation—that can also be openly hostile toward books (see Sweeney 19–53).

We are aware that accounts of educational experiences in prison can romanticize literacy and misrepresent the sources of and solutions to trauma, dislocation, and separation (see Ginsburg 1–17; Rodríguez 75–112; McCorkel and DeFina). The structural inequities that deprive people of education, health care, housing, and employment; the criminalization of poverty, addiction, and mental illness; the hypersurveillance of Black, brown, LGBTQ+, and poor people; the massive failure to hold police accountable for injury, terror, and death; the devastation caused by the drug war; the legal discrimination that awaits released people: these conditions are not resolved by a really good book.

As we advocate for imprisoned people's right to education, we are committed to critical reflection on our work. Well-intentioned prison volunteerism has the potential, as Rebecca Ginsburg observed, "to take on the values and imperatives of the carceral state" and "to become yet another repressive force in incarcerated individuals' lives" (1). We are also alert to the ethical shortcomings of using recidivism as a rationale for education in prison. We agree with Erin Castro that "[t]racking recidivism is not a neutral endeavor . . . the evidence demonstrates that recidivism reveals less about an individual's behavior than about a social system that systemically disadvantages people of Color" (9). Education should be available, regardless of release date, classification of conviction, or disciplinary status. The Second Chance pilot program, for instance, recommended that Pell grants be extended to qualified students who would be released within five years (Ositelu).

APBP book clubs are open to people of all educational levels and to those who might be ineligible for higher education. We have had conversations in book club and with staff members about not excluding people convicted of sex crimes. The national Alliance on Higher Education in Prison encourages programs to uphold, "as a matter of principle, a commitment to inclusivity in all its forms; and steadfastly challenging the notion that either current or prior incarceration status, or any particular commitment offense or type of sentence, disqualifies anyone from quality education" (Erzen et al. 3). APBP adheres to this principle.

The book club can serve as a path toward or away from formal education—either way, a learning path in a country that, among developed ones, "combines the highest level of incarceration with the lowest level of postsecondary education provision" (Lockard and Rankins-Robertson 25). This educational model, a blend of college-level literary studies and the popular form of a book club, offers ways for all members to strengthen reading, analytical, collaborative, and communication skills. As importantly, the book club builds community and confers responsibility. For volunteers, this responsibility includes holding home institutions accountable for policies that strengthen the carceral regime, such as the use of criminal background checks, shares in private prison companies, contracts with prison-involved vendors, and minimal involvement with programs for incarcerated and formerly incarcerated people.

While this is not an optimistic essay, it is a determined one that confirms the vitality of literary and writing studies, offers an adaptable model, and documents the history of an evolving practice. APBP book clubs take place in a precarious interstice between higher education and the carceral regime—and often physically occur in spaces designed for manufacturing: cavernous, bleak, ostensibly unsuitable to learning. That's where we learn and where we build.

Where We Began

Our vision for a book club extended from our original work as a prison book project: to get books into the hands of people who are locked up. Each week, APBP receives approximately two hundred letters from people in prison who are looking for something to read: poetry, Indigenous histories, thrillers, African American literature, sacred books, world philosophy, books in Spanish, instruction on how to draw or to play music.

The most requested book, at APBP and at book projects across the country, is a dictionary.

The form letter that APBP includes with every outgoing book begins, "This book is free and yours to keep." When we composed that sentence sixteen years ago, we had no idea how radical it was or would become. Many prisons only accept books shipped from a publisher, a distributor, or a contracted vendor. APBP is unable to send books to several prisons and jails across our region. In response to censorship and restrictions on books, several organizations—among them the Human Rights Defense Center, PEN America, and the American Civil Liberties Union—are challenging barriers to reading, and an alliance of prison book projects has formed to ensure people's right to information and to education.[3] With Patrick Elliot Alexander, we consider the absence of education inside prisons a violation of international human rights (10).

APBP is a volunteer-driven organization funded by donations and small grants. We work hard to send people books they have requested, books they really want to read. Our approach to book clubs is the same. Book club members select what we read in a process that extends over two or three meetings and concludes with a vote.[4] The first book we read in the women's book club was Octavia E. Butler's novel *Kindred*. This was followed by over seventy novels, story collections, graphic novels, and plays, including Chimamanda Ngozi Adichie's *Americanah*, Ernest Gaines's *A Lesson before Dying*, Michelle Alexander's *The New Jim Crow*, Bryan Stevenson's *Just Mercy*, Zitkala-Ša's *American Indian Stories*, Toni Morrison's *God Help the Child*, Edwidge Danticat's *Farming of the Bones*, Julia Alvarez's *In the Time of the Butterflies*, Marjane Satrapi's *Persepolis*, Jhumpa Lahiri's *Unaccustomed Earth*, August Wilson's *Two Trains Running*, Rachel Carson's *Silent Spring*, Kazuo Ishiguro's *Never Let Me Go*, and Leonard Peltier's *Prison Writings: My Life Is My Sun Dance*. We have discussed poetry by Maya Angelou, Reginald Dwayne Betts, Lucille Clifton, Langston Hughes, Nikki Giovanni, Etheridge Knight, Adrienne Rich, and Rainer Maria Rilke.

Although membership changes as people are transferred or released and new people join, group demographics consistently reflect national trends. The majority of members are Black, and there are roughly equal numbers of Latinx and white members. Prisons in Appalachia invert outside racial demographics, confirming what we know about the most marginalized being the most criminalized. A significant number of the women's book club members are nonbinary or identify as male or trans. Many are parents, and mothers in the federal system are usually located farther from their children than fathers and are more likely to lose custody (see Hager and Flagg; Halter; Schenwar; Kaba).

Changes in policy and policing strategies continue to drive the rise in women's incarceration despite variation among states and attempts to decarcerate "the 'total' prison population" through legislative reforms (Sawyer). Gender-specific prison pipelines—trauma, sexual abuse, and mental health issues—point to a shared story in which the common denominator is pain. Donna Hylton's memoir, *A Little Piece of Light*, describes how lives can be derailed by sexual abuse and harassment. Hylton has said, "Too often, by the time a woman commits a crime, her only goal has been survival" (qtd. in Sered 75).

Early on, members of both the women's and men's book clubs arrived at meetings with notes that sounded like—that were—poems, and with books heavily annotated, highlighted, and dog-eared. They had looked up unfamiliar words and reread difficult passages. Although book clubs are known for being "less text-driven" than classrooms (Beach and Yussen 121), we have spent half an hour discussing one paragraph.[5] In ways similar to those identified by Sweeney, members use literature as a "vehicle for self-education, peer education, politicization, and empowerment" (21).

The goal of the facilitator is to keep the conversation flowing and equitable. We have noticed that book club inspires collective facilitation. Once, as we sat down to discuss the day's material, inside members informed us that we had not finished discussing the previous book. We launched into round two and never got around to the novel for that day. Some conversations meander as we step away from the text to speak of our own lives. One inside member, Antonio, described the group as thinkers "who simply enjoy taking long walks through the well-kept garden of other people's minds."[6] Other days yield literary analysis on par with graduate-level seminars. The group dictates the balance.

The book club does not lead to a certificate. To confer certificates, our work would need an end date, and members have agreed that they would rather be part of an ongoing learning community. As one member, Jazz, explains when inviting people to join, "It's not about that. It's about self-preservation." As outside facilitators, we stress, "This is your space"—and we return to this statement often. While we acknowledge the impossibility of incarcerated persons fully controlling space or time, our goal has been to foster an environment that is not structured by the preset goals of an institution or instructor. We do not grade. We do not assess. We do not arrive with course objectives, book lists, or lesson plans. We arrive with books.

A Reading Community

Historically, the egalitarian structure of book clubs made them popular choices for community building and organizing among people denied access to education. Reading groups and other literacy circles are often born of the desire to secure a space for the relational experiences of reading and literacy and, in some cases, the awakening of social movements (see Long; Jack; Scheil; Twomey). Elizabeth McHenry has documented the history of African American literary societies that galvanized people to assert citizenship and create "durable communities" (24). Belinda Jack has detailed all-female literacy circles that have been met, for centuries, with suspicion and condemnation.

The majority of book clubs in the United States are women's groups (Clarke et al. 173; Long). This gendered association was not lost on the men who showed up to learn about this new program. After two years in the group, Antonio reflected, "I remember the very first session we had just like it were yesterday. Initially I had butterflies in my stomach because I really didn't know what to expect, because my notion of a Book Club (back then) was something that only women did. But boy was I wrong. I have since discovered that a Book Club is something that human beings do." Jeannie, an original member of the women's group, described meetings as a "sacred escape": "Time spent in book club meetings was time out of the prison milieu, mentally and spiritually. To the extent possible, we were 'free' from standard prison surroundings, in a room that did not have the feel of barbed wires, guards, uniforms, and oppression." This description syncs with Anita Wilson's idea of a third space forged by people who cannot go home and who want "to resist the negativity of the site in which they find themselves" (198–199; see also Malakki 18). Members give similar reasons for attendance. They also always add, "I really like to read."[7]

As a non-credit-bearing, non-certificate-granting program, the book club can be undervalued and misrecognized. Trying to describe it can lead to a series of deferrals: not a classroom, not a social club, not like other educational spaces in prisons (and that is not a homogenous category). Book clubs are vulnerable to staff changes and shortages, book restrictions, and lack of institutional funding on both sides of the wall.[8] Most volunteers do not receive a course release or academic credit. The openness of the structure can also challenge outside members' (specifically, teachers') assumptions about their role. But, over time, an understanding of what the book club *isn't* has evolved into an understanding of what the book club *is*: a space for reflection, collaboration, preparation, and reading in community.

S. J. Stout, a graduate student, recounts how the book club compelled her to rethink what it means to read with others:

> I was eager to get involved with the book club, but nervous too. How could I prepare? Should we provide discussion questions, secondary readings? Are there strategies for moderating? Does someone lecture?
> "We aren't there to teach," Katy told me. "Our role is to create the space and bring resources, like books and paper, to them."
> When we discussed Kazuo Ishiguro's *Never Let Me Go*, the women leapt into action. They debated characters and plot structure; they posed questions and dove back and forth between book pages and stories from their own lives. Later, prompted by Butler's *Kindred*, Katy asked us, "What do you need to pack with you to survive?"
> And I realized how these novels, poems, and short stories were transformed in these women's hands into tools—not unlike paper clips and flashlights—to survive in the world. Best yet, as our discussions continued from losses and reunions to activism, Buddhism, and police violence, the sense of *us* and *them* melted away. Emerging was a curious, kind, apprehensive, brave, encouraging, funny *we*.
> I am still thinking about this dynamic, wise *we*. Maybe this *we* is the response to our dystopian present. The *we*—like the double heads of playing cards, somersaulting between asking and answering, a Swiss army knife of voices and visions—is our way to survive.

S. J. discovered a social resource and, to borrow from Patrick Berry, "a *contextual now* that we can all inhabit" (15). At its best, this is the defining ethos of the book club.

Our insistence on a shared space has taken us in directions we did not plan and could not have anticipated. On their initiative, members began to read their writing aloud, and we started to alternate sessions between book discussions and writing workshops. Writing is now fully integrated into our practice. In 2017, we created a collection of the women's stories, poems, letters, essays, and artwork. In response to Ross Gay's poem "A Small Needful Fact," a meditation on Eric Garner's last words, we asked one another, "What helps you breathe?" and wrote answers on slips of paper. These handwritten pieces of paper, scanned and arranged, became the quilted centerpiece of the collection. After choosing the title *Women of Wisdom* for the anthology, the members decided to adopt the same name for the book club itself.[9] The following year, the men produced a one-hundred-page compilation of creative writing and visual art, *Holding onto Sand*.

In a later discussion on gender fluidity and nonconformity, we revisited our name, Women of Wisdom, and considered whether the term *women* remained accurate. Jazz, who identifies as male, said, "I love it. I tell people I am a woMAN." Rayna Momen wrote a poem, "Jazz," in response to this moment.

> To the woMAN of wisdom
> who on a Tuesday in May
> after talking about authentic selves stood up and said,
> "I love the person that I am,"
> while wearing a smile
> bigger than a full blood moon and brighter,
> thank you for being
> (such a stud).

We decided that day that our full name should be Women of Wisdom: Figuring Shit Out.

Members create space for one another and assure one another that they are not alone. Celeste joined the group, she explained, because she was afraid in prison she would lose her ability to communicate:

> What I really got was so much more. [People] who were not judgmental, who came just to bring hope and share their love of books, people that are now etched in my heart forever. . . . I gained a group of friends on the compound that had a positive common denominator. The most amazing part, the magic, was that we were able to open up and get into some really deep conversations that were probably more effective than any personal therapist in my past.

In feedback, members continue to name these elements—the chance to listen and to learn from others—as especially valuable. The book club has become, as Jeannie wrote, "a catalyst for friendships and conversations throughout the compound."

Prison employees can perceive the bonds that form between members as a threat. At best, these perceptions make it more difficult for us to get in; at worst, we fear retaliation against members. As Ann Folwell Stanford pointed out, developing a group identity, "a 'we' within the confines of the razor wire," is dangerous because it "disrupts the individualistic discourse and practice on which any system of oppression depends" (165). We engage critically with the emphasis on individual transformation that dominates correctional and popular discourse and rely on the historical elements of literature, language, and writing to offset the constant stress on personal choice.[10]

This model can lessen structural hierarchies, but it does not dissolve them. We do not imagine that we have created utopian spaces within prison. We do not know everything that happens, and we constantly consider, with the help of inside members, whether it makes sense to continue. Breea Willingham observed that women writing in prison "may not dismantle the system," but "they find their voice and educate themselves" (57). That is the key: the capacity of people to educate themselves, in and outside prison, with space and support.

Building Outward

The book club extends far beyond our reading circle. Books are shared and donated to prison libraries. Discussions about literature, history, and science continue long after we leave. Staff members use our materials in classes they teach. Inside members teach classes on communication, intimate partner violence, parenting, addiction, and recovery. The book club is not responsible for the incredible leadership of these individuals, but it does set in motion a circulation of resources.[11] Released members send book recommendations to APBP, and in that way we still read together.

In contrast to the image of the solitary reader,[12] the book club is grounded in collective discovery. On campus and in our community, we work to build "literacy on the outside" (Hinshaw and Jacobi 77) and "to inform and to incite movement" (Tapia 2). Many of us incorporate into classrooms strategies, perspectives, and readings from the book club. In 2017, Beth Staley and Valerie Surrett created a podcast, *Contact across the Divide*, that features over a dozen APBP volunteers.[13] All of us feel an increased responsibility to work toward decarceration. As one graduate student volunteer, Gabriella Pishotti, put it, "Talking about the work is fifty percent of the work" (see Lockard 28).

We never underestimate the impact and reach of reading. In the words of one book club member, Antoine, "[T]he Language Art's net of companionship reveals itself to be fathomless." After taking a literature class with Katy and becoming involved in the book club, Kevin wrote:

> I felt more accountable about everything—my life, my family, the community—but especially accountable for justice. I became more

conscious of the world around me. . . . The literature I read in class led me to have certain conversations with my family that helped me cope with things that happened in my life. I was for sure able to heal from this class. I believe this to be one of the most authentic things, and most selfish, that I got.

When another member read *Writing Down the Bones*, by Natalie Goldberg, she found the courage to write a letter to her adult son. He wrote back. They talked on the phone for the first time in years, and soon he visited her. Another member's son was reading Lorraine Hansberry's *A Raisin in the Sun* for a high school English class when we were discussing the play. It was wonderful, she said, to talk to him about Beneatha and Walter, to debate the ending, and, for a minute, not talk about prison.

When APBP shared the writing anthology with Kirsten, a released contributor, she responded within minutes, "This is amazing!!! Let the women know I think about them all the time and miss the group. Reading everyone's writing reminds me how much I miss everyone. I can't wait to sit down this evening and read every story." Feedback from Bryan and Michael confirm this mix of community building and collaborative learning. In Bryan's words, "I have found comfort now in reading whereas before it was for study only. The family feeling we created in this book club has made me a stronger writer and also an 'expert' analyst on every[thing] I read." Michael echoes, "I don't think I can find something as unique and equally mentally stimulating and intellectually challenging as the book club" ("Reflections" 89, 87).

We began our reading community five years ago by time-traveling to the antebellum south with Butler's fictional characters Dana and Kevin, collapsing past and present to better understand how we have come to this place. On her last day before she was released, Leslie read a personal essay about book club:

> I initially came for the books, then for the peace, and the company of outsiders. . . . As I continued to show up, in time it was no longer about books, or programs, or peace. I began to realize that it was about me, and millions of others like me. . . . Many of us end up in prisons, mental institutions, or as drug addicts—or in cemeteries. And many just give up. Today, however, there will be no giving up. I think back to Bryan Stevenson in *Just Mercy*. Broken. Crying into the night and wanting to give up, but continuing to forge ahead, to help one more incarcerated individual.
>
> No, I cannot give up. I can accept personal responsibility and not allow outside voices to become inside voices. Besides, my own con-

viction is much greater than my felony conviction, and in the words of the great Assata Shakur:

> If I know anything at all
> It's that a wall is just a wall
> And nothing more at all
> It can be broken down.

Unfinished

In constructing her biographical note for the writing collection, Tanisha asked others to describe her in one or two words and listed their responses: "Beautiful, spicy, loving, funny, sassy, sarcastic, realistic, bold, brass, intelligent, interesting, fierce, caring, loyal, weird, friend. Who am I? What's my life's score? I am all that they say and a little bit more. I am UNFINISHED" ("Contributors' Biographies" 88).

Much of what we do, and are, in the book club, feels unfinished. Discussions are interrupted by moves, friendships disrupted by transfers, writing projects upended. A longtime member took the lead in composing a performance piece called *Book Club* about a place where you can "book" whatever you need: a vacation, a good book, an escape, a night out. The members had begun to rehearse a script when the playwright was transferred. Months later, the women began work on a new collaborative script, inspired by their friend's vision and Ntozake Shange's *for colored girls who have considered suicide / when the rainbow is enuf.*

We keep going. Holding onto sand. We know the book club could go in an instant.[14] We hope it doesn't. Like everyone doing this work, we know we need to have a backup plan.

NOTES

1. For more information on the environmental dangers facing incarcerated people in the United States, see Schept; Campaign to Fight Toxic Prisons (fighttoxicprisons.wordpress.com).

2. Raymond Thompson's photography documentary, *The Divide*, deals specifically with travel to state prisons in Virginia.

3. See Jensen; Freedom to Learn Campaign (freedom-to-learn.net); National Coalition against Censorship (ncac.org/about-us); Library Services to the Incarcerated and Detained (ala.org/asgcla/interestgroups/iglsid).

4. See Long 114–43 on the significance of book selection.

5. On close reading as a countercultural practice, see Boccio 432–34.

6. Quotations from book club members are from written feedback and are used with participants' permission, along with preferred first names.

7. See Clarke and Nolan 123–24 for an overview of book club research.

8. See "Literature Locked Up" on book restrictions in prison.

9. On self-representation and the ethics of facilitation, publication, and consent, see Hinshaw and Jacobi; Lawston.

10. See Karlsson on how personal choice structures autobiographical narratives.

11. See Kilgore on "invisible teachers" inside prison.

12. See Barstow 10–11; for analysis of the race-, gender-, and class-based image of the solitary reader, see Long 1–30.

13. The full podcast is available at appalachianprisonbookproject.org/connect/podcast/.

14. This line has haunted us. As we finished this essay in summer 2019, the book club at the women's prison was unable to continue because of prison staff shortages.

WORKS CITED

Alexander, Patrick Elliot. "Education as Liberation: African American Literature and Abolition Pedagogy in the Sunbelt Prison Classroom." *South: A Scholarly Journal*, vol. 50, no. 1, 2017, pp. 9–21.

Antonio. "Dear Family." *Holding onto Sand*, p. 91.

Barstow, Jane Missner. "Reading in Groups: Women's Clubs and College Literature Classes." *Publishing Research Quarterly*, vol. 18, no. 4, 2003, pp. 3–15.

Beach, Richard, and Steven Yussen. "Practices of Productive Adult Book Clubs." *Journal of Adolescent and Adult Literacy*, vol. 55, no. 2, 2011, pp. 121–131.

Berry, Patrick W. *Doing Time, Writing Lives: Refiguring Literacy and Higher Education in Prison*. Southern Illinois UP, 2017.

Boccio, Rachel. "Toward the Soul of a Transformational Praxis: Close Reading and the Liberationist Possibilities of Prison Education." *Pedagogy*, vol. 17, no. 3, Oct. 2017, pp. 423–48.

Castro, Erin L. "Racism, the Language of Reduced Recidivism, and Higher Education in Prison: Toward an Anti-Racist Praxis." *Critical Education*, vol. 9, no. 17, 2018, pp. 2–18.

Clarke, Robert, and Marguerite Nolan. "Book Clubs and Reconciliation: A Pilot Study on Book Clubs Reading the Fictions of Reconciliation." *Australian Humanities Review*, vol. 56, 2014, pp. 121–40.

Clarke, Robert, et al. "Reading in Community, Reading for Community: A Survey of Book Clubs in Regional Australia." *Journal of Australian Studies*, vol. 41, no. 2, 2017, pp. 171–83.

"Contributors' Biographies." *Women of Wisdom*, pp. 87–89.

Erzen, Tanya, et al. *Equity and Excellence in Practice: A Guide for Higher Education in Prison*. Alliance for Higher Education in Prison and Prison University Project, June 2019, www.higheredinprison.org/publications/equity-and-excellence-in-practice-report.

Gay, Ross. "A Small Needful Fact." *Split This Rock*, 30 Apr. 2015, splitthisrock.org/poetry-database/poem/a-small-needful-fact.

Ginsburg, Rebecca, editor. *Critical Perspectives on Teaching in Prison: Students and Instructors on Pedagogy behind the Wall.* Routledge, 2019.

Hager, Eli, and Anna Flagg. "How Incarcerated Parents Are Losing Their Children Forever." *The Marshall Project*, 2 Dec. 2018, themarshallproject .org/2018/12/03/how-incarcerated-parents-are-losing-their-children-forever.

Halter, Emily. "Parental Prisoners: The Incarcerated Mother's Constitutional Right to Parent." *The Journal of Criminal Law and Criminology*, vol. 108, no. 3, 2018, pp. 539–67.

Hinshaw, Wendy Wolters, and Tobi Jacobi. "What Words Might Do: The Challenge of Representing Women in Prison and Their Writing." *Feminist Formations*, vol. 27, no. 27, 2015, pp. 67–90.

Holding onto Sand. Appalachian Prison Book Project, 2018, appalachianpris onbookproject.org/wp-content/uploads/2019/05/Holding-onto-Sand.pdf.

Jack, Belinda. *The Woman Reader.* Yale UP, 2013.

Jensen, Kelly. "Ohio Becomes Latest State to Attempt to Stop Book Donations to Incarcerated." *BookRiot*, 9 May 2019, bookriot.com/2019/05/09/ohio -prison-book-ban.

Kaba, Mariame. "Circles of Grief, Circles of Grieving." *The Long Term: Resisting Life Sentences Working toward Freedom*, edited by Alice Kim et al., Haymarket Books, 2018, pp. 184–91.

Karlsson, Lena. "'This Is a Book about Choices': Gender, Genre and (Auto)Biographical Prison Narratives." *NORA—Nordic Journal of Feminist and Gender Research*, vol. 21, no. 3, 2013, pp. 187–200.

Kilgore, James. "From Africa to High Desert State Prison: Journeys of an Invisible Teacher." Ginsburg, pp. 48–59.

Lawston, Jodie Michelle. "From Representations to Resistance: How the Razor Wire Binds Us All." *Razor Wire Women: Prisoners, Activists, Scholars, and Artists*, edited by Lawston and Ashley E. Lucas, State U of New York P, 2011, pp. 1–17.

Leslie. "A Flicker of Light." *Women of Wisdom*, pp. 39–40.

"Literature Locked Up: How Prison Book Restriction Policies Constitute the Nation's Largest Book Ban." PEN America, Sept. 2019, pen.org/wp-content/ uploads/2019/09/literature-locked-up-report-9.24.19.pdf.

Lockard, Joe. "Prison Writing Education and US Working-Class Consciousness." *Prison Pedagogies: Learning and Teaching with Imprisoned Writers*, edited by Joe Lockard and Sherry Rankins-Robertson, Syracuse UP, 2018, pp. 11–31.

Lockard, Joe, and Sherry Rankins-Robertson. "The Right to Education: Prison-University Partnerships, and Online Writing Pedagogies in the U.S." *Critical Survey*, vol. 23, no. 3, 2011, pp. 23–29.

Long, Elizabeth. *Book Clubs: Women and the Uses of Reading in Everyday Life.* U of Chicago P, 2003.

Malakki [Ralph Bolden]. "An Open Letter to Prison Educators." Ginsburg, pp. 17–18.

McCorkel, Jill, and Robert DeFina. "Beyond Recidivism: Identifying the Liberatory Possibilities of Prison Higher Education." *Critical Education*, vol. 10, no. 7, 2019, pp. 1–17.

McHenry, Elizabeth. *Forgotten Readers: Recovering the Lost History of African American Literary Societies.* Duke UP, 2002.

Ositelu, Monique O. *How Would a Five-Year Restriction on Pell Eligibility Impact Incarcerated Adults If the Pell Ban Is Lifted?* New America, January 2020.

"Reflections: Holding onto Sand." *Holding onto Sand*, pp. 87–90.

Rodríguez, Dylan. *Forced Passages: Imprisoned Radical Intellectuals and the U.S. Prison Regime.* U of Minnesota P, 2006.

Sawyer, Wendy. "The Gender Divide: Tracking Women's State Prison Growth." *Prison Policy Initiative*, 9 Jan. 2018, prisonpolicy.org/reports/women_overtime.html.

Scheil, Katherine West. *She Hath Been Reading: Women and Shakespeare Clubs in America.* Cornell UP, 2012.

Schenwar, Maya. *Locked Down, Locked Out: Why Prison Doesn't Work and How We Can Do Better.* Berrett-Koehler Publishers, 2014.

Schept, Judah. *Coal, Cages, Crisis: The Rise of the Prison Economy in Central Appalachia.* New York UP, 2022.

Sered, Danielle. *Until We Reckon: Violence, Mass Incarceration, and the Road to Repair.* New Press, 2019.

Solinger, Rickie, et al. *Interrupted Life: Experiences of Incarcerated Women in the United States.* U of California P, 2010.

Stanford, Anne Fowell. "Lit by Each Other's Light: Women's Writing at Cook County Jail." Solinger et al., pp. 165–77.

Stevenson, Bryan. *Just Mercy.* Spiegel and Grau, 2015.

Sweeney, Megan. *Reading Is My Window: Books and the Art of Reading in Women's Prisons.* U of North Carolina P, 2010.

Tapia, Rudy C. "Certain Failures: Representing the Experiences of Incarcerated Women in the United States." Solinger et al., pp. 1–6.

Thompson, Raymond. *The Divide. Raymond Thompson, Jr., Photography*, raymondthompsonjr.com/divide.

Twomey, Sarah. "Reading 'Woman': Book Club Pedagogies and the Literary Imagination." *Journal of Adolescent and Adult Literacy*, vol. 50, no. 5, 2007, pp. 398–407.

Wagner, Peter. "Why Is West Virginia the Federal Prison Capital of the Country?" *Prison Policy Initiative*, 10 June 2014, prisonpolicy.org/blog/2014/06/10/wv-prison-capital/.

Willingham, Breea C. "Black Women's Prison Narratives and the Intersection of Race, Gender, and Sexuality in US Prisons." *Critical Survey*, vol. 23, no. 3, 2011, pp. 55–66.

Wilson, Anita. "'I Go to Get Away from the Cockroaches': Educentricity and the Politics of Education in Prisons." *Journal of Correctional Education*, vol. 58, no. 2, 2007, pp. 185–203.

Women of Wisdom. Appalachian Prison Book Project, 2017, appalachianprisonbookproject.org/wp-content/uploads/2022/04/women-of-wisdom-collection-2018.pdf.

Narrating Captivity, Imagining Justice: Reading Mary Shelley's *Frankenstein* in Prison

Laura E. Ciolkowski

In the words of Ursula K. Le Guin, "The exercise of imagination is dangerous to those who profit from the way things are because it has the power to show that the way things are is not permanent, not universal, not necessary" ("War without End" 219). Le Guin never taught literature in prison, but she understood intuitively the dangers and pleasures of animating the literary imagination within carceral spaces. For Le Guin, the imagination is "an essential tool of the mind . . . an indispensable means of becoming and remaining human" ("Operating Instructions" 4). For the student in prison, whose carceral life ensures that the daily labor of "becoming and remaining human" is both risky and necessary, the literature classroom is invested with enormous power and possibility. This is because it is in the classroom that the dreams and imagined futures of students, who elsewhere are compelled to exist frozen in time, suspended in a criminalized past, can be fully animated. It is in the classroom that fugitive tales of survival and violence, often concealed but never fully erased, can be remembered, created, and shared in community with others.

I here relate the remarkable journey of reading and thinking about Mary Shelley's *Frankenstein* in a college literature classroom in prison. This particular classroom was nested within a medium security facility for women in New York State. It was brought to life by a group of Black, brown, white, queer, straight, and gender nonconforming daughters, mothers, and grandmothers, ranging in age from twenty-five to seventy-five. It is by now trite to observe how the literature we read bends under the pressures of our present desires and is reshaped by the critical poking and prodding of students whose lived experience demands something different or exposes something unexpected from the materials we read and think about in the classroom. Nevertheless, the lived experiences, critical insights, and emotional investments of the women in this classroom bent Shelley's text out of shape in especially meaningful and, perhaps, unexpected ways, opening up fundamental questions about the continuing legacy of anti-Black racism in America; our investment in the civil, social, and physical death of several million justice-involved people in this country every year; and our ferocious appetite for punishment (Lamble 244).[1] As Danielle Sered has observed, "In all the world and all recorded time, no country has locked up their own people at the rate we do. . . . [I]ncarceration is not just a dimension of how we punish crime in our country. It exists at such a scale that it is a defining feature of our culture. It is who we are, who we have become" (7–8). In raising the nuanced and complicated issues of monstrosity, gendered racial violence, and the specter of disposable life and the exploitability of racialized bodies under capitalism, *Frankenstein* became the occasion for us to think critically, read deeply, and imagine justice from within the walls of the prison.

Scene 1

"Hideous progeny" (10) is Shelley's playful but ambivalent term of endearment for the Romantic, proto-sci-fi novel *Frankenstein; or, The Modern Prometheus*, which she published in 1818 as a first-time novelist. It is also the language of disfigurement and disgust so closely associated with the abandoned creature at the heart of the novel, the "hideously deformed and loathsome" (123) being who would endure in literature and on stage and screen as an embodiment of the first great modern myth of the nineteenth century. Written when Shelley was only nineteen and published anonymously with an unsigned preface by Shelley's celebrated poet-husband Percy Shelley, *Frankenstein* would remain its author's most lasting legacy, defining her in life—as a young author goaded by her husband to "prove myself worthy of my parentage, and enroll myself on the page of fame" (6)—and also long after her death in 1851 at the age of fifty-three.[2] Heavily edited for publication by Percy in 1818, and then further revised by Mary and republished in 1831 under her own name, *Frankenstein* sold over seven thousand copies during Mary's lifetime, far exceeding the sale of all of Percy's many volumes of poetry combined (Hitchcock 82). Over two hundred years after it was written, the novel continues to speak to us about our equivocal attachment to and strange fascination with monstrosity and violence. In the figure of the scientist Victor Frankenstein's accursed creation, cast off by his maker and left "wretched, helpless, and alone" (Shelley 132), is the familiar tale of the outcast, the monstrous other. Like so many of the students, who know too well what it is like to be expected to survive in an environment that refuses to sustain them, the creature is forced to find his way in a world that deals out punishment and pain rather than the love and nurturing that he craves.

The human capacity for love and the desire for attachment that Shelley infuses so deeply into the core of her "solitary and abhorred" (133) creature is a central focus of class discussions and a source of concern for students whose capacity and need for love and attachment is also routinely discounted or erased inside prison. Outside the space of the classroom, they are criminals, defined by their history rather than by their present or future. They are, in short, dehumanized by a criminal legal system that denies the essential humanity and individual complexity of those it confines to living in cages. It is from this particular point of entry into the novel that students insist upon reading a kind of humanity into the figure of Shelley's miserable creature, many emphatically identifying with and drawing attention to the creature's persistent "[yearning] to be known and loved" (134) in spite of the relentlessness with which he is denied the most basic right to personhood by his creator. Perhaps even more importantly, the students also sense that the creature's greatest offense to the universe, even more grievous than the crimes of violence that he subsequently commits, is quite simply that he lives. The creature himself comes to see that his original sin against his creator is not that he has harmed members of Victor's family but that he survives. Victor fantasizes about murdering "the demoniacal corpse to which I had so miserably given life" (59) and ardently desires "to extinguish that life which I had so thoughtlessly bestowed" (95). And yet Shelley's creature still lives.

The sin of survival is an unsettling but important element of Shelley's tale that carries a particular weight within a carceral space in which many of the women are serving sentences for surviving violence—most commonly, child sexual abuse, intimate partner violence, rape, and sexual abuse. According to the Vera Institute for Justice, an astonishing eighty-six percent of women in US jails report having experienced sexual violence in their lifetime (Swavola et al. 11). A 1999 study of women incarcerated at Bedford Hills Correctional Facility found that more than eighty percent have a childhood history of physical and sexual abuse (Browne, et al. 316). Often referred to as the "abuse-to-prison pipeline," the journey from sexual abuse to entanglement in the criminal legal system is well documented (see, for example, Saar et al.). This trajectory is especially common for the most vulnerable women, who are already marginalized by, for example, racism, immigration status, homophobia, or transphobia, and are surviving under dangerous conditions made even more precarious by some combination of poverty, homelessness, unemployment, disability, and physical or behavioral illness. As the Combahee River Collective understood, a person's "lived experience" of violence, poverty, and oppression is a source of critical knowledge that can become the ground for resistance and struggle. Each and every student in the prison classroom lives in some way with this knowledge. They know, for example, that power and violence are not democratic forces but are mapped unevenly onto differently positioned bodies. They know that certain kinds of people (usually white) are entitled to make mistakes, while others (usually Black and brown) are seen as acting out deep-seated pathologies that are hardwired into their souls. The students' life narratives bear out these truths. Our work in the classroom therefore engages critically with the literature we read in order to name the conditions of racialized violence and gender oppression and collectively develop a language to imagine and build something different. I believe this is what Audre Lorde meant when she wrote that "[p]oetry is the way we help give name to the nameless so it can be thought. The farthest horizons of our hopes and fears are cobbled by our poems, carved from the rock experiences of our daily lives" ("Poetry" 37).

For students who come to *Frankenstein* already "survived and punished," who come into the classroom as people who have been criminalized for surviving violence, the creature's survival is both a cause for celebration and a source of great pain.[3] What does it mean to survive violence only to be sentenced to a life of agony and isolation and, in the case of the students in the class, captivity? The creature speaks directly to this carceral and existential dilemma: "'Cursed, cursed creator! Why did I live?'" (Shelley 138). If "death by incarceration" is an apt description of what it really means for a person to endure the punishment of a life sentence, then perhaps, as Guillermo del Toro has proposed in his own meditations on Shelley's novel, it is not death but "the impossibility of death" that is "the greatest of the tragedies for the monster: the fact that his creator made him well and gave him a body that endures in spite of himself—his self, his lonely, desperate self" (xv).[4]

Like the creature, who urgently desires "love and fellowship" (224) but is instead forced to live alone, with "none to lament my annihilation" (131), abandoned by his creator and "united by no link to any other being in existence" (132), many of the students in the classroom have themselves been called upon to survive a childhood unnurtured, an adolescence under siege, or an adult life in prison, estranged or cut off from their communities. As Ruth Wilson Gilmore and others have argued, prisons are essentially an extractive industry. They extract people from their communities and deposit them often hundreds of miles away, in facilities located in isolated, rural areas far from home. John Eason notes that in 2002, seventy percent of prisons were located in rural areas (22), representing the efforts of a range of state actors to, as Jackie Wang has explained, "revive the economies of rural white America through the construction of prisons and the employment of displaced white workers as prison guards" (81). This is yet another way in which the prison economy deepens and extends rather than reduces violence. As Sarah Lamble has put it, "Prisons remove people from their communities, isolate them from social support, and disconnect them from frameworks of accountability" (245). The pervasive sense of loneliness and isolation in Shelley's novel is often difficult for students to sit with and hold, particularly those who come into the class newly severed from their own networks of love and support or who fear the weakening of bonds to those they love and depend upon and to those who love and depend upon them.

This is especially true for those students in the class who come to the text as mothers, typically a majority every semester. According to the Prison Policy Initiative, in 2022, over half of all women in US prisons were mothers, most of them primary caretakers of their children (Sawyer and Bertram, "Prisons"). In jails, the number of women who are mothers rises to eighty percent. In 2008, 2.7 million children had a parent who was incarcerated. One in nine of those children were Black, a racial disparity that is mirrored in much of the data around incarceration in the United States (Western and Petit 18; Sawyer and Bertram, "Beyond the Count"). The students' engagement with Shelley's text is often shaped by their experience of forced separation from their children. Their rage and agony over this loss are frequently directed in the novel toward Victor Frankenstein, the unwilling parent, whose "abhorrence" for his creation "cannot be conceived" (95). The language Victor uses at this point in the text is important and is a crucial flash point in the class. Victor can barely contain himself. He is physically transformed by his rage into another monstrous version of the being he has created: "When I thought of him I gnashed my teeth, my eyes became inflamed . . . my hatred and revenge burst all bounds of moderation" (95). Victor openly expresses the profound horror and disgust that he feels toward the creature he has made and, as many students quickly observe, he unapologetically shirks the parental duties of which he himself has been a happy beneficiary as a beloved child in the care of an attentive mother and father. Over the course of the novel, Victor frequently recalls the nurturing, benevolence, and love exhibited toward him by his parents, and he disavows the contradiction between his own refusal to care for and support the creature he has made and the debt he believes he owes his mother and father:

> My mother's tender caresses and my father's smile of benevolent
> pleasure while regarding me, are my first recollections. I was their

> plaything and their idol, and something better—their child, the
> innocent and helpless creature bestowed on them by Heaven, whom
> to bring up to good, and whose future lot it was in their hands to
> direct to happiness or misery, according as they fulfilled their duties
> towards me. (35)

These immensely powerful emotional investments and identifications in
the classroom, born of lived experience, deep trauma, and multiple forms
of physical and psychological violence, become the wedge that calls
into question Victor's frantic assurances, to himself and to others, that
the creature is not a victim of harm but a demon who must be destroyed.
Victor refuses to recognize the humanity of the being he has created, yet
students point out that it was Victor-as-author who fashioned the creature's heart to be "susceptible of love and sympathy" (222). This generative paradox necessarily turns the conversation about justice and punishment, harm and repair fully inside out.

And yet, like our own dystopian American dreamscape, dotted with
cages that hold over two million people (Sawyer and Wagner), the universe of the novel persists in turning creatures into monsters, humans
into objects to be used or caged or hidden away in a system that exploits
and also annihilates those bodies judged undesirable, dangerous, and
disposable. The novel also continues to mystify the messy reality lived by
students who know that people cannot be divided neatly into victims and
perpetrators, creatures who love and care for others and monsters who
murder. Rather, as Sered puts it, "Nearly everyone who commits violence
has also survived it" (4). This is not a justification for violence—whether
perpetrated by the creature or by the students in the class—but is instead
a reckoning with the conditions that grow violence. The antiviolence advocacy organization Generation Five reminds us, "People that commit
violence are not born that way; they are created by their histories and
given permission by the inequitable practices and arrangements of power
within the society in which we live" (Kershnar et al. 28). In short, no
one—not Shelley's creature or any of the students in the class—is born
a monster, although the mythic tale of monstrosity—the racialized and
gendered fiend, the murderer, the "superpredator"—is at the core of the
story we continue to tell ourselves about violence in America (see Bogert
and Hancock).

The creature's fatal mis-recognition of himself as monster is, for students, one of the most moving and powerful moments in the text. It has
the curious effect of redirecting our attention from the "miserable de-
formity" (Shelley 117) that appears to seal the creature's fate as vengeful

murderer and "filthy daemon" (77) in the novel, to the unforgiving world that casts him out and refuses to recognize and sustain him. The creature recalls, "When I became fully convinced that I was in reality the monster that I am, I was filled with the bitterest sensations of despondence and mortification" (116–17). This is a decisive moment for students who live this monstrosity as the business-as-usual of gendered racial power both within and outside prison. They understand, as the creature does, that in the absence of sustenance, care, and community, life is, in fact, hell.

Scene 2

Teaching in carceral spaces is an exercise of love and tolerance. It is about love because it rests on the persistent, repeated, and deliberate act of recognition and witnessing of the humanity of others—namely, those whose humanity has been appropriated from them. And it is about tolerance because it is riddled with interruptions, with noise—constant and consuming—and with the random and unpredictable expressions of gendered racial power that must be dismantled if one is to survive. This essay is divided into parts to signal the discontinuities of the work we do and the myriad structural challenges of the spaces in which we must do it. I want to share the experience of one interruption in particular, mainly because it represents one of the many ways Shelley's text was opened up, stretched, and bent out of shape by the students in the prison classroom.

Questions of silence and speech, of whose story matters and whose voice can be heard, which history can be spoken and what this means for all of us in our ongoing struggles to survive in a carceral regime, pervade Shelley's text. These questions also define the fundamental experience of "human being" (as verb, not noun), as Sylvia Wynter might put it, in a range of carceral spaces—not only in the space of the prison but also in the innumerable racialized criminalized spaces breathing with insurgent life in, around, and outside it. Silence, like power and privilege, agency and personhood, is always unevenly allocated. As Rebecca Solnit has written, "Silence is a pervasive force, distributed differently to different categories of people" (29). At the center of Shelley's novel is a raging battle over silence and speech. A creature struggles to be heard, fully understanding that his claim to personhood rests upon his ability to speak truth to power ("I intreat you to hear me" [102]), and his creator intuitively understands the threat posed by his creature's entreaty and simply turns away ("Begone! I will not hear you" [103]). In Solnit's words,

"Liberation is always in part a storytelling process: breaking stories, breaking silences, making new stories. A free person tells her own story. A valued person lives in a society in which her story has a place" (19).

The interruption to our classroom meditations on silence and speech in *Frankenstein* took the form of a mock presidential election. The month was November, the year 2016. Donald Trump was elected the forty-fifth president of the United States. Incarcerated people in the state of New York (and in every state except the two whitest states in the nation, Maine and Vermont) are prohibited from voting. This means that the students in the class have no voice in the public sphere of electoral politics even as their bodies and lives are weaponized by white supremacist "law and order" campaign strategies; bitter debates over race, immigration, and reproductive justice; and proposals for welfare and criminal justice reform, among other things. Against the backdrop of the analysis of dehumanization, silence, and speech in *Frankenstein*, the students' inability to be heard, their sense that their voices and stories and life narratives do not have a place in the world, and that, following Solnit, they are neither free nor valued, came to feel intolerable.

How does one sit with the intolerable? What does one do in the face of that which is experienced as intolerable?

The classroom in this moment becomes a space of profound discomfort and pain, not in order to shut down speech or to reproduce the gendered and racialized conditions of silence but in order to engender agency and to collectively imagine transformation and change. As Lorde observed, "As we get in touch with the things that we feel are intolerable, in our lives, they become more and more intolerable. If we just once dealt with how much we hate most of what we do, there would be no holding us back from changing it" (Hammond 20).

The following week, the class staged a mock election, exercising voice and activating hope, despair, and citizenship. The experience was not just intellectual and emotional but physical as well—the performance of citizenship as a fully embodied act, proudly entangled (as it always is) with the material lives, emotional investments, and imaginative horizons of bodies firmly located in space. It is significant that, as required by the prison facility, our election has left no trace. There is no paper trail, no audiotape, no video recording of the creative performances of citizenship on that day, and of course the belated ballots we cast would never be counted by the state. But the work had been done. The muscles that carceral life is designed to atrophy—imagination, dreamwork, belief in futurity and possibility, desire, hope, and love—had been toned, stretched, and strengthened by our work in the classroom. It is in community that we work out together precisely how to live with, against, and beyond that which we experience as intolerable.

Scene 3

In the literature classroom in prison and outside it, we regularly muse over "big questions"—not just the many variations of the creature's agonized and desperate inquiries into Self: "What did this mean? Who was I? What was I? Whence did I come? What was my destination?" (131)—but also questions about justice and care, about harm and repair. Students observe with anger and frustration that Victor holds on tight to the ego-driven fictions of his own suffering and, even more tightly, to his own innocence—"I was guiltless," he insists (167). He does this in ways that are very dark but also familiar to students who know what it means to live with harm—harms directed against others and also the harms experienced oneself. Students' strong identification with the creature who must bear the burden of great pain, shoulder it over many chapters in Shelley's text, and carry it with him as he travels across several continents as well, opens up a nuanced exploration of accountability and the challenge, as Mia Mingus has put it, of embracing one's humanity in all its flaws. Mingus asks, "What if our own accountability wasn't something we ran from, but something we ran towards and desired, appreciated, held as sacred . . . what if we embraced accountability as a reflection of our undeniable, incredible, tender humanity? As a magnificent example of what it means to be human and flawed and in relationship with one another?" Victor steadfastly refuses accountability for the harm he has caused the creature, resisting attachment to him and concluding, incorrectly, "There can be no community between you and me" (Shelley 103). Up until the final moments of his life, Victor clings to the grotesque distortion of human relationship that is at the heart of the model of retributive justice we worship in this country and that, in turn, lingers always in the classroom as a grievous reality of carceral life and the larger culture of punishment in which we live. Victor instructs Walton, the ship captain who has rescued Victor from the Arctic Sea: "Yet, when I am dead, if [the creature] should appear, if the ministers of vengeance should conduct him to you, swear that he shall not live" (212). Ultimately repudiating the creature's experience of indignity and pain, his own life-narrative, his human spirit, Victor remains unwilling to build the relationship of mutual care and recognition on which justice and repair depend: "trust him not," Victor commands Walton; "[H]is soul is hellish as his form, full of treachery and fiendlike malice. *Hear him not*" (212; emphasis mine).

As the students know well, and as they find confirmed in Shelley's text and rarely need to persuade or point out to one another, it is not vengeance or violence or harm to his creator that the creature craves. As unhappy beneficiaries of a prison system that does not eliminate violence or make us safe from harm but is instead a primary agent of violence and harm, these students know that it is not punishment or retribution that heals.[5] It is love. Left solitary and alone after Victor's death, now truly desolate and without parent or relation, the creature reveals his tragically unsatisfied desire for love and community, a human craving that the exercise of violence or the expression of vengeance can never appease: "For while I destroyed his hopes, I did not satisfy my own desires. They were forever ardent and craving; still I desired love and fellowship . . ." (224).

Epilogue

This account of our collective work in the prison classroom is less the final word on *Frankenstein*, on prison education, or on literature, than it is an invitation or, better, a provocation to translate the insights, insurgencies, and visionary lives that were nurtured and grown together over the course of a semester. Salman Rushdie reminds us that the word *translation* derives from the Latin for "bearing across" (17). We bear across the prison walls and barbed wire, in joyous translation, the freedom dreams of the imaginary monsters who are exiled, degraded, dehumanized, and locked away in cages. In so doing, we redraw the map of the future and work together to reenvision our history otherwise. Thinking about the generative and truly revolutionary practice of freedom dreaming, Robin D. G. Kelley asks, "What shall we build on the ashes of a nightmare?" (196).

NOTES

1. Lamble explains, "The prison system is literally killing, damaging, and harming people from our communities. Whether we consider physical death caused by self-harm, medical neglect, and state violence; social death caused by subsequent unemployment, homelessness, and stigmatization; or civil death experienced through political disenfranchisement and exclusion from citizenship rights, the violence of imprisonment is undeniable" (244).

2. Much has been written about the relationship between Shelley's artistic and philosophical concerns in *Frankenstein* and her literary heritage, especially in connection to the life and work of her mother, Mary Wollstonecraft, author of *A Vindication of the Rights of Woman*, and her father, the political philosopher William Godwin. Shelley's hefty and imposing name—Mary Wollstonecraft Godwin Shelley—reflects the weight, sometimes burdensome,

of her family attachments. It also stands as a perpetual reminder of the multiple traumas Mary endured in life, including the death of her mother from complications a little more than a week after her birth; the loss of three children, none of whom lived more than a year; and the death of her husband at sea in 1822 at the age of twenty-nine. There are many now classic books and articles exploring the intersections between the theme of birth and death in *Frankenstein* and in Mary Shelley's personal history, including early feminist interventions by Ellen Moers and Anne K. Mellor's biography *Mary Shelley: Her Life, Her Fiction, Her Monsters.*

3. Kaba argues that survivors of abuse are "systematically punished for taking action to protect themselves and their children while living in unstable and dangerous conditions. Survivors are criminalized for self-defense, failing to control abusers' violence, migration, removing their children from situations of abuse, being coerced into criminalized activity and securing resources needed to live day to day while suffering economic abuse." Kaba is a cofounder of Survived and Punished, a national coalition that "organizes to de-criminalize efforts to survive domestic and sexual violence, support and free criminalized survivors, and abolish gender violence, policing, prisons, and deportations" (survivedandpunished.org).

4. The term "death by incarceration" has been embraced by incarcerated and formerly incarcerated organizers and their families and allies in the fight against sentences of life without the possibility of parole (see Cozzens and Grote).

5. Rodríguez and others have emphasized the violence perpetrated and reproduced by the prison system. Rodríguez defines incarceration as "legitimated state violence, mobilizing the power of law, policing and (gendered racial) common sense to produce, fortify, and/or militarize the geographic isolation and (collective) bodily immobilization of targeted human groups" (1584).

WORKS CITED

Bogert, Carroll, and Lynnell Hancock. "Superpredator: The Media Myth That Demonized a Generation of Black Youth." *The Marshall Project*, 2020, themarshallproject.org/2020/11/20/superpredator-the-media-myth-that -demonized-a-generation-of-black-youth.

Browne, Angela, et al. "Prevalence and Severity of Lifetime Physical and Sexual Victimization among Incarcerated Women." *International Journal of Law and Psychiatry*, vol. 22, nos. 3–4, pp. 301–22.

Combahee River Collective. "A Black Feminist Statement." *WSQ: Women's Studies Quarterly*, vol. 42, nos. 3–4, pp. 271–80.

Cozzens, Quinn, and Brett Grote. "A Way Out: Abolishing Death by Incarceration in Pennsylvania." Abolitionist Law Center, 2018, abolitionistlawcenter .org/wp-content/uploads/2018/09/ALC_AWayOut_27August_Full1.pdf.

Del Toro, Guillermo. "Introduction: Mary Shelley, or the Modern Galatea." *The New Annotated Frankenstein*, edited by Leslie S. Klinger, W. W. Norton, 2017, pp. xi–xvii.

Eason, John. "Prisons as Panacea or Pariah? The Countervailing Consequences of the Prison Boom on the Political Economy of Rural Towns. " *Social Sciences*, vol. 6, no. 1, pp. 1–23.

Gilmore, Ruth Wilson. *Golden Gulag: Prisons, Surplus, Crisis, and Opposition in Globalizing California*. U of California P, 2007.

Hammond, Karla. "An Interview with Audre Lorde." *American Poetry Review*, Mar.-Apr. 1980, pp. 18–21.

Hitchcock, Susan Tyler. *Frankenstein: A Cultural History*, W. W. Norton, 2007.

Kaba, Mariame. "Black Women Punished for Self-Defense Must Be Freed from Their Cages." *The Guardian*, 3 Jan. 2019, theguardian.com/commentis free/2019/jan/03/cyntoia-brown-marissa-alexander-black-women-self -defense-prison.

Kelley, Robin D. G. *Freedom Dreams: The Black Radical Imagination*. Beacon Press, 2003.

Kershnar, Sara, et al. *Toward Transformative Justice: A Liberatory Approach to Child Sexual Abuse and Other Forms of Intimate and Community Violence*. Generation FIVE, June 2007.

Lamble, Sarah. "Transforming Carceral Logics." *Captive Genders: Trans Embodiment and the Prison Industrial Complex*, edited by Eric Stanley and Nat Smith, AK Press, 2011, pp. 235–65.

Le Guin, Ursula K. "The Operating Instructions." *Words Are My Matter: Writings about Life and Books, 2000–2016*, by Le Guin, Small Beer Press, 2016, pp. 3–6.

———. "A War without End." *The Wave in the Mind: Talks and Essays on the Writer, the Reader, and the Imagination*, by Le Guin, Shambhala Publications, 2004, pp. 211–20.

Lorde, Audre. "Poetry Is Not a Luxury." *Sister Outsider*, by Lorde, Ten Speed Press, 1984, pp. 36–40.

Mellor, Anne K. *Mary Shelley: Her Life, Her Fiction, Her Monsters*. Routledge, 1989.

Mingus, Mia. "Dreaming Accountability." *Leaving Evidence*, 5 May 2019, leavingevidence.wordpress.com/2019/05/05/dreaming-accountability -dreaming-a-returning-to-ourselves-and-each-other/.

Moers, Ellen. "Female Gothic." *The Endurance of Frankenstein*, edited by George Levine and U. C. Knoepflmacher, U of California P, 1974, pp. 77–87.

Rodríguez, Dylan. "Abolition as Praxis of Human Being: A Foreword." *Harvard Law Review*, vol. 132, no. 6, 2019, pp. 1575–612.

Rushdie, Salman. "Imaginary Homelands." *Imaginary Homelands: Essays and Criticism, 1981–1991*. Penguin Books, 1992, pp. 9–21.

Saar, Malika Saada, et al. *The Sexual Abuse to Prison Pipeline: The Girls' Story*. Georgetown Center on Poverty and Inequality, genderjusticeand opportunity.georgetown.edu/wp-content/uploads/2020/06/The-Sexual -Abuse-To-Prison-Pipeline-The-Girls%E2%80%99-Story.pdf.

Sawyer, Wendy, and Wanda Bertram. "Beyond the Count: A Deep Dive into State Prison Populations." Prison Policy Initiative, Apr. 2022, prisonpol icy.org/reports/beyondthecount.html.

———. "Prisons and Jails Will Separate Millions of Mothers from Their Children in 2022." Prison Policy Initiative, May 2022, prisonpolicy.org/blog/2022/05/04/mothers_day/.

Sawyer, Wendy, and Peter Wagner. "Mass Incarceration: The Whole Pie 2022." Prison Policy Initiative, Mar. 2022, prisonpolicy.org/reports/pie2022.html.

Sered, Danielle. *Until We Reckon: Violence, Mass Incarceration, and a Road to Repair*. New Press, 2019.

Shelley, Mary. *Frankenstein; or, the Modern Prometheus*. Edited by Maurice Hindle, Penguin Books, 1992.

Solnit, Rebecca. "A Short History of Silence." *The Mother of All Questions*, by Solnit, Haymarket Books, 2017, pp. 17–67.

Swavola, Elizabeth, et al. *Overlooked: Women and Jails in an Era of Reform*. Vera Institute of Justice, 2016.

Wang, Jackie. *Carceral Capitalism*. Semiotext(e), 2018.

Western, Bruce, and Becky Petit. *Collateral Costs: Incarceration's Effect on Economic Mobility*. Pew Charitable Trusts, 2010, pewtrusts.org/~/media/legacy/uploadedfiles/pcs_assets/2010/collateralcosts1pdf.pdf.

Wynter, Sylvia. "The Pope Must Have Been Drunk, The King of Castile a Madman: Culture as Actuality, and the Caribbean Rethinking Modernity." *Reordering of Culture*, edited by Alvina Ruprecht and Cecilia Taiana, Queen's School of Policy Studies, 1995, pp. 17–41.

From a Public Defender Office to a Prison Classroom: Why I Teach Writing in Prison

Patrick Filipe Conway

When I think about why I teach writing in prison, I remember a woman who called herself Sunshine.[1] I met Sunshine in my first job out of college, working as a criminal investigator at the public defender office in Washington, DC. Public defender offices run on tight budgets, tending to hire young and eager investigators. I could also speak Spanish, which was a need within the office. I viewed it as important work: interviewing witnesses, photographing crime scenes, testifying in court. I was glad to be helping in the legal representation of clients who didn't have the money to hire private attorneys.

I was also disturbed by much of what I encountered. In courtroom after courtroom, it was mostly a procession of young Black and Hispanic men, shackled and wearing orange jumpsuits, brought to stand in front of gray-haired judges. I often felt like I was watching gears churn. It was grim, the utter routineness of it all. Of the countless clients I helped represent over my three years with the office, only two were white. The jail was crowded and dirty, filled with the poorest in our communities, and almost everyone was a person of color.

I often thought about what these outcomes in our nation's capital said about our society at large. African Americans make up twelve percent of the population of the United States but constitute nearly thirty-three percent of its prison population (U.S. Department of Justice). The correlation of poverty and incarceration rates is also noted on a national scale. In 2018, the Brookings Institution reported that boys who grow up in families within the bottom ten percent of income distribution are twenty times more likely to be imprisoned in their early thirties than those raised within the top ten percent. Nearly one out of every ten boys born in the lowest-income families are incarcerated at age thirty, accounting for about twenty-seven percent of the incarcerated population at that age (Looney and Turner 2).

By the time I met Sunshine, I was working for attorneys who represented clients accused of murder, rape, and abuse—cases of desperation, anger, and sometimes almost unimaginable violence. It was difficult to reconcile the clients I met with regularly at the DC jail, who often seemed like genuinely good—even if flawed—people, with the crimes they were accused of committing. Believing I wanted to be a public defender myself, I had applied to law schools and been accepted, but now I dreaded choosing among them, having come to feel akin to a cog in the grand machine of the criminal justice system.

Sunshine was a witness in an armed robbery case that I was investigating. She had been listed in the police report as having observed the crime, but we didn't know much else about her. We spoke on the street, late at night, as the occasional car or truck rolled slowly past. She claimed not to know much about the case. She said she didn't know how the police had gotten her name or why she would have ended up in the report. She told me she hadn't been witness to anything, which may have been the truth. It's also possible that she simply did not want to become involved in a court case, a sentiment I had grown to easily understand. At times, the courts can be as unkind to witnesses as they can be to defendants.

While Sunshine did not have much to say about my client's guilt or innocence, she shared many details from her life. She told me she had moved to DC when she was just a teenager and explained how a series of deaths in her family and a resulting drug addiction had derailed her life for a number of years. She made a point of reiterating that she came from a "good family" and that people shouldn't judge the decisions she had made. "Things get confusing at times," she said. "I don't know, honey. I can't help you with your case." She paused briefly, looking down at the ground. "I know my life doesn't mean much. I know that's what people think. I know that's how my name ends up being thrown out into silly police reports. But I'm not going to apologize for who I am. Life is messy, honey. I'm like anyone else, just trying to figure this world out."

When our time together was over, I walked back toward my car and Sunshine walked in the opposite direction along the sidewalk, her high heels clicking against the pavement. Investigators step into the lives of others for a few moments and then usually step right back out. My client's case was soon dismissed, and so too was my work on it. The experience of meeting Sunshine, however, has stayed with me. Not long before my interview with her, I had begun writing about my experiences as an investigator. In writing, I found an opportunity to explore how my own life and work connected to the city around me. I wrote about the contradictory nature of interviews, which on the one hand were a necessary part of representing those who are the most vulnerable in our society but on the other hand could cause discomfort for witnesses and victims. I wrote about representing a client who was guilty of a truly disturbing murder, for whom I nonetheless found myself feeling compassion. I also explored systemic issues in what I came to observe as a painfully imperfect and unjust judicial system, where money and skin color seemed to determine important aspects of how one was viewed and treated by the law.

Contained within Sunshine's comment to me, I now recognize, was the reason I felt so unsatisfied with my work at the time. I longer believed in the capacity of the legal system to address the problems I observed. It was a system that had forgotten that it was dealing with human lives. It seemed purely a mechanism for processing people out of society. The work of a public defender is vitally important, but I came to view it as serving the role of a stopgap. To me, writing allowed one to do what the legal system did not: to care for and explore the human condition. Writing starts from a place—to borrow a line from Sunshine—that admits that we don't always have ourselves or our communities "figured out" just yet. It wasn't long after that interview that I turned down my admissions to law schools, deciding instead to begin down a route that would eventually lead me to teaching college-level writing and literature courses in prison, first through Boston University and now through Boston College.

During my second year of teaching in prison, I was again reminded of Sunshine. Midway through the fall semester, I lost my brother suddenly to an undetected heart condition. It was the first real tragedy on that level that I had ever experienced. My own writing and my teaching of writing in prison were some of the only activities I was able to approach with any real motivation. As my students learned of the news and offered their condolences, the stories of loss they shared made me realize how fortunate I had been. I had grown up in a safe city, with a good public school system, and in a supportive family. I hadn't encountered too many roadblocks. Many of the students in my courses, much like Sunshine, had never had those benefits. Many had experienced tragedies much earlier in life, and many had been faced with roadblock after roadblock after roadblock.

These interactions reinforced the reason teaching writing in prison had become so important to me. As scholarship suggests, the loss of self-determination often experienced by imprisoned people can lead to a form of "institutionalized dehumanization," in which correctional facilities implicitly—and often explicitly—deprive the incarcerated of their individual identities and personhoods (Rodríguez 8). As Ragnhild Utheim explains, "Incarcerated students live under very controlled circumstances. They are told what to do and say at all times throughout the day: when and how to sleep, eat, shower, use the bathroom, talk, and move" (95). As they shared insights from their personal histories, my students were fighting to keep those identities alive.

Many advocates of prison education point to a 2013 RAND Corporation study as a primary justification for providing higher education in prison. The study found that participants in prison education had forty-three percent lower odds of recidivating, which translates to a reduction in the risk of recidivating of thirteen percent (Davis et al. 32). It concluded that for every dollar spent on prison education, taxpayers save five dollars on what would be spent on reincarcerating repeat offenders (40). The study, however, is a meta-analysis and includes many studies that do not effectively account for selection bias. It also includes studies covering all levels of prison education, not just the postsecondary level, and "cannot say with certainty that the programs grouped in each category are pure examples of a given program type (e.g., adult basic education or postsecondary education)" (35).

The usefulness of the RAND Corporation's study in terms of justifying the involvement of higher education in prison is limited. Such justifications, regardless of whether or not they are convincing for the general public, also potentially inhibit efforts to fight against the types of "institutionalized dehumanization" that prisons often produce. A focus on reduced recidivism reinforces and strengthens the compulsory dynamic of redemption and gratitude (the notion that prison education is strictly for the purpose of employment and that incarcerated students should be grateful for it) often underlying the types of educational experiences offered within prisons. In order to have a more fully humanizing educational program, one that prioritizes critical thought and the work of reclaiming human dignity, it is important, as Simone Weil Davis and Bruce Michaels emphasize, that incarcerated students not be "required to shape [their] goals or pursuits around correctional definitions of rehabilitation" (153).

Writing programs, of course, cannot even come close to resolving the many injustices within our criminal justice system, but they help allow spaces within prisons to become slightly more humane. Such programs represent a recognition that our communities and our judicial system are imperfect, overly punitive, and often unjust. While the legal system tends to dismiss, discard, and dehumanize, writing classrooms create a space where incarcerated people have a chance to reconceptualize themselves as students and writers (Evans 3; Shafer 76). As Adam Key and Matthew May suggest, "When prisoners enroll in classes, they are participating in a discourse that produces them as scholars instead of inmates, learners instead of threats, people instead of numbers" (14). Teaching strategies should aim to bolster these potential outcomes rather than merely reinforce a conception of incarcerated students as being either less than deserving or only deserving if their education leads toward reduced recidivism.

The basic aims inside a prison writing classroom are not all that different from those in writing courses on college campuses. We cover rules of grammar and sentence structure, critical reasoning, and clarity. We work to develop skills relating to personal narratives, critical analysis, argument construction, and incorporating research into essays. We use each semester as an opportunity not only to gain valuable tools as writers and thinkers but also to explore issues within our own lives, aiming to place our experiences within the context of the world around us.

Yet it is important to remember that the context in which such learning takes place is far different from a "typical" college campus. In prison classrooms, students undertake the responsibility of their education within a setting that often seeks to constrain and limit their educational opportunities (Davis and Michaels 147). Students come to the classroom from a variety of backgrounds, with a variety of different life experiences, ranging in age from teenagers to retirees. In response to these realities, my teaching methodology is heavily influenced by the tenets of andragogy, the methods and principles used in adult education.

Malcolm Knowles, the preeminent theorist in the field, lays out six assumptions relating to adult education, among which are that adults' self-conception typically moves from that of a dependent personality toward one of self-direction. Knowles notes that adults accumulate a growing reservoir of experience that serves as a rich resource for learning. As Sharan Merriam and Laura Bierema note, "While a pedagogical model emphasizes content—content determined, organized, delivered, and evaluated by the teacher—an andragogical model emphasizes process" (47). An andragogical teaching approach is one in which the instructor facilitates an environment where adult learners are involved in the planning, delivery, and assessment of their own learning (Knowles et al. 116).

Investigating for a public defender office gave me insight into the way in which the legal and carceral systems routinely ignore defendants and imprisoned people as individuals. Such disempowerment is in many ways the very aim of the criminal justice system. Self-direction no longer exists in practical terms, as the fate of individuals is often determined by attorneys, judges, and juries; then, in the case of a conviction, by wardens and correctional officers. Fighting against this sense of disempowerment is part of what prison education can help offer. The last thing any of my students need is a pedagogy (the art and science of teaching children) that stresses content over process or my own "expertise" over their "inexperience." If adulthood, as Knowles suggests, is a process leading toward self-direction (65), I want my syllabi to reflect that right of self-direction.

The expectation of imprisoned people is almost exclusively that they repeatedly follow orders. Such expectation can have potentially debilitating effects. Disrupting that pattern, however, can at times be difficult. At the outset of a semester, I offer short assignments and paper topics that are highly structured, touchstones we can then return to as a class throughout the semester—a textual analysis or argument essay, for example, in which students select from among a limited number of offered topics. But as the course continues, the assignments themselves become more self-directed on the part of students. So long as the self-direction relates to the purpose of developing writing skills, students are encouraged to pursue their own learning objectives. As an instructor, I set a number of goals throughout the semester for student learning, but I also promote and provide space and opportunity within the syllabus for students to set their own goals. By the end of the semester, I view my role as one of facilitator, providing feedback, helping brainstorm ideas or discuss questions, and suggesting potential strategies for structuring and developing essays.

Brainstorming essay topics is often one of the more engaging aspects of the class. If experience, as Knowles suggests, is a rich resource for learning (66), the makeup of students in a prison classroom offers a wide array of perspectives and experiences to draw upon. Rather than restrict the use of such diverse experience by limiting options for exploration through tightly bounded assignments, I instead hope to push students toward pursuing their own interests. As Robert Scott contends, "radical" instructors (those cognizant of the isolation, oppression, and power dynamics at work within carceral settings) are more likely to value student perspectives, thus encouraging "intercultural exchange in opposition to the regressive stratification of society that has occurred under mass incarceration" (29). Students can be encouraged to draw upon their own experiences and unique perspectives through research assignments that are self-directed in terms of subject matter, textual analysis assignments in which the given texts are not necessarily predetermined by the instructor, and personal narratives that explore issues relevant to the particular student's own life. As the educational opportunities become more individualized, the strategies and mechanics of good writing become more meaningful.

Self-direction also plays a part in the evaluation of student work. It is a higher priority, according to Knowles, for adult learners to understand at a personal level the reasons for learning something (64). Internal motivation takes priority over external factors such as grades or instructor approval. Students in my class take part in determining how they will be evaluated, what their goals are for the semester as writers and learners, and what they hope to get out of the course in terms of both work product and content learning. As Valerie McGrath observes, teachers who allow students to participate in the evaluation and assessment of their own work place them in a position of greater autonomy: "By using the andragogical method they can encourage students to return to education and by allowing them to participate they are treating them like equals and the student is no longer dependent on them for learning as they would have been when they were children in primary and secondary school" (108).

One major method of enabling self-directed learning within prison classrooms is the creation of learning contracts. Learning contracts help resist the more compulsory traits of education embodied within traditional pedagogies. As Jodi Meadows notes, "[C]ompulsory experiences are rarely joyful and generally contribute to the transactional model of education. To develop self-efficacy, individuals must feel they have an appropriate level of autonomy, of self-direction" (59). Within prison contexts, transactional models of education are especially troublesome, given the many dehumanizing aspects already present within the lived reality of incarceration.

A learning contract can help promote a level of autonomy in the learning process, since in creating the contract students actively participate not only in setting their own particular learning objectives but also in establishing how their work will be assessed and evaluated. Such a process is accomplished through one-on-one conversations between instructor and student so that both have a say in setting goals for the course. Learning contracts for each student are agreed upon after the first few weeks of class—whereupon both the instructor and the individual student sign the document as a way to formalize the process—and then are returned to at the end of the semester, enabling both parties to evaluate the progress that was made. Beyond promoting a process of self-direction, a benefit of such contracts is that grades themselves become more meaningful for students, because they are determined through a process of discussion and dialogue rather than merely received as a mark or letter grade.

Such a design, of course, also requires a degree of flexibility on the part of instructors. In helping students take ownership over their own educational pursuits, instructors must be aware that students in prison classrooms are often at different points in their own development as learners. Some students are perfectly prepared to be self-directed, eager to set learning goals for themselves and pursue those goals over the course of a semester. Others may prefer a more traditional, rubric-style assessment in order to gauge their own progress as writers. Under the tenets of andragogy, an instructor must be flexible, prepared to meet students at their own level of engagement with course material.

During that late-night interview, Sunshine explained to me how she felt that the broader world was telling her that her life didn't matter, that her experiences were unimportant and dispensable. Prisons often indicate as much to incarcerated people. Writing programs create a space in which to offer the opposite perspective, a space that aims to reaffirm that our lives and experiences matter and have meaning. The guiding principles of andragogy reinforce this perspective. In prison writing classrooms, I've come to fully embrace what Sunshine told me that night in DC: "Life is messy, honey." Writing programs in prison offer a chance for those involved to explore life's messiness on their own terms.

NOTE

1. Any potentially identifying information has been altered for the sake of privacy.

WORKS CITED

Davis, Lois, et al. *Evaluating the Effectiveness of Correctional Education.* RAND Corporation, 2013.

Davis, Simone Weil, and Bruce Michaels. "Ripping Off Some Room for People to 'Breathe Together': Peer-to-Peer Education in Prison." *Social Justice*, vol. 42, no. 2, 2015, pp. 146–58.

Evans, David. "The Elevating Connection of Higher Education in Prison: An Incarcerated Student's Perspective." *Critical Education*, vol. 9, no. 11, 2018, pp. 1–13.

Key, Adam, and Matthew May. "When Prisoners Dare to Become Scholars: Prison Education as Resistance." *Review of Communication*, vol. 19, no. 1, 2019, pp. 1–18.

Knowles, Malcolm, et al. *The Adult Learner: The Definitive Classic in Adult Education and Human Resource Development.* Elsevier, 2005.

Looney, Adam, and Nicholas Turner. *Work and Opportunity before and after Incarceration.* Brookings Institution, 2018.

McGrath, Valerie. "Reviewing the Evidence on How Adult Students Learn: An Examination of Knowles' Model of Andragogy." *Adult Learner: The Irish Journal of Adult and Community Education*, 2009, pp. 99–110.

Meadows, Jodi. "Resisting Commodification in Honors Education." *Journal of National Collegiate Honors Council*, vol. 20, no. 1, 2019, pp. 57–62.

Merriam, Sharan, and Laura Bierema. *Adult Learning: Linking Theory and Practice.* Jossey-Bass, 2014.

Rodríguez, Dylan. "The Disorientation of the Teaching Act: Abolition as Pedagogical Position." *Radical Teacher*, vol. 88, no. 1, 2010, pp. 7–19.

Scott, Robert. "Distinguishing Radical Teaching from Merely Having Intense Experiences While Teaching in Prison." *Radical Teacher*, vol. 95, no. 1, 2012, pp. 22–32.

Shafer, Gregory. "Composition and a Prison Community of Writers." *The English Journal*, vol. 90, no. 5, 2001, pp. 75–81.

U.S. Department of Justice, Bureau of Justice Statistics. "Prisoners in 2018." Government Printing Office, 2018.

Utheim, Ragnhild. "The Case for Higher Education in Prison: Working Notes on Pedagogy, Purpose, and Preserving Democracy." *Social Justice*, vol. 43. no. 3, 2016, pp. 91–106.

Writing Our Lives into the World
Benjamin J. Hall, Rhiannon M. Cates, and Vicki L. Reitenauer

Prisons stand in incontrovertible ways as sites where the dominator logics of power and control are on full display. For those who are or have been incarcerated, or who have been in relationship with persons who are or have been incarcerated, these logics create a felt and lived experience of power at work to order and constrain human lives. For those who have not been incarcerated, an understanding of these logics remains intellectual at best. Courses offered in the Inside-Out model bring "outside" college students and "inside" incarcerated students together inside prison settings, offering a learning opportunity across the social divide that is prison through a shared experience of engagement within the carceral context.[1]

In this essay, we—who are, at the time of this writing, a currently incarcerated student and teaching assistant, a university staff member with experience as a student and teaching assistant, and an instructor of women, gender, and sexuality studies—examine strategies for conceptualizing, building, and nurturing the power-sharing approaches we take in the Inside-Out course Writing as Activism. The essay traces the grounding of this course in the centering of every participant—both those who are incarcerated and those who process into the carceral facility twice weekly from a large urban state university—as author and authority on their work and in the processes and practices that catalyze the making of that work. We reveal how we have collaborated to build a co-created space across difference within which the active redistribution of power drives a shared responsibility for developing course content and facilitating class activities, establishing trusting critical relationships as writing coaches and feedback partners, and engaging in rigorous self- and community reflection, including the use of self-grading as a mechanism to promote individual accountability within the group.

We have engaged equitably to co-create this essay and our course. Given that two of us are employed at a large urban-serving state university and that one of us is incarcerated at a minimum security prison in the same city, we have experienced the making of this written work as both an individually driven, compartmentalized process and a collectively held and collaboratively developed one. This essay therefore includes both individually authored sections and collaboratively constructed ones and strives to convey the fractured and fraught nature of working across the fiercely drawn institutional boundaries we intentionally cross, over and over again, in our attempt to know and support one another as learners, as teachers, as writers, and as persons. We recount our individual experiences as participant-writers in the learning space and share our collective vision for the ways teaching and learning writing in prison settings, including through approaches that demand a sharing of power among incarcerated and nonincarcerated individuals, create the conditions in which we (all) may practice agency, responsibility, and accountability for writing ourselves into our lives and writing our lives into the world.

Despite the Fissures: Vicki

I can feel the fissure that runs through the foundation of this essay beneath me as I write. I am sitting in a swanky space (or at least a space that passes for swanky at my chronically underfunded state university), trying to find a handhold, a way into this piece. At this faculty writing retreat, I am surrounded by eleven colleagues searching for their own grip as writers on their own projects. I am a veteran of these retreats, drawn by the spaciousness of a day away from other responsibilities and, if I'm being honest, magnetized as a former first-in-family student and working-class-reared woman in the academy to the breakfast, lunch, and bottomless coffee provided to keep us going. The working-class girl in me still feels like she's getting away with something on days like this—and most days. That girl still feels like she's going to get caught.

Rhiannon is sitting perpendicular to me, a first-timer at one of these events. I'm taking the first crack at this piece while she finishes another project this morning; then we'll do the handoff at lunch. We're not allowed to talk—we're reminded by a posted list of rules that this is to be a silent space—but every now and then we text to keep each other going.

I can't stop thinking about Ben. I'm contributing to an essay about teaching and learning about writing in prisons in a quiet space, surrounded by real-deal academics doing their smarty-pants things, being fed yogurt and granola and fresh fruit and hard-boiled eggs and breakfast sandwiches of all sorts—and that's just for starters. I'm here in material comfort and ease, absolutely free to come and free to go, encouraged in every way to wrestle these words onto the page.

I picture Ben in his milieu: he's at his prison job in the chaplain's office, in my mind's eye. I can see that space, and I can see the chapel across the hall where the three of us meet when Rhiannon and I go inside to advance our collaborative work. We're scheduled to be there together on Monday at 8:00 a.m., and we'll have to use our every minute inside wisely and efficiently to get this shared writing done.

So whether or not I'm comfortable using my power to put these first words on the page; whether or not my chair teeters, its legs metaphorically astride the crack in the foundation; whether or not the use of my power in this way makes that crack wider and deeper, I take a deep breath and begin.

Processes of Processing: Rhiannon

It happens in the spring—or, rather, has happened to happen in the spring: our course, the one the three of us have set out to write about together. Spring, marked by its particular dynamism of dramatic weather, explosive growth, suddenly restored belief in the possibility of summer, shed layers, graduations, resurrections, feels right for our course. That feeling of stepping outside at the end of a day and reeling in the fact that it is still light out, that the world is still there; that there is still time.

For a term, half of our cohort enters prison from the outside to join the other half inside. Some of us have spent time inside before, here or elsewhere, briefly or more than briefly. Others are led to this experience by credit requirements, evening availability, curiosity urged by a neatly phrased course description, or a persuasive friend. Some of us are just tagging along. Circumstance and luck, informed and complicated by multitudes, have determined which half of the class we each find ourselves a part of, which way we turn in the hallway once class ends, and why we aren't walking the same way.

Vicki, who designed this course, serves as the guide through this ten-week endeavor, working with corrections officials to bring all of us together, with the readings and materials we need, for each course session. In the weeks leading up to the start of the term, both inside and outside students, after registering online or by "kyte" (correspondence between

inside students and carceral staff), have the opportunity, through informal interviews, to determine if this unique course is a mutually good fit.
The first week of the term, students meet separately in their settings of
origin to collectively prepare for our time together. At the carceral facility, inside students gather to spend an evening with our teaching team
to ask questions and clarify expectations as we break in the classroom
space we will convene in for the next ten weeks. On the outside, at the
downtown campus of our giant commuter school, Vicki and I, missing a
third of our team, answer many of the same questions about the course
before walking the outside students through what (not) to wear, what
(not) to bring, and how to navigate the logistics of meeting for class a mere
ten miles away—ten miles meant to feel a world away.

Moving from "I" to "We": Ben

I remember where this all started for me. As I enter the room there are
fifteen outside students, strangers to me. I have met the instructor only
once, in a short interview. I know nothing about the course or even what
the word *pedagogy* means. I am a first-time college student who is incarcerated and terrified of interacting with the public, knowing only that the
course will focus on criminology in some way. I imagine this class will
be like any other I've taken, with the usual power dynamic: the professor
teaches, and the students read the material. Only later will I learn that
this course will involve transformative learning.

In organizing we often talk about power: *power over*, *power within*,
and *power among*, concepts I knew very little about during my first college
course. Perhaps more than any institution, prison is the ultimate expression of *power over*, with its ideology built on human abjection. Teaching
writing and the humanities inside prison is vital to building power within
and among those subjected, to empowering prisoners to reconstitute and
assert their humanity, if those involved challenge the typical power dynamics in the classroom. This prompts the question, How can professors
and students navigate and accomplish that in a space that dehumanizes?

Following the many Inside-Out courses I've now taken, I've had the
privilege of being a teaching assistant (TA) in several. My first experience
as a TA consisted simply of setting up chairs and passing out papers.
Later, another professor I assisted told me he would use me for much
more than that. During this particular course he went out of town one
week and said, "You and Katie [the other, outside, TA] figure it out." This
was my first experience of sharing power in a class setting. When writing

is taught—or, rather, learned—in this manner, it not only opens possibilities but shifts the power in the classroom.

Creating a space of learning and autonomy within a prison first reminds us of our power within—the power that asserts that no one can take away our ability to contemplate, to imagine a better world, and to work to create it. Although this power is intangible, it is what reminds us of our value and that each of us has pieces of the puzzle we can engage toward collective liberation. This inner power helps us learn fluidity in this restricted space we must move in. Our intentionality in exercising this power (sometimes by restraining it) creates a *power among* that is transformative.

It had been over ten years since I first enrolled in Writing as Activism when I returned to it as a TA. I am now a member of a teaching team with my colleagues Vicki and Rhiannon—we explicitly name ourselves in this way—with an expectation that through this shared power (and through sharing this power) something magical will transpire. I bring an earned experience to the room, knowing I will learn and teach as Octavia E. Butler prescribed: "Belief initiates and guides action—or it does nothing" (47). This is part of the power we share and build within an ethic of community. What sets Writing as Activism apart from any course that I've taken in prison is the complete collaboration among all of us—students and teaching assistants and instructor—as teachers and learners and our intentionality in building relational power.

The humanities ask us to examine the ways human beings experience and interact in the world and also challenge me to live more intentionally in an unjust world. That we have to even teach inside prisons throughout this country suggests that something is terribly wrong. Considering prisons and the oppressive ideologies that built them, I have come to believe they cannot be destroyed by focusing on tearing them down, nor by protesting or loud screaming. Rather, we must build something that counters the greater systemic injustices that fill them up. Our co-creating relational power in a classroom inside a prison made up of incarcerated and nonincarcerated students, incarcerated and nonincarcerated teaching assistants, and an instructor—truly, teachers and learners, all—begins this small but dynamically powerful construction that chips away at the prison's foundations, that allows us to act as "accomplices in postcarceral world-building" (Hall et al. 1).

As adrienne maree brown argues, "[W]e must become the systems we need—no government, political party, or corporation is going to care for us, so we have to remember how to care for each other" (113). Week after week, around our circle, we do. Today, when I walk into the classroom of the world, it is no longer "I" but "we."

Power-Sharing across Difference: Pedagogy, Practice, and Process

But how does that individual "I" get transformed into being part of a collective "we"? In the case of Writing as Activism, a number of intentional course design and delivery elements constitute the mechanisms through which an explicit power-sharing across difference may take place. In this coauthored section, we identify six of those elements, and we weave considerations from the literature together with our lived experiences as (collaborative) teachers and learners.

Shared Ownership of Course Content

At the very beginning of our course, as names are learned, expectations discussed, and ground rules agreed upon, it is made clear that our course content, the prompts answered, and the activities carried out in our circle of writers will, after our first few sessions, be collaboratively selected by every person in the room. The week-by-week schedule included with the syllabus resembles a fresh Mad Libs, with plenty of spaces ready to be filled and read back to the room.

Once the course is revealed as a co-created experience, "there is a much stronger sense that the class belongs to everyone," as every participant is instantly vested and invested in this collaborative process by its very design (Weimer 31). This shared ownership engages every student not only as a contributor but also as an authority of information, redistributing the curricular power typically reserved for the instructor equally around the circle. At its core, this leveling of authority is informed by a belief that each student is capable and qualified, coming into the space with "valuable insights and experiences that could contribute to discussions" and the ability to create together as both teachers and learners (Ropers-Huilman 99).

This participatory and collaborative element of Writing as Activism fosters an environment of enriched discussion, consensus, and adaptability as the content of the course evolves to embody the subject matter that drives our small community of activist-writers. The content, direction, and success of the course begin and remain in everyone's power to make our own as we claim ownership of the experience by deeply trusting in one another and the work we have set out to do.

Individually Chosen Writing Projects

A key component of the coursework in Writing as Activism is the individual course plan (ICP). For this assignment, each member of our circle, we three authors included, outlines what our individual writing project will entail, how it will be accomplished, and why. Through this reflective narrative exercise, each writer self-assigns explicit expectations for the work they will hold themselves to complete over the course of the term, including accompanying texts and concrete routines they will incorporate into their practice, such as a certain amount of time dedicated to writing or revising each day or a number of pages to generate between each class session. By developing appropriate and attainable goals, each student retains the power and assumes the responsibility to track and determine their own success in fulfilling, or revising and fulfilling, their ICP by the conclusion of our time together.

Self-direction ensures that projects will be not only personally achievable but also meaningful. The ICP requires critical engagement with the collaboratively developed framework and goals of the course to effectively identify how each student will contribute to, and in turn benefit from, the success of our community in their personal projects. These stakes position our course to be leveraged to its highest advantage: agency functions as an inherent opportunity for students "to pursue matters they are passionate about and/or to write something relevant to a professional aspiration or future pursuit" in their work (Eodice et al. 35).

Replacing the demands of identical assignments doled out by any singular person in power, this accountability to an individual writing practice preserves authority and authorship of our narratives as well as our experiences of learning. In the profoundly immovable and marshaled setting of prison, the freedom of this responsibility feels especially vital and monumentally worthwhile.

Shared Facilitation of Writing Workshops

Starting on the second full class meeting (and continuing every second meeting of every week), we all take turns in small groups to design, plan, and facilitate writing workshops—essentially, ways for each of us to make things new and to make new things—for the whole group. The teaching team conducts the first workshop to offer a sense of one way it might be done; then, passing the baton to small teams of students to conduct the remaining workshops, we participate fully as students. Since we're in a prison, where half of us live and half of us do not, we've got to do this designing and planning during our first class meetings of the week. We dream up activities that we hope will inspire our colleagues to engage in the workshops with enthusiasm, with goodwill, and with a sense of play. We practice being together in this literal and figurative space of collaboration, believing each of us is an agent and expert on our own experience. We get good at using our precious time well.

Week after week, the writing workshops are colorful and diverse. Our writing practice one week has us collaboratively making children's books on activist topics that excite us; another week, we write our way into deeply reflective prompts that ask us to put words around our experiences of loss or to imagine what a world without prison might look and be like. We generate poems together in the form of an "exquisite corpse" and, as we read them, marvel at the collective unconscious at work among us.

We will take some of this work with us into our individually chosen writing projects; some of it will languish in our notebooks. No matter: in our second class session of the week we experience the power and delight of playing with words, of collective imagining, of collaborative making, of forging our practices on the page, in the room, and in the world.

Engaging as Writing Coaches and Feedback Partners Together

Through weekly practice on our individual projects and participation in writing workshops, we each generate pages and pages of writing. One way that we seek to understand what "writing as activism" might be and mean for us is to share that work with one another to see what kind of impact it has on an audience of readers.

With much intentionality, we set up a number of feedback groups within the class to provide a container for giving and receiving feedback inside a growing sense of trust. Some of us have never experienced feedback groups before; some of us have been wounded in them by careless, cutting critique; some of us love to engage in rigorous critique, cutting or not. Through reflection, each of us identifies the level of critical engagement we're looking for in our feedback groups. Those for whom simply sharing work is a big, vulnerable stretch find their way to others who feel similarly; those who want their work torn apart so they can put it back together again, better than before, find others who want that too. Once we're in those groups, we practice a decidedly author-centered process in that we empower each writer to direct the focus and type of the feedback we receive.

In this way, we take responsibility for ourselves and our development as writers, asking for the sharing of insight we can and will actually use.

In this way, we practice a discipline, a care, and an accountability with one another to center each writer in their work and each person in their own experience.

Collaborative Development of Projects

A feature of all Inside-Out courses, including Writing as Activism, is co-creation of one or more collaborative projects intended to carry on into the world. Given the fully relational, power-sharing intention of our course, we create and practice community by collaboratively brainstorming possible projects, deciding on one or more of them to pursue, and completing them together during the second half of the term.

Each of us gathered around the circle begins to imagine our project possibilities through considering the contexts we are operating in, identifying our interests, and determining both what gifts we would like to bring to the project and what skills and capacities we would like to build through our collaborative work. In this way, we leave something behind that also passes on, and we leave having experienced growth and learning in the process.

One way we have left something behind at the end of our time together is through the making of a class-wide zine, a self-published volume of writing and art produced by every class so far. Connected to the zine, each class has opted to host a reading inside the correctional facility, which facility and university staff members attend. Last year, Ben and Rhiannon led a process to create a facilitation resource manual of promising practices to pass on to women incarcerated at another institution. These student-driven and student-created projects allow for a spaciousness in our course, a way for us to work with autonomy and interdependence—a way to literally speak and write ourselves into the world.

Self-Grading

Grades, at base, are accountability measures. Most educational settings posit accountability to outside standards held up by someone deemed an authority. Far too often, bias is built into those standards, into the teaching that intends to compel students to perform to those standards, and into the evaluation and assessment strategies used to determine how convincing, or not, that performance has been.

As in each of Vicki's courses, grades in Writing as Activism are generated through a rigorous self-grading process (Reitenauer; Cates et al.).

Students are, through this model, invited to be accountable to themselves and to one another by determining their own learning and growth goals for the course, being in formative conversation with their colleagues and instructors about their experiences in working toward those goals, and engaging in critical self-reflection around what they accomplished, how they accomplished it, how they affected and contributed to the success of others and to the learning community as a whole, and what they are taking from this course experience to be applied in the future. Essentially, each person in the circle identifies how they chose to engage with themselves, their writing, and the collaborative work of the class; how those choices contributed to making personal, interpersonal, and community-level change; and how they might commit to the continued practice of that agency going forward.

At the end of all that formal and informal reflection, students determine the grade they have earned in the course—with the caveat that the instructor may ask them to have a conversation about the grade if their choice seems significantly over- or underinflated. Many teaching practitioners assume that students will always give themselves an A, whether they have earned it or not—yet nothing could be further from our observations of students acting with integrity in self-grading. With few exceptions, Vicki's conversations around grades come about because students—both incarcerated and not, so many of whom occupy one or more target identities and have been socialized to an internalized undervaluing of their intelligences, their efforts, and their positive impacts on others—are at least as hard on themselves as the oppressive forces they have encountered in the classroom and in the world.

In Solidarity

We are now preparing, sometimes together, but mostly apart, for another offering of Writing as Activism. As we complete this writing project and begin a new term, the synchronicity feels right: it has been through our interactions as co-teachers and co-learners in a course integrated with both incarcerated and nonincarcerated folks and held within a prison that has allowed us to build our relationship across difference and our affinity for collaboration as writers.

We have come to believe that this building of relationship is key to the kind of learning and growth that allows all persons to become true agents in their lives and truly accountable to one another to co-construct the world as we wish it to be. We have also come to believe that, in order to build these sorts of transformative relationships across difference, an active engagement with power and, even under constraint, a lived sharing of power must occur. With this writing, we offer some of the approaches and methods we have used to forward this agenda. And we live and act and write in solidarity with all of you who work to forward this agenda too.

NOTES

The authors are deeply grateful to all those who made this essay possible, including the students and facility staff members, past and present, without whose shared insights and active support this essay could not have been written.

1. Temple University's Inside-Out Prison Exchange Program offers courses inside correctional facilities. In its integrated class sessions, half the students are incarcerated at the facility and half the students enter the facility from the sponsoring college or university. For more information, see insideoutcenter.org.

WORKS CITED

brown, adrienne maree. *Emergent Strategy: Shaping Change, Changing Worlds.* AK Press, 2017.

Butler, Octavia E. *Parable of the Sower.* 1993. Warner Books, 2000.

Cates, Rhiannon K., et al. "'Locations of Possibility': Critical Perspectives on Partnership." *International Journal for Students as Partners*, vol. 2, no. 1, 2018, pp. 33–46, doi.org/10.15173/ijsap.v2i1.3341.

Eodice, Michele, et al. *The Meaningful Writing Project: Learning, Teaching, and Writing in Higher Education.* Utah State UP, 2016.

Hall, Benjamin J., et al. "Out of Time: Accomplices in Post-carceral World-Building." *Humanities*, vol. 8, no. 2, 2019, doi.org/10.3390/h8020064.

Reitenauer, Vicki L. "'A Practice of Freedom': Self-Grading for Liberatory Learning." *Radical Teacher*, vol. 107, 2017, pp. 60–63, doi.org/10.5195/rt.2017.354.

Ropers-Huilman, Becky. *Feminist Teaching in Theory and Practice: Situating Power and Knowledge in Poststructural Classrooms.* Teachers College Press, 1998.

Weimer, Maryellen. *Learner-Centered Teaching: Five Key Changes to Practice.* Jossey-Bass, 2002.

Erasure or Exploitation? Considering Questions in Prison Publications

Sarah Shotland

On Halloween 2016, I received an e-mail from the mother of a former student I had taught at the Allegheny County Jail. It was short, thanking me for publishing a chapbook of the class's work. Her son, Jacob, had a poem featured in the publication. Attached to her message was a copy of the poem along with a photo of Jacob, which had been distributed at his funeral.

In the final two months of 2016, I received phone calls, e-mails, and *Facebook* messages from seven different families, requesting copies of other chapbooks featuring their loved ones' writings. Their children, spouses, and cousins had been students in the Words Without Walls program, which has brought creative writing classes to jails, prisons, and drug treatment centers in Pittsburgh since 2009. I cofounded the program, and as the program coordinator I am the de facto archivist of all our class publications. We teach about eighteen classes per year, and each of those classes is tasked with creating a collective chapbook. Since we have been publishing these for nearly a decade, my home and office are filled with the records of our students' work.

Before 2016, I rarely received requests for additional copies of the chapbooks. Occasionally, someone would contact me once they had been released from jail or prison to ask for some extra copies, but most students seemed satisfied with the three or four copies they were given at the end of the class—at least one to keep for themselves and a few to send to family or friends or to pass out in the housing units.

Since 2016, however, I have been contacted by more than two dozen families asking for chapbooks. The opioid crisis continues to ravage the country, and it has hit the Rust Belt, where I work, hard. Because of our ongoing, failed War on Drugs, vast majorities of my incarcerated students are serving sentences directly or tangentially related to buying, selling, and using drugs. When a person finishes treatment or leaves jail or prison, they are at their most vulnerable for overdose. Their previous tolerance to a drug has dropped, and the strength of that drug on the streets has grown—a deadly combination. This alarming uptick in the deaths of my students has led me to think differently about publishing their work.

Preparing students to publish and giving them practice revising for an audience is at the heart of what we do as creative writing teachers—writing for readers is the crucial distinction between professional writing and personal writing. It is the motivation behind such fundamental concepts as clarity, continuity, purpose, and beauty. Without the reader, we would have no reason to revisit our writing in the confines of our notebooks.

Students are told to consider an audience; the stories we tell, the rhetorical moves we make, are largely determined by the readers we aim to reach. When teaching these classes in prisons and jails, publication must be considered if we are to offer incarcerated scholars the same respect and expectations we offer our students on college campuses.

But after 2016, my reasons for incorporating publication became more complicated and urgent. Yes, publication is about finding an audience and revising for them, but it is also about leaving evidence of a life. This evidence is important for incarcerated writers for many cultural and political reasons, including the creation of primary historical sources that document the realities of the US legal system in an age of mass incarceration. Creating first-person accounts and documentation of this era is an important part of the work that academics and universities can do to help the broader society bear witness to these spaces, especially given the ways literacy complicates the creation of primary sources, leaving profound gaps in the historical record where we lack accounts from those unable or forbidden to write.

Beyond historical and cultural documentation, publishing the work of incarcerated students is profoundly important for more intimate reasons. This became starkly obvious to me once I started mailing chapbooks to the children and parents who survived my students. Sending family members these publications gave evidence that their loved ones were more than their struggles, their worst mistakes, or their criminal records. Since the beginning of the written word, writers have been working toward legacy—an artifact or idea that will outlast our flimsy mortality. The families I work with are grateful to have a written legacy of their absent ones—a small poem to distribute at a funeral, something to read to a surviving child. *This was your mother, and this is the poem she wrote about the depth of her love for you.*

While most of this essay deals with the practicalities of publishing, I urge educators and editors who work with incarcerated writers to consider the fragility of our work and the importance of remaining committed to a publishing practice even when the readership of student work may be a micro audience of family, friends, and fellow incarcerated writers and scholars.

The logistics around facilitating the publication of incarcerated students' work are challenging. They can be tedious. Some of them are frustrating, and all of them take more time to facilitate than on-campus work. I offer this personal introduction to a practical guide because these families are people I think about when I feel overwhelmed by the challenges of these projects. The stakes and urgency of publishing the work of incarcerated writers and scholars make it worth the extra time.

As prison educators who are usually coming from universities, we have distinct questions to consider in our prison classrooms. One simple question I return to frequently is, How can I be useful?

I've found my usefulness is measured by my ability to transport information. I can bring information into a prison classroom, which is highly restricted when it comes to Internet access, research materials, or creative and scholarly opportunities. I can also carry information outside the prison classroom, amplifying incarcerated voices to those who never pass through prison gates. With the privilege of free passage I assume the responsibility of information transport as one of my most valuable uses.

Bringing information into the prison is simpler than transporting it out. I wonder how the material changes once it travels through the walls. How does language transform when it receives an audience? How are we preparing incarcerated writers for an audience? How, with our access to the worlds both inside and outside the gates, are we preparing our university communities to receive and read these scholars' work? And how are we working in our lives outside the university to prime editors and publishers in the literary world to read the work of our students with historical context, social awareness, and genuine interest and open-mindedness? In the following pages, I offer questions to consider and strategies to employ when working to publish the voices of incarcerated writers. I hope that for prison educators aiming to be more efficient and thoughtful transporters, this will be a useful resource.

Paving Pathways: Options for Class Publications

While prison educators aim to offer similar experiences on campus and in carceral spaces, we all know that the two can never be identical. One of the ways this distinction manifests in the creative writing classroom is through publication. It is an ethical imperative for educators to consider the specificities that our incarcerated students face when publishing their work.

The challenges and risks associated with publishing student work can seem daunting. Resources such as computers and typewriters are limited and unpredictable. Students are often transient, making sustained work on a project difficult. Complicated policies governing prisons may limit readership by restricting what can leave the prison walls. The constant interruptions that come with prison can mean a loss in momentum for projects. Depending on the parameters of a program—whether it awards college credit or not—the interests, styles, and skills of students may vary wildly, creating challenges in curating a cohesive class publication, which is the kind of publishing opportunity I most frequently offer students. Despite these challenges, it is important for prison educators to continue presenting meaningful and professional publishing opportunities for incarcerated students.

Whenever possible, build a team. My graduate students have aided me tremendously by typing, copyediting, designing, and typesetting class publications. Teamwork offers university students opportunities to be of service and gain skills, and it gives incarcerated students experience working with a publishing team.

There are some practical concerns to consider when planning a class publication. First, the facility administration needs to know a publication is being planned. This is less about gaining permission from authorities (though that's important) than it is about protecting students from retribution and punishment if they are found to be working on an unauthorized project. Materials can be confiscated or destroyed if writers don't have permission to work on such projects, and sometimes even if they do. Obtaining written records of permission from administrators is crucial. Administrators can also advise on the use of incarcerated writers' names in publications or announcements of publication, which victim's rights laws in some locations may forbid. I recommend working with administrators from the education unit at a facility rather than applying to general administrative staff members. Getting the permission of a principal, education coordinator, or social worker inside the programming department will offer an additional layer of protection if the administration or leadership at the facility abruptly changes (a frequent occurrence). Try to make sure someone inside the system is willing to support the class project, since these full-time prison educators and social workers understand the language and internal politics of the Department of Corrections much better than educators from the outside.

Approved publications might include chapbooks, magazines or zines, newspapers, podcasts, anthologies, dramatic scripts for performance, book reviews, op-eds and letters to the editor, and scholarly articles or proposals. There are also questions of how the publication might be distributed. It is important to center the considerations of the writers in this decision, as they are the experts about the consequences of readership. The options presented below may serve as a starting point for discussion.

Class-Only Publication

The first option is the publication equivalent of "What happens in Vegas stays in Vegas." Copies are distributed only to class participants and instructors. The class should agree on the number of copies to be printed for a micro-run after considering how many copies each member of the class wants for personal use, whether the facility requires a copy, and how many copies the educator should keep for the archive. If desired, a nonbinding publishing contract could be created—for example, a compact that serves as a commitment between class members but doesn't grant permission to distribute the work (permission that might be negotiated in one of the other models discussed below).

In-House Publication

An in-house publication could be distributed to a select audience consisting of friends, family members, program supporters, prospective instructors, grant funders, and those inside the facility whom writers personally deem interested in the material, like cellmates, coworkers, friends, or other educators. Distribution outside the class introduces additional considerations, such as the use of pen names. For any number of reasons, students may not wish to publish work under their documented names. A brief discussion of the literary history of pseudonyms offers students a range of choices about their creation of a literary identity.

Since educators will likely use an in-house publication to provide evidence of course outcomes, train future teachers, or amplify program goals, a binding contract may be necessary. Our program uses a simple template we modified from a university press contract. When entering into publishing contracts with students, take care to explain publishing terms for the sake of expanding literary vocabulary and offer students the explicit opportunity to decline the contract. I provide examples from former students who have declined, explaining their rationales to begin a discussion about the implications of publishing in a prison setting. Some writers worry that their work could be used against them. Others prefer to wait for larger publication opportunities that might not be available if the work is deemed "previously published." There are also considerations of whether a writer wants to risk further stigma by being included in a publication explicitly for incarcerated writers. Discussing these reasons and inviting further contemplation allows students to make more informed and thoughtful decisions about their writing lives.

There may be opportunities to hold a reading or performance of the class publication inside the facility or to organize a public reading outside the prison in cooperation with the sponsoring organization or university. If there is a public reading, consider whether videoconferencing will be available so that the incarcerated writers can participate. If the writers are not able to perform their own work, note that the choice of readers is important to the work's reception. In our program, we try to find local writers and performers whose work reflects or intersects with the specific incarcerated writers who are featured in a publication. For example, we invited a local comedian to perform one incarcerated writer's comedic monologues and a journalist reporting on local issues to read from another writer's political essays about racism in prisons. For many new writers, reading work to an audience is the first opportunity to receive audience feedback and to feel the sense of accomplishment that comes with finishing a work and presenting it to readers. While on-campus students can likely organize these events on their own, incarcerated students usually don't have that option. Your on-campus students, or a local organization you choose to partner with, may be able to help produce a public reading of your incarcerated students' work.

Small Press Publication

Some student publications may be distributed by a university program or organization at conferences, panel presentations, university events, literary festivals, and so on. Such projects can create opportunities for students to gain skills as editors and publishers of their own small press. Consider how the members of an editorial board, or the author of a volume introduction, might be chosen or elected from the class and what responsibilities might be involved. Explore whether the press can set rules or recommendations for distribution and whether, if the sponsoring organization receives donations related to the publication, those funds are earmarked for programs that support your students' education.

Facility-Specific Publication

Student writers and publishers can also create and circulate a pamphlet or newsletter within their facility or even between prisons. There are some excellent examples of prison newspapers, including the *San Quentin News*, which maintains an outstanding website at sanquentinnews. com. Enquiring at their website will allow you to connect with incarcerated publishing experts.

It is important to reserve class time for a full discussion and deliberation about the risks and rewards of creating and distributing a publication on any scale. As mentioned above, whenever possible, include your students in the editorial process, including the selection of the title, the written content, and any artwork, especially if there will be author photos; the creation of style guides; and the determination of layout and design. This kind of instruction increases students' understanding of publishing and editorial standards as well as their agency in framing and broadcasting their stories and images, no matter the scale or scope.

Risks and Rewards of Reaching Out

There are distinct questions to consider when students begin to submit for publication to outside journals, contests, and conferences. Instructors and students creating class publications control many aspects of the publishing process that writers submitting work elsewhere do not. Writers in the latter group therefore have fewer means at their disposal of ensuring that the publication of their work reflects their intentions.

As with students in any setting, preparing writers for industry standards is an important part of publishing instruction. For incarcerated students, this often means the instructor needs to print and make copies of complete submission guidelines for students. Limited Internet access in prison also puts much of the burden and responsibility of finding and curating submission opportunities on the instructor.

Some opportunities are created specifically for incarcerated writers. The best-known of these is the PEN America Prison Writing Contest, which takes into consideration the restrictions incarcerated writers face and offers a user-friendly website featuring clear guidelines and submission deadlines as well as excerpts from winning works ("Annual Prison Writing Contest"). This contest is open to all incarcerated writers as well as those who have been released from incarceration within the last year.

While such opportunities are important ways for incarcerated writers to be recognized, we also want our incarcerated students to have broader

opportunities that encompass their wide-ranging interests, both scholarly and creative. The world of publication is so vast that it is impossible
for a single instructor to offer students the full breadth of the Internet or
of a platform like *Submittable*. Curating a possible list of reasonable and
relevant submission venues and deadlines is one way to offer students
options. I usually pick five to ten deadlines that will fall near the end of
the course at publications I know and respect. Researching the journal
masthead is one of the most important parts of determining whether I
can recommend the journal in good conscience. In a world that increasingly does not accept mailed submissions, I have often contacted journals
to ask if I might submit pieces on behalf of a student or send a batch of
submissions by mail. This contact has always been revealing about the
journal's attitudes toward receiving unconventional submissions. I have
spoken with many editors who are thrilled to receive work from writers
that fall outside their usual submission queue and who have been generous and accommodating, often coming up with creative solutions so that
my students can be fairly considered for publication.

My incarcerated students show the same enthusiasm and motivation
to do the work of submission as my on-campus students. Those who are
beginning to identify as writers will show tremendous interest, which
allows me to differentiate instruction and curate opportunities specific
to their interests and skills. Those who are still in the beginning stages
of building a writing practice often intuitively understand that they are
not ready to send work out yet. I approach this situation as I would on
campus for the most part, supportively offering instruction and information for those not yet ready and pushing those who are to make the leap
into publication.

Both populations of students also face the emotional risk of rejection—an inevitable part of becoming a writer or scholar—but the stigma
and stereotypes associated with the prison system can weight the odds
against incarcerated writers. When a submission arrives in a Department
of Corrections envelope, it will be read in a different light than something
that arrives on university stationery. Handwritten submissions, too, will
call attention to themselves. Whenever possible, I try to minimize these
factors by finding students on the outside who are willing to type and
send submissions so that incarcerated scholars are not at an immediate disadvantage based on first impressions. After working to minimize
technological issues, psychologically preparing students for possible rejection is important. I usually share stories about my own rejections as a
writer, but the sting still burns. Many of the incarcerated writers I have
worked with have already suffered a profound and excruciating amount

of rejection in their lives. Some also have very little to look forward to and can attach an outsized expectation to the possibility of external validation. This situation isn't unique to incarcerated writers, but I have noticed it more in my prison classrooms than on campus. Because of this, I am careful to be brutally honest with students about the rates of acceptance to various journals.

Many of my incarcerated students have had work published in scholarly volumes, literary journals, and newspapers. The satisfaction of success shines twice as bright in these classrooms because we know the hurdles were twice as high. The pride I have witnessed after publication is contagious, the kind that inspires other students to take creative risks themselves. I have never seen the kind of academic competitiveness that universities are known for when one student receives publication while others don't. Instead, what I have seen is a collective pride that the class itself is contributing to everyone's continued excellence and achievement. This phenomenon is one of the strongest pieces of evidence I have seen to support a vigorous argument for prioritizing these publication opportunities despite the profound challenges.

Exploit Me or Erase Me: Working with Journalists

Journalists have an interest in prison education stories, and in recent years working with journalists has become a hotly debated topic among prison educators and incarcerated scholars, particularly regarding issues of exploitation, sensationalism, language, and incomplete narratives that focus on criminal records rather than scholarship or creative achievement.

There is a risk in working with journalists. Incarcerated students already know this. They are intimately familiar with distortions of their cases, their stories, and their lives in the press. Many them have already been burned by journalists who covered their trials. Despite this, several of my incarcerated students have made conscious decisions to work with journalists, whether acting as sources or subjects or in cowriting situations. They know that the press can be a powerful tool for sharing their stories and potentially writing new narratives of their lives. I too have made the decision to give journalists access to our program to write about our teachers and students.

The results have been mixed.

My decisions and mistakes are my own, but as an educator, I feel a responsibility to reserve class time to discuss the risks of working with journalists, which gives students opportunities to build skills in media literacy, critical thinking, debate, and textual analysis. Among the examples we have discussed in class is the hotly debated *New York Times* article by Eli Hager "From Prison to Ph.D.: The Redemption and Rejection of Michelle Jones," various pieces from the Marshall Project (www.themarshall project.org), and the "Voices Unlocked" series, written by Brittney Hailer for the nonprofit news outlet Public Source (publicsource.org/category/se ries/voices-unlocked/). Analyzing these articles allows students to imagine different outcomes and to consider their own framing techniques when writing complicated stories.

What students know, most of all, is that if they cannot access the media, their lives become almost entirely invisible to people outside their immediate sphere of influence. Though they haven't disappeared to their families or friends, they are physically and psychically separated from the rest of our society. Sometimes the calculus suggests that it is worth the risk to work with journalists who might get their stories wrong, who might lead with their convictions, or who might sensationalize or exaggerate the transformative power of education.

This exaggeration of transformation is one of the dangers I consider when determining whether to work with media outlets. I am aware of the transformational power of education in my own life, and I obviously advocate for it as a prison educator. I also know the limitations of this redemption cliché. I know that my role as instructor makes me a prime beneficiary of such coverage. Often journalists paint prison educators as saviors, saints, or some version of a salvation cliché themselves. I am supportive of my students making whatever decision they have calculated is wise for them when working with journalists, but I am less certain when it comes to coverage that involves me as a character or Words Without Walls as an organization. For now, I have suspended efforts to garner media attention for our program. I have worked with journalists to bring attention to writing by individual students, but profiles of the program feel off-limits to me for now.

I am optimistic, though. Projects like the Berkeley Underground Scholars at the University of California, Berkeley, give me hope. They have created a resource for those who are communicating about people involved in the carceral system. It is a language guide created by formerly incarcerated people for journalists and writers (Mason et al.). I have passed it along to every journalist I know, hoping they will take it into account. I am also buoyed by the ongoing conversation about how journalists might approach stories about the carceral system with more nuance and context. I have faith that journalists will become better communicators when it comes to telling the stories of incarceration, and as an educator who occasionally teaches college students who are studying journalism, I have an additional responsibility to train them to be at the forefront of changing our media norms.

I wonder if or when I will lift my personal ban. For now, it has been a useful boundary to set. It encourages me to be more critical of my own work, to question my own strategies and motivations, and it requires me to interrogate my ego. Moving in and out of prison is complicated, no matter what your position in life. The longer I have done this work, the more complex it has become for me, but most of the media coverage of our program has been reductive in some sense. I don't blame individual journalists or news outlets. I simply set this boundary until I have time to live in these questions longer or until the urgency of my own story or program becomes such that the rewards of exposure outweigh the risks.

I conclude with a short account of an end-of-semester reading at Allegheny County Jail. We had organized a semipublic performance to celebrate the printing of the class chapbooks, but the day before the reading, the campus print shop told me the binding of the books had been delayed. Then I was called to a last-minute on-campus meeting that conflicted with the reading at the jail. Still, I knew I had to be there with the cardboard box of chapbooks in my trunk that the printers had finally finished after hours. I knew that if the students didn't receive their chapbooks that morning, many of them wouldn't have another opportunity. I knew that the reading wouldn't be possible without the chapbooks, since the students wouldn't be allowed to return to their cells to retrieve their notebooks. I knew that if I didn't arrive with the chapbooks, I would have failed to live up to the standards I set for my students.

Beyond all its other benefits, publishing offers everyone involved accountability to our own values and ideas. Revision and submission are processes that hold us accountable to readers, to editors, and, more importantly, to ourselves. My commitment to building publication opportunities into prison classrooms is as much about me as it is about my students. I need accountability in my life. I need more ways to show up, on time, and to deliver what I've promised. I made it to the jail with the chapbooks the morning of the reading. We passed them around the room before the performance, fingers over fresh ink, evidence.

WORKS CITED

"Annual Prison Writing Contest." *PEN America*, 3 Dec. 2012, pen.org/annual -prison-writing-contest/.

Hager, Eli. "From Prison to Ph.D.: The Redemption and Rejection of Michelle Jones." *The New York Times*, 13 Sept. 2017, nytimes.com/2017/09/13/us/ harvard-nyu-prison-michelle-jones.html.

Mason, Joshua, et al. *Language Guide for Communicating about Those Involved in the Carceral System*. Underground Scholars Initiative, UC Berkeley, 2019.

Self-Care as Ethical Practice for Teachers and Volunteers Working with Writers behind Bars

Shelby D. Tuthill and Tobi Jacobi

Viva and Hazel were volunteer teachers in weekly SpeakOut! writing workshops in a county jail and youth rehabilitation center. Like many writing teachers working in carceral spaces, they revealed feelings of pride, guilt, sadness, and solidarity when asked to reflect upon the work of writing with and responding to writers behind bars. In interviews about the program, they articulated some of its personal challenges. "I had a really tough time just going there, the physical space of the jail," Viva commented. "The way we're situated when we go pick up the women in their cells and walk in a line. It was all really awful [and] hard to talk about because we are in such privileged positions . . . we don't get to feel shitty about being there because we don't have to stay." Hazel explained, "I get really attached to people. . . all of a sudden they are gone and I don't know how they are doing, if they are on the streets, if they are on drugs or clean, if they are getting the help that they need, so that's really hard." Bringing together research on secondary trauma, empathy, and mindfulness in writing practice with data drawn from qualitative interviews with SpeakOut! program volunteers, this essay articulates a set of self-care strategies for teachers working in prison. Ongoing support for strategies such as deliberate community connection, active reflection, and intentional boundary setting is necessary for the development of sustainable carceral teaching and writing work.

We begin by recognizing the compassion fatigue, collective trauma, and feelings of alienation, allyship, anger, empathy, and helplessness that often arise with working in contexts like prison. Mere recognition, however, does little to equip volunteers, teachers, and administrators with the tools they need to ensure the health of their programs, their students, and their own capacity for commitment to teaching inside. Access to ongoing and varied self-care strategies can provide the support that prison teachers and students require in order to maintain participation in the movement toward more equitable educational access for people both free and confined.

Recognizing Secondary Trauma and the Exigence of Self-Care

Through their work witnessing and responding to writing that reveals deep emotion, centralizes injustice, and elucidates histories of trauma, teachers working in prison are prone to vicarious or secondary trauma, burnout, and exhaustion. Researchers have regularly found that incarcerated people, especially women, experience higher rates of trauma relative to the nonincarcerated general population (e.g., Baranyi et al.; Green et al; Grella et al.). This reality creates a dynamic wherein traumatic or violent life experiences described in student writing may be unfamiliar to or triggering for teachers. Community literacy practitioners such as Jennifer Horsman and Pat Schneider suggest methods whereby workshop facilitators can best meet the needs of writers as they collectively grapple with these topics, making visible many of the ways in which literacy work touches on trauma, trust, control, and boundaries—concepts that are central to work in prisons. While it is important to safeguard the emotional well-being of writers by competently dealing with trauma and boundaries, less attention is paid to the impacts of these constant negotiations on educators. Irena Michals and Suzanne Kessler assert that while the satisfaction and gains of prison teaching are high, teachers regularly grapple with not only institutional barriers to teaching practices (e.g., lack of resources, unstable access) but also emotional stressors such as "the difficult burden of knowing" when students disclose trauma or are transferred to another facility without warning (53–54). What guidelines are there for those who teach writing to care for themselves in addition to the writers they work with? How might increased attention to educator self-care contribute to sustainable teaching practices behind bars and empathy for writers inside?

Self-care, a term that has grown in popularity in recent years, is conceptualized broadly as individualized practices of monitoring and attending to one's own emotional, mental, and spiritual functioning. Self-care is critical to the well-being of students preparing for careers in fields such as counseling psychology and social work (Colman et al.; Napoli and

Bonifas) and has been considered necessary for the ethical provision of human services; in acknowledgment of the idea that a therapist or social worker cannot maintain professional competence in the face of burnout or exhaustion, scholars have called for the institutionalization of self-care practices in graduate training programs (Bamonti et al.). Fields such as psychology, social work, and hospice care propose mindfulness—the practice of openly and nonjudgmentally attending to the present moment and one's internal experience—as helpful for those in professional settings that may otherwise induce burnout (Bruce and Davies; Napoli and Bonifas; Shapiro et al.; Lipsky and Burk). Brittany Sansbury, Kelly Graves, and Wendy Scott suggest that training in trauma recovery concepts and the fostering of resiliency as a normalized organizational practice support individuals and promote a workplace culture that actively recognizes work within challenging contexts (119–20). Thomas Fabisiak argues that adopting an "ethos of self-compassion would mean acknowledging the difficult realities involved in prison education, recognizing that we are limited human beings operating in complex, irrational environments" (69). Such mindsets are useful models for those committed to literacy-based work behind bars.

In recent years, English studies has joined conversations on affect, mindfulness, and contemplative practice in theory, pedagogy, and professional development (Usler; Mathieu, "Being There" and "Excavating Indoor Voices"). Graduate teacher trainings and guidebooks acknowledge the need for attention to work-life balance through what Paula Mathieu calls "mindful awareness practices" ("Being There" 18); Sean Ruday's *The First-Year English Teacher's Guidebook: Strategies for Success*, for example, includes a chapter titled "Make Time for Self-Care," which highlights familiar practices of scheduling downtime and countering overload with physical and social activity. Writing centers have also become sites for enacting self-care practices (Giaimo). Acknowledging that sharing writing can be weighty and emotional, writing centers and their staff are encouraged to allow for open discussion of mental health issues (Degner et al.). Others advocate for the practice of mindfulness, intentionality, and empathy when hearing and responding to writing (Mack and Hupp; Perry) and advise partnering with community resources, including counseling centers (Perry). These recognitions, across disciplines, of the presence of individual and sociocultural traumas and the need for intentional self-care response suggest that attention to such matters within carceral literacy spaces is a relevant and timely alignment with pedagogical work occurring across varied locations in English studies.

Developing Self-Care Principles in the SpeakOut! Writing Workshops

While some professional organizations offer scholars and practitioners disciplinary guidelines for conduct (e.g., counselors and therapists in the United States look to the American Psychological Association's *Ethical Principles of Psychologists and Code of Conduct*), teaching writing behind bars exists in an interdisciplinary gray area, and often it is up to individual literacy programs to establish and support ethical practices for volunteer conduct and training. While some attention has been paid to self-care surrounding the teaching and facilitating of writing behind bars (Jacobi and Roberts; Yenne et al.), its ethical urgency in maintaining teacher satisfaction and program viability has not been apparent in most community literacy or prison teaching scholarship. Our review of literature and our lived experience as workshop facilitators and as a program director in English studies and a doctoral student in counseling psychology suggest that a reframing of self-care practices as community-based and contextually sensitive has much to offer teachers working behind bars. To establish this, we draw upon relational-cultural theory (RCT), a framework for psychotherapy that shares ideological values with approaches within materialist feminism, intersectional theory, and decolonial practice. RCT underscores the importance of empathic connection with others as a way of maintaining a sense of energy and ability to stay connected in all relationships (Comstock et al.).

Furthermore, we draw upon the lived experience of program facilitators through qualitative data from the SpeakOut! writing program. SpeakOut! is a community-based writing initiative sponsored by the Colorado State University English department's Community Literacy Center and its College of Liberal Arts. From humble beginnings with one group of women writers in a halfway house in 2005, it now includes seven weekly writing workshops for people affiliated with youth rehabilitation, community corrections, and a county jail. Each workshop meets for sixty to ninety minutes for twelve weeks in the spring and fall. Our dataset draws from twenty-five semistructured interviews conducted with current and past SpeakOut! facilitators who had volunteered in the program for at least one semester between 2010 and 2019 and is complemented by thirteen years of program evaluations.

Interviews focused primarily on motivation for participation, perceptions of impact and benefit, experience of challenge, and awareness of self-care strategies. Interviewees included female and male participants and identified as traditional or returning college students, current and retired faculty members, and community members interested in literacy outreach. Selected portions of the full interview transcripts were coded for thematic commonalities and disparities. Data analysis affirmed teachers' commitment to working with confined writers and suggested self-care practices that they had used or envisioned. Participants shared positive feelings about community engagement, the development of community and relationships across teaching peer groups, and opportunities for creative interaction with other writers; they also described challenges around hearing, responding to, and processing difficult disclosures as well as grappling with the complicity in the carceral system that working behind bars requires. Our analysis suggests several core principles for establishing guidelines for self-care as ethical practice within confined spaces:

>Self-care should occur at the inception of and throughout teachers' experiences rather than being reduced to a set of practices undertaken upon exiting prison or jail.

>Self-care should function as a recursive rather than linear set of practices. Since the experience of working inside a carceral space is itself unpredictable and fraught with institutional tensions, the practices we use to understand those experiences must be responsive and dynamic rather than fixed.

>Self-care practices that work toward sustaining teachers and volunteers should also be available to writers behind bars. While incarcerated writers will not have access to all the same tools and contexts as nonincarcerated facilitators, we can and should make efforts to incorporate practices that encourage mindful engagement into our program design, facilitation and teaching, professional development opportunities, extracurricular activities, and assessment plans.

Utilizing Empathy and Mutuality as Self-Care Practice

To realize these core principles, we have identified three interconnected practices that can inform and guide development of self-care plans for teachers and writers in confined spaces: fostering connection, engaging active reflection, and setting intentional boundaries. We include strategies for applying each practice to demonstrate the breadth of possibility for support. Drawing from relational cultural theory and participant responses, we suggest that programs promote growth-fostering relationships between teachers and writers by adopting intentional self-care practices, a step we see as critical to moving toward ethical practice both for our teacher-selves and for the writers we work with inside.

Fostering Connection

Concepts of community and connection with others emerged as both a benefit of the program and a strategy for self-care. Connection happens naturally upon first contact with writers and other facilitators and often grows deeply throughout the course of the semester, showing itself in moments of laughter, crying, gratitude, empathic silence, encouragement, awe, and inspiration. Relational cultural theory posits that, despite a broader culture that values individualism and self-sufficiency as markers of mature functioning, we are wired to be in connection with one another, and that health is instead indicated by engagement in mutually empathic relationships (Comstock et al. 280). Volunteers attest to these benefits, describing experiences of support and community with workshop writers, other facilitators, and extended networks of support beyond SpeakOut! Maddie mused, "We're going through things together as a community, and that's one of the powerful parts about SpeakOut!" Sarah added, "You have to be really careful because we're not therapists. . . . I think, for me, it was very important to be working with people that I trusted and could have conversations with." Several volunteers noted that carpooling to and from the jail facility helped them connect and process shared experience with other facilitators. Olive expressed the benefit of talking about her workshops, and about other "life stuff," with a family friend after leaving the jail. Per RCT, connecting with others in this empathic way leads to increased energy and vitality as well as heightened desire to connect more deeply to others. Considering that burnout and compassion fatigue tend to be associated with withdrawal from social relationships—and that burnout is eased by social support—practices that increase social connectedness are critical for self-care (Maslach and Leiter 109). Volunteers also commented on the importance of learning experientially, as Frank reflects: "I can't help but feeling like whatever takes place in the workshop is part of the healing. Whatever it is. So, as difficult as the stuff is in the moment, I feel like the big-picture perspective is, 'Great, I'm glad you could share that. I'm glad we could all share that experience.'" Others extended the importance of connection to local community, mentioning a sense of educational responsibility; Karen said, "I do think it's important for people who do these workshops to take that knowledge in some way and do something with it, so people start to understand."

Whereas many volunteers expressed the benefits of these connections, others also indicated a desire for more opportunities to create and maintain such relationships. Some noted that it can be difficult to discuss SpeakOut! with people who are not involved in it; connecting by way of shared experience may at times be the most helpful way to hold space for workshop content. And while these informal connections can help alleviate some of the heaviness of grappling with some writers' work, programs can also provide more explicit opportunities for volunteers to connect at scheduled meetings and trainings. Underscoring this need for connection, volunteers noted that some of the challenges included desensitization to the content of writing, taking on the pain of others, and fearing judgment from writers about perceived privilege—all experiences that can feel overwhelming in the absence of space to process with others. Volunteers like Viva called for increased interaction with peers: "Even once a semester to have a coming-together to discuss this would be really important. To do this in a structured way where there is writing and reflecting; to be in a safe space to talk about this stuff."

The interactions between facilitators and writers during workshop supply additional connection, both energizing and draining. The nature of literacy programs is such that facilitators and teachers fall into a hierarchical role above writers and students. Although this power dynamic results inevitably from structural aspects of privilege and access, the boundary it creates need not be a barrier to connection between facilitators and writers (see the section on setting intentional boundaries). Connecting meaningfully and empathically with writers, rather than fearing and avoiding authentic exchanges, is one strategy for self-care, consistent with the concepts of RCT. It is achieved by sharing authentically and being mindfully attuned and empathic in responding to writers' narratives. To the first point, Olive said, "Write about what you truly need to write about right now. . . . [T]hat's how you can make even deeper connections—if you write about what's important to you and not what you think will be most well-received by the group that you're with." In regard to empathic engagement with writers' disclosures, Eli shares, "I try my very best to find [a] way to give gravity to it and to honor it and not move on too fast from that piece of information." These experiences of connection within and outside of workshop give rise to a series of best practices, below, for creating and deepening connection that will allow teachers to better sustain themselves and their work inside:

> Set up opportunities for connecting with other teachers or volunteers at meetings and trainings (e.g., coffee hours, digital meetups, monthly trainings responsive to program concerns).
> Encourage teachers to hold space for organic connections between writers in the classroom, even when interactions feel "off-topic."
> Create lesson plans collaboratively and include invitations to write individually and collectively.

Support and encourage informal networks of connection (i.e., recommend that volunteer groups carpool, organize monthly coffees to discuss workshop joys and challenges, set up private online discussion spaces).

Engaging Active Reflection

Many interview responses implied the importance of reflection and subsequent reflection-based actions as necessary to sustainable work in carceral settings. Making meaning of their experience through reflection appears to help volunteers move forward from the difficult moments of workshops; volunteers like Maddie expressed the power of recognizing, naming, and processing experiences, honing the ability to "reflect instead of absorb . . . to be there in the moment and just move through. . . . [I]t won't benefit you to dwell." Facilitators can employ reflective techniques in workshop by encouraging writers to reflect on prompts and on pieces shared. Shaheed, a volunteer with a youth facility, explained, "What's difficult is the process of planning lessons or planning prompts, because until you really get to know the group that you're working with, you don't know what will work well." His words highlight the utility of checking in with the group as workshop progresses, using reflection to modify prompts and future lesson plans.

Many interviewees recommended reflective journaling practices. Mindful and reflective writing can be used before workshop to center oneself before entering the space, during workshop while writing with the group members, and after workshop to process the workshop itself, one's positionality and privilege, one's emotions—whatever is alive and ready to be reflected upon. Olive said, "Journaling has been really good. So coming home and giving myself limited amounts of time . . . describing one challenging thing of the night . . . and then responding to that. . . . If I truly believe in the power of writing, the power of journaling, why am I not using it myself?" Although journaling emerged as an individual practice for some volunteers, programs can provide instruction on specific journaling techniques that have been shown in other groups, such as nursing students and counseling psychology trainees, to promote meaningful reflection (e.g., Epp; Hubbs and Brand; Poon and Danoff-Burg; Adams). Our SpeakOut! training and materials encourage written reflections at the opening of each staff meeting (biweekly) as well as through distributed resources such as the volunteer handbook and exit surveys (see Jacobi and Roberts for examples).

RCT emphasizes that therapists should connect client struggles with broader structures and systems in order to do justice to their full experiences; the same can certainly be said for volunteers reflecting on their experiences with writers. Reflection through writing or conversation may include grappling with systems such as race, ethnicity, gender, class, and the prison-industrial complex. Lily expressed a desire for more explicit education and instruction on managing these larger reflections, stating, "Sometimes I wonder what is the exact mission of SpeakOut! . . . I don't know if we as facilitators are supposed to be doing more in terms of bringing out heavier material or material about experiences in jail or how they've been treated . . . like shedding light on that institution as a whole." Although the program demonstrated openness to these conversations by hosting relevant guest speakers and reflective opportunities at trainings, Lily requested operationalization of those reflections in workshop and accountability for the continuation of such conversations. It is recommended that literacy programs provide clear and consistent opportunities to read about and reflect upon personal and program-wide ways of grounding into the work. In the absence of such education and guidance, volunteers are left without tools for contending with crucial questions.

As other self-care techniques are attempted, those explorations can be reflected upon in the same ways. Reflexivity in approaches to self-care is crucial; strategies that work well for one volunteer may fall flat for another, and certain combinations of practices may address a volunteer's needs more comprehensively than single strategies can. Encouraging volunteers to be mindful, observant, and curious about their evolving self- and community-care practices is likely to help them more meaningfully reflect on what works for their own specific needs and preferences. We therefore recommend the following strategies:

Call out reflective practice regularly by making space for volunteers and writers to reflect together during workshop about the prompts and the pieces shared.

Provide research-informed guidance to teachers (and students, when possible) on mindful journaling practice, and include prompts about personal reactions, possible adjustments to workshop, and the broader context of mass incarceration.

Establish guidelines for keeping volunteers accountable to continuing and applying their reflections, as appropriate to the program structure (e.g., digital dialogues, volunteer newsletters, program e-mail messaging).

Setting Intentional Boundaries

Many interviewees articulated a need for healthy, intentional boundaries in order to work inside sustainably. While they mapped their boundaries variously, they generally distinguished three categories—emotional, physical, and intellectual—for understanding their experience and potential self-care. RCT suggests upending entrenched social understandings of boundaries as barriers with an alternative notion of boundaries as places "of meeting and exchange with surrounding milieu rather than as a place of protection from it" (Jordan 93). Some volunteers noted that the time commitment (approximately three evening workshop hours plus preparation time) felt "just right," noting that a greater expectation would have felt overwhelming in terms of both contact inside and life balance. Others, like Maddie, suggested a will to create a set of intentional actions for working through engagement with writers inside: "I just know what my boundaries need to be for it. If I've done everything that I can, I have to say 'Okay. I hope everything's well with her.' Maybe say a prayer or have a short discussion with someone else and then try to ground myself and find something else that I could focus on." Establishing such boundaries can be challenging, however, when teachers become deeply invested in students' lives and success, a process that writing together enables. Ruth, for example, felt bewildered when, without explanation, writers stopped returning for workshop sessions, and Hazel lamented the loss of connection: "When someone disappears, you hope they've gone home . . . but they completely disappear. . . . You feel like you know them really well and they're gone." Others, like Samantha, held tight to hopeful (imagined) futures: "You desperately want them all to get out and find happiness and success." The most recurrent challenge named by facilitators centered on the emotional experience of hearing and processing writers' stories. Frank said, "There's been times where I've read something and sat in here and had a little cry . . . and then typed it up for them." Matt similarly noted, "They're constantly [saying,] 'Here,' 'Here,' 'Here,' 'Here's more,' 'I want more feedback,' which is kind of great to want and have, but at the same time . . . I take it as almost this personal burden." For facilitators like Frank and Matt, the accumulation of difficult narratives and the pressure to respond to and manage them was palpable; both went on to cite the importance of interactions with peers as central to maintaining motivation to continue working with the program in sustainable ways.

Similarly, multiple interviewees noted the importance of creating critical distance from their time inside, often enacted as literal and figurative space between their workshop time and the other demands of life, citing a need to simply drive, to go grocery shopping, or to talk about life with a family friend before moving from the creative space of workshop into dense graduate school reading or academic writing. Olive described "spending a long time looking at a computer screen until I was ready to write something academic rather than something creative." Other facilitators transitioned from the workshop through physical activity and familiar comforts (e.g., "taking a barre exercise class," "eat well, exercise," "shower and getting into comfy pajamas"). As the teachers grapple with their concerns about individual writers, practicing regular reflection through private writing, paired or group conversation, or protected digital spaces offers them ways to understand and contextualize workshop moments within the larger program aims and the more global context of incarceration. Additionally, facilitator comments, in addition to a decade of program evaluations, affirm the need for regular, scheduled training opportunities in verbal and written response techniques, lesson plan development in carceral contexts, and the creation of boundaries with semipermeable walls so teachers and writers can embrace writing as a viable tool for healing and change. The strategies below support these goals:

> Design program goals and practices that can be responsive to specific participants' needs.
> Encourage teachers and writers to consider workshop boundaries as a meeting space where all participants can choose to be present (and not stymied).
> Encourage teachers and writers to collaboratively develop a set of guidelines for responding to difficult topics and contexts. Make these shared guidelines available to all participants.
> Encourage teachers and writers to create a continuum of individual and group activities that facilitate emotional, physical, and intellectual self-care.
> Develop clear program language to help teachers and writers recognize how their work contributes to positive change and works toward social justice.

Moving toward Sustainability and Social Justice

After more than a dozen years of facilitating creative writing workshops in spaces of confinement, we feel certain that intentional self-care is central to sustainable practice in teaching within the larger US system of mass incarceration. Whether we engage with students through well-supported and -defined prison college programs, arts-based nonprofit groups, or one of the many more ad hoc opportunities to write alongside people experiencing imprisonment, attention to how and when we make sense of the experience is necessary. The practices and strategies we offer here contribute to a growing body of interdisciplinary research on sustainability, engagement, and mindfulness—one that scholars and teachers in English and literacy studies have begun to adapt as we recognize the need to offer self-care training to teachers working in diverse contexts.

At a recent SpeakOut! reading, we witnessed more than a dozen writers steadily make their way to the front of the workshop room to speak out their words. Stories, poems, one-liners, and even songs filled the rooms used for anger management, parenting, and Bible study during other hours of the day. Writers moved each other with words of love gained and lost, with calls for justice, and with observations on life, including the tragic, the joyful, the unexpected burst of laughter that permeates all walls. As teachers, we have come to cherish such moments, holding onto them as we wade through the bureaucracy of the higher education and justice systems. We carry writers' words out of doors and into our cars, into the grocery store, the coffee shop, and the shower. The weight of those words, and the heaviness of a broken system mired in racial and gender inequities, poverty of access, and historical privilege, can feel overwhelming. We advocate for increased attention to the ways that the principles and practices that guide our SpeakOut! program might guide others engaged in both emergent and long-standing prison teaching and program development in establishing a continuum of self-care for participants.

NOTE

The authors recognize with deep appreciation the contributions of those interviewed.

WORKS CITED

Adams, Kathleen. *Scribing the Soul: Fourteen Essays on Journal Therapy.* Center for Journal Therapy, 2004.

American Psychological Association. *Ethical Principles of Psychologists and Code of Conduct. American Psychological Association*, Mar. 2017, www .apa.org/ethics/code/.

Bamonti, Patricia M., et al. "Promoting Ethical Behavior by Cultivating a Culture of Self-Care during Graduate Training: A Call to Action." *Training and Education in Professional Psychology*, vol. 8, no. 4, 2014, pp. 253–60.

Baranyi, Gergő, et al. "Prevalence of Posttraumatic Stress Disorder in Prisoners." *Epidemiologic Reviews*, vol. 40, no. 1, 2018, pp. 134–45.

Bruce, Anne, and Betty Davies. "Mindfulness in Hospice Care: Practicing Meditation-in-Action." *Qualitative Health Research*, vol. 15, no. 10, 2005, pp. 1329–44.

Colman, Douglas E., et al. "The Efficacy of Self-Care for Graduate Students in Professional Psychology: A Meta-Analysis." *Training and Education in Professional Psychology*, vol. 10, no. 4, 2016, pp. 188–97.

Comstock, Dana L., et al. "Relational Cultural Theory: A Framework for Bridging Relational, Multicultural, and Social Justice Competencies." *Journal of Counseling and Development*, vol. 86, no. 3, 2008, pp. 279–87.

Degner, Hillary, et al. "Opening Closed Doors: A Rationale for Creating a Safe Space for Tutors Struggling with Mental Health Concerns or Illnesses." *Praxis: A Writing Center Journal*, vol. 13, no. 1, 2015, pp. 28–38.

Epp, Sheila. "The Value of Reflective Journaling in Undergraduate Nursing Education: A Literature Review." *International Journal of Nursing Studies*, vol. 45, no. 9, 2008, pp. 1379–88.

Fabisiak, Thomas. "On the Practice and Ethos of Self-Compassion for Higher Educators in Prisons." *Critical Perspectives on Teaching in Prison: Students and Instructors on Pedagogy behind the Wall*. Routledge, 2019, pp. 68–79.

Giaimo, Genie. "Working towards the Trifecta: A WLN Special Issue on Wellness and Self-Care." *WLN: A Journal of Writing Center Scholarship*, Apr. 2018, wlnjournal.org/blog/2018/04/working-towards-the-trifecta/. Accessed 19 May 2019.

Green, Bonnie L., et al. "Trauma Experiences and Mental Health among Incarcerated Women." *Psychological Trauma: Theory, Research, Practice, and Policy*, vol. 8, no. 4, 2016, pp. 455–63.

Grella, Christine E., et al. "Relationships among Trauma Exposure, Familial Characteristics, and PTSD: A Case-Control Study of Women in Prison and in the General Population." *Women and Criminal Justice*, vol. 23, no. 1, 2013, pp. 63–79.

Horsman, Jennifer. "'But I'm Not a Therapist': The Challenge of Creating Effective Literacy Learning for Survivors of Trauma." *Australian Council for Adult Literacy 21st National Conference: Literacy on the Line*, edited by Sue Shore, U of South Australia, 1998, pp. 1–5, files.eric.ed.gov/fulltext/ED430143.pdf.

Hubbs, Delaura L., and Charles F. Brand. "The Paper Mirror: Understanding Reflective Journaling." *Journal of Experiential Education*, vol. 28, no. 1, 2005, pp. 60–71.

Jacobi, Tobi, and Lara Rose Roberts. "Developing Support and Self-Care Strategies for Volunteers in a Prison Writing Program." *The Voluntary Sector in Prisons*, edited by Laura Abrams et al., Palgrave Macmillan, 2016, pp. 331–61.

Jordan, Judith V. "A Relational-Cultural Model: Healing through Mutual Empathy." *Bulletin of the Menninger Clinic*, vol. 65, no. 1, 2001, pp. 92–103.

Lipsky, Laura van Dernoot, with Connie Burk. *Trauma Stewardship: An Everyday Guide to Caring for Self While Caring for Others*. Las Olas Press, 2007.

Mack, Elizabeth, and Katie Hupp. "Mindfulness in the Writing Center: A Total Encounter." *Praxis: A Writing Center Journal*, vol. 14, no. 2, 2017, pp. 9–14.

Maslach, Christina, and Michael P. Leiter. "Understanding the Burnout Experience: Recent Research and Its Implications for Psychiatry." *World Psychiatry*, vol. 15, no. 2, 2016, pp. 103–11.

Mathieu, Paula. "Being There: Mindfulness as Ethical Classroom Practice." *Journal of the Assembly for Expanded Perspectives on Learning*, vol. 21, no. 1, 2015, pp. 14–20.

———. "Excavating Indoor Voices: Inner Rhetoric and the Mindful Writing Teacher." *Journal of Advanced Composition*, vol. 34, nos. 1–2, 2014, pp. 173–90.

Michals, Irena, and Suzanne Kessler. "Prison Teachers and Their Students: A Circle of Satisfaction and Gain." *The Journal of Correctional Education*, vol. 66, no. 3, 2015, pp. 47–62.

Napoli, Maria, and Robin Bonifas. "From Theory toward Empathic Self-Care: Creating a Mindful Classroom for Social Work Students." *Social Work Education*, vol. 30, no. 6, 2011, pp. 635–49.

Perry, Alison. "Training for Triggers: Helping Writing Center Consultants Navigate Emotional Sessions." *Composition Forum*, vol. 34, 2016, compositionforum.com/issue/34/training-triggers.php.

Poon, Alvin, and Sharon Danoff Burg. "Mindfulness as a Moderator in Expressive Writing." *Journal of Clinical Psychology*, vol. 67, no. 9, 2011, pp. 881–95.

Ruday, Sean. *The First-Year English Teacher's Guidebook: Strategies for Success*. Routledge, 2018.

Sansbury, Brittany, et al. "Managing Traumatic Stress Responses among Clinicians: Individual and Organizational Tools for Self-Care." *Trauma*, vol. 17, no. 2, 2015, pp. 114–22.

Schneider, Pat. *Writing Alone and with Others*. Oxford UP, 2003.

Shapiro, Shauna L., et al. "Teaching Self-Care to Caregivers: Effects of Mindfulness-Based Stress Reduction on the Mental Health of Therapists in Training." *Training and Education in Professional Psychology*, vol. 1, no. 2, 2007, pp. 105–15.

Usler, Christina. *In Contemplative Consideration of Colorado State University's First-Year Composition Curriculum*. Colorado State University, 2019, MA thesis.

Yenne, Elise, et al. "Lockstep Literacies: The Challenge of Social Justice Volunteer Work behind Bars." *Peace and Social Justice Education on Campus*, edited by Laura Finley and Kelly Concannon, Cambridge Scholars Publishing, 2015, pp. 133–52.

Notes on Contributors

Patrick Elliot Alexander is associate professor of English and African American studies at the University of Mississippi. He is the author of *From Slave Ship to Supermax: Mass Incarceration, Prisoner Abuse, and the New Neo-slave Novel* (2018), and his articles on teaching African American literature in prison appear in *Humanities*, the *Journal of African American History, South: A Scholarly Journal*, and *Reflections: A Journal of Writing, Service-Learning, and Community Literacy*. Alexander is the director of the Prison-to-College Pipeline Program, a college-in-prison program he cofounded in 2014 that won the 2018 Mississippi Humanities Award from the Mississippi Humanities Council for offering high-quality for-credit college courses for imprisoned men at the Mississippi State Penitentiary at Parchman and for imprisoned women at Central Mississippi Correctional Facility. In 2020, Alexander was honored with the University of Mississippi Humanities Teacher of the Year Award, and in 2021 he received the University of Mississippi Elsie M. Hood Outstanding Teacher Award.

Molly Dooley Appel is assistant professor of English at Nevada State College. She has been an educator for fifteen years, first as a K–12 ESL teacher and now as a professor of Latinx and Latin American literature. Her research and teaching examine how literature and other forms of media work as a space of pedagogical thinking and practice for human rights and social justice. She was a 2018 MLA Connected Academics Fellow, is the recipient of a 2021 NEH Humanities Connections Grant, and is cofounder of the Educators' Alliance Caucus for the American Studies Association. Her work appears in *Chiricú Journal*, the edited volume *Human Rights, Social Movements, and Activism in Contemporary Latin American Cinema, Paste Magazine, Nevada Humanities*, and the Scholar at Large series on *Interfolio*'s blog.

David Bennett is a former Prison University Project student who has been a California prisoner for the past thirty-three years. Before coming to San Quentin, he taught himself about history and ethnic studies through extensive reading and many a jailhouse scholarly debate in maximum security institutions. David and his coauthor, Courtney Rein, believe in doing away with the traditional hierarchies of higher education. They both hope that the experience they describe in this volume will be replicated by many more teachers and students.

Rachel Boccio is associate professor of English at LaGuardia Community College in the City University of New York. Her scholarly interests range widely across the American nineteenth century with a focus on literature, education, incarceration, and social justice. Her work has appeared in *Pedagogy*, *Rethinking Schools*, *The Edgar Allan Poe Review*, *The Nathaniel Hawthorne Review*, and the edited collection *Critical Insights: Frederick Douglass*. Before joining the faculty at LaGuardia, Boccio taught English and American literature for two decades at John R. Manson Youth Institution, a maximum security prison in Connecticut.

C. Fausto Cabrera is a multigenre writer and artist incarcerated since 2003. He is coauthor, with Alex Soth, of *The Parameters of Our Cage*. His work also appears in the *Washington Post Magazine*, *Colorado Review*, *Water-Stone Review*, *The Missouri Review*, and elsewhere.

Paméla Cappas-Toro is associate professor of Spanish, Latin American, and Latinx studies at Stetson University. She is the cofounder and codirector of the university's Community Education Project, a higher-education-in-prison program that provides high-quality liberal instruction to individuals who are incarcerated in a men's maximum security prison in Florida. Her research focuses on second language acquisition and curricular development in Latin American and Latinx studies in carceral spaces.

Rhiannon M. Cates works in Special Collections and University Archives at Portland State University (PSU) and teaches community-based courses centered on LGBTQ+ oral and archival history in PSU's university studies program. She is a volunteer and cofacilitator of educational and leadership programming conducted inside Oregon state correctional facilities and a founding coeditor of *Amplify: A Journal of Writing-as-Activism*, and her work can be found in the *International Journal for Students as Partners*, *Humanities*, *Collaborative Librarianship*, *Higher Education Accessibility behind and beyond Prison Walls*, *Radical Teacher*, and other venues.

Laura E. Ciolkowski is senior lecturer in the Department of Women, Gender, Sexuality Studies at the University of Massachusetts, Amherst. Her work lies at the intersection of literary studies, gender and sexuality studies, and critical prison studies. She writes about gender-based violence, social justice feminisms, literature, and prison education. Her work has been published in *Twentieth Century Literature*, *Studies in the Novel*, *Genders*, *Novel: A Forum on Fiction*, *Public Books*, *Victorian Studies*, and *Victorian Literature and Culture*, among other places. Her "Rape Culture Syllabus," published in *Public Books*, was widely shared and circulated by scholars and activists across the country. In addition to teaching graduate and undergraduate courses at UMass, she teaches college humanities courses in prison and jail, in programs enrolling incarcerated students pursuing bachelor's or associate's degrees.

Patrick Filipe Conway is director of the Boston College Prison Education Program and earned his PhD in higher education at Boston College's Lynch School of Education and Human Development. His research interests relate to the development and expansion of higher education opportunities in prison, including policy and media coverage analysis, effective teaching practices, and the exploration of student experiences in prison. His scholarship has appeared in the *Harvard Educational Review*, *Adult Education Quarterly*, and *Sociological Forum*. His work and research were featured on the *Have You Heard* podcast when he won the 2021 *Have You Heard* Graduate Student Research Contest.

Anne Dalke tutors writing, co-teaches classes, and facilitates workshops in several Philadelphia county jails and Pennsylvania state prisons as an affiliate of the Petey Greene Program, the Inside-Out Prison Exchange Program, and the restorative justice project Let's Circle Up. For thirty-five years, she taught English and gender studies at Bryn Mawr College, where she worked with a colleague and students to establish a reading and writing program in a local women's jail. An abolitionist and a Quaker with a particular interest in resistant teaching practices, Dalke is the author of *Teaching to Learn / Learning to Teach: Meditations on the Classroom* (2002), coeditor of *Minding the Light: Essays in Friendly Pedagogy* (2004), a contributor to *Critical Perspectives on Teaching in Prison: Students and Instructors on Pedagogy behind the Wall* (2019) and *Failure Pedagogies: Systems, Risks, Futures* (2020), and coauthor of *Steal This Classroom: Teaching and Learning Unbound* (2020).

Jenna Dreier completed her PhD at the University of Minnesota, where she conducted doctoral research on prison arts programs dedicated to the study and performance of Shakespeare, and now leads a college-in-prison initiative known as TREC (Transformation and Reentry through Education and Community).

Rivka Eckert is an abolitionist and community-based theater artist exploring the intersections of theater and social justice. She has taught theater and English in prisons, high schools, and middle schools and worked with the Peace Corps in Samoa and Liberia. As assistant professor in the Department of Theatre and Dance at State University of New York, Potsdam, Eckert teaches Theatre and Community, Devising Theatre, Applied Theatre, Directing, Acting / Scene Study, and Play Interpretation and Analysis.

Shannon Frey works with a community and university literacy partnership through Penn State University. She proposed and co-organized a creative writing class for incarcerated women in a county correctional facility in 2012 and has continued to be involved in education in carceral settings. Her background is in adult education, and her research interests focus on creating space for adult critical pedagogy, building learning communities, centering student perceptions of success in correctional settings and educational institutions, and supporting peer-led pedagogical practices.

Jess A. Goldberg is assistant professor of American literature at New Mexico Highlands University. Before Highlands, they taught at Longwood University and worked with the Restorative Justice Initiative at Penn State University. While in graduate school, they taught courses in writing instruction, introductory literature, world literature, and American drama and theater with the Cornell Prison Education Program. With Marquis Bey, they are a coeditor of *Queer Fire: Liberation and Abolition*, a special issue of *GLQ: A Journal of Lesbian and Gay Studies* on prison abolition. Their scholarship appears in the journals *ASAP/Journal*, *Women's Studies*, *College Literature*, *Public Culture*, *Women and Performance*, *Callaloo*, *MELUS*, and *CLA Journal* as well as the edited collections *Unsettling Poetry Pedagogy*, *Against a Sharp White Background: Infrastructures of African American Print*, *Toni Morrison on Mothers and Motherhood*, and *The Routledge Handbook of CoFuturisms*.

R. Michael Gosselin is associate professor of English at Genesee Community College. He has been teaching college composition and literature classes inside New York state prisons since 2011. Previous papers include "Toward a Student-Centered Prison Pedagogy," at the New York College English Association Conference, Rochester, NY; "Pedagogy and the Panopticon: Teaching inside Attica Correctional Facility," at Fitchburg State

University; and "College Success in Attica," a paper on prison education that was read before the New York State Assembly Standing Committee on Corrections.

Ann E. Green is the Dirk Warren '50 Sesquicentennial Chair and professor of English at Saint Joseph's University in Philadelphia, where she teaches writing and service-learning. She has published in *College Composition and Communication*, *The Michigan Journal of Community Service Learning*, a number of edited collections, and the *Philadelphia Inquirer*. She is the recipient of the 2017 Outstanding Leader in Experiential Education award from the National Society of Experiential Education and the Lindback Lifetime Teaching Award.

Richard Sean Gross is currently studying for his bachelor's degree from Villanova University and participates in many programs like Alternatives to Violence. Richard was awarded second place in the essay category in the 2019 PEN America Prison Writing Contest for his piece "Death by Incarceration: Cruel and Unusual."

Benjamin J. Hall was incarcerated for twenty-two years. In pursuing higher education inside, Benjamin took and served as a teaching assistant in more than fifteen Inside-Out courses and, at the Oregon State Penitentiary, was a founding member of the Inside-Out Think Tank / Another Chance at Education program and the Penned Thoughts writers' group. His writing appears in the anthologies *Ebb and Flow* and *Men Still in Exile* as well as the magazines *Contexts* and *All Rise*. Passionate about writing as a form of nonviolent resistance, Benjamin was released on parole in April 2020, enrolled at Portland State University, and died in December 2020.

Elizabeth Hawes is the recipient of six national PEN America prizes in drama, poetry, and memoir; three Minnesota Broadsides in prose and poetry; and a Fielding A. Dawson award for drama. She was a 2018 finalist for PEN America's Writing for Justice Fellowship, and her work has been published in *American Theatre Magazine*, *Exchange*, *Hunger Mountain*, *Truthout*, and *A World without Cages*.

Tobi Jacobi is professor of English and director of the Community Literacy Center at Colorado State University. She coordinates the SpeakOut! writing program for confined writers and has published scholarship on prison literacy in journals such as *Reflections*, *Community Literacy Journal*, *The Journal of Correctional Education*, *Feminist Formations*, and *Radical Teacher* and in edited collections. Her coedited book *Women, Writing, and Prison* came out in 2014, and she is currently working on a collaborative literacy remix project that blends contemporary pedagogy with archival prison texts.

James King is a state campaigner for the Ella Baker Center. As a person who has seen firsthand the harm the US legal system causes, James is committed to abolishing prisons and to championing reinvestment in communities most directly impacted by such harm. He is also a writer whose works have been published by Witness LA, the Marshall Project, Vice Media, and Re:Store Justice.

Meghan G. McDowell is assistant professor of criminology and criminal justice at Northern Arizona University and cofounder of Humanities Behind Bars.

Seth Michelson is associate professor in the Romance Languages Department at Washington and Lee University, where he teaches the poetry of the hemispheric Americas. He has taught poetry to people in maximum security prisons and detention centers for almost twenty years. In addition to teaching poetry, he writes and translates it. To date he has published nineteen books of original poetry and poetry in translation, as well as numerous book chapters and articles on poetry and carcerality, and is frequently engaged internationally as a speaker on these topics.

Rayna Momen is a Black, transgender poet, queer criminologist, and abolitionist from West Virginia. They are a longtime volunteer with the Appalachian Prison Book Project.

Anna Plemons is associate vice chancellor for academic and student affairs at Washington State University Tri-Cities as well as a faculty member in the Department of Digital Technology and Culture. From 2009 to 2019, she taught workshops and courses for incarcerated students through the California Arts in Corrections program and the Incarcerated Students Program at Lake Tahoe Community College. She has published on prison education in *Teaching Artist Journal*, *Community Literacy Journal*, and the edited collections *Prison Pedagogies: Learning and Teaching with Imprisoned Writers* (2018) and *Critical Perspectives on Teaching in Prison: Students and Instructors on Pedagogy behind the Wall* (2019). Her book, *Beyond Progress in the Prison Classroom: Options and Opportunities* (2019), explores the possibilities and impossibilities of teaching inside with a selection of narrative nonfiction by incarcerated and formerly incarcerated writers in the Arts in Corrections program at New Folsom Prison.

Alison Rose Reed is currently associate professor of English at Old Dominion University in Norfolk, Virginia, where she cofounded Humanities Behind Bars. Her critical and creative work has appeared in *GLQ: A Journal of Lesbian and Gay Studies*, *Frontiers: A Journal of Women Studies*, *Cimarron Review*, *No Tea, No Shade: New Writings in Black Queer Studies* (2016), and elsewhere. She is the author of *Love and Abolition: The Social Life of Black Queer Performance* (2022). With Felice Blake and Paula Ioanide, she coedited *Antiracism Inc.: Why the Way We Talk about Racial Justice Matters* (2019).

Courtney Rein has spent the last twenty-two years teaching high school English, and she has taught and learned in incarcerated communities since 2015. This work has transformed her sense of what education can and should be. Courtney and her coauthor, David Bennett, believe deeply in the power of proximity to aid the process of equitable and transformative collaboration.

Vicki L. Reitenauer serves on the faculty of the Women, Gender, and Sexuality Studies Department at Portland State University, employing participatory pedagogies and reflective practice for integrative, transformative, liberatory learning; building and sustaining community partnerships; facilitating relational faculty support processes; and co-creating faculty-led assessment practices. She is a founding coeditor of *Amplify: A Journal of Writing-as-Activism*, and alongside scholarly writing she publishes creative nonfiction and poetry. She developed the course Writing as Activism, which she has taught inside a state correctional facility in Portland, Oregon, since 2016.

Antonio Rosa is a student, participant, and co-instructor of Spanish in Stetson University's Community Education Project (CEP). He has presented his research at the National Conference on Higher Education in Prison; the Southeast Conference on Foreign Languages, Literatures and Films; and the Thirty-Sixth International Conference of the Latin American Studies Association. He helped lead CEP's Public History Research Collective's work on slavery and Indian removal in east Florida, and his work has been published in *Southern Cultures* and *Process*, the blog of the Organization of American Historians.

Katy Ryan is professor of English and Eberly Family Professor of Outstanding Teaching at West Virginia University. She is the founder of the Appalachian Prison Book Project.

Anastazia Schmid is an artist, activist, and PhD student in ethnic studies at the University of California, Riverside. She is a founding member of the Indiana Women's Prison History Project, a research team engaged in rewriting the history of women's prisons and institutions. Her area of emphasis is nineteenth-century gender and sexuality. She also works in collaboration with *Abolition Journal Collective*, the IDOC Watch anarchist collective, the Lumina Foundation, the National Council of Incarcerated and Formerly Incarcerated Women and Girls, Constructing Our Future, Focus Re-entry Initiative, Silent Cry, Underground Scholars, and Memento Mori Paranormal History Hunters. In 2016, she won the American Studies Association's Gloria E. Anzaldúa Award for her independent scholarship in women's studies.

Amber Shields was a teacher and tutor with Mount Tamalpais College at San Quentin State Prison from 2017 to 2019. Her most recent published work is the edited collection *Refocus: The Films of Zoya Akhtar* (2022). She is assistant professor of film studies at Diablo Valley College.

Sarah Shotland is the author of the novel *Junkette* and the nonfiction work *Abolition Is Everything*. She is cofounder of Words Without Walls, which brought creative writing workshops to jails, prisons, and drug treatment centers in Pittsburgh, Pennsylvania, from 2009 to 2022. Her work has been supported with grants and fellowships from the National Endowment for the Arts, the National Endowment for the Humanities, the Creative Nonfiction Foundation, and the Heinz Endowments. She is assistant professor of English at Carlow University, where she directs the Madwomen in the Attic program.

Ken Smith has been a student and participant in Stetson University's Community Education Project (CEP) since 2015. In 2016, he became a tutor for the Spanish program, and in 2017 he joined the course as a co-instructor. He has presented his research at the Brown Center Spotlight Series and the Thirty-Sixth International Conference of the Latin American Studies Association, and he is actively involved in CEP's Public History Research Collective's work on slavery, family separation, and Indian removal.

Sheila Smith McKoy is vice provost of equity, inclusion, and faculty excellence at the University of San Francisco. Smith McKoy previously taught literature and writing at North Carolina Correctional Institution for Women. She is a poet, literary critic, fiction writer, and documentary filmmaker whose books include *When Whites Riot: Writing Race and Violence in American and South African Cultures* (2001), *The Elizabeth Keckley Reader: Writing Self, Writing Nation* (2016), *The Elizabeth Keckley Reader: Artistry, Culture and Commerce* (2017), and the poetry collection *The Bones Beneath*, forthcoming from Nomadic Press in 2023; she is coauthor of *One Window's Light: A Haiku Collection*. With LaJuan Simpson-

Wilkey and Eric Bridges, Smith McKoy is coeditor of *Recovering the African Feminine Divine in Literature, the Arts, and Practice: Yemonja Awakening* (2020). Smith McKoy is actively involved in mental health reform, faculty and BIPOC leadership initiatives, education in prisons, restorative and research justice, and international and transnational engagement.

Valerie Surrett is assistant professor of English at the University of North Georgia. As a graduate student and lecturer at West Virginia University, she served as a board member and volunteer coordinator for Appalachian Prison Book Project (APBP) and, along with Yvonne Hammond, Elissa Momen, and Alex Kessler, facilitated APBP's book clubs. Valerie has continued working with APBP from Georgia and is currently assisting with APBP's tablet campaign.

Rachel Swenarton is a quality analyst for Agilent Technologies. She holds a bachelor's degree in chemical biology from Saint Joseph's University and a master's degree in secondary education from Temple University.

Shelby D. Tuthill is a doctoral student in counseling psychology at Colorado State University. She was a SpeakOut! writing workshop facilitator for three years, writing with a women's group in jail and a men's group at a halfway house. Her research primarily focuses on mental health outcomes among LGBTQ+ people.

Index